HOW GREAT IS OUR GOD

HOW
GREAT
IS OUR
GOD

Classic Writings from
History's Greatest Christian Thinkers

IN CONTEMPORARY ENGLISH

WORTHY
PUBLISHING

Copyright © 2011 by Mark Gilroy Creative LLC
www.markgilroy.com

Published by Worthy Publishing, a division of Worthy Media, Inc.,
134 Franklin Road, Suite 200, Brentwood, Tennessee 37027.

HELPING PEOPLE EXPERIENCE THE HEART OF GOD

eBook available at www.worthypublishing.com

Audio distributed through Oasis Audio; visit www.oasisaudio.com

Library of Congress Control Number: 2011935242

Scripture quotations in some of the older writings come from archaic versions of the Bible that are no
longer available. Where possible, we have included a note in the text with a scripture for reference.

Scripture quotations marked ASV are from the *American Standard Version*, © 1901. Public domain.

Scripture quotations marked KJV are from the *King James Version*. Public domain.

Scripture quotations marked NIV are from the Holy Bible, *New International Version®, NIV®* Copyright
© 1973, 1978, 1984 by Biblica, Inc.™ Used by permission of Zondervan. All rights reserved worldwide.

Scripture quotations marked NRSV are from the *New Revised Standard Version* Bible, copyright 1989,
Division of Christian Education of the National Council of the Churches of Christ in the United States
of America. Used by permission. All rights reserved.

For foreign and subsidiary rights, contact Riggins International Rights Services, Inc.; www.rigginsrights.com

Hardcover ISBN: 978-1-936034-60-4 (hardcover)

Project created by Mark Gilroy
Project Editor: Christina M. Honea
Cover Design: Greg Jackson, ThinkPen Design, Inc.
Interior Design and Typesetting: Marjorie Jackson, ThinkPen Design, Inc.

Printed in the United States of America
11 12 13 14 15 16 17 LBM 8 7 6 5 4 3 2 1

Contents

INTRODUCTION
IT'S A GLORIOUS FAITH

Is the Christian faith primarily believing the right things about God? Or is it a lifestyle? Or is it about trusting your life into the hands of God? The answer is incredibly simple. It is, of course, *yes*. The Christian faith is a set of propositions, a new way of walking through life, and a personal encounter with God.

But even if there is a certain simplicity in saying "all of the above," the answer to the question of what defines the Christian faith becomes incredibly complex and messy when expressed by different people and in different ages. Which set of beliefs is true? Christians through the ages have held different tenets—sometimes with such conviction that they've been willing to go to war against each other. And what are the rules for daily living? What does it mean to trust one's life to God? Though it would seem each aspect of faith should be straightforward and clear, the answers to these questions have been defined differently by separate traditions, cultures, and ages.

Perhaps in the myriad of emphases and convictions we can discover a significant part of what makes the Christian faith so glorious. For throughout the centuries there has been enough agreement and commonality to establish a mystical connection and love for one another that endures. We discover that there's so much that we agree on in heart and mind that even if differences are real and don't go away, they take a backseat in importance—and in our commitment to one another—to what binds us together and encourages us to walk humbly with God.

After spending a year reading the daily selections from *How Great Is Our God* you will have been inspired—and on occasion bewildered or bemused—by writings from every century and every major tradition of the Christian faith. You will have heard what was on the hearts and minds of Early Church Fathers under great persecution, Egyptian monastics hidden in the desert, American frontier evangelists trying to reach a scattered congregation, ministers that still preach every Sunday in our day, and many others.

Will you agree with everything you read? Of course not. But you might be surprised by the poignancy and encouragement you receive from voices that are not as familiar to you and your background of instruction in the faith.

   Most of all it is my intent and prayer that all of these selections taken as a whole—though a multifaceted mosaic—will sparkle with the light of God's truth in your soul and renew your sense of wonder at our glorious faith and the greatness of our God.

                                          ~ MARK GILROY, GENERAL EDITOR

NOTES ABOUT THE SELECTIONS

First and foremost, *How Great Is Our God* is compiled to take you on a journey through every century and every tradition of the Christian faith. We want you to experience the heart and thoughts of Christians from the birth of the church until today.

You will find daily readings that have been selected because they are considered great and enduring thoughts that have contributed to the spiritual growth of Christians in every age, but also because some of the readings represent seminal moments in the history of Christian thought and Western civilization. That's why you'll find an excerpt from the sermon that launched the first crusade next to a sermon from a Puritan evangelist. There are a few selections from non-Christian sources that provide insight into the Christian faith as well. Be prepared to be inspired—but also challenged to understand how Christianity has interacted with itself and the world at large.

In putting together the daily selections we had several goals:

1. To be true to the meaning of the author;
2. To be clear and understandable to the modern reader;
3. To pull out representative themes and messages from the writers.

When possible, we have cited the translation used—many going back more than a thousand years—and have noted in the bibliography when we have edited and paraphrased to make the meaning clearer. In many cases, we have cut and pasted the selections from a longer treatise, letter, or sermon to focus on a single or narrower topic. We have noted which work of the author the selections came from, should something spark a particular interest and you want to find and read a selection in its entirety.

In the cases of creeds and poetic works—for example, Milton's *Paradise Lost*—we have not attempted to rework the translation available, lest we damage the beauty of the original language or introduce potential confusion or inaccuracy. For that reason, you will find a few selections that are more difficult to understand—but worth digging into.

Each selection includes a sentence or two to place it in historical context. We would love to have provided more depth but didn't want to take too much space from the writers.

If you prefer to read *How Great Is Our God* in historical sequence, there is a reading plan in the back of the book.

January 1

The Humble Heart

Saint Benedict | 6th century

Saint Benedict of Nursia is a Christian saint, honored by the Roman Catholic Church as the patron saint of Europe and students.

If we do not dare approach men who are in power, except with humility and reverence, when we wish to ask a favor, how much more must we beseech the Lord God of all things with all humility and purity of devotion? And let us be assured that it is not in many words, but in the purity of heart that we are heard.

The Holy Scripture cries out, saying: "Every one that exalteth himself shall be humbled; and he that humbles himself shall be exalted" (see Luke 14:11). This shows us that every exaltation is a kind of pride. The Prophet declares that he guards himself against this, saying: "Lord, my heart is not puffed up; nor are my eyes haughty. Neither have I walked in great matters nor in wonderful things above me" (see Psalm 131:1).

Therefore, if we wish to reach the greatest height of humility, we must erect the ladder that appeared to Jacob in his dream, by which angels were shown ascending and descending. We understand this to be nothing else but that we descend by pride and ascend by humility. The erected ladder, however, is our life in the present world, which, if the heart is humble, the Lord lifts up to heaven. For our body and soul are the two sides of this ladder; and into these sides the divine calling has inserted various degrees of humility or discipline that we must mount.

We must, therefore, guard against evil desires. If the eyes of the Lord observe both good and bad, and our actions are reported to the Lord by the angels who are appointed to watch over us daily, we must ever be on our guard, that God may at no time see us "gone aside to evil and become unprofitable" (see Psalm14:3), and, because He is kind and waits for us to be changed for the better, may say to us in the future: "These things thou hast done and I was silent" (see Psalm 50:21).

Read: Luke 14:11

THE WISDOM OF PATIENCE

CHARLES SPURGEON | 19TH CENTURY

Charles Haddon (C. H.) Spurgeon (1834-1892) was a British Particular Baptist preacher and a prolific author who is still known as the "Prince of Preachers."

Patience is better than wisdom: an ounce of patience is worth a pound of brains. All men praise patience, but few enough can practice it. When one's flesh and bones are full of aches and pains, it is as natural for us to murmur as for a horse to shake his head when the flies tease him, or a wheel to rattle when a spoke is loose. But nature should not be the rule with Christians, or what is their religion worth?

We expect more fruit from an apple tree than from a thorn, and we have a right to do so. The disciples of a patient Savior should be patient themselves. Grin and bear it is the old-fashioned advice, but sing and bear it is a great deal better.

Many people are born crying, live complaining, and die disappointed; they chew the bitter pill which they would not even know to be bitter if they had the sense to swallow it whole in a cup of patience and water. They think every other man's burden to be light and their own feathers to be heavy as lead. Yet, if the truth were known, it is their fancy rather than their fate which makes things go so hard with them.

When troubles come, it is of no use to fly in the face of God by hard thoughts of providence: that is kicking against the pricks and hurting your feet. The trees bow in the wind, and so must we. If one door should be shut, God will open another. There's a bright side to all things, and a good God everywhere.

"All things work together for good to them that love God" (Romans 8:28 KJV). Losses and crosses are heavy to bear, but when our hearts are right with God, it is wonderful how easy the yoke becomes. All's well that ends well; therefore, let us plow the heaviest soil with our eye on the sheaves of harvest, and learn to sing at our labor while others murmur.

READ: JAMES 1:2-4

January 3

The Mystery of the Kingdom

George Eldon Ladd | 1959

George Eldon Ladd (1911-1982) was an American Baptist minister and professor whose best-known work, A Theology of the New Testament, *has been used by thousands of seminary students since its publication in 1974.*

The Word of God says that the Kingdom of God is a present spiritual reality. Righteousness and peace and joy are fruits of the Spirit which God bestows now upon those who yield their lives to the rule of the Spirit. They have to do with the deepest springs of spiritual life, and this, says the inspired apostle, is the Kingdom of God.

At the same time, the Kingdom is an inheritance which God will bestow upon His people when Christ comes in glory. "Then the King will say to those on His right hand, 'Come, you blessed of My Father, inherit the kingdom prepared for you from the foundation of the world'" (Matthew 25:34). How can the Kingdom of God be a present spiritual reality and yet be an inheritance bestowed upon God's people at the second coming of Christ?

The very complexity of the biblical teaching about the Kingdom of God is one of the reasons why such diverse interpretations have arisen in the history of theology. Isolated verses can be quoted for most of the interpretations which can be found in our theological literature. The Kingdom is a present reality (Matthew 12:28), and yet it is a future blessing (1 Corinthians 15:50). It is an inner spiritual redemptive blessing (Romans 14:17) which can be experienced only by way of the new birth (John 3:3), and yet it will have to do with the government of the nations of the world (Revelation 11:15). The Kingdom is a realm into which men enter now (Matthew 21:31) , and yet it is a realm into which they will enter tomorrow (Matthew 8:11). It is at the same time a gift of God which will be bestowed by God in the future (Luke 12:32) and yet which must be received in the present (Mark 10:15). Obviously no simple explanation can do justice to such a rich but diverse variety of teaching.

Read: Romans 14:17

JANUARY 4

THE LORD EXALTED

GEORGE FOX | 17TH CENTURY

George Fox (1624-1691) was an English Dissenter and a founder of the Religious Society of Friends, commonly known as the Quakers or Friends.

Upon the Fourth-day of the First month, 1650,
I felt the power of the word spread over all the world in praise.
Praise, honor, and glory be to the Lord of heaven and earth!
Lord of peace, Lord of joy!
Your countenance makes my heart glad.
Lord of glory, Lord of mercy, Lord of strength,
Lord of life, and of power over death,
and Lord of lords, and King of kings!
In the world there are lords many,
but to us there is but one God the Father, of whom are all things;
and one Lord Jesus Christ, by whom are all things:
to whom be all glory, who is worthy!
In the world are many lords, and many gods,
and the earth makes lords, coveting after riches,
and oppressing the creatures;
and so, the covetous mind getting to itself, lords it above others.
This nature of lordly pride is head, until subdued by the power of God:
for everyone, in that state, strives to be above another;
few will strive to be the lowest.
Oh, that everyone would strive to put down, in themselves, mastery
    and honor,
so that the Lord of heaven and earth might be exalted!

READ: PSALM 99:9

January 5

The Sin of Impatience

Catherine of Siena | c. 1374

Saint Catherine of Siena (1347-1380) was a tertiary of the Dominican Order, a scholastic philosopher, and theologian. She is one of the two patron saints of Italy, together with Francis of Assisi.

I write to you with the desire to see you established in true patience, since I consider that without patience we cannot please God. For just as impatience gives much pleasure to the devil and to one's own lower nature, and revels in nothing but anger when it misses what the lower nature wants, so it is very displeasing to God. It is because anger and impatience are the very pith and sap of pride that they please the devil so much.

Impatience loses the fruit of its labor and deprives the soul of God; it begins by knowing a foretaste of hell: for in hell the evil perverted will burns with anger, hate, and impatience. It burns and does not consume, but is evermore renewed. It has indeed parched and consumed grace in the souls of the lost, but it has not consumed their being, and so their punishment lasts eternally.

There is no sin nor wrong that gives a man such a foretaste of hell in this life as anger and impatience. It is hated by God, it holds its neighbor in aversion, and has neither knowledge nor desire to bear and forbear with its faults. And whatever is said or done to it, it poisons quickly, and its impulses blow about like a leaf in the wind. It becomes unendurable to itself, for perverted will is always gnawing at it, and it craves what it cannot have; it is discordant with the will of God and with the rational part of its own soul. And all this comes from the tree of Pride, from which oozes out the sap of anger and impatience. The man becomes an incarnate demon, and it is much worse to fight with these visible demons than with the invisible. Surely, then, every reasonable being ought to flee this sin.

Read: Ecclesiastes 7:8-9

JANUARY 6

A LONG REPENTANCE

DANIEL DEFOE | 1719

Daniel Defoe (c. 1659-1731), born Daniel Foe, was an English writer and journalist, who was famous for his popular pamphlets on numerous topics and later for his novel Robinson Crusoe.

Being one day at Hull, and one of my companions being about to sail to London in his father's ship, and prompting me to go with them with the common allurement of seafaring men, I consulted neither father nor mother, nor so much as sent them word of it; but without asking God's blessing or my father's, without any consideration of circumstances or consequences, on the first of September 1651, I went on board a ship bound for London.

Never any young adventurer's misfortunes, I believe, began sooner, or continued longer than mine. The ship was no sooner out of the Humber than the wind began to blow and the sea to rise in a most frightful manner; and, as I had never been at sea before, I was most inexpressibly sick in body and terrified in mind. I began now seriously to reflect upon what I had done, and how justly I was overtaken by the judgment of Heaven. My conscience, which was not yet come to the pitch of hardness to which it has since, reproached me with the contempt of advice, and the breach of my duty to God and my father.

To make short this sad part of my story, we went the way of all sailors; the punch was made and I was made half drunk with it: and in that one night's wickedness I drowned all my repentance, all my reflections upon my past conduct, all my resolutions for the future. In a word, as the sea was returned to its smoothness of surface and settled calmness by the abatement of that storm, I entirely forgot the vows and promises that I made in my distress.

But I was to have another trial for it still; and Providence, as in such cases generally it does, resolved to leave me entirely without excuse; for if I would not take this for a deliverance, the next was to be such a one as the worst and most hardened wretch among us would confess both the danger and the mercy of.

READ: PROVERBS 14:12-13

January 7
Stand and Defend
Ambrose | 4th century

Aurelius Ambrosius (c. 337-397), better known in English as Saint Ambrose, was a bishop of Milan who became one of the most influential ecclesiastical figures of the fourth century. He was one of the four original Doctors of the Church.

Make yourselves then to appear worthy that Christ should be in your midst. For where peace is, there is Christ, for Christ is Peace; and where righteousness is, there is Christ, for Christ is Righteousness. Let Him be in the midst of you, that you may see Him, lest it be said to you also: "There standeth one in the midst of you, whom ye see not" (John 1:26 KJV). The Jews saw not Him in Whom they believed not; we look upon Him by devotion, and behold Him by faith.

Let Him therefore stand in your midst, that the heavens, which declare the glory of God, may be opened to you, that you may do His will, and work His works. He who sees Jesus, to him are the heavens opened as they were opened to Stephen, when he said: "Behold I see the heavens opened and Jesus standing at the right hand of God" (see Acts 7:56). Jesus was standing as his advocate, He was standing as though anxious, that He might help His athlete Stephen in his conflict, He was standing as though ready to crown His martyr.

Let Him then be standing for you, that you may not be afraid of Him sitting; for when sitting He judges, as Daniel says: "The thrones were placed, and the books were opened, and the Ancient of days did sit" (see Daniel 7:9). But in the eighty-second Psalm it is written: "God stood in the congregation of gods, and decideth among the gods." So then when He sits He judges, when He stands He decides, and He judges concerning the imperfect, but decides among the gods. Let Him stand for you as a defender, as a good shepherd, lest the fierce wolves assault you.

Read: Romans 8:34

JANUARY 8
COUNTING THE COST
ROBERT HAWKER | 1801

Robert Hawker (1753-1827) was a prominent vicar of the Anglican Church who was called the "Star of the West" for his superlative preaching that drew thousands.

"For which of you, intending to build a tower, does not sit down first and count the cost?" (Luke 14:28). Ponder, my soul, over this very striking image concerning the divine life. The picture of a builder is most aptly chosen; for the Christian builder is building for eternity. And the figure of a warrior, which our Lord also joins to it, is no less so, for the battle is for life, and that life is eternal. Have you counted the cost? Have you entered upon the work? Is the foundation stone, which God hath laid in Zion, the rock on which you are building?

Pause and examine. Be the cost what it may: the loss of earthly friends; the parting with every worldly pursuit; the scorn, contempt, and derision of all mankind; indeed, the loss of life itself: if these become competition, are you ready to give them all up? When you have answered these inquiries, go on, and see that your foundation be really fixed on Christ.

If so, it must have been previously sought for, by digging deep into the natural state in which you were born. Jesus must have been first determined to be most essentially necessary and precious, before the spiritual building of the soul was made to rest upon him. And, when found, unless the whole of the building rests entirely upon him, it will, like an off-center column, still totter.

Oh! It is blessed to make Christ the all in all of the spiritual temple; blessed to make him the first in point of order; blessed to make him the first in point of strength, to support and bear the weight of the whole building; blessed to make him the grand cement, to unite and keep together, in one harmonious proportion and regularity, every part of the building; and blessed to bring forth the capstone of the building, by his strength and glory, crying, "Grace, grace unto it."

READ: LUKE 14:28

THE BLISS OF UTTER HELPLESSNESS

WILLIAM BARCLAY | 1956

William Barclay (1907-1978) was a Scottish minister, author, professor, and radio and television presenter.

If people have realized their own utter helplessness, and have put their whole trust in God, there will enter into their lives two elements which are opposite sides of the same coin. They will become completely detached from material things, for they will know that things do not have the power to bring happiness or security; and they will become completely attached to God, for they will know that God alone can bring them help, hope, and strength. Those who are poor in spirit are men and women who have realized that things mean nothing, and that God means everything.

We must be careful not to think that this beatitude calls actual material poverty a good thing. Poverty is not a good thing. Jesus would never have called blessed a state where people live in slums and do not have enough to eat, and where health deteriorates because conditions are all against it. It is the aim of the Christian gospel to remove that kind of poverty. The poverty which is blessed is the poverty *of spirit*, when people realize their own utter lack of resources to meet life, and find their help and strength in God.

Jesus says that to such a poverty belongs the kingdom of heaven. Why should that be so? If we take the two petitions of the Lord's Prayer and set them together,

Your kingdom come.

Your will be done in earth as it is in heaven.

We get the definition: the kingdom of God is a society where God's will is as perfectly done in earth as it is in heaven. That means that only those who do God's will are citizens of the kingdom; and we can only do God's will when we realize our own utter helplessness, our own utter ignorance, our own utter inability to cope with life, and when we put our whole trust in God.

So, the first beatitude means: *O the bliss of those who have realized their own utter helplessness, and who have put their whole trust in God, for thus alone can they render to God that perfect obedience which will make them citizens of the kingdom of heaven!*

READ: MATTHEW 5:3

JANUARY 10

TRUE HAPPINESS

JOHN CALVIN | 16TH CENTURY

John Calvin (1509-1564) was born into a wealthy family in Noyon, France. Never formally ordained, once he converted to Protestantism, his life was given to ministry.

Many are pressed down by distress, and yet continue to swell inwardly with pride and cruelty. But Christ pronounces those to be happy who, chastened and subdued by afflictions, submit themselves wholly to God, and, with inward humility, turn to him for protection.

We see that Christ does not swell the minds of his own people by any unfounded belief, or harden them by unfeeling obstinacy, but leads them to entertain the hope of eternal life, and assures them, that in this way they will pass into the heavenly kingdom of God. It deserves our attention, that only he who is reduced to nothing in himself, and relies on the mercy of God, is poor in spirit: for they who are broken or overwhelmed by despair murmur against God, and this proves them to be of a proud and haughty spirit.

The ordinary belief is that calamities render a man unhappy. This arises from the thought that they constantly bring along with them mourning and grief. Now, nothing is supposed to be more inconsistent with happiness than mourning. But Christ does not merely affirm that mourners are not unhappy. He shows that their very mourning contributes to a happy life, by preparing them to receive eternal joy, and by furnishing them with motives to seek true comfort in God alone. Accordingly, Paul says, "We glory in tribulations also: knowing that tribulation worketh patience; and patience, experience; and experience, hope: and hope maketh not ashamed" (Romans 5:3-5 KJV).

The children of this world never think themselves safe, except when they fiercely revenge the injuries that are done them, and defend their life by the "weapons of war" (Ezekiel 32:27). But as we must believe that Christ alone is the guardian of our life, all that remains for us is to "hide ourselves under the shadow of his wings" (see Psalm 17:8). We must be sheep, if we wish to be reckoned a part of his flock.

READ: ROMANS 5:3-5

JANUARY 11
TEACH ME TO SEEK
ANSELM OF CANTERBURY | 12TH CENTURY

Anselm of Canterbury (c. 1033-1109) was a Benedictine monk, philosopher, and a prelate of the church who held the office of Archbishop of Canterbury from 1093 to 1109.

Up now, slight man! Cast aside, for now, thy burdensome cares, and put away thy toilsome business. Yield room for some little time to God; and rest for a little time in him. Enter the inner chamber of thy mind; shut out all thoughts save that of God, and such as can aid thee in seeking him; close thy door and seek him. Speak now, my whole heart!

Lord, if thou art not here, where shall I seek thee, being absent? I have never seen thee, O Lord, my God; I do not know thy form. What shall this man do, an exile far from thee? It is thou that hast made me, and hast made me anew, and hast bestowed upon me all the blessing I enjoy; and not yet do I know thee. I was created to see thee, and not yet have I done that for which I was made.

O wretched lot of man, when he hath lost that for which he was made! O hard and terrible fate! Man once did eat the bread of angels, for which he hungers now; he eateth now the bread of sorrows, of which he knew not then.

But alas! Wretched that I am, one of the sons of Eve, far removed from God! Be it mine to look up to thy light, even from afar, even from the depths. Teach me to seek thee, and reveal thyself to me, when I seek thee, for I cannot seek thee, except thou teach me, nor find thee, except thou reveal thyself. Lord, I acknowledge and I thank thee that thou hast created me in thine image, in order that I may be mindful of thee, may conceive of thee, and love thee; but that image has been so consumed and wasted away by vices, and obscured by the smoke of wrong-doing, that it cannot achieve that for which it was made, except thou renew it, and create it anew.

READ: HEBREWS 2:5-9

JANUARY 12

ON THE EXISTENCE OF GOD

DESCARTES | 1641

René Descartes (1596-1650) was a French philosopher and writer who spent most of his adult life in the Dutch Republic. He has been called the "Father of Modern Philosophy."

I realize that I shouldn't be surprised at God's doing things that I can't explain. I shouldn't doubt His existence just because I find that I sometimes can't understand why or how He has made something. I know that my nature is weak and limited and that God's is limitless, incomprehensible, and infinite. From this, I can infer that He can do innumerable things for reasons that are unknown to me.

If I suspend judgment when I don't clearly and distinctly grasp what is true, I obviously do right and am not deceived. But, if I either affirm or deny in such a case, I misuse my freedom of choice. If I affirm what is false, I deceive myself, and if I stumble onto the truth, I'm still blameworthy since the light of nature reveals that a perception of the understanding should always precede a decision of the will. In these misuses of freedom of choice lies the deprivation that accounts for error.

I find in myself innumerable ideas of things that, although they may not exist outside me, can't be said to be nothing. While I have some control over my thoughts of these things, I do not make them up: they have their own real and immutable natures. Suppose, for example, that I have a mental image of a triangle. While it may be that no figure of this sort does exist or ever has existed outside my thoughts, the figure has a fixed nature (essence or form) which hasn't been produced by me and isn't dependent of my mind.

Thus I plainly see that the certainty and truth of all my knowledge derives from one thing: my thought of the true God. Before I knew Him, I couldn't know anything else perfectly. But now I can plainly and certainly know innumerable things, not only about God and other mental beings, but also about the nature of physical objects, insofar as it is the subject matter of pure mathematics.

READ: ISAIAH 55:8

JANUARY 13
YOU ARE EVER WITH ME
THOMAS MERTON | 20TH CENTURY

Thomas Merton (1915-1968) was an Anglo-American Catholic writer and a Trappist monk. He was ordained to the priesthood in 1949 and given the name Father Louis.

My Lord God,
I have no idea where I am going.
I do not see the road ahead of me.
I cannot know for certain where it will end.

Nor do I really know myself,
and the fact that I think I am following
your will does not mean that I am actually doing so.
But I believe that the desire to please you
does in fact please you.

And I hope I have that desire in all that I am doing.
I hope that I will never do anything apart from that desire.
And I know that if I do this you will lead me by the
right road, though I may know nothing about it.

Therefore will I trust you always though I may
seem to be lost and in the shadow of death.
I will not fear, for you are ever with me, and
you will never leave me to face my troubles alone.

READ: PSALM 23:1-4

A CALL TO DEFEND

POPE URBAN II | 1095

Urban II (c. 1035-1099) was Pope from March 12, 1088, until his death. He is most known for starting the First Crusade and setting up the modern-day Roman Curia.

Sons of God, although you have promised to keep the peace among yourselves and to preserve the rights of the church, there remains an important work for you to do. You must apply the strength of your righteousness to another matter that concerns you as well as God. For your brethren who live in the east are in urgent need of your help, and you must hasten to give them the aid that has often been promised them.

For, as most of you have heard, the Turks and Arabs have attacked them and have conquered the territory of Romania. They have occupied more and more of the lands of those Christians, they have killed and captured many, and have destroyed the churches and devastated the empire. If you permit them to continue thus, the faithful of God will be much more widely attacked by them. On this account I, or rather the Lord, beseech you as Christ's heralds to publish this everywhere and to persuade all people of whatever rank, poor and rich, to carry aid promptly to those Christians and to destroy that vile race from the lands of our friends.

All who die by the way, shall have immediate remission of sins. This I grant them through the power of God with which I am invested. Oh what a disgrace if such a despised and base race, which worships demons, should conquer a people that has the faith of omnipotent God and is made glorious with the name of Christ! With what reproaches will the Lord overwhelm us if you do not aid those who profess the Christian religion! Let those who go not put off the journey, but rent their lands and collect money for their expenses; and as soon as spring comes, let them eagerly set out on the way with God as their guide.

READ: JOHN 15:13

JANUARY 15
UNFINISHED THINGS
BILLY SUNDAY | 20TH CENTURY

William Ashley "Billy" Sunday (1862-1935) was a professional baseball player who later became the most celebrated and influential American evangelist during the early twentieth century.

If you live wrong you can't die right. Emerson said: "What you are speaks so loudly that I cannot hear what you say." This is an age of incompleteness of unfinished things. Life is full of half done things. Education is begun and abandoned. Obedience to the law of God is begun—and given up. People start in business—and fail. They attempt to learn a trade—and don't do it thoroughly.

A hound once started running after a stag and after running for a while it saw a fox and turned after it. A little farther along it saw a rabbit and ran after that, and finally wound up holing a field mouse. So it is with so many who enter the Christian life. They started to hunt and compromised on a glass of booze. They enter a royal race, but compromised on a glass of beer or on some little gain through dishonesty.

Not every backslider is an apostate, but every apostate is a backslider. Peter was a backslider, but he came back and preached that sermon at Pentecost. Judas was a backslider, and what he did so preyed upon his mind that he did not want it. He went out but he never came back.

I can imagine a man being untrue in business. I can imagine him being untrue in politics. I can even—though it is difficult—imagine him being untrue to the vows made at the altar. But to be untrue to God! Be untrue to God and you will lose heaven and lose all. Be true to God and you will lose hell. I pray that God will so work upon your consciences that you will cry salty tears upon your pillow and seek a dry spot that he may reproach you until you have been stung into a return to the God to whom you have been false.

READ: ACTS 20:24

January 16

A Love for Worthy Things

Richard Rolle | 1347

Richard Rolle (1290-1349) was an English religious writer, Bible translator, and hermit.

Be it known to all manner of people living in this wretched dwelling place of exile, that no man may be filled with endless life, nor be anointed with heavenly sweetness, unless he truly be turned to God. Only by love is this turning done; so that he loves that which is worthy to be loved, and loves not that which is unworthy; that he burn more in love of those things that are most worthy, and less in them that are less worthy.

Truly turning from worldly goods that deceive, stands in want of fleshly desire, and hatred of all wickedness; so that they savor not earthly things, nor desire to hold to worldly things beyond their basic need. For they that heap up riches and know not for whom they gather, finding solace in them, are not worthy to be gladdened in the joy of heavenly love. All love that ends not in God is sinful and makes its possessors evil. Loving worldly things, they are set on fire with sinful love, and are further from heavenly heat than is the space between the highest heaven and the lowest place of the earth.

For while the love of temporal things occupies the heart of any man, truly the love of God and of this world may never be together in one soul, but whichever love is stronger puts out the other. Thus it may openly be known who loves the world and who is Christ's follower. Certainly as Christ's lovers behave themselves towards the world, and the flesh, so lovers of the world behave themselves towards God and their own souls.

They that are chosen eat and drink with their focus on God, and do not lust for earthly things, but seek only what they need. The remainder of time they yield to God's service; not standing in idleness nor running to plays nor wonders—that is the token of the rejected—but rather behaving themselves honestly, speaking, doing, and thinking only those things that long to God.

Read: John 12:25

JANUARY 17

OF STRIFE AND ENVY

CLEMENT OF ROME | C. 96

Pope Clement I (d. 99), also known as Saint Clement of Rome, was Bishop of Rome and a leading member of the church during the late first century.

Every kind of honor and happiness was bestowed upon you, and then was fulfilled that which is written, "But Jeshurun grew fat and kicked. . . . Then he forsook God *who* made him, and scornfully esteemed the Rock of his salvation" (Deuteronomy 32:15). Hence flowed emulation and envy, strife and sedition, persecution and disorder, war and captivity. For this reason righteousness and peace are now far departed from you, inasmuch as everyone abandons the fear of God, nor acts a part becoming a Christian but walks after his own wicked lusts.

Let us take the noble examples in our own generation. Through envy and jealousy, the greatest and most righteous pillars of the church have been persecuted and put to death. Peter endured numerous labors and when he had at length suffered martyrdom, departed to the place of glory due to him. Paul also obtained the reward of patient endurance, after being seven times thrown into captivity, compelled to flee, and stoned. Having taught righteousness to the whole world, and suffered martyrdom under the prefects, he was thus removed from the world, and went into the holy place, having proved himself a striking example of patience.

To these men there is to be added a great multitude of the elect, who, having endured many indignities and tortures, furnished us with a most excellent example. Envy has alienated wives from their husbands. Envy and strife have overthrown great cities and rooted up mighty nations.

These things, beloved, we write unto you, not merely to admonish you, but also to remind ourselves. For we are struggling in the same arena, and the same conflict is assigned to both of us. Wherefore let us give up vain and fruitless cares and attend to what is good, pleasing, and acceptable in the sight of Him who formed us. Let us look steadfastly to the blood of Christ, and see how precious that blood is to God, which, having been shed for our salvation, has set the grace of repentance before the whole world.

READ: 1 TIMOTHY 6:3-11

JANUARY 18

WORD AND SPIRIT

MARTIN LUTHER | 1566

Martin Luther (1483-1546) was a German priest and professor of theology who initiated the Protestant Reformation.

The Holy Ghost has two offices. First, he is a Spirit of grace, that makes God gracious unto us, and receive us as his acceptable children, for Christ's sake. Secondly, he is a Spirit of prayer, that prays for us, and for the whole world, to the end that all evil may be turned from us, and that all good may happen to us. The Spirit of grace teaches people; the Spirit of prayer prays.

We do not separate the Holy Ghost from faith; neither do we teach that he is against faith; for he is the certainty itself in the world, that makes us sure and certain of the Word; so that, without all wavering or doubting, we certainly believe that it is even so and not otherwise than as God's Word says and is delivered unto us. But the Holy Ghost is given to none without the Word.

Mohammed, the pope, papists, Antinomians, and other sects, have no certainty at all, neither can they be sure of these things; for they depend not on God's Word, but on their own righteousness. And they always stand in doubt, and say: "Who knows whether this which we have done be pleasing to God or not, or whether we have done works enough or not?" They must continually think with themselves, *We are still unworthy.*

But a true and godly Christian, between these two doubts, is sure and certain, and says: "I neither look upon my holiness, nor upon my unworthiness, but I believe in Jesus Christ, who is both holy and worthy. For my part, I am a poor sinner, and that I am sure of out of God's Word. Therefore, the Holy Ghost only and alone is able to say: Jesus Christ is the Lord; the Holy Ghost teaches, preaches, and declares Christ." For we must first hear the Word, and then afterwards the Holy Ghost works in our hearts; he works in the hearts of whom he will, and how he will, but never without the Word.

READ: ISAIAH 55:10-11

JANUARY 19

A HOLY METAPHOR

JOHN OF DAMASCUS | 745

Saint John of Damascus (c. 676-749) was a Syrian Christian monk and priest. Born and raised in Damascus, he died at his monastery, Mar Saba, near Jerusalem.

Since we find many terms used symbolically in the Scriptures concerning God that are more applicable to that which has a body, we should recognize that it is quite impossible for men clothed about with this dense covering of flesh to understand or speak of the divine, lofty, and immaterial energies of the Godhead, except by the use of images and types and symbols derived from our own life.

By God's eyes and eyelids and sight we are to understand His power of overseeing all things and His knowledge, that nothing can escape. God's ears and hearing mean His readiness to be propitiated and to receive our petitions. God's mouth and speech are His means of indicating His will, as we make clear the thoughts that are in the heart. And God's sense of smell is His appreciation of our thoughts and goodwill towards Him, like a sweet fragrance.

God's countenance is the demonstration and manifestation of Himself through His works. His hands represent the effectual nature of His energy, for it is with our own hands that we accomplish our most useful and valuable work. His right hand is His aid in prosperity, for it is the right hand that we also use when making anything of beautiful shape or value, or where much strength is required. His feet and walk are His advent and presence, either for the purpose of bringing succor to the needy, or to perform any other action, for it is by using our feet that we come to arrive at any place.

All the statements made about God that imply body have some hidden meaning and teach us what is above us by means of something familiar to ourselves, with the exception of any statement concerning the bodily sojourn of the God-Word. For He for our safety took upon Himself the whole nature of man, the thinking spirit, the body, and all the properties of human nature, even the natural and blameless passions.

READ: JOB 16:26

JANUARY 20
THE BIRTH OF A KING
SAMUEL WILLARD | 1701

Samuel Willard (1640-1707) was a colonial clergyman. He published many sermons and served as acting president of Harvard from 1701 until his death.

We are to begin at his life, for he both lived for us as well as died for us. He had to come into the world, because here were they who were to be redeemed by him, and here was that work to be done, which must save them. Because this work could not be accomplished in a moment, but required time to be completed, he was required to tarry here a while and dwell among men for such a period as was necessary for its performance. He sojourned here, as one absent from his home, until he had fulfilled the business his Father sent him here to do.

Let me invite you to come to the birth of your Savior: see the King of Glory, veiled in obscurity and entering into the world under a cloud. He is the Lord of Heaven and Earth entering into his dominion, in the lowest and most obscure situation imaginable. He who made both Heaven and Earth, not accommodated with so much as a house to be born in, but turned out among the beasts.

And why? Our sins procured it; we lost our right to all, we deserved poverty and misery, we deserved to be turned out of house and home. We were under this curse. The Son of God was a great king; he could have commanded all the world, and with a word built a stately palace, and furnished it in magnificence for himself. But how would he be our redeemer then? It was "for your sakes He became poor" (2 Corinthians 8:9). It was for this reason he was born. Was not this condescension a disclosure of his great love? Let this stable and manger make him exceedingly precious to us.

And if we enjoy any benefits in our birth, let us acknowledge them to him. For in the day of patience, God allows this favor even to wicked men, yet God's people should understand that all their mercies flow through Christ, and ascribe them to him.

READ: LUKE 2:6-7

JANUARY 21
THE ART OF ENTICEMENT
WILLIAM GURNALL | 1655

William Gurnall (1617-1679) was an English author who signed the declaration required by the Act of Uniformity 1662, on account of which he was the subject of a libelous attack, published in 1665.

Satan will come on the scene when you are on some notable errand for God's glory. He will raise himself up like a snake in your path, hissing his venomous lies. What a handsome excuse he served the Jews: "The time is not come!" God's time was come, but not the devil's; and therefore he perverted the sense of Providence, as if it were not yet time for the Messiah.

Two periods stand out in Christ's life: His entrance into public ministry at His Baptism, and the culmination of it at His Passion. At both He had a fierce encounter with the devil. This should give you an idea of how the master tempter works. The more public your place, and the more eminent your service for God, the greater the probability that Satan is at that very moment hatching some deadly scheme against you. If even the cadet corps need to be armed against Satan's bullets of temptation, how much more the commanders and officers, who stand in the front line of battle!

Satan will not always wait until you are on an important mission to tempt you, however; he will seize every opportunity along the way to practice his enticing skills. Thus he took Eve when she was looking with longing at the tree. Since her own eye first enticed her, it was that much easier for Satan to take the object of her affection, polish it to a high gloss, and with it quicken a lust which lay dormant in her heart. If we do not wish to yield to sin, we must take care not to walk by or sit at the door of the occasion. Do not look on temptation with a wandering eye, nor allow your mind to dwell on that which you do not want lodged in your heart.

READ: MATTHEW 26:41

January 22

Stranger in the Land

Robert McCheyne | 1839

Robert Murray McCheyne (1813–1843) was a minister in the Church of Scotland from 1835 to 1843, until his early death during an epidemic of typhus.

The Lord Jesus has been making Himself known and the Holy Spirit has been quickening whom He will. Still in most parts of our land, it is to be feared that God is a stranger. How few conversions are there in the midst of us? When God is present with power in any land, then there are always many awakened to a sense of sin and flocking to Christ.

One godly minister, speaking of such a time, says, "There were tokens of God's presence in almost every house. It was a time of joy in families, on account of salvation being brought to them. Parents were rejoicing over their children as newborn, husbands over their wives, and wives over their husbands." Alas! What a dismal contrast do most of our families present. How many families where there is not one living soul!

How much deadness there is among true Christians! In times of reviving, when God is present with power in any land, not only are unconverted persons awakened to Christ, but those who were in Christ before receive new measures of the Spirit; they are brought into the palace of the King, and say, "let him kiss me with the kisses of his mouth: for thy love is better than wine" (Song of Solomon 1:2 kjv). How little of this feeling is there among us! How plain that God is a stranger in the land!

How great is the boldness of sinners in sin. When God is present with power, then open sinners, though they may remain unconverted, are often much restrained. There is an awe of God upon their spirits. Alas! It is not so amongst us. The floodgates of sin are opened. "They declare their sin as Sodom, they hide it not" (Isaiah 3:9 kjv). Is it not, then, a time to cry, "Oh the hope of Israel, the saviour thereof!" (Jeremiah 14:8 kjv).

Should we not solemnly ask ourselves, "Why is God such a stranger in this land?"

Read: 2 Chronicles 7:14

JANUARY 23

THE ONE TRUE SON

HILARY | 4TH CENTURY

Hilary of Poitiers (c. 300-c. 368) was Bishop of Poitiers and is a Doctor of the Church. He is sometimes referred to as the "Hammer of the Arians" and the "Athanasius of the West."

At length, with the Holy Ghost speeding our way, we are approaching the safe, calm harbor of a firm faith. We are in the position of men, long tossed about by sea and wind, to whom it very often happens, that while great heaped-up waves delay them for a time around the coasts near the ports, at last that very surge of the vast and dreadful billows drives them on into a trusty, well-known anchorage.

Yet we do not rest, like sailors, on uncertain or on idle hopes: whom, as they shape their course to their wish, and not by assured knowledge, at times the shifting, fickle winds forsake or drive from their course. But we have by our side the unfailing Spirit of faith, abiding with us by the gift of the only-begotten God, and leading us to smooth waters in an unwavering course. For we recognize the Lord Christ as no creature, for indeed He is none such; nor as something that has been made, since He is Himself the Lord of all things that are made; but we know Him to be God, God the true generation of God the Father.

All we indeed, as His goodness has thought fit, have been named and adopted as sons of God: but He is to God the Father the one, true Son, which abides only in the knowledge of the Father and the Son. But this alone is our religion, to confess Him as the Son not adopted but born, not chosen but begotten. For we do not speak of Him either as made, or as not born; since we neither compare the Creator to His creatures, nor falsely speak of birth without begetting. He does not exist of Himself, Who exists through birth; nor is He not born, Who is the Son; nor can He, Who is the Son, come to exist otherwise than by being born, because He is the Son.

READ: COLOSSIANS 1:15-20

JANUARY 24

THE RISE AND FALL OF KINGDOMS

SIR WALTER RALEIGH | 1614

Sir Walter Raleigh (1552-1618) was an English aristocrat, writer, poet, soldier, courtier, spy, and explorer.

We plainly behold living now that great world—the wise work of a great God—as it was then, when but new to itself. By it I say, that we live in the very time when it was created: we behold how it was governed; how it was covered with waters, and again repopulated; how kings and kingdoms have flourished and fallen.

And it is not the least debt which we owe unto history, that it has made us acquainted with our dead ancestors; and, out of the depth and darkness of the earth, delivered us their memory and fame. But it has neither made us remember that the infinite eye and wisdom of God pierces through all our pretenses; nor that the justice of God requires no other accuser than our own consciences.

To repeat God's judgments in particular, upon those which have played with his mercies would require a volume apart: for the sea of examples has no bottom. The marks, set on private men, are with their bodies cast into the earth; and their fortunes, written only in the memories of those that lived with them: so as they who succeed, and have not seen the fall of others, do not fear their own faults.

God's judgments upon the greater and greatest have been left to posterity; first, by those happy hands which the Holy Ghost has guided; and secondly, by their virtue, who have gathered the acts and ends of men mighty and remarkable in the world. For who has not observed what labor, practice, peril, bloodshed, and cruelty the kings and princes of the world have committed to make themselves and their offspring masters of the world? And yet hath Babylon, Persia, Syria, Macedon, Carthage, Rome, and the rest no fruit, flower, grass, nor leaf, springing upon the face of the earth; no, their very roots and ruins do hardly remain.

READ: DANIEL 7:14

JANUARY 25

DISCIPLINE OF THE SOUL

JOHN OF THE CROSS | 16TH CENTURY

John of the Cross (1542-1591), born Juan de Yepes Alvarez, at Fontiveros, Old Castile, was a major figure of the Counter-Reformation.

It must be known that the soul, after it has surrendered to the service of God, is nurtured and loved by Him, even as the newborn child is nurtured by its loving mother, who keeps it warm and cared for in her arms. But as the child grows bigger, the mother sets the child down from her arms and makes it walk upon its feet, so that it may lose the habits of a child and take on more important and substantial occupations. The loving mother is like the grace of God, for, as soon as the soul is revived by its new warmth and fervor, God treats it in the same way. He gives it spiritual milk, sweet and delectable, in all the things of God, without any labor of its own.

Therefore, such a soul finds its delight in spending long periods—possibly whole nights—in prayer; it finds joy in occupying itself with spiritual things. Yet these new souls, even though taking part with great efficacy, persistence, and care, often find themselves, spiritually speaking, very weak and imperfect. For since they are moved to these things by the consolation and pleasure that they find in them, and since they have not been prepared for them through the practice of discipline, they have many faults and imperfections.

After all, any man's actions correspond to the habit of perfection attained by him. And, as these individuals have not had the opportunity to acquire these habits of strength, it will be clearly seen how like children they are in all they do. And it will also be seen how many blessings the dark night brings with it, since it cleanses the soul and purifies it from all these imperfections.

READ: HEBREWS 12:7-11

JANUARY 26

AWARE OF MY UNBELIEF

SAINT PATRICK | 5TH CENTURY

Saint Patrick (c. 387-460) was a Christian missionary who is the most generally recognized patron saint of Ireland.

I, Patrick, a sinner, was taken captive at about sixteen years of age. I did not know the true God; and I was taken into captivity in Ireland with many thousands of people, for we did not keep his precepts, nor were we obedient to our priests who used to remind us of our salvation. And the Lord brought down on us the fury of his being and scattered us among many nations, even to the ends of the earth, where I, in my smallness, am now to be found among foreigners.

There the Lord made me aware of my unbelief, that I might remember my transgressions and turn with all my heart to the Lord my God. He watched over me before I knew him, before I learned sense or even distinguished between good and evil, and he protected me, consoling me as a father would his son.

Therefore, I cannot keep silent, so many favors and graces has the Lord bestowed on me in the land of my captivity. For there is no God but God the Father, unbegotten and without beginning, in whom all things began; and his son Jesus Christ, who manifestly always existed with the Father, and all things visible and invisible were made by him. He was made man, conquered death, was received into Heaven, and given all power over every name in Heaven and on Earth and in Hell, so that every tongue should confess that Jesus Christ is Lord and God. And he poured out his Holy Spirit on us in abundance, which makes the believers and the obedient into sons of God and co-heirs of Christ.

Thus I give untiring thanks to God who kept me faithful in the day of my temptation, so that today I may confidently offer my soul as a living sacrifice for Christ my Lord. Whatever befalls me, be it good or bad, I should accept it equally, and give thanks always to God who revealed to me that I might trust in him, implicitly and forever.

READ: ISAIAH 12:2

The Nature of Mercy

John Wycliffe | 14th century

John Wycliffe (c. 1328-1384), also known as Wycliffe John, was an English theologian, lay preacher, translator, reformer, and university teacher. He is considered the founder of the Lollard movement, a precursor to the Protestant Reformation.

And therefore, Christ bids all men to be merciful, for their Father in Heaven that shall judge them is merciful. But we should understand that this mercy is nothing against reason, and so by this just mercy men should sometimes forgive, and sometimes punish; but always guided by mercy. The reason of mercy stands in this: that which men might do cruelly they may do justly for God's sake, to change the hearts of men; and men may mercifully reprove men, and punish them, and require them to pay what they owe, for the sake of their own improvement.

In this way, God, who is full of mercy, says that He reproves and chastises His wayward children that He loves; and thus Christ reproved Pharisees, and punished priests with other people, and punishes mercifully all damned men in hell, for He could not punish any way but mercifully.

But here men should beware that all the goods that they have be goods of their God, and that they are naked servants of God; they should avoid taking their own vengeance, but avenge injury of God, with the intention to change. Thus Christ, meekest of all, suffered through two temptations of the devil, but in the third He said, "Go, Satan," and reproved him sharply by authority of God. Thus Moses, mildest man of all, killed many thousand of his people, for they worshipped a calf as they should worship God. And thus in our works of mercy lies much discretion, for often our mercy seeks to avenge and punish men, and else justices of man's law should never punish men to the death, but often they do amiss, and they know not when they do well, and so religion of priests should leave such judgments.

Read: Proverbs 3:12

JANUARY 28

ABOUT REMITTANCE OF SIN

ZWINGLI | 1522

Huldrych (or Ulrich) Zwingli (1484-1531) was a pastor and leader of the Reformation in Switzerland.

God alone remits sin through Jesus Christ, his Son, and alone our Lord.

Anyone who assigns this to creatures detracts from the honor of God and gives it to him who is not God; this is real idolatry.

Therefore the confession that is made to a priest or neighbor shall not be declared to be a remittance of sin, but only seeking for advice.

Works of penance coming from the counsel of human beings do not cancel sin; they are imposed as a menace to others.

Christ has borne all our pains and labor. Therefore whoever assigns to works of penance what belongs to Christ errs and slanders God.

Whoever pretends to remit any sin to a penitent being would not be a vicar of God or St. Peter, but of the devil.

Whoever remits any sin only for the sake of money is the companion of Simon and Balaam, and the real messenger of the devil personified.

READ: JOHN 14:6

JANUARY 29

THE GIFT OF THE SPIRIT

THEOGNOSTUS OF ALEXANDRIA | 3RD CENTURY

Theognostus (c. 210-270) was a late third-century Alexandrian theologian who presided over the School of Alexandria.

The substance of the Son is not a substance devised extraneously, nor is it one introduced out of nothing; but it was born of the substance of the Father, as the reflection of light or as the steam of water. For the reflection is not the sun itself, and the steam is not the water itself, nor yet again is it anything alien; neither is He Himself the Father, nor is He alien, but He is an emanation from the substance of the Father, this substance of the Father suffering the while no partition.

For as the sun remains the same and suffers no diminution from the rays that are poured out by it, so neither did the substance of the Father undergo any change in having the Son as an image of itself.

As the Savior converses with those not yet able to receive what is perfect, condescending to their littleness, while the Holy Spirit communes with the perfected, and yet we could never say on that account that the teaching of the Spirit is superior to the teaching of the Son, but only that the Son condescends to the imperfect, while the Spirit is the seal of the perfected; even so it is not on account of the superiority of the Spirit over the Son that the blasphemy against the Spirit is a sin excluding impunity and pardon, but because for the imperfect there is pardon, while for those who have tasted the heavenly gift, and been made perfect, there remains no plea or prayer for pardon.

READ: EPHESIANS 4:30

January 30

Savior, Lead Us by Thy Power

Williams Pantycelyn | 18th century

William Williams Pantycelyn (1717-1791), also known as Williams Pantycelyn, was a poet and writer and is generally acknowledged as Wales' most famous hymn writer. He was also one of the key leaders of the eighteenth-century Welsh Methodist revival.

Savior, lead us by Thy power
Safe into the promised rest;
Choose the path, the way whatever,
Seems to Thee, O Lord, the best;
Be our guide in every peril,
Watch and keep us night and day,
Else our foolish hearts will wander
From the straight and narrow way.

Since in Thee is our redemption
And salvation full and free,
Nothing need our souls dishearten
But forgetfulness of Thee;
Nought can stay our steady progress,
More than conquerors we shall be,
If our eye, whate'er the danger,
Looks to Thee, and none but Thee.

In Thy presence we are happy,
In Thy presence we're secure;
In Thy presence all afflictions
We can easily endure;
In Thy presence we can conquer,
We can suffer, we can die;
Wandering from Thee, we are feeble;
Let Thy love, Lord, keep us nigh.

Read: Psalm 31:3

JANUARY 31

PRESENT WITH THE LORD

VATICAN II | 1964

The Second Vatican Council, commonly known as Vatican II, was the twenty-first
Ecumenical Council of the Catholic Church, opening on October 11, 1962, and closing
on December 8, 1965.

To accomplish so great a work, Christ is always present in His church. By His
power He is present in the sacraments, so that when a man is baptized it is really
Christ Himself who baptizes. He is present in His Word, since it is He Himself
who speaks when the holy scriptures are read. He is present, lastly, when the
church prays and sings, for He promised: "Where two or three are gathered
together in my name, there am I in the midst of them" (Matthew 18:20 KJV).

Christ indeed always associates the church with Himself in this great work
wherein God is perfectly glorified and men are sanctified. The church is His
beloved Bride who calls to her Lord, and through Him offers worship to the
Eternal Father.

Rightly, then, the liturgy is considered as an exercise of the priestly office of
Jesus Christ. In the liturgy the sanctification of the man is signified by signs
perceptible to the senses, and is effected in a way that corresponds with each of
these signs.

In the earthly liturgy we take part in a foretaste of that heavenly liturgy which
is celebrated in the holy city of Jerusalem toward which we journey as pilgrims,
where Christ is sitting at the right hand of God, a minister of the holies and of
the true tabernacle; we sing a hymn to the Lord's glory with all the warriors of
the heavenly army; we eagerly await the Savior, Our Lord Jesus Christ, until He
shall appear and we too will appear with Him in glory.

But before men can come to the liturgy they must be called to faith and to
conversion: "How then are they to call upon him in whom they have not yet
believed? How are they to believe him whom they have not heard? And how
are they to hear if no one preaches? And how are men to preach unless they be
sent?" (see Romans 10:14-15).

READ: MATTHEW 18:20

FEBRUARY 1

A HOLY BROTHERHOOD

JOHN KNOX | 1559

John Knox (c. 1510-1572) was a Scottish clergyman and a leader of the Protestant Reformation who is considered the founder of the Presbyterian denomination in Scotland.

For that same Eternal God and Father, who of mere grace elected us in Christ Jesus his Son, before the foundation of the world was laid, appointed him to be our Head, our Brother, our Pastor, and great Bishop of our souls. But because the enmity between the justice of God and our sins was such that no flesh by itself could or might have attained unto God, it became necessary that the Son of God should descend unto us, and take himself a body of our body, flesh of our flesh, and bone of our bones, and so become the perfect Mediator between God and man; giving power to so many as believe in him to be the sons of God.

By this most holy fraternity, all we have lost in Adam is restored to us again. And for this reason we are not afraid to call God our Father, not so much because he has created us (which we have in common with the reprobate), as that he has given to us his only Son to be our brother, and given us grace to acknowledge and embrace him for our only Mediator.

It was further necessary for the Messiah and Redeemer to be truly God and Man, because he was to underlie the punishment due for our transgressions, and to present himself in the presence of his Father's judgments, in our stead, to suffer for our transgression and disobedience, by death, to overcome him that was author of death.

But because the only God could not suffer death, neither yet could man overcome the same, he joined both together in one person, that the weakness of the one should suffer and be subject to death (which we deserved), and the infinite and invincible power of the other should triumph and purchase for us life, liberty, and perpetual victory. And so we confess, and most undoubtedly believe.

READ: JOHN 1:14

February 2

Happy Forevermore

Samuel Rutherford | 17th century

Samuel Rutherford (c. 1600-1661) was a Scottish Presbyterian theologian and author, and one of the Scottish Commissioners to the Westminster Assembly.

Happy forevermore are those who are fully submerged in the love of Christ, and know no sickness but lovesickness for Christ, and feel no pain but the pain of an absent and hidden Beloved. We run our souls out of breath and tire them in chasing and galloping after our own dreams, to get some created good thing in this life. We would rather stay and spin out a heaven to ourselves, on this side of death; but sorrow, poverty, changes, crosses, and sin are both woof and warp in that ill-spun web.

Oh, how sweet and dear are those thoughts that are still upon the things that are above! And how happy are they who can cry to Christ, "Lord Jesus, have over; come and fetch the sorrowful passenger!" Alas, there is such a scarcity of love, and of lovers, to Christ amongst us all!

Shame on us, who love fair things, like gold, houses, lands, pleasures, honors, and persons, and do not pine and melt away with love for Christ! If those frothy, fluctuating, and restless hearts of ours would become all about Christ, and look into His bottomless love, to the depth of mercy, to the unsearchable riches of His grace, to inquire after and search into the beauty of God in Christ, they would be swallowed up in the depth and height, length and breadth of His goodness.

There is nothing better than to count up the worth of Christ; to take Him up and weigh Him again and again: and after this have none other to court your love, and to woo your soul's delight, but Christ. He will be found worthy of all your love, even if it should swell from the earth to the uppermost circle of the heaven of heavens. To our Lord Jesus and His love I commend you.

Read: Ephesians 3:17-19

A STRAIGHTFORWARD MATTER

THE SCILLITAN MARTYRS | 180 A.D.

The Scillitan Martyrs were a company of twelve North African Christians who were tried and executed for their beliefs on July 17, 180.

On the seventeenth day of July, at Carthage, there were set in the judgment hall Speratus, Nartzalus, Cittinus, Donata, Secunda, and Vestia.

Saturninus the proconsul said: Ye can win the indulgence of our lord the Emperor, if ye return to a sound mind.

Speratus said: We have never spoken ill, but when ill-treated we have given thanks; because we pay heed to our Emperor.

Saturninus said: We swear by the genius of our lord the Emperor.

Speratus said: The empire of this world I know not; but rather I serve that God, whom no man hath seen, nor with these eyes can see.

Saturninus said: Be not partakers of this folly.

Cittinus said: We have none other to fear, save only our Lord God.

Donata said: Honour to Cæsar as Cæsar: but fear to God.

Saturninus said to Speratus: Dost thou persist in being a Christian?

Speratus said: I am a Christian. *And with him they all agreed.*

Saturninus said: Will ye have a space to consider?

Speratus said: In a matter so straightforward there is no considering.

Saturninus said: Have a delay of thirty days and bethink yourselves.

Speratus said a second time: I am a Christian. *And with him they all agreed.*

Saturninus read out the decree from the tablet: Having confessed that they live according to the Christian rite, since after opportunity offered them of returning to the custom of the Romans they have obstinately persisted, it is determined that they be put to the sword.

They all said: Thanks be to God.

And so they all together were crowned with martyrdom; and they reign with the Father and the Son and the Holy Ghost, forever and ever. Amen.

READ: PHILIPPIANS 1:21

THE SIN OF INGRATITUDE

FRANCIS ASBURY | 1812

Francis Asbury (1745-1816) was a pioneer bishop of American Methodism.

The sin of the age, among all classes and nations, is ingratitude to God. If heaven would pass away and hell would burn up, every man and woman in the universe should serve God anyway, for His great benefits bestowed upon them daily. And what unmerited favors are these?

First: We are out of hell; if we had justice dealt to us, we would have been in hell already. Think of the many times we have sinned against God by breaking His laws time and again, yet He has spared us. We are yet in the land of Mercy and Pardon. O, the marvelous goodness of God!

Second: God in His great mercy granted us a second chance, by giving His Son to die for us. Satan would give a million worlds, if he had them, to pray, repent, and obtain the favor of God, but it can never be granted. You and I have offended God times without number, and still the door of mercy is open to us.

Third: Our lives are prolonged. Friend, it is actually a miracle to be alive, when we observe the many instruments of death that are thick in the land to hurry mortals home. Oh, it is only by the goodness of God that we are alive!

Fourth: We still enjoy health. Men do not realize what a God-given blessing it is to have health. It is not properly appreciated until it is gone. But when we visit the sickrooms and see the hundreds of souls that are there, then we know the goodness of God by giving us health.

Fifth: God keeps the lamp of hope burning in our breast. Oh, what a miserable world this would be if the lamp of hope were blown out! Amidst sorrow's bitterest cup and disappointment's gloomiest vale, we are encouraged to hope for a brighter day.

Now, do you think that God is making any unfair demand on you by requiring a wholehearted service? From this hour surrender yourself to Him completely and you will be greatly benefited both in this world and the world to come. Amen.

READ: JUDE 1:24-25

FEBRUARY 5

SEARCH THE SCRIPTURES

WILLIAM WILBERFORCE | 1797

William Wilberforce (1759-1833) was a British politican, philanthropist, and a leader of the movement to abolish the slave trade.

The diligent study of Scripture would reveal to us our past ignorance. We should cease to be deceived by superficial appearances, and to confound the Gospel of Christ with the systems of philosophers; we should become impressed with that weighty truth, that Christianity calls on us, as we value our immortal souls, to be religious and moral, but especially to believe the doctrines, imbibe the principles, and practice the precepts of Christ.

It may be sufficient here to remark that Christianity is always represented in Scripture as the grand, unparalleled instance of God's bounty to mankind. It was graciously held forth in the original promise to our first parents; it was predicted by a long continued series of prophets, the subject of their prayers, inquiries, and longing expectations. In a world that opposed and persecuted them, it was their source of peace, hope, and consolation.

At length it approached—the Desire of all Nations—the long-expected Star announced its presence. "Lord, now let thou thy servant depart in peace, for mine eyes have seen thy salvation," was the exclamation with which it was welcomed by the pious Simeon (see Luke 2:29); and it was universally received and professed among the early converts with thankfulness and joy.

Yet, in vain have we studied "line upon line and precept upon precept" (see Isaiah 28:13). Thus predicted, prayed, and longed for, announced and characterized and rejoiced in, this heavenly treasure poured into our lap in rich abundance we scarce accept. We turn from it coldly, or at best possess it negligently, as a thing of no account or estimation.

Revelation commands, "Faith comes by hearing, and hearing by the word of God." "Search the Scriptures." "Be ready to give to every one a reason of the hope that is in you." Is it not undeniable that with the Bible in our houses, we are yet ignorant of its contents; and that therefore the bulk of the Christian world knows so little, and mistakes so greatly what regards the religion which they profess?

READ: 2 TIMOTHY 3:16-17

A RETURN TO INNOCENCE

ST. GREGORY OF NYSSA | 4TH CENTURY

St. Gregory of Nyssa was a fourth-century bishop who wrote on theology, philosophy, ethics, oration, and asceticism.

Christ was baptized by John so that He might cleanse him who was defiled; that He might bring the Spirit from above, and exalt man to heaven; that he who had fallen might be raised up and he who had cast him down might be put to shame. Do not marvel: for it was with care on the part of him who did us wrong that the plot was laid against us; it is with forethought on the part of our Maker that we are saved.

And he, that evil charmer, framing his new device of sin against our race, drew a disguise worthy of his own intent—dwelling in that creeping thing. But Christ, the repairer of his evildoing, assumes manhood in its fullness, and saves man, and becomes the type and figure of us all, to leave His servants no doubt in their zeal for the tradition. Baptism, then, is a purification from sins, a remission of trespasses, a cause of renovation and regeneration—though not discerned by bodily sight.

For we shall not change the old man, who is wrinkled and gray-headed, to tenderness and youth, by bringing him back again into his mother's womb. But we do bring back, by royal grace, him who bears the scars of sin, and has grown old in evil habits, to the innocence of the babe. For as the newborn child is free from accusations and from reproof, so too the child of spiritual rebirth has nothing for which to answer, being released by royal bounty.

This gift is not the water itself, but the command of God, and the visitation of the Spirit that comes to set us free. But water serves to express the cleansing. As we wash in water to clean our body when it is soiled by dirt or mud, we also apply it in the sacramental action, and display the spiritual brightness in a way that is visible to our senses.

READ: ROMANS 6:4

FEBRUARY 7

THE BLOOD AND THE CROSS

WATCHMAN NEE | 1957

Watchman Nee (1903-1972) was a Chinese Christian author and church leader during the early twentieth century. He spent the last twenty years of his life in prison and was severely persecuted by the Communists in China.

What is the normal Christian life? The Apostle Paul gives us his definition in Galatians 2:20. It is "no longer I, but Christ," which can be summarized: I live no longer, but Christ lives His life in me. God makes it quite clear in His Word that He has only one answer to every human need—His Son, Jesus Christ. He works by taking us out of the way and substituting Christ in our place. The Son of God died instead of us for our forgiveness: He lives instead of us for our deliverance. So we have a Substitute on the Cross, who secures our forgiveness, and a Substitute within, who secures our victory.

When God's light first shines into my heart, my cry is for forgiveness; but once I have received forgiveness I realize that I have not only committed sins before God, but that there is something wrong within. I discover that I have the nature of a sinner. I may seek and receive forgiveness, but then I sin once more. So life goes on in a vicious circle of sinning and being forgiven and then sinning again. I appreciate God's forgiveness, but I want something more: I want deliverance. I need forgiveness for what I have done, but I need also deliverance from what I am.

The first part of Romans speaks of the work of the Lord Jesus which is represented by "the Blood" shed for our justification through "the remission of sins." Later we read of His work represented by "the Cross," and our union with Christ in His death, burial, and resurrection. This distinction is a valuable one. The Blood deals with what we have done, whereas the Cross deals with what we are. The Blood disposes of our sins, while the Cross strikes at the root of our capacity for sin.

READ: 1 CORINTHIANS 1:18

FEBRUARY 8

THE NICENE CREED

FIRST COUNCIL OF NICEA | 325

The Nicene Creed is the creed, or profession of faith, that is most widely used in Christian liturgy. It is called Nicene because, in its original form, it was adopted in the city of Nicaea by the first ecumenical council, which met there in the year 325.

We believe in one God, the Father Almighty, Maker of all things visible and invisible. And in one Lord Jesus Christ, the Son of God, begotten of the Father, the only-begotten; that is, of the essence of the Father, God of God, Light of Light, very God of very God, begotten, not made, being of one substance with the Father;

By whom all things were made both in heaven and on earth;

Who for us men, and for our salvation, came down and was incarnate and was made man;

He suffered, and the third day he rose again, ascended into heaven;

From thence he shall come to judge the quick and the dead.

And in the Holy Ghost.

But those who say: "There was a time when he was not;" and "He was not before he was made;" and "He was made out of nothing," or "He is of another substance" or "essence," or "The Son of God is created," or "changeable," or "alterable"—they are condemned by the holy catholic and apostolic Church.

READ: EPHESIANS 4:1-6

FEBRUARY 9

BLESSED ASSURANCE

FANNY CROSBY | 1873

Frances Jane Crosby (1820-1915), commonly known as Fanny Crosby but sometimes by her married name, Frances van Alstyne, was an American Methodist rescue mission worker, poet, and lyricist known for her Christian hymns. She wrote more than 8,000 hymns, despite being blind from infancy.

Blessed assurance, Jesus is mine!
O what a foretaste of glory divine!
Heir of salvation, purchase of God,
Born of His Spirit, washed in His blood.

This is my story, this is my song,
Praising my Savior, all the day long;
This is my story, this is my song,
Praising my Savior, all the day long.

Perfect submission, perfect delight,
Visions of rapture now burst on my sight;
Angels descending bring from above,
Echoes of mercy, whispers of love.

This is my story, this is my song,
Praising my Savior, all the day long;
This is my story, this is my song,
Praising my Savior, all the day long.

Perfect submission, all is at rest,
I in my Savior am happy and blessed,
Watching and waiting, looking above,
Filled with His goodness, lost in His love.

This is my story, this is my song,
Praising my Savior, all the day long;
This is my story, this is my song,
Praising my Savior, all the day long.

READ: HEBREWS 10:21-23

February 10

The Lonely Heart

Alexander Maclaren | 19th century

Alexander Maclaren (1826-1910) was an English nonconformist preacher, pastor, and minister of Scottish origin.

Jesus was the loneliest man that ever lived. He knew the pain of unappreciated aims, unaccepted love, unbelieved teachings, a heart thrown back upon itself. No man understood Him, no man knew Him, no man thoroughly loved Him or sympathized with Him, and He dwelt apart. He felt the pain of solitude more sharply than sinful men do. Perfect purity is keenly susceptible; a heart fully charged with love is wounded terribly when the love is rejected; with even greater pain the more unselfish it is.

Solitude was no small part of the pain of Christ's passion. Remember the pitiful appeal in Gethsemane, "Wait here and watch with Me." Remember the three vain returns to the sleepers in the hope of finding some sympathy from them. Remember the emphasis with which He foretold the loneliness of His death. And then let us understand how the bitterness of the cup that He drank had, for not the least bitter of its ingredients, the sense that He drank it alone.

Some of us, no doubt, have to live outwardly solitary lives. We all live alone after fellowship and communion. We die alone, and in the depths of our souls we all live alone. So let us be thankful that the Master knows the bitterness of solitude, and has Himself walked that path.

Jesus Christ's union with the Father was deep, close, constant; altogether transcending any experience of ours. But still He sets before us the path of comfort for every lonely heart: "I am not alone, for the Father is with Me." If earth be dark, let us look to Heaven. If the world holds no friend, let us turn to Him who never leaves us. If dear ones are torn from our grasp, let us grasp God. Solitude is bitter; but, like other bitters, it is a tonic. All is not lost if the trees that shut out the sky from us are felled, revealing the blue.

Read: Deuteronomy 31:8

FEBRUARY 11

AT THE END OF THE DAY

ROBERT LOUIS STEVENSON | 1910

Robert Louis Balfour Stevenson (1850-1894) was a Scottish novelist, poet, essayist, and travel writer. His best-known books include Treasure Island, Kidnapped, *and* Strange Case of Dr. Jekyll and Mr. Hyde.

We come before Thee, O Lord, in the end of thy day, with thanksgiving.

Our beloved in the far parts of the earth, those who are now beginning the labors of the day at what time we end them, and those with whom the sun now stands at the point of noon—bless, help, console, and prosper them.

Our guard is relieved, the service of the day is over, and the hour has come to rest. We resign into thy hands our sleeping bodies, our cold hearths, and open doors. Give us to awake with smiles, give us to labor smiling. As the sun returns in the east, so let our patience be renewed with dawn; as the sun lightens the world, so let our loving-kindness make bright this house of our habitation.

Lord, receive our supplications for this house, family, and country. Protect the innocent, restrain the greedy and the treacherous, lead us out of our tribulation into a quiet land.

Look down upon us and upon our absent dear ones. Help us and them; prolong our days in peace and honor. Give us health, food, bright weather, and light hearts. In what we meditate of evil, frustrate our will; in what of good, further our endeavors. Cause injuries to be forgotten and benefits to be remembered.

Let us lie down without fear and awake and arise with exultation. For his sake, in whose words we now conclude.

READ: PSALM 141:2

JUDGMENT OF THE HEART

AMBROSE | 4TH CENTURY

Ambrose (c. 337-397) is considered one of the original Doctors of the Church. He played an important role in the conversion of Augustine.

Many refrain from showing active mercy, because they believe that God does not care about the actions of men, or that He does not know what we think and do in secret. Some think that His judgment seems unjust; for they see that sinners have abundance of riches and enjoy honors, health, and children; while, on the other hand, the just live in poverty and are without children, sickly in body, and often in grief.

That is no small point. Those three royal friends of Job declared him to be a sinner, because they saw that he, after being rich, became poor; that after having many children, he had lost them all, and that he was now covered with sores and was a mass of wounds from head to foot. But Job made the matter plain, stating that the lamp of the wicked is put out, that their destruction will come; that God, the teacher of wisdom and instruction, is not deceived, but is a judge of the truth.

Therefore the blessedness of individuals must not be determined by the value of their known wealth, but according to the voice of their conscience within them. For this, as a true and uncorrupted judge of punishments and rewards, decides between the innocent and the guilty.

You see the enjoyments of the sinner—but remember to question his conscience. You behold his joy, you admire the bodily health of his children, and the amount of his wealth; but look within at the sores and wounds of his soul, the sadness of his heart. And what shall I say of his wealth? "For a man's life consisteth not in the abundance of the things which he possesseth" (Luke 12:15 KJV). Thus the wicked man is a punishment to himself, but the upright man is a grace to himself—and to either, whether good or bad, the reward of his deeds is paid in his own person.

READ: 1 SAMUEL 16:7

FEBRUARY 13

THE ROMANCE OF RELIGION

G. K. CHESTERTON | 1908

Gilbert Keith Chesterton (1874-1936) was an English writer. His prolific and diverse writings included philosophy, poetry, playwriting, journalism, public lecturing and debate, biography, fiction, and Christian apologetics.

All I had heard of Christian theology had alienated me from it. I was a pagan at the age of twelve; a complete agnostic by age sixteen. It was Huxley, Herbert Spencer, and Bradlaugh who brought me back to orthodox theology, sowing in my mind my first wild doubts of doubt. Our grandmothers were quite right when they said that free-thinkers unsettle the mind. They do. They unsettled mine horribly.

If Christianity was, as these people said, a thing purely pessimistic and opposed to life, then I was quite prepared to blow up St. Paul's Cathedral. They proved to me that Christianity was too pessimistic; and then, they began to prove that it was a great deal too optimistic. This puzzled me. The state of the Christian could not be at once so comfortable that he was a coward to cling to it, and so uncomfortable that he was a fool to stand it.

This is the thrilling romance of orthodoxy. People have fallen into a foolish habit of speaking of orthodoxy as something heavy, humdrum, and safe. There never was anything so perilous or exciting. It was the equilibrium of a man behind madly rushing horses, seeming to stoop this way and to sway that, yet in every attitude having the grace of statuary and the accuracy of arithmetic.

The church in its early days went fierce and fast; swerving to the left and right to avoid enormous obstacles. The orthodox church never took the tame course or accepted the conventions; it was never respectable. It is always easy to let the age have its head; the difficult thing is to keep one's own. To have fallen into any one of the fads from Gnosticism to Christian Science would indeed have been obvious and tame. But to have avoided them all has been one whirling adventure; and in my vision the heavenly chariot flies thundering through the ages, the dull heresies sprawling and prostrate, the wild truth reeling but erect.

READ: HEBREWS 4:12

FEBRUARY 14

THE GREATEST GIFT

HENRY DRUMMOND | C. 1874

*Henry Drummond (1851-1897) was a Scottish evangelist, scientific lecturer,
and author who is best remembered for assisting Dwight L. Moody during his
revival campaigns.*

We have been accustomed to being told that the greatest thing in the religious
world is faith. That great word has been the keynote for centuries of the popular
religion; and we have easily learned to look upon it as the greatest thing in the
world. Well, we are wrong. If we believe that, we miss the mark.

The Bible tells us, "The greatest of these is love." It is not an oversight. Paul
was speaking of faith just a moment before. He says, "If I have all faith, so that I
can remove mountains, and have not love, I am nothing." So far from forgetting,
he deliberately contrasts them, "Now abideth faith, hope, love," and without a
moment's hesitation, the decision falls, "The greatest of these is love."

And it is not prejudice. A man is apt to recommend to others his own strong
point. Love was not Paul's strong point. The observing student can detect a
beautiful tenderness growing and ripening all through his character as Paul gets
old; but when we first meet the hand that wrote, "The greatest of these is love," it
is stained with blood.

Do you remember the profound remark which Paul makes elsewhere, "Love
is the fulfilling of the law"? Did you ever think what he meant by that? In
those days men were working their passage to Heaven by keeping the Ten
Commandments, and the hundred and ten other commandments which they
had manufactured out of them. Christ said, "I will show you a more simple way."
If you do one thing, you will do these hundred and ten things, without ever
thinking about them. If you love, you will unconsciously fulfill the whole law. It
is the rule for fulfilling all rules, the new commandment for keeping all the old
commandments—Christ's one secret of the Christian life. Now Paul had learned
that; and he has given us Love defended as the supreme gift.

READ: 1 CORINTHIANS 13:13

A REASON TO LOVE

BERNARD OF CLAIRVAUX | 12TH CENTURY

Bernard of Clairvaux (1090-1153) was a French abbot and the primary builder of the reforming Cistercian order.

You want me to tell you why God is to be loved and how much. I answer, the reason for loving God is God Himself; and the love due to Him is immeasurable. Is this plain? We are to love God for Himself, for two reasons: nothing is more reasonable, nothing more profitable.

Could any reason be greater than this, that He gave Himself for us unworthy wretches? And being God, what better gift could He offer than Himself? Therefore, if anyone seeks for God's claim upon our love here is the greatest: because He first loved us.

Ought He not to be loved in return, when we think who loved, whom He loved, and how much He loved? For it was God who loved us, freely, and loved us while we were yet enemies. And how great was this love of His? St. John answers: "God so loved the world that he gave his only begotten Son, that whosoever believeth in Him should not perish, but have everlasting life" (John 3:16 KJV).

Those who admit the truth of what I have said know why we are bound to love God. But if unbelievers will not admit it, their ingratitude is at once confounded by His innumerable benefits, lavished on our race, and plainly discerned by the senses. Who is it that gives food to all flesh, light to every eye, air to all that breathe? These are not God's best or only gifts, but they are essential to bodily life. Man must seek for the highest gifts—dignity, wisdom, and virtue. By dignity I mean free will, whereby he not only excels all other earthly creatures, but has dominion over them. Wisdom is the power whereby he recognizes this dignity, and perceives also that it is no accomplishment of his own. And virtue impels man to seek eagerly for Him who is man's Source, and to lay fast hold on Him when He has been found.

READ: 1 JOHN 4:19

FEBRUARY 16

GOD AND HUMAN REASON

COPERNICUS | 1543

*Nicolaus Copernicus (1473-1543) was a Renaissance astronomer and the first person
to formulate a comprehensive heliocentric cosmology, which displaced Earth from the
center of the universe.*

I can easily conceive that as soon as some people learn that in this book which
I have written concerning the revolutions of the heavenly bodies, I ascribe
certain motions to the Earth, they will cry out at once that I and my theory
should be rejected. For I am not so much in love with my conclusions as not
to weigh what others will think about them, and although the philosopher's
endeavor is to seek out the truth in all things, so far as this is permitted by God
to the human reason, I still believe that one must avoid theories altogether
foreign to orthodoxy.

When I considered in my own mind how absurd it must seem to those who
know that the judgment of many centuries has approved the view that the Earth
remains fixed as center in the midst of the heavens, if I should, on the contrary,
assert that the Earth moves; I was for a long time at a loss to know whether I
should publish the commentaries which I have written in proof of its motion.
When I considered this carefully, the contempt which I had to fear because of
the novelty and apparent absurdity of my view, nearly induced me to abandon
utterly the work I had begun.

My friends, however, withheld me from this decision. Several eminent and
scholarly men urged that I should no longer refuse to give out my work for the
common benefit of students of mathematics because of fear. They said that
the more absurd most men now thought this theory of mine concerning the
motion of the Earth, the more admiration and gratitude it would command after
they saw the mist of absurdity cleared away by most transparent proofs. So,
influenced by these advisors and this hope, I have at length allowed my friends
to publish the work, as they had long encouraged me to do.

READ: PROVERBS 2:6

FEBRUARY 17

THE ART OF CONTENTMENT

JEREMIAH BURROUGHS | 17TH CENTURY

Jeremiah Burroughs (c. 1600-1646) was an English Congregationalist and a well-known Puritan preacher.

A man who has learned the art of contentment is the most contented with any low condition that he has in the world, and yet he cannot be satisfied. Here is the mystery of it: though his heart is so enlarged that the enjoyment of all the world and ten thousand worlds cannot satisfy him for his portion; yet he has a heart quieted under God's disposal, if he gives him but bread and water. To join these two together is indeed a great art and mystery.

Though he is contented with God in a little, yet those things that would content other men will not content him. The men of the world seek after wealth, and think they would be content. But a gracious heart says that if he had the quintessence of all the excellences of all the creatures in the world, it could not satisfy him; and yet this man can sing, and be merry and joyful when he has only a crust of bread and a little water in the world. Great is the mystery of godliness, not only in the doctrinal part of it, but in the practical part of it also.

A soul that is capable of God can be filled with nothing else but God. Though a gracious heart knows that it is capable of God, and was made for God, carnal hearts think without reference to God. But a gracious heart, being enlarged to be capable of God, and enjoying somewhat of him, can be filled by nothing in the world; it must only be God himself.

As in Psalm 73:25, "Whom have I in heaven but thee, and there is none upon earth that I desire beside thee" (KJV). If God gave you not only earth but heaven, that you should rule over sun, moon, and stars, and have the rule over the highest of the sons of men, it would not be enough to satisfy you, unless you had God himself.

READ: PHILIPPIANS 4:11-13

FEBRUARY 18

DESIRE ONE THING

SØREN KIERKEGAARD | 1843

Søren Aabye Kierkegaard (1813-1855) was a Danish Christian philosopher,
theologian, and religious author interested in human psychology.

Father in Heaven! What is a man without You! What is all that he knows, vast accumulation though it may be, but a chipped fragment if he does not know You! What is all his striving, even if it could encompass the world, but a half-finished work if he does not know You—the One, who is one thing and who is all!

May You give to the intellect, wisdom to comprehend that one thing; to the heart, sincerity to receive this understanding; to the will, purity that wills only one thing. In prosperity may You grant perseverance to will one thing; amid distractions, collectedness to will one thing; in suffering, patience to will one thing.

Oh, You who give both the beginning and the completion, at the dawn of day, give to the young man the resolution to will one thing. As the day wanes, give to the old man a renewed remembrance of his first resolution, that the first may be like the last, the last like the first, in possession of a life that has willed only one thing. Alas, but this has indeed not come to pass. The separation of sin lies in between. Each day, something is being placed in between: delay, blockage, interruption, delusion, corruption. So in this time of repentance may You give the courage once again to will one thing.

True, it is an interruption of our daily tasks, when the penitent is alone before You in self-accusation. This is indeed an interruption. But it is an interruption that searches back into its very beginnings that it might bind up anew that which sin has separated, that in its grief it might atone for lost time, that in its anxiety it might bring to completion that which lies before it. Oh, give victory in the day of need so that what a man cannot achieve by his burning wish nor his determined resolution, may be granted unto him in the sorrowing of repentance: to will only one thing.

READ: PSALM 27:4

FEBRUARY 19

JUST DISCIPLINE

LEO THE GREAT | 5TH CENTURY

Pope Leo I (c. 400-461), or Pope Saint Leo the Great, was an Italian aristocrat best known for persuading Attila the Hun to turn back from his invasion of Italy.

Excommunication should be inflicted only on those who are guilty of some great crime, and even then not hastily. No Christian should lightly be denied communion, nor should that be done at the will of an angry priest which the judge's mind ought to a certain extent unwillingly and regretfully to carry out for the punishment of a great crime. For we have ascertained that some have been cut off from the grace of communion for trivial deeds and words, and that the soul for which Christ's blood was shed has been exposed to the devil's attacks and wounded, disarmed, so to say, and stripped of all defense by the infliction of so savage a punishment as to fall an easy prey to him.

Of course if ever a case has arisen of such a kind as in due proportion to the nature of the crime committed to deprive a man of communion, only he who is involved in the accusation must be subjected to punishment: and he who is not shown to be a partner in its commission ought not to share in the penalty.

Wherefore, because we are anxious that the settled state of all the Churches and the harmony of the priests should be maintained, exhorting you to unity in the bond of love, we both entreat and admonish you, in the interests of your peace and dignity, to keep what has been decreed by us at the inspiration of God. But in our anxiety we are claiming for you that no further innovations should be allowed, and that for the future no opportunity should be given for the usurper to infringe your privileges. For we acknowledge that it can only redound to our credit, if in our maintenance of Apostolic discipline we do not allow what belongs to your position to fall to the ground through unscrupulous aggressions.

READ: GALATIANS 6:1-3

THE BLESSING OF SORROW

OCTAVIUS WINSLOW | 1858

Octavius Winslow (1808-1878) was one of the foremost evangelical preachers of the nineteenth century in England and America.

God's family is a sorrowing family. "I have chosen you," He says, "in the furnace of affliction." "I will leave in the midst of you a poor and an afflicted people." The history of the Church finds its fittest emblem in the burning yet unconsumed bush that Moses saw. Man is "born to sorrows;" but the believer is "appointed thereunto." It would seem to be a condition inseparable from his high calling. If he is journeying to the heavenly kingdom, his path lies through "much tribulation." If he is a follower of Jesus, it is to "go unto Him without the camp, bearing His reproach."

But, if his sufferings abound, much more so do his consolations. God comforts His sorrowful ones with the characteristic love of a mother. See the tenderness with which that mother alleviates the suffering and soothes the sorrow of her mourning one. So does God comfort His mourners. Oh, there is a tenderness and a delicacy of feeling in God's comforts which distances all expression. There is no harsh reproof—no unkind upbraiding—no unveiling of the circumstances of our calamity to the curious and unfeeling eye. God meets our case in every sorrow. Go, then, and breathe your sorrows into God's heart, and He will comfort you.

Blessed sorrow! If in the time of your bereavement, your grief, and your solitude, you are led to Jesus, making Him your Savior, your Friend, your Counselor, and your Shield. Blessed loss! If it be compensated by a knowledge of God, if you find in Him a Father now, to whom you will transfer your ardent affections—upon whom you will repose your bleeding heart. But let your heart be true with Him. Love Him, obey Him, confide in Him, serve Him, live for Him; and in all the unknown, untrodden, unveiled future of your history, a voice shall gently whisper in your ear— "As one whom his mother comforts, so will I comfort you" (Isaiah 66:13).

READ. MATTHEW 5:3-10

February 21

The Blind Lead the Blind

Gilbert Tennent | 1739

Gilbert Tennent (1703-1764) was one of the religious leaders of the Great Awakening, along with Jonathan Edwards and George Whitefield.

Is it a strange thing to think that God does not ordinarily use the ministry of His enemies to turn others to be His friends, seeing He works by suitable means? I cannot think that God has given any promise that He will be with and bless the labors of natural (non-spiritual) ministers for, if He had, He would be surely as good as His Word. But I can neither see nor hear of any blessing upon these men's labors, unless it is a rare, wonderful instance of chance! Whereas, the ministry of faithful men blossoms and bears fruit as the rod of Aaron.

From such as have a form of godliness and deny the power thereof, we are enjoined to turn away. And are there not many such? Our Lord advised His disciples to beware of the leaven of the Pharisees (Matthew 16:6), by which He shows that He meant their doctrine and hypocrisy, which were both sour enough.

Memorable is the answer of our Lord to His disciples in Matthew 15:12-14: "Then came his disciples and said unto him, Knowest thou that the Pharisees were offended . . .? But he answered and said, Every plant, which my heavenly Father hath not planted, shall be rooted up. Let them alone: they be blind leaders of the blind. And if the blind lead the blind, both shall fall into the ditch" (KJV). If it is objected that we are bid to go to hear those who sit in Moses' chair (Matthew 23:2-3), I would answer this, in the words of a body of dissenting ministers: "Sitting in Moses' chair signifies a succeeding of Moses in the ordinary part of his office and authority; so did Joshua and the seventy elders (Exodus 18:21-26). Now, Moses was no priest (say they) though of Levi's tribe, but king in Jeshurun, a civil ruler and judge, chosen by God (Exodus 18:13)."

Therefore, no more is meant by the Scripture in the objection but that it is the duty of people to hear and obey the lawful commands of the civil magistrate, according to Romans 13:5.

Read: Matthew 23:2

FEBRUARY 22

HIS INVISIBLE POWER

TATIAN | 2ND CENTURY

Tatian the Assyrian (c. 120-180) was an early Christian writer and theologian of the second century.

For what reason, men of Greece, do you wish to bring the government, as in a boxing match, into collision with Christians? And, if I am not inclined to comply with these tactics, why am I to be abhorred as a villain? If the sovereign orders the payment of tribute, I am ready to render it. Should my master command me to act as a bondsman and to serve, I acknowledge the serfdom. Man is to be honored as a fellow man; but God alone is to be feared—He who is not visible to human eyes, nor comes within the capacity of human art and expression. Only when I am commanded to deny Him, will I not obey, but would rather die than show myself false and ungrateful.

Our God did not begin to be in time: He alone is without beginning, and He Himself is the beginning of all things. God is a Spirit, not inhabiting matter, but the Maker of everything; He is invisible, impalpable, being Himself the Father of both sensible and invisible things. Him we know from His creation, and apprehend His invisible power by His works. I refuse to worship that workmanship which He has made for our sakes. The sun and moon were made for us: how, then, can I worship my own servants? How can I speak of animals and stones as gods?

For the spirit that inhabits matter is inferior to the more divine Spirit and not to be honored equally with the perfect God. Nor even ought the ineffable God to be presented with gifts; for He who is in want of nothing is not to be misrepresented by us as though He were in need. I hope I have set forth our views distinctly and clearly.

READ: ISAIAH 37:16

FEBRUARY 23

A HOLY PARADOX

AUGUSTINE | 398

Augustine (354-430) was Bishop of Hippo Regius and one of the most important figures in the development of Western Christianity. He believed that the grace of Christ was indispensable to human freedom.

Great are You, O Lord, and greatly to be praised; great is Your power, and Your wisdom is infinite. You awaken us to delight in Your praise; for You made us for Yourself, and our heart is restless, until it rests in You. They that seek the Lord shall praise Him: for they that seek shall find Him, and they that find shall praise Him.

I will seek You, Lord, by calling on You; and will call on You, believing in You; for to us You have been preached. My faith, Lord, shall call on You, which You have given me, wherewith You have inspired me, through the Incarnation of Your Son, through the ministry of the Preacher.

How shall I call upon my God, my God and Lord, since, when I call for Him, I shall be calling Him to myself? And what room is there within me, where my God can come into me, God who made heaven and earth? Is there, indeed, O Lord my God, anything in me that can contain You?

I could not be then, O my God, could not be at all, were You not in me; or, rather, unless I was in You, of whom are all things, by whom are all things, in whom are all things. For where can I go beyond heaven and earth, that my God should come into me, God who hath said, "I fill the heaven and the earth"?

Do the heaven and earth contain You, since You fill them? Or do You fill them and yet overflow, since they do not contain You? But do You, who fills all things, fill them with Your whole self? Or, since all things cannot contain You wholly, do they contain part of You? And all at once the same part? Or each its own part, the greater more, the smaller less? And is, then, one part of You greater, another less? Or, are You wholly everywhere, while nothing contains You wholly?

READ: 1 KINGS 8:27

FEBRUARY 24

HE COMES QUICKLY

AIMEE SEMPLE MCPHERSON | 1927

Aimee Semple McPherson (1890-1944) was an evangelist and media celebrity in the 1920s and 1930s. She founded the Foursquare Church and was a pioneer in the use of modern media, especially radio.

That the Lord Jesus Christ is coming back to this earth some day, no honest believer in the Word of God can doubt. Most emphatically and unmistakably does the sacred page declare it. In the Old Testament, there are twenty times as many references to the second coming of Christ, as to His first coming. That is, twenty times as many references to His coming as a crowned King, seated upon the throne of David, ruling with a rod of iron, bringing victory and glory unto Jerusalem, and peace upon earth: as to His coming—a meek and lowly Jesus, wounded for our transgressions, bruised for our iniquities, and bleeding as a slain Lamb upon the cursed tree.

Thus it was that the Jews, who had been looking for the mighty King, failed to recognize the lowly Nazarene; and refuse to recognize Him to this day. And yet, the cross must ever precede the crown. He came with the cross, fulfilling Isaiah 53; and now He is coming with a crown, the Messiah and King. Not only did He come to the earth once—Christ offered to bear the sins of many; but "unto them that look for him shall he appear the second time" (Hebrews 9:28 KJV).

Every time you repeat the Lord's prayer, you are praying for Christ's return. "Thy kingdom come, Thy will be done, on earth as it is in Heaven." How can there be a kingdom without a King, or His righteous reign be established upon the earth till Christ returns to rout the hosts of darkness, cast down Satanic rules, and wield His own dear scepter over the lands?

The last prayer in the Bible is a great heart throbbing cry for His return. "Even so, Lord Jesus, come quickly" (see Revelation 22:20). And the answer still rings from Heaven—"Surely I come quickly; and My reward is with Me" (see Revelation 22:12).

READ: REVELATION 22:20

FEBRUARY 25

THE ACT OF CONTRITION

JAMES GIBBONS | 1884

James Gibbons (1834-1921) was a cardinal of the Roman Catholic Church, only the second American to receive that distinction.

O my God,
I am heartily sorry for
Having offended Thee,
And I detest all my sins,
Because I dread the loss of heaven,
And the pains of hell;
But most of all because
They offend Thee, my God,
Who are all good and
Deserving of all my love.
I firmly resolve,
With the help of Thy grace
To confess my sins,
To do penance
And to amend my life.
Amen.

READ: PSALM 41:4

DECEPTION AND CORRUPTION

WILLIAM GURNALL | 1655

William Gurnall (1617-1679) was an English author who signed the declaration required by the Act of Uniformity 1662, on account of which he was the subject of a libelous attack, published in 1665.

Satan singles out persons of prominence and power. They may be either in the state or in the church. If he can, he will secure both the throne and the pulpit, as the two generals that command the whole army. A head of state may influence thousands; therefore, Paul said to Elymas, when he tried to dissuade the deputy from the faith, "O full of all subtilty and all mischief, thou child of the devil" (Acts 13:10 KJV). As if he had said, "You have learned this from your father the devil—to haunt the courts of princes and wield your influence over rulers."

Satan doubles his leverage in gaining such leaders to his side. First of all, they have the power to draw others to their way. Corrupt the captain, and he will bring his troops with him. Let Jeroboam set up idolatry, and all Israel is soon in a snare. Second, should the sin stay at court and the infection go no further, yet a whole kingdom may pay dearly for the sin of its leader. David succumbed to Satan's temptation to number the people, but the entire nation suffered the plague of punishment with him (1 Chronicles 21).

Besides trying to infiltrate the ranks of government, Satan also aims at those in office in the church. What better way to infect the whole town than to poison the cistern where they draw their water? He takes special delight in corrupting the heart of a minister. If he can wiggle into a pastor's heart, then he is free to roam among God's flock undetected—a devil in shepherd's clothing. How may the worship of God be discredited? Let the world observe the scandalous conduct of a minister, and many, both good and bad, will reject the truth of the Gospel on the strength of the lie his life tells.

READ: 1 TIMOTHY 2:1-3

IN PERFECT HARMONY

ORIGEN | 246-248 A.D.

Origen (c. 185-254) was an early Christian African scholar and theologian, and one of the most distinguished writers of the early church.

There is in the Divine oracles nothing crooked or perverse, for they are all plain to those who understand. But the Word is the one Shepherd of things rational which may have an appearance of discord to those who have not ears to hear, but are truly at perfect concord. For as the different chords of the psalter or the lyre, each of which gives forth a certain sound of its own which seems unlike the sound of another chord to a man who is not musical, so those who are not skilled in hearing the harmony of God in the sacred Scriptures think that the Old is not in harmony with the New, or the Prophets with the Law, or the Gospels with one another, or the Apostle with the Gospel, or with himself, or with the other Apostles.

But he who comes instructed in the music of God, being a man wise in word and deed, and, on this account, like another David—which is, by interpretation, skilful with the hand—will bring out the sound of the music of God, having learned from this at the right time to strike the chords, now the chords of the Law, now the Gospel chords in harmony with them, and again the Prophetic chords, and, when reason demands it, the Apostolic chords which are in harmony with the Prophetic, and likewise the Apostolic with those of the Gospels.

For all the Scripture is the one perfect and harmonized instrument of God, which from different sounds gives forth one saving voice to those willing to learn, which stops and restrains every working of an evil spirit, just as the music of David laid to rest the evil spirit in Saul.

READ: PSALM 18:30

FEBRUARY 28

OF INCOMPARABLE WORTH

JOHN PAUL II | 1995

John Paul II (1920-2005) reigned as pope of the Roman Catholic Church from October 16, 1978, until his death on April 2, 2005.

Man is called to a fullness of life which far exceeds the dimensions of his earthly existence, because it consists in sharing the very life of God. Even in the midst of difficulties and uncertainties, every person sincerely open to truth and goodness can come to recognize in the natural law written in the heart the sacred value of human life from its very beginning until its end, and can affirm the right of every human being to have this primary good respected to the highest degree.

In a special way, believers in Christ must defend and promote this right. This reveals to humanity not only the boundless love of God who "so loved the world that he gave his only Son" (John 3:16), but also the incomparable value of every human person. Therefore every threat to human dignity and life must necessarily be felt in the Church's very heart.

Today this proclamation is especially pressing because of the extraordinary increase and gravity of threats to the life of individuals and peoples, especially where life is weak and defenseless. In addition to the ancient scourges of poverty, hunger, endemic diseases, violence and war, new threats are emerging on an alarmingly vast scale.

The Second Vatican Council, in a passage which retains all its relevance today, forcefully condemned a number of crimes against human life: "Whatever is opposed to life itself, such as murder, genocide, abortion, euthanasia, or willful self-destruction; whatever violates the integrity of the human person; whatever insults human dignity, such as subhuman living conditions, arbitrary imprisonment, deportation, slavery, prostitution; wherever people are treated as mere instruments of gain rather than as free and responsible persons; all these things and others like them are infamies indeed. They poison human society, and moreover, they are a supreme dishonor to the Creator."

READ: MATTHEW 25:45

LIFE FOR SINNERS

ROBERT TRAILL | 17TH CENTURY

Robert Traill (1642-1716) was a Scottish Presbyterian minister. He was repeatedly persecuted for his beliefs and imprisoned for refusing to take an unlawful oath.

When clear light about the law shines upon a man's conscience, then all the Babel-building of their own works—their praying, reading, hearing, and holiness—is all thrown to the ground by the law of God. The law condemns them utterly in point of righteousness. Indeed it commands them in point of practice, and it commends them as things pleasing to God; but in point of righteousness before God, the law condemns them utterly. The only language of the law is this, "Do all, and live; fail in the least, and die"—and thus the man sees all his own righteousness is gone.

When a poor awakened sinner, who never knew the grace of God, is brought under some conviction of sin and duty, he then sets about praying, reading, and reforming; in the meantime he is an utter stranger to Jesus Christ. Now what a great matter is it for a man to forego all this, as if it had no worth? But why should not a man be willing to part with it?

"I count all things but loss . . . and [dung]," says the apostle, "that I may win Christ" (Philippians 3:8 KJV). This blasphemous frame is expressed in Ezekiel, "When I shall say to the righteous, that he shall surely live; if he trust to his own righteousness, and commit iniquity, all his righteousnesses shall not be remembered; but for his iniquity that he hath committed, he shall die for it" (Ezekiel 33:13 KJV).

When the sinner learns he must forego all that he has gained, that he has no hopes at all of a righteousness by the law, he is sorry to part with the rotten props of his own righteousness, as if taking it away was what cast him into hell; when it is the only way to save him from it. No man can be a believer on Jesus Christ, but he that despairs of righteousness by his own doings. The law can give eternal life to a sinless man; but it can give no life to a sinner.

READ: ROMANS 3:21-24

MARCH 1

WHAT IS THE TRUE FAITH?

THE HEIDELBERG CATECHISM | 1563

The Heidelberg Catechism is a Protestant confessional document taking the form of a series of questions and answers, for use in teaching Reformed Christian doctrine. It has been translated into many languages and is regarded as one of the most influential of the Reformed catechisms.

WHAT IS TRUE FAITH?

True faith is not only a certain knowledge, whereby I hold for truth all that God has revealed to us in his word, but also an assured confidence, which the Holy Ghost works by the gospel in my heart; that not only to others, but to me also, remission of sin, everlasting righteousness and salvation, are freely given by God, merely of grace, only for the sake of Christ's merits.

WHAT ARE THESE ARTICLES?

1. I believe in God the Father, Almighty, Maker of heaven and earth:
2. And in Jesus Christ, his only begotten Son, our Lord:
3. Who was conceived by the Holy Ghost, born of the Virgin Mary:
4. Suffered under Pontius Pilate; was crucified, dead, and buried: He descended into hell:
5. The third day he rose again from the dead:
6. He ascended into heaven, and sitteth at the right hand of God the Father Almighty:
7. From thence he shall come to judge the quick and the dead:
8. I believe in the Holy Ghost:
9. I believe in a holy catholic church: the communion of saints:
10. The forgiveness of sins:
11. The resurrection of the body:
12. And the life everlasting.

READ: 1 TIMOTHY 4:6

TO SEE HIS ESSENCE

THOMAS AQUINAS | 1270

Thomas Aquinas (1225-1274) was an Italian Dominican priest and, along with Augustine, the most influential Christian philosopher and theologian through the Middle Ages.

"The grace of God is life everlasting" (see Romans 6:23). But life everlasting consists in the vision of the Divine essence, according to the words: "This is eternal life, that they may know Thee the only true God" (see John 17:3). Therefore to see the essence of God is possible to the created intellect by grace, and not by nature.

It is impossible for any created intellect to see the essence of God by its own natural power. For knowledge is regulated according as the thing known is in the knower, and according to the mode of the knower. Hence the knowledge of every knower is ruled according to its own nature. If therefore the mode of anything's being exceeds the mode of the knower, it must result that the knowledge of the object is above the nature of the knower.

To God alone does it belong to be His own subsistent being. Therefore what exists only in individual matter we know naturally, for our soul, whereby we know, is the form of certain matter. Now our soul possesses two cognitive powers; one is the act of a corporeal organ, which naturally knows things existing in individual matter. But there is another kind of cognitive power in the soul, called the intellect; and this is not the act of any corporeal organ. The intellect naturally knows natures, not as they exist in individual matter, but as they are abstracted by consideration; hence it follows that through the intellect we can understand these objects as universal; and this is beyond the power of the sense.

The angelic intellect naturally knows natures beyond the power of the intellect of our soul in the state of its present life, united as it is to the body. It follows therefore that to know self-subsistent being is beyond the natural power of any created intellect. Therefore the created intellect cannot see the essence of God, unless God by His grace unites Himself to the created intellect, as an object made intelligible to it.

READ: 1 CORINTHIANS 13:12

THE LEAST OF THESE

RON SIDER | 1977

Ronald James Sider (1939–) is a Canadian-born American theologian and
Christian activist.

According to Scripture, defending the weak, the stranger, and the oppressed is
as much an expression of God's essence as creating the universe. Because of who
he is, Yahweh lifts up the mistreated. The foundation of Christian concern for
the hungry and oppressed is that God cares especially for them.

God not only acts in history to liberate the poor, but in a mysterious way that
we can only partly fathom, the Sovereign of the universe identifies with the
weak and destitute. Proverbs 19:17 says: "Whoever is kind to the poor lends to
the Lord" (NRSV). What a statement! Assisting a poor person is like helping the
Creator of all things with a loan.

Only in the Incarnation can we begin to perceive what God's identification
with the weak, oppressed, and poor really means. "Though he was rich," Paul
says of our Lord Jesus, "yet for your sakes he became poor" (2 Corinthians
8:9 KJV).

Jesus was born in a small, insignificant province of the Roman Empire. His
first visitors, the shepherds, were viewed by Jewish society as thieves. His parents
were too poor to bring the normal offering for purification. Jesus was a refugee.
Since Jewish rabbis received no fees for their teaching, Jesus had no regular
income during his public ministry. Nor did he have a home of his own.

When asked if he were the long-expected Messiah, Jesus simply pointed to his
deeds: he was healing the sick and preaching to the poor. But the clearest statement
about Jesus' compassion for the poor is found in Matthew 25: "I was hungry and
you gave me food, I was thirsty and you gave me something to drink . . . I was
naked and you gave me clothing . . . Truly I tell you, just as you did it to one of the
least of these who are members of my family, you did it to me" (35-36, 40 NRSV).

READ: MATTHEW 25:40

MARCH 4

A PEACE CONVENTION

WILLIAM LLOYD GARRISON | 1838

*William Lloyd Garrison (1805-1879) was a prominent American abolitionist,
journalist, and social reformer. He wrote the following declaration after taking part in
a discussion on the means of suppressing war in the Society for the Establishment of
Peace among Men.*

We the undersigned, regard it as due to ourselves, to the cause which we
love, to the country in which we live, to publish a declaration expressive of
the purposes we aim to accomplish and the measures we shall adopt to carry
forward the work of peaceful, universal reformation.

We cannot acknowledge allegiance to any human government. We recognize
but one King and Lawgiver, one Judge and Ruler of mankind. Our country is the
world, our countrymen are all mankind. We love the land of our nativity only
as we love all other lands. The interests and rights of American citizens are no
more dear to us than those of the whole human race. Hence we can allow no
appeal to patriotism to revenge any national insult or injury.

The dogma that all the governments of the world are approvingly ordained
of God, and that the powers that be in the United States, in Russia, in Turkey,
are in accordance with his will, is no less absurd than impious. It makes the
impartial Author of human freedom and equality unequal and tyrannical. It
cannot be affirmed that the powers that be in any nation are actuated by the
spirit or guided by the example of Christ in the treatment of enemies; therefore
they cannot be agreeable to the will of God; and therefore their overthrow by a
spiritual regeneration of their subjects is inevitable.

We believe that the penal code of the old covenant—an eye for an eye, and
a tooth for a tooth—has been abrogated by Jesus Christ, and that under the
new covenant the forgiveness instead of the punishment of enemies has been
enjoined on all his disciples in all cases whatsoever. To extort money from
enemies, cast them into prison, or execute them, is obviously not to forgive but
to take retribution.

READ: LUKE 6:35

THE WESTMINSTER CONFESSION OF FAITH

1646

The Westminster Confession of Faith was drawn up by the 1646 Westminster Assembly, becoming the "subordinate standard" of doctrine in the Church of Scotland and influencing Presbyterian churches worldwide.

The authority of the holy Scripture, for which it ought to be believed and obeyed, depends not upon the testimony of any man or church, but wholly upon God (who is truth itself), the Author thereof; and therefore it is to be received, because it is the Word of God.

We may be moved and induced by the testimony of the Church to a high and reverent esteem of the holy Scripture; and the efficacy of the doctrine, the majesty of the style, the consent of all the parts, the scope of the whole (which is to give all glory to God). Yet, notwithstanding, our full assurance of the infallible truth and divine authority of Scripture comes from the inward work of the Holy Spirit, bearing witness by and with the Word in our hearts.

The whole counsel of God, concerning all things necessary for his own glory, man's salvation, faith, and life, is either expressly set down in Scripture, or by good and necessary consequence may be deduced from Scripture: unto which nothing at any time is to be added, whether by new revelations of the Spirit, or traditions of men. Nevertheless we acknowledge the inward illumination of the Spirit of God to be necessary for the saving understanding of such things as are revealed in the Word; and that there are some circumstances concerning the worship of God, and government of the Church, common to human actions and societies, which are to be ordered by the light of nature and Christian prudence, according to the general rules of the Word, which are always to be observed.

All things in Scripture are not alike plain in themselves, nor equally clear unto all; yet those things which are necessary to be known, believed, and observed, for salvation, are so clearly propounded and opened in some place of Scripture or other, that not only the learned, but the unlearned, in a due use of the ordinary means, may attain unto a sufficient understanding of them.

READ: PSALM 119.105

MARCH 6

AVOID IDLE WORDS

IGNATIUS | 1548

St. Ignatius of Loyola (1419-1556) was the founder of the Jesuits and was canonized by Pope Gregory XV in 1622. His Spiritual Exercises *are a central part of the first-year training of Jesuit novitiates, although they are increasingly being used by lay people and non-Catholics.*

One must not speak an idle word. By idle word I mean one that does not benefit either me or another, and is not directed to that intention. Therefore words spoken for any useful purpose, or meant to profit one's own or another's soul, the body or temporal goods, are never idle, not even if one were to speak of something foreign to one's state of life, as, for instance, if a religious person speaks of wars or articles of trade; but in all that is said there is merit in directing well, and sin in directing badly, or in speaking idly.

Nothing must be said to injure another's character or to find fault, because if I reveal a mortal sin that is not public, I sin mortally; if a venial sin, venially; and if a defect, I show a defect of my own. But if the intention is right, in two ways one can speak of the sin or fault of another.

First, when the sin is public, as in the case of a public prostitute, and of a sentence given in judgment, or of a public error that is infecting the souls with whom one comes in contact. Secondly, when the hidden sin is revealed to some person that he may help to raise him who is in sin—supposing, however, that he has some probable conjectures or grounds for thinking that he will be able to help him.

READ: JAMES 1:26

March 7

The Conciliation of Peace

Dionysius | 5th century

Dionysius the Areopagite is the name given to the anonymous author of a number of fifth-century Christian texts. Debates about the identity of the author continue to this day.

Come, then, let us extol the Peace Divine, and Source of conciliation, by hymns of peace! For this it is which unifies all, and engenders, and effects the agreement and fellowship of all. Wherefore, even all things aspire to it, which turns their divided multiplicity into the thorough Oneness, and unifies the tribal war of the whole into a homogeneous dwelling together, by the participation of the divine Peace.

With regard, then, to the more reverend of the conciliating powers, these indeed are united to themselves and to each other, and to the one Source of Peace of the whole; and the things that are under them, these they unite also to themselves and to each other, and to the One and all-perfect Source and Cause of the Peace of all, which, passing indivisibly to the whole, limits and terminates and secures everything, as if by a kind of bolts, which bind together things that are separated; and do not permit them, when separated, to rush to infinity and the boundless, and to become without order, and without stability, and destitute of God, and to depart from the union amongst themselves, and to become intermingled in each other, in every sort of confusion.

Concerning then, this, the Divine Peace and Repose, as compared with every known progression, immobility, how it rests and is at ease, and how it is in itself, and within itself, and entire, and to itself entire is super-united, and when entering into itself, and multiplying itself, neither loses its own Union, but even proceeds to all, while remaining entire within, by reason of excess of its Union surpassing all, it is neither permitted, nor attainable to any existing being, either to express or to understand. But, having premised this, as unutterable and unknowable, as being beyond all, let us examine its conceived and uttered participations, and this, as possible to men, and to us, as inferior to many good men.

Read: Ephesians 4:3

March 8
The Universal Church
John Huss | 14th century

John Huss (c. 1369-1415) was a Czech priest, philosopher, reformer, and master at Charles University in Prague. He was burned at the stake for heresy against the doctrines of the Catholic Church.

Likewise the church of the righteous is on the one hand catholic, that is, universal, which is not a part of anything else. On the other hand, it is particular, a part with other parts, as the Savior said: "Where two or three are gathered together in my name, there am I in the midst of them" (Matthew 18:20 kjv). From this it follows that two righteous persons congregated together in Christ's name constitute, with Christ as the head, a particular holy church, and likewise three or four and so on to the whole number of the predestinate. In this sense the term church is often used in Scripture, as when the apostle says, "To the church which is in Corinth, to the sanctified in Jesus Christ" (see 1 Corinthians 1:2).

But the holy catholic—that is, universal—church is the totality of the predestinate—present, past, and future. For Augustine says: "The church which brought forth Abel, Enoch, Noah, and Abraham, also brought forth Moses, and at a later time the prophets before the Lord's advent and she, which brought forth these, also brought forth the apostles and our martyrs and all good Christians. For she has brought forth all who have been born and lived at different periods, but they have all been comprised in a company of one people. And the citizens of this city have experienced the toils of this pilgrimage."

From these words of Augustine we deduce that the universal church is one, praising God from the beginning of the world to the end; that the holy angels are a part of the holy catholic church; that the part of the church called pilgrim or militant is helped by the church triumphant; that the church triumphant and the church militant are bound together by the bond of love; that the whole church and every part of it are to worship God, and that neither she nor any part of it wishes to be worshipped as God.

Read: Romans 12:5

MARCH 9
THE VALUE OF KNOWLEDGE
J. GRESHAM MACHEN | 1913

John Gresham Machen (1881-1937) was an American Presbyterian theologian in the early twentieth century.

One of the greatest problems that has agitated the Church is the relationship between knowledge and piety, between culture and Christianity. Some men have devoted themselves chiefly to the task of forming right conceptions as to Christianity and its foundations. To them no fact, however trivial, has appeared worthy of neglect; by them truth has been cherished for its own sake.

Some, on the other hand, have emphasized the essential simplicity of the gospel. The world is lying in misery, we ourselves are sinners, men are perishing in sin every day. So desperate is the need that we have no time to engage in vain babblings. While we are discussing the exact location of the churches of Galatia, men are perishing under the curse of the law; while we are settling the date of Jesus' birth, the world is doing without its Christmas message.

Christianity is the proclamation of an historical fact—that Jesus Christ rose from the dead. Modern thought has no place for that proclamation. It prevents men even from listening to the message. Yet the culture of today cannot simply be rejected as a whole. It is either subservient to the gospel or else it is the deadliest enemy of the gospel. For making it subservient, religious emotion is not enough; intellectual labor is also necessary. And that labor is being neglected. The Church has turned to easier tasks. And now she is reaping the fruits of her indolence. Now she must battle for her life.

The Church is waiting for men to fight her battles and solve her problems. They need not all be men of conspicuous attainments. But they must all be men of thought. To them theology must be something more than a task. It must be a matter of inquiry. It must lead not to successful memorizing, but to genuine convictions.

READ: 2 PETER 1:5

MARCH 10

A VIEW OF ETERNITY

ALBERT BARNES | 1839

Albert Barnes (1798-1870) was an American theologian and Presbyterian pastor.

All men have some scheme of salvation. Except the very few cases where individuals are thrown into a state of despair, there are none who do not expect to be happy beyond the grave. The proof of this is found in the composure with which most men look at eternity; and in their indifference when warned of a coming judgment.

Yet it is perfectly clear that there can be but one scheme of salvation that is true. If the Christian plan is *true,* then all others are *false.* If others are true, then there was no need of the sacrifice on the cross, and the scheme is an imposition. The admission then, that the Christian religion is true, is a condemnation of all other systems and shuts out all who are not interested in the gospel from all hope of heaven.

God's plan of saving men is based on the fact that the race is destitute of holiness. If it were not so, men would have possessed full capability of saving themselves. But it is important to be understood that it is not asserted that all men are as bad as they can be; or that one man is as bad as another; or that there is no morality; no parental or filial affection; no kindness or compassion in the world; no love of truth, and no honest dealing among men. Yet all these things may exist, and still there would be an utter destitution of right feeling toward God.

Christianity does not charge men with crimes of which they are not guilty. It does not say that the sinner is held personally responsible for the transgressions of any other man; or that God has given a law which man has no power to obey. Such a charge, and such a requirement, would be most clearly unjust. The law requiring love toward God and man is fully within the reach of every mortal, if there is first a willing mind; be he in heaven, earth, or hell; be he a king on the throne, or a beggar in the streets; be he slave or free.

READ: JOHN 14:1-6

MARCH 11

JUST WAR THEORY

4TH CENTURY

Just War Theory is an official doctrine of the Catholic Church formulated to say when it is permissible for a Christian or Christian nation to go to war.

The fifth commandment forbids the intentional destruction of human life. All citizens and all governments are obliged to work for the avoidance of war. However, "as long as the danger of war persists and there is no international authority with the necessary competence and power, governments cannot be denied the right of lawful self-defense, once all peace efforts have failed.

The strict conditions for legitimate defense by military force include:

- The damage inflicted by the aggressor on the nation or community of nations must be lasting, grave, and certain;
- All other means of putting an end to it must have been shown to be impractical or ineffective;
- There must be serious prospects of success;
- The use of arms must not produce evils and disorders graver than the evil to be eliminated.

Those who are sworn to serve their country in the armed forces are servants of the security and freedom of nations. If they carry out their duty honorably, they truly contribute to the maintenance of peace. Authorities should make equitable provision for those who for reasons of conscience refuse to bear arms; these are nonetheless obliged to serve the human community in some other way.

The Church and human reason both assert the permanent validity of the *moral law during armed conflict*. Non-combatants, wounded soldiers, and prisoners must be treated humanely. Actions deliberately contrary to the law of nations and to its universal principles are crimes, as are the orders that command such actions. Blind obedience does not suffice to excuse those who carry them out. Thus the extermination of a people or ethnic minority must be condemned as a mortal sin. One is morally bound to resist orders that command genocide.

READ: MICAH 6:8

MARCH 12

HEALING WOUNDS

RICHARD SIBBES | 1630

Richard Sibbes (1577-1635) was an English theologian who was a representative of "mainline Puritanism."

God's children are bruised reeds before their conversion and oftentimes after. And as there are differences with regard to temperament, gifts, and manner of life, so there are in God's intention to use men in the time to come; for usually he empties such of themselves, and makes them nothing, before he will use them in any great services.

The bruised reed is a man who for the most part is in some misery, as those who came to Christ for help, and by misery he is brought to see sin as the cause of it, for, whatever pretences sin makes, they come to an end when we are bruised and broken. He is sensible of sin and misery; and, seeing no help in himself, is carried with restless desire, with some hope, which a little raises him out of himself to Christ. This is such a one as our Savior Christ terms "poor in spirit," who sees his wants, and also sees himself indebted to divine justice.

After conversion we need bruising so that we may know ourselves to be reeds, and not oaks. The heroic deeds of great worthies do not comfort the church so much as their falls and bruises do. Thus David was bruised until he came to a free confession, without guile of spirit (Psalm 32:3-5). Thus Hezekiah complained that God had "broken his bones" as a lion (Isaiah 38:13). Thus the chosen vessel Paul needed the messenger of Satan to buffet him, lest he should be lifted up above measure (2 Corinthians 12:7).

Hence we learn that we must not pass too harsh judgment upon ourselves or others when God exercises us with bruising upon bruising. There must be a conformity to our head, Christ, who "was bruised for us" (Isaiah 53:5) that we may know how much we are bound unto him. Ungodly spirits, ignorant of God's ways in bringing his children to heaven, censure broken-hearted Christians as miserable persons, whereas God is doing a gracious, good work with them.

READ: MATTHEW 12:20

A CHANGE OF HEART

CHARLES DICKENS | 1843

Charles John Huffam Dickens (1812-1870) was the most popular English novelist of the Victorian era. He is responsible for some of English literature's most iconic characters.

The finger pointed from the grave to him, and back again.

"No, Spirit! Oh no, no!"

The finger still was there.

"Spirit!" he cried, tight clutching at its robe, "Hear me! I am not the man I was. I will not be the man I must have been but for this intercourse. Why show me this, if I am past all hope!"

For the first time the hand appeared to shake.

"Good Spirit," he pursued, as down upon the ground he fell before it: "Your nature intercedes for me, and pities me. Assure me that I yet may change these shadows you have shown me, by an altered life!"

The kind hand trembled.

"I will honor Christmas in my heart, and try to keep it all the year. I will live in the Past, the Present, and the Future. The Spirits of all three shall strive within me. I will not shut out the lessons that they teach."

In his agony, he caught the spectral hand. It sought to free itself, but he was strong in his entreaty, and detained it. Holding up his hands in a last prayer to have his fate reversed, he saw an alteration in the Phantom's hood and dress. It shrunk, collapsed, and dwindled down into a bedpost. . . . Scrooge was better than his word. He did it all, and infinitely more; and to Tiny Tim, who did NOT die, he was a second father. He became as good a friend, as good a master, and as good a man, as the good old city knew.

Ever afterwards it was always said of him, that he knew how to keep Christmas well, if any man alive possessed the knowledge. May that be truly said of us, and all of us! And so, as Tiny Tim observed, God bless Us, Every One!

READ: MATTHEW 3:2

MARCH 14

THE VULNERABLE MINORITY

ISAAC BACKUS | 1773

Isaac Backus (1724-1806) was a leading Baptist preacher during the era of the American Revolution who campaigned against state-established churches in New England.

God has appointed two kinds of government in the world, which are distinct in their nature and ought never to be confounded together; one of which is called civil, the other ecclesiastical government. All acts of executive power in the civil state are to be performed in the name of the king or state they belong to; while all our religious acts are to be done in the name of the Lord Jesus; and so are to be performed heartily as to the Lord, and not unto men. Now who can hear Christ declare that his kingdom is not of this world, and yet believe that this blending of church and state together can be pleasing to him?

The effects of the constitution of our country are such that it emboldens the majority of the people to usurp God's judgment seat, and they daringly give out their sentence, that for a few to profess a persuasion different from the majority, it must be from bad motives. The first fathers of the Massachusetts so embraced this evil that they were moved to imprison, whip, and banish men, only for denying infant baptism, and refusing to join in worship that was supported by violent methods: yet they were so blind as to declare that there was this vast difference between these proceedings and the coercive measures which were taken against them in England.

Our Lord tells us plainly that few find the narrow way, while many go in the broad way; yet the scheme we complain of has given the many such power over the few, that if the few are fully convinced that one causes people to err, and is so far from bringing the pure gospel doctrine, that they should break the divine command, and become partakers of his evil deeds. The many are prepared with such instruments of war against them, as to seize their goods, or cast them into prison, where they may starve and die, in spite of what the constitution has provided for them.

READ: JOHN 18:36

MARCH 15

A VISION OF SUFFERING

EUSEBIUS | 314

Eusebius of Caesarea (c. 263-339), the first Christian historian, was an exegete and one of the more renowned church fathers.

It is fitting to add to these accounts the true prediction of our Savior in which he foretold these very events: "For then shall be great tribulation, such as was not since the beginning of the world to this time, no, nor ever shall be" (Matthew 24:21 KJV).

Reckoning the whole number of the slain, 1.1 million perished by famine and sword, and the rest of the rioters and robbers were slain. But the tallest of the youths and those distinguished for beauty were preserved for the triumph. Of the rest, those that were over seventeen years of age were sent as prisoners to labor for Egypt, while still more were scattered through the provinces to meet their death in the theaters by the sword and by beasts. Those under seventeen years of age were sold as slaves, and these alone numbered ninety thousand.

These things occurred in the second year of the reign of Vespasian, in accordance with the prophecies of our Lord Jesus Christ, who by divine power saw them beforehand, and wept and mourned, saying, "For the days shall come upon thee, that thine enemies shall cast a rampart about thee, and compass thee round, and keep thee in on every side, and shall lay thee and thy children even with the ground" (see Luke 19:43-44).

"For there shall be great distress in the land, and wrath upon this people. And they shall fall by the edge of the sword, and shall be led away captive into all nations: and Jerusalem shall be trodden down of the Gentiles, until the times of the Gentiles be fulfilled. . . . When ye shall see Jerusalem compassed with armies, then know that the desolation thereof is nigh" (Luke 21:23-24, 20 KJV).

How can one fail to wonder, and to admit that the prophecy of our Savior was truly divine and marvelously strange, concerning those calamities that befell the whole Jewish nation after the Savior's Passion and after the multitude of the Jews begged the release of the robber and murderer, but besought that the Prince of Life should be taken from their midst.

READ: MARK 13:2

MARCH 16

A FEW WORDS

DR. NORMAN VINCENT PEALE | 1952

Dr. Norman Vincent Peale (1898-1993) was a minister and author, most notably of
The Power of Positive Thinking.

Believe in yourself! Without a humble but reasonable confidence in your own
abilities you cannot be successful or happy. But with sound self-confidence you
can succeed.

After speaking to a convention of businessmen, I was on stage when a man
approached me and asked, "May I talk with you about a matter of desperate
importance to me? I'm in town to handle the most important business deal of my
life," he explained. "If I succeed, it means everything to me. If I fail, I'm done for."

I suggested that he relax a little, that nothing was quite that final. If he
succeeded, that was fine. If he didn't, well, tomorrow was another day.

"I have no confidence," he said dejectedly. "I am very discouraged and depressed.
In fact, I'm just about sunk. I want to ask how I can get some faith in myself."

"There are two steps to take," I replied. "First, it is important to discover why
you have these feelings. We must approach the maladies of our emotional life
as a physician probes to find something wrong physically. This cannot be done
immediately, and it may require treatment. But tonight I suggest that you repeat
certain words which I shall give you. Say them several times after you get into
bed. Tomorrow, repeat them three times before arising. On the way to your
appointment, say them three additional times. Do this with an attitude of faith
and you will receive sufficient strength and ability to deal with this problem."

I gave him the following affirmation: "I can do all things through Christ which
strengtheneth me" (Philippians 4:13 KJV). I wrote it on a card and had him read
it aloud three times. "Now, follow that prescription, and I am sure things will
come out all right."

He stood quietly for a moment, then said with considerable feeling, "O.K.,
Doctor. O.K."

Later, he reported that this simple formula "did wonders" for him and added, "It
seems incredible that a few words from the Bible could do so much for a person."

READ: ISAIAH 55:11

MARCH 17

APPEAL TO A KING

ARISTIDES | 128

Aristides the Athenian was a second-century Greek Christian author who is primarily known for the Apology of Aristides.

Christians trace their origin from the Lord Jesus Christ, who is acknowledged by the Holy Spirit to be the Son of the most high God, who came down from heaven for the salvation of men. Born of a pure virgin, unbegotten and immaculate, He assumed flesh and revealed Himself among men that He might recall them to Himself from their wandering after many gods. By voluntary choice He tasted death on the cross, and after three days came to life again and ascended into heaven.

He had twelve disciples, who went forth into the provinces of the world and declared His greatness. From this, they who observe the righteousness enjoined by their preaching are called Christians. And these, more than all the nations on the earth, have found the truth. They have the commands of the Lord Jesus Christ engraved upon their hearts; and they observe them, looking forward to the resurrection of the dead and life in the world to come.

They do not commit adultery nor fornication, nor bear false witness, nor covet the things of others; they honor father and mother, and love their neighbors; they judge justly, and they never do to others what they would not wish to happen to themselves; they abstain from all unlawful conversation and impurity; and they are ready to sacrifice their lives for the sake of Christ.

Rightly then, did your son apprehend, and justly was he taught to serve the living God and to be saved for the age that is destined to come upon us. Great and wonderful are the sayings and deeds of the Christians; for they speak not the words of men but those of God. Let your foolish sages cease their idle talk against the Lord; for it is profitable for you to worship God the Creator, and to give ear to His incorruptible words, that you may escape from condemnation and punishment, and be found to be heirs of life everlasting.

READ: ROMANS 2:15

March 18
To Walk with God
Andrew Murray | 19th century

Andrew Murray (1828-1917) was a South African writer, teacher, and Christian pastor. Murray considered missions to be "the chief end of the church."

Man was created for fellowship with God. God made him in His own image and likeness, that he might be capable of understanding and enjoying God, entering into His will, and delighting in His glory. Because God is the everywhere-present and all-pervading One, he could have lived in the enjoyment of unbroken fellowship amidst whatever work he had to do.

Sin robbed us of this fellowship. Nothing else can satisfy the heart of man or God. It was this Christ came to restore; to bring back to God His lost creature, and man to all he was created for. This communication with God is meant to be ours all day, whatever be our condition or the circumstances that surround us. But its enjoyment depends upon the reality in the inner chamber. Our Lord teaches: "Shut thy door, pray to thy Father which is in secret" (Matthew 6:6 KJV).

Christian! There is a terrible danger of substituting prayer and Bible study for living fellowship with God. Your needs, your desire to pray humbly and earnestly, may so occupy you, that the light of His countenance and the joy of His love cannot enter you. Your Bible study may so interest you, and waken pleasing religious sentiment, that—yes—the very Word of God may become a substitute for God Himself, keeping the soul occupied instead of leading it to God Himself.

What a difference it would make in the life of many, if everything in the closet were subordinate to this one thing: I want through the day to walk with God; God has taken charge of me, He is going with me Himself; I am going to do His will all day in His strength; I am ready for all that may come. Yes, what if secret prayer were not only an asking for some new sense of comfort, light, or strength, but the giving away of life just for one day into the sure and safe keeping of a mighty and faithful God.

Read: 1 Corinthians 1:9

MARCH 19

LIVING WATER

TERESA OF ÁVILA | 1577

St. Teresa of Ávila (1515-1582) was a prominent Spanish mystic, Roman Catholic saint, Carmelite nun, and theologian of contemplative life through mental prayer.

Let us imagine we see two fountains with basins that fill with water. These two basins are filled in different ways: the one with water from a distance flowing into it through many pipes and waterworks, while the other basin is built near the source of the spring itself and fills quite noiselessly. If the fountain is plentiful, like the one we speak of, after the basin is full the water overflows in a great stream that flows continually. No machinery is needed here, nor does the water run through aqueducts.

Such is the difference between the two kinds of prayer. The water running through the aqueducts resembles sensible devotion, which is obtained by meditation. We gain it by meditating on created things, and by the labor of our minds; in short, it is the result of our endeavors, and so makes the commotion I spoke of, while profiting the soul. The other fountain receives the water from the source itself, which signifies God. As usual, when His Majesty wills to bestow on us any supernatural favors, we experience the greatest peace, calm, and sweetness in the inmost depths of our being; I know neither where nor how.

This joy is not, like earthly happiness, at once felt by the heart; after gradually filling it to the brim, the delight overflows throughout all the mansions and faculties, until at last it reaches the body. Therefore, I say it arises from God and ends in ourselves, for whoever experiences it will find that the whole physical part of our nature shares in this delight and sweetness. This joy does not appear to me to originate in the heart, but in some more interior part and, as it were, in the depths of our being. I think this must be the center of the soul. O my Lord and my God! How stupendous is Thy grandeur!

READ: JOHN 7:38

MARCH 20

TRULY PERFECT

WILHELMUS À BRAKEL | 17TH CENTURY

Wilhelmus à Brakel (1635-1711) was a Reformed minister in the Netherlands and arguably the most esteemed representative of the Dutch Second Reformation.

The perfection of the creature man consists in the possession of a measure of goodness which God has given and prescribed to all His creatures. All creatures, whatever the degree of their perfection may be, are dependent upon an external source for their being and well-being.

God's perfection, however, excludes such a possibility, as He has no need of anything. No one can add to or subtract anything from His being, neither can anyone increase or decrease His felicity. His perfection consists in His self-sufficiency, His self-existence, and that He is the beginning—the first (Revelation 1:8). His all-sufficiency is within and for Himself, *El Shaddai*, the All-Sufficient One (Genesis 17:1). "Neither is worshipped with men's hands, as though he needed any thing" (Acts 17:25 KJV); "Is it any pleasure to the Almighty, that thou art righteous? or is it gain to him, that thou makest thy ways perfect?" (Job 22:3 KJV). "My goodness extendeth not to thee" (Psalm 16:2 KJV).

Thus there is no common ground between the perfection of God and of creatures—except in name. That which is in man is contrary to the perfection of God, however, and thus the perfection of God is an incommunicable attribute (one that cannot be given to men) of God. The salvation of man consists in knowing, honoring, and serving God.

Such is our God, who not only is all-sufficient in Himself but who with His all-sufficiency can fill and saturate the soul to such an overflowing measure that it has need of nothing else but to have God as its portion. The soul so favored is filled with such light, love, and happiness, that it desires nothing but this. "Whom have I in heaven but thee? and there is none upon earth that I desire beside thee" (Psalm 73:25 KJV).

READ: REVELATION 22:13

THE WEAK NATURE

JAN VAN RUYSBROECK | 14TH CENTURY

Jan van Ruysbroeck (c. 1293-1381) was a Flemish mystic. He founded a congregation in Groenendaal, and his writings were widely circulated during his lifetime, influencing an entire generation of Christian mystics.

Now, if we wish to possess these virtues, and to cast out their opposites, we must possess righteousness, and we must practice and preserve it in purity of heart unto death; for we have three powerful adversaries, who tempt us and make war on us at all times, in all places, and in many ways. If we make peace with one of these three, and become subject to him, we are vanquished; for the three of them agree together in all iniquity.

These three adversaries are the devil, the world, and our own flesh; and this last is the nearest to us and often the worst and most harmful; for our fleshly lusts are the weapons with which our enemies make war on us. The weakness of our nature, our carelessness, and ignorance of truth; these are the swords with which our enemies often wound, and sometimes conquer us.

For this reason we should build up a wall and make a separation within ourselves. And the lower part, which is beastly and contrary to the virtues, and which wills our separation from God, we should hate and persecute, and we should torment it by means of penances and austerity of life; so that it be always repressed, and subject to reason, that thereby righteousness and purity of heart may always have the upper hand in all the works of virtue.

And all the suffering, grief, and persecution, which God sends us through these enemies of virtue, we should gladly bear for the glory of God, and for the honor of the virtues, that we may obtain and possess righteousness in purity of heart. For Christ says: "Blessed are they which are persecuted for righteousness' sake: for theirs is the kingdom of heaven" (Matthew 5:10 KJV). For a righteousness that is maintained in suffering and in virtuous deeds is like the penny that is counted as heavy as the kingdom of God; and with it is bought eternal life.

READ: 2 CORINTHIANS 12:10

MARCH 22

WHAT IS TO COME . . .

ST. NILUS | 5TH CENTURY

Saint Nilus the Elder (died c. 430) was one of the many disciples and defenders of St. John Chrysostom. By his own account, his prophecy is to take place 1,900 years after the death of Christ.

When the time for the Advent of the Antichrist approaches, people's minds will grow cloudy from carnal passions, and dishonor and lawlessness will grow stronger. Then the world will become unrecognizable. People's appearances will change, and it will be impossible to distinguish men from women due to their shamelessness in dress and style of hair.

There will be no respect for parents and elders, love will disappear, and Christian pastors, bishops, and priests will become vain men. At that time the morals and traditions of Christians and the Church will change. People will abandon modesty, and dissipation will reign. Falsehood and greed will attain great proportions; and lust, adultery, homosexuality, secret deeds, and murder will rule in society.

At that future time, the churches of God will be deprived of God-fearing and pious pastors, and woe to the Christians remaining at that time; they will completely lose their faith because they will lack the opportunity of seeing the light of knowledge from anyone at all.

And all this will result from the fact that the Antichrist wants to be Lord and ruler of the whole universe, and he will produce miracles and fantastic signs. He will also give depraved wisdom to an unhappy man so that he will discover a way by which one man can carry on a conversation with another from one end of the earth to the other. Men will also fly through the air like birds and descend to the bottom of the sea like fish. And, the impious one will so complete science with vanity that it will go off the right path and lead people to lose faith in the existence of God in three persons.

Then God will see the downfall of the human race and will shorten the days for the sake of those few who are being saved, because the enemy wants to lead even the chosen into temptation . . . then the sword of chastisement will suddenly appear and kill the perverter and his servants.

READ: REVELATION 12:10-12

THE PRODIGAL HEART

JOHN DARBY | 19TH CENTURY

John Nelson Darby (1800-1882) was an Anglo-Irish evangelist who is considered to be the father of modern Dispensationalism.

If we look at man as he is in himself, he could never get back to God. But look at what *God is in Himself*, and who or what can resist His grace? Still it is the joy of the finder, and not of the thing found. "Rejoice with *me*, for I have found my sheep that was lost" (Luke 15:6 KJV, emphasis added).

All caught the joy of the father's heart, except the unhappy, self-righteous elder brother (the Pharisee, the Jew), to whom the father replied, "It was meet that we should make merry, and be glad: for this thy brother was dead, and is alive again" (Luke 15:32 KJV). It is the joy God has in receiving a sinner back to Himself.

When the young man left his father's house it was but a display of the evil in his heart. He was just as wicked when he asked for his portion of goods and crossed his father's threshold as when he ate husks with the swine in the far country. He was, doubtless, more miserable then, but his heart was gone before. One man may run further into riot than another, but if we have turned our backs upon God we are utterly bad. In this sense there is no difference.

Every man has turned his back upon God, though all have not run to the same excess of riot, nor fallen into the same degradation. The famine never draws back to the father's house. When the prodigal thinks of his father's house, the whole work is morally done, though he is not back there yet. He turns, his heart is changed, and thus his whole desire is to get back to his father's house from whence he had departed. He is brought to a sense of his guilt, and what was it? Feeding with the swine? No; that was the fruit of it, but his guilt was in leaving his father's house, turning away from God. When he came to himself he desired to return.

READ: LUKE 15:17-24

MARCH 24

THE IMMUTABLE CHURCH

JOHN FOXE | 1559

John Foxe (1517-1587) was an English historian and martyrologist, the author of what is popularly known as Foxe's Book of Martyrs. *The book helped mold British popular opinion about the Catholic Church for several centuries.*

Christ our Savior, hearing the confession of Simon Peter, who first openly acknowledged Him to be the Son of God, and perceiving the secret hand of His Father therein, called him (alluding to his name) a rock, upon which rock He would build His Church so strong that the gates of hell should not prevail against it. In these words three things are to be noted: First, that Christ will have a Church in this world. Secondly, that the same Church should mightily be impugned, not only by the world, but also by the uttermost strength and powers of all hell. And, thirdly, that the same Church, notwithstanding the uttermost of the devil and all his malice, should continue.

We see Christ's prophecy wonderfully verified, insomuch that the whole course of the Church to this day may seem nothing else but a verifying of the said prophecy. First, that Christ hath set up a Church, needs no declaration. Secondly, what force of princes, kings, monarchs, governors, and rulers of this world, with their subjects, publicly and privately, and with all their strength and cunning, have bent themselves against this Church! And, thirdly, how in spite of all this, the Church has yet endured and held its own!

As it is not our business to enlarge upon our Savior's history, either before or after His crucifixion, it is only necessary to remind our readers of the discomfiture of the Jews by His subsequent resurrection. Although the apostles betrayed, denied, and forsook him, with the exception of "the disciple who was known unto the high-priest," the history of His resurrection gave a new direction to all their hearts, and, after the mission of the Holy Spirit, imparted new confidence to their minds. The powers with which they were endued emboldened them to proclaim His name, to the confusion of the Jewish rulers and the astonishment of Gentile proselytes.

READ: MATTHEW 16:13-18

MARCH 25

BEYOND OURSELVES

KARL BARTH | 1933

Karl Barth (1886-1968) was a Swiss Reformed theologian who is believed to be one of the most important Christian thinkers of the twentieth century.

Within the Bible there is a strange new world, the world of God. This answer is the same that came to the first martyr, Stephen: "Behold, I see the heavens opened, and the Son of man standing on the right hand of God" (Acts 7:56 KJV). Neither by the earnestness of our belief nor by the depth and richness of our experience have we deserved the right to this answer. But if we wish to come to grips with the contents of the Bible, we must dare to reach far beyond ourselves. The Book admits nothing less.

For, besides giving to every one of us what we rightly deserve, it leaves us no rest whatever. Before long the Bible says to us, with regard to the "versions" we make of it: "These may be you, but they are not I! They may perhaps suit you, meeting the demands of your era and your 'circle,' of your religious or philosophical theories. You wanted to be mirrored in me, and now you have really found in me your own reflection. But now I bid you come seek *me*, as well. Seek what is here."

It is the Bible itself that drives us out beyond ourselves and invites us, without regard to our worthiness or unworthiness, to reach for the last highest answer. And that answer is: a new world, the world of God. There is a spirit in the Bible that allows us to stop a while—but presently it begins to press us on. There is a river in the Bible that carries us away, once we have entrusted our destiny to it. We need only dare to follow this drive, this spirit, this river, to grow out beyond ourselves toward the highest answer. This daring is *faith*; and we read the Bible rightly when we read it in faith. The Bible unfolds to us as we are met, guided, drawn on, and made to grow by the grace of God.

READ: LUKE 12:31

MARCH 26

A FITTING HOME

FREDERIC FARRAR | 1870

Frederic Farrar (1831-1903) was a well-known British preacher who served as minister at Westminster Abbey and later as dean of Canterbury.

St. Matthew tells us that in the settlement of the Holy Family at Nazareth, was fulfilled that which was spoken by the prophets, "He shall be called a Nazarene." It is well known that no such passage occurs in any extant prophecy. If the name implied an inherent dislike—as may be inferred from the proverbial question of Nathaniel, "Can any good thing come out of Nazareth?"—certainly to this day "Nazarene" has continued to be a term of contempt.

But the explanation which refers to those passages of prophecy in which Christ is called "the Branch" (*nêtser*) seems far more probable. The village may have derived this name from abundant foliage; but the Old Testament is full of proofs that the Hebrews attached immense and mystical importance to mere resemblances in the sound of words. St. Matthew, a Hebrew of the Hebrews, would without any hesitation have seen a prophetic fitness in Christ's residence at this town of Galilee, because its name recalled the title by which He was addressed in the prophecy of Isaiah.

"Shall Christ come out of Galilee?" asked the wondering people. "Search, and look," said the rabbis to Nicodemus, "for out of Galilee ariseth no prophet" (John 7:41,52 KJV). It would not have needed very deep searching or looking to find that these words were ignorant or false; for Barak the deliverer, Elon the judge, and Anna the prophetess—and those prophets of the highest eminence, Jonah, Elijah, Hosea, and Nahum—had been born, or had exercised much of their ministry, in the precincts of Galilee.

And in spite of the supercilious contempt with which it was regarded, the little town of Nazareth, situated as it was in a healthy and secluded valley, yet close upon the confines of great nations, and in the center of a mixed population, was eminently fitted to be the home of our Savior's childhood, the scene of that quiet growth "in wisdom, and stature, and favor with God and man."

READ: MATTHEW 2:21-23

MARCH 27

ALL FOR OUR GOOD

PETER ABELARD | 12TH CENTURY

Peter Abelard (1079-1142) was a medieval French scholastic philosopher and theologian, described as the "keenest thinker and boldest theologian of the twelfth century."

And now, it should suffice for your sorrows and the hardships you have endured that I have written this story of my own misfortunes, amid which I have toiled almost from the cradle. For so shall you come to regard your tribulation as nought, or at any rate as little, in comparison with mine, and so shall you bear it more lightly in measure as you regard it as less.

Take comfort ever in the saying of our Lord, what he foretold for his followers at the hands of the followers of the devil: "If they have persecuted me, they will also persecute you. If the world hate you, you know that it hated me before it hated you. If you were of the world, the world would love his own" (see John 18:20).

Commenting on this, St. Jerome, whose heir it seems to me I am in the endurance of foul slander, says in his letter to the monk Heliodorus: "You are wrong, brother, if you think there is ever a time when the Christian does not suffer persecution. For our adversary goes about as a roaring lion seeking what he may devour, and do you still think of peace? Nay, he lies in ambush among the rich."

We should endure our persecutions all the more steadfastly the more bitterly they harm us. We should not doubt that even if they are not what we deserve, at least they serve for the purifying of our souls. And since all things are done in accordance with the divine ordering, let everyone of true faith console himself amid all his afflictions with the thought that the great goodness of God permits nothing to be done without reason, and brings to a good end whatsoever may seem to happen wrongfully. Great is the consolation to all lovers of God in the word of the Apostle when he says: "We know that all things work together for good to them that love God" (Romans 8:28 KJV).

READ: 1 PETER 1:6-7

MARCH 28

THE ROAD TO PERFECTION

THE UNKNOWN MYSTIC | 14TH CENTURY

The Unknown Mystic, an anonymous English monk, is referenced as the author of
The Cloud of Unknowing, *a medieval spiritual guidebook that focused on a mystical approach to Christian prayer, where God is not found through rote knowledge but through "blind love."*

Ghostly friend in God, you shall well understand that I find, in my boisterous beholding, four degrees and forms of Christian men's living: Common, Special, Singular, and Perfect. Three of these may be begun and ended in this life; and the fourth may by grace be begun here, but it shall ever last without end in the bliss of Heaven.

And as they are set here in order—first Common, then Special, after Singular, and last Perfect—so I think that in the same order and in the same course our Lord has of His great mercy called you and led you unto Him by the desire of your heart. For first you were well, living in the Common degree of Christian men's living in the company of your worldly friends, yet it seemed to me that the everlasting love of His Godhead might not suffer you to be so far from Him in form and degree of living.

And therefore He kindled your desire graciously, and fastened by it a leash of longing, and led you by it into a more Special state and form of living, to be a servant among His special servants; where you might learn to live more specially and more ghostly in His service than you did in the common degree of living before.

Yet it seems that He would not leave you thus lightly, for love of His heart. Do you not see how mistily and how graciously He has pulled you to the third degree and manner of living, which is called Singular? That in solitary form and manner of living, you may learn to lift up the foot of your love; and step towards that state and degree of living that is Perfect, and the last state of all.

READ: 2 SAMUEL 22:31

MARCH 29

GOD'S SOVEREIGNTY

ARTHUR PINK | 1918

Arthur Walkington Pink (1886-1952) was an English Christian evangelist and biblical scholar known for his staunchly Calvinist and Puritan-like teachings.

Who is regulating affairs on this earth today—God, or the Devil? That God reigns supreme in Heaven, is generally conceded; that He does so over this world, is almost universally denied—if not directly, then indirectly. More and more are men relegating God to the background. Not only is it denied that God created everything, but few believe that He has any immediate concern in regulating the works of His own hands. Everything is supposed to be ordered according to the (impersonal and abstract) "laws of Nature." Thus is the Creator banished from His own creation.

Therefore we need not be surprised that men exclude Him from the realm of human affairs. Throughout Christendom, the theory is held that man is "a free agent," and therefore, the determiner of his destiny. That Satan is to be blamed for much of the evil in the world is freely affirmed by those who often deny their own responsibility, by attributing to the Devil what, in fact, proceeds from their own evil hearts (Mark 7:21-23).

What a scene of confusion and chaos confronts us on every side! Sin is rampant; thrones are creaking and tottering, ancient dynasties are being over-turned. Unrest, discontent, and lawlessness are rife everywhere, and none can say how soon another great war will be set in motion. Statesmen are perplexed. Men's hearts are "failing them for fear, and for looking after those things which are coming on the earth"(Luke 21:26 KJV). Do these things look as though God had full control?

Because God is God, He does as He pleases. He is the Supreme Being, and therefore Sovereign of the universe. He declares, "My thoughts are not your thoughts, neither are your ways my ways, saith the LORD. For as the heavens are higher than the earth, so are my ways higher than your ways, and my thoughts than your thoughts" (Isaiah 55:8-9 KJV). In light of this, it is only to be expected that much of the Bible conflicts with the sentiments of the carnal mind, which is at enmity against God.

READ. PSALM 99:1

MARCH 30

A SIGN FROM HEAVEN

SOZOMENUS | 449

Salminius Hermias Sozomenus (c. 400-c. 450) was a historian of the Christian church who was born into a wealthy Christian family of Palestine.

Constantine was led to honor the Christian religion by the concurrence of several different events, particularly by the appearance of a sign from heaven.

When he first formed the resolution of entering into a war against Maxentius, he was beset with doubts as to the means of carrying on his military operations, and as to what quarter he could look for assistance.

In the midst of his perplexity, he saw, in a vision, the sight of the cross shining in heaven. He was amazed at the spectacle, but some holy angels who were standing by, exclaimed, "Oh, Constantine! By this symbol, conquer!" And it is said that Christ himself appeared to him, and showed him the symbol of the cross, and commanded him to construct one like unto it, and to retain it as his help in battle, as it would insure the victory.

This vision met him by the way, when he was perplexed as to whither he should lead his army. While he was reflecting on what this could mean, night came; and when he fell asleep, Christ appeared with the sign which he had seen in heaven, and commanded him to construct a representation of the symbol, and to use it as his help in hostile encounters. There was nothing further to be elucidated; for the emperor clearly apprehended the necessity of serving God.

At daybreak, he called together the priests of Christ, and questioned them concerning their doctrines. They opened the sacred Scriptures, and expounded the truths relative to Christ, and showed him from the prophets how the signs which had been predicted had been fulfilled. The sign which had appeared to him was the symbol, they said, of the victory over hell; for Christ came among men, was stretched upon the cross, died, and returned to life the third day. For God, in his love towards man, bestows forgiveness on those who have fallen into sin, on their repentance, and the confirmation of their repentance by good works.

READ: MARK 16:20

LOVE YOUR NEIGHBOR

ISAAC | 7TH CENTURY

Isaac of Nineveh (died c. 700), also known as Isaac the Syrian, was a seventh-century bishop and theologian best remembered for his written work.

Do not demand love from your neighbor, because you will suffer if you don't receive it; but better still, indicate your love toward your neighbor and you will settle down. In this way, you will lead your neighbor toward love.

Don't exchange your love toward your neighbor for some type of object, because in having love toward your neighbor, you acquire within yourself Him Who is most precious in the whole world. Forsake the petty so as to acquire the great; spurn the excessive and everything meaningless so as to acquire the valuable.

Shelter the sinner if it brings you no harm. Through this you will encourage him toward repentance and reform—and attract the Lord's mercy to yourself. With prayers and sorrow of your heart, share your lot with the aggrieved and the source of God's mercy will open to your entreaties. When giving, give magnanimously with a look of kindness on your face, and give more than what is asked of you.

Do not distinguish the worthy from the unworthy. Let everyone be equal to you for good deeds, so that you may be able to also attract the unworthy toward goodness, because through outside acts, the soul quickly learns to be reverent before God.

He who shows kindness toward the poor has God as his guardian, and he who becomes poor for the sake of God will acquire abundant treasures. God is pleased when He sees people showing concern for others for His sake. When someone asks you for something, don't think: "Just in case I might need it, I shall leave it for myself, and God—through other people—will give that person what he requires." These types of thoughts are peculiar to people that are iniquitous and do not know God.

READ: 1 JOHN 4:7-11

APRIL 1

THE MANIFESTED MYSTERY

JOHN FLETCHER | 1777

John William Fletcher (1729-1785), born in Switzerland of French Huguenot descent, was a contemporary of John Wesley and one of Methodism's first great theologians.

The revelation of Christ, by which an unconverted man becomes a holy and a happy possessor of the faith, is a supernatural, spiritual, experimental manifestation of the spirit, power, and love of God, manifest in the flesh, whereby He is known and enjoyed in a manner which is altogether new. It is as new as the knowledge that a man has when he first tastes honey and wine, if he had eaten nothing but bread and water previously.

This manifestation comes to every sincere seeker, though it may be in a gradual or an instantaneous way, according to God's good pleasure. As soon as the veil of unbelief is rent by the power of the Holy Spirit, the Lord Jesus Christ comes in and reveals Himself as being full of grace and truth; only then is the tabernacle of God with man. His kingdom has come with power; righteousness, peace, and joy in the Holy Spirit are spread through the newborn soul; eternal life has begun.

If, by God's grace, this general manifestation is improved upon, the effects are glorious: now, drawn by the love of Jesus, the believer's heart pants after greater conformity to God's holy will, and mounts up to Him in prayer and praise. Having found the great I AM, the eternal Lord, he considers all created things to be as mere shadows.

In fact, he counts all things but loss, for the excellency of the knowledge of Christ Jesus his Lord. He casts his sins and miseries upon Jesus; and in return Jesus bestows His righteousness and happiness upon him. He puts on Christ and becomes a partaker of the divine nature. Thus, to use Paul's illustration, they are espoused and married. Joined by the double band of redeeming love and saving faith, they are one Spirit, even as Adam and Eve—by matrimony—were one flesh. "This is a great mystery," wrote the Apostle, but thanks be to God, it is made manifest to his saints.

READ: EPHESIANS 5:30-32

APRIL 2

A SHINING LIGHT

MALCOM MUGGERIDGE | 1968

Thomas Malcolm Muggeridge (1903-1990) was an English journalist, author, media personality, and satirist.

"I am the light of the world," the founder of the Christian religion said. What a stupendous phrase! And how particularly marvelous today when one is conscious of so much darkness in the world! "Let your light shine before men," he exhorted us. Sometimes I am asked what I should most like to do in the little that remains of my life, and I always truthfully answer, "I should like my light to shine, even if only very fitfully, like a match struck in a dark cavernous night and then flickering out."

How I should love to be able to speak with the certainty and luminosity of St. Paul, when he and his companions were, in the most literal sense, turning the world upside down by insisting, contrary to Caesar's decrees, that there was another king, one Jesus. Golden words: a bright and shining light indeed. Now something had happened to him, as it had to Christ's disciples, transforming them from rather inarticulate cowardly men who ran away for cover when their leader was arrested, into the most lion-hearted, eloquent, quick-witted, and even joyful evangelists the world has ever known.

Well, what had happened to them? They were reborn. They were new men with a new allegiance, not to any form of earthly authority but to this other king, this Jesus. Ever since their time, with all the ups and downs, this notion has persisted, of being reborn, of dying in order to live, and I want to consider whether such a notion, as I understand it the very heart of the Christian religion, has any point or validity today.

So I come back to where I began, to the Christian notion that man's efforts to make himself happy in earthly terms are doomed to failure. He must indeed, as Christ said, be born again, be a new man, or he's nothing. So at least I have concluded, having failed to find in past experience, present dilemmas, and future expectations, any alternative proposition. As far as I am concerned, it is Christ or nothing.

READ: MATTHEW 5:16

April 3

Evidence of Grace

Archibald Alexander | 1844

Archibald Alexander (1772-1851) was an American educator, theologian, and pastor. He is most known as founder and first principal of Princeton Seminary.

Growth in grace is evidenced by a more habitual vigilance against besetting sins and temptations, and by greater self-denial in regard to personal indulgence. A growing conscientiousness in regard to what may be called minor duties is also a good sign. The counterfeit of this is a scrupulous conscience, which sometimes haggles at the most innocent gratifications, and has led some to hesitate about taking their daily food.

Increasing spiritual mindedness is a sure evidence of progress in piety; and this will always be accompanied by deadness to the world. Continued aspirations to God, in the house and by the way, in lying down and rising up, in company and in solitude, indicate the indwelling of the Holy Spirit, by whose agency all progress in sanctification is made.

Increasing solicitude for the salvation of men, sorrow on account of their sinful and miserable condition, and a disposition tenderly to warn sinners of their danger, evince a growing state of piety. It is also a strong evidence of growth in grace when you can bear injuries and provocations with meekness and when you can from the heart desire the temporal and eternal welfare of your bitterest enemies.

An entire and confident reliance on the promises and providence of God, however dark may be your horizon, or however many difficulties environ you, is a sign that you have learned to live by faith; and humble contentment with your condition shows that you have profited by sitting at the feet of Jesus. Diligence in the duties of our calling, with a view to the glory of God, is an evidence not to be despised. Indeed there is no surer standard of spiritual growth than a habit of aiming at the glory of God in everything. That mind which is steady to the main end gives as good evidence of being touched by divine grace as the tendency of the needle to the pole proves that it has been touched by the magnet.

Read: Philippians 1:6

APRIL 4

THE CHOSEN

THE SYNOD OF DORT | 1618-1619

The Synod of Dort was a national synod held in Dordrecht in 1618-1619 by the Dutch Reformed Church to settle a serious controversy in the Dutch churches instigated by the rise of Arminianism.

Election is the unchangeable purpose of God, whereby, before the foundation of the world, He has chosen from the whole human race, which had fallen through its own fault from the primitive state of rectitude into sin and destruction, a certain number of persons to redemption in Christ. This elect number, though by nature neither better nor more deserving than others, God has decreed to give to Christ to be saved by Him, and effectually to call and draw them to His communion by His Word and Spirit; to bestow upon them true faith, justification, and sanctification; and having powerfully preserved them in the fellowship of His Son, finally to glorify them for the demonstration of His mercy, and for the praise of the riches of His glorious grace.

As it is written, "For he chose us in him before the creation of the world to be holy and blameless in his sight. In love he predestined us to be adopted as his sons through Jesus Christ, in accordance with his pleasure and will—to the praise of his glorious grace, which he has freely given us in the One he loves" (Ephesians 1:4-6 NIV). And elsewhere: "And those he predestined, he also called; those he called, he also justified; those he justified, he also glorified" (Romans 8:30 NIV).

This election was not founded upon foreseen faith and the obedience of faith, holiness, or any other good quality or disposition in man, as the prerequisite, cause, or condition of which it depended; but men are chosen to faith and to the obedience of faith, holiness, etc. Therefore election is the fountain of every saving good, from which proceed faith, holiness, and the other gifts of salvation, and finally eternal life itself, as its fruits and effects, according to the testimony of the apostle: "For he chose us in him before the creation of the world to be holy and blameless in his sight" (Ephesians 1:4 NIV).

READ: JOHN 15:16

April 5

God Always Is

Gregory | 381

Gregory of Nazianzus (c. 329-389) was an Archbishop of Constantinople. Along with Basil the Great and Gregory of Nyssa, he is known as one of the Cappadocian Fathers.

God always was, and always is, and always will be. Or rather, God always Is. For *was* and *will be* are fragments of our time, and of changeable nature, but He is Eternal Being. For in Himself He sums up and contains all Being, having neither beginning in the past nor end in the future; like some great Sea of Being, limitless and unbounded, transcending all conception of time and nature.

Not one image being got from one source and another from another, and combined into some sort of presentation of the truth, which escapes us before we have caught it, and takes to flight before we have conceived it, as the lightning flash which will not stay its course, does upon our sight. As I conceive by that part of it which we can comprehend to draw us to itself (for that which is altogether incomprehensible is outside the bounds of hope, and not within the compass of endeavor), and by that part of it which we cannot comprehend to move our wonder, and as an object of wonder to become more an object of desire, and being desired to purify, and by purifying to make us like God; so that when we have thus become like Himself, God may, to use a bold expression, hold converse with us as gods, being united to us, and that perhaps to the same extent as He already knows those who are known to Him.

The Divine Nature then is boundless and hard to understand; and all that we can comprehend of Him is His boundlessness; even though one may conceive that because He is of a simple nature He is therefore either wholly incomprehensible, or perfectly comprehensible. For it is quite certain that this simplicity is not itself its nature, just as composition is not by itself the essence of compound beings.

Read: Revelation 1:8

APRIL 6

GOD AMONG US

JOHN DARBY | 19TH CENTURY

John Nelson Darby (1800-1882) was an Anglo-Irish evangelist who is considered to be the father of modern Dispensationalism.

When God is pleased to occupy Himself with the world, and to take a part in what passes therein, it is marvelous to see how He acts and the instruction He gives. There is no agreement, but a total opposition between His ways and those of men. The Emperor and his decree are but insignificant instruments. Caesar Augustus acts in view of his subjects; yet he is, without knowing it, the means of accomplishing the prophecy that Jesus should be born in Bethlehem.

How wondrous! All the world is in movement to bring about this event, needed to fulfill prophecy, that the poor carpenter, with Mary his espoused wife, should be in the city of David, and David's heir should be born there and then. God is accomplishing His purpose of love, but man was blind to it. Who cared to notice the poor Jew, though he might be of the house and lineage of David? The things that are perfectly indifferent to man fill the heart and eye of God.

Still we are in Jewish atmosphere. *Promises* are being accomplished; the babe must be born in Bethlehem. On earth the babe is the object of God's counsels; angels and all Heaven are occupied with His birth; but there is no place in the world for Him! Go where the great world registers every individual, go to the little world of an inn, but there is no room *for Jesus*. And the manger led, in due time, to the lowest place—the Cross.

Our true wisdom is through what God reveals. But we never get God's fullest blessings till we are where the flesh is brought down and destroyed. We cannot get into the simple joy and power of God till we accept the place of lowliness and humiliation, till the heart is emptied of what is contrary to the lowliness of Christ. From the manger to the Cross, all in Christ was simple obedience. Christ did all in God's way, and we must do so too.

READ: JOHN 1:14

Thoughts of Devotion

Hesychius | 5th century

Hesychius of Jerusalem was a Christian presbyter and exegete, probably of the fifth century.

Attentiveness is the heart's stillness, unbroken by any thought.

Through His incarnation God gave us the model for a holy life and recalled us from our ancient fall. In addition to many other things, He taught us, feeble as we are, that we should fight against the demons with humility, fasting, prayer, and watchfulness.

Prayer is a great blessing, and it embraces all blessings, for it purifies the heart, in which God is seen by the believer.

Just as it is impossible to fight battles without weapons, or to swim a great sea with clothes on, or to live without breathing, so without humility and the constant prayer to Christ it is impossible to master the art of inward spiritual warfare or to set about it and pursue it skillfully.

As you sail across the sea of the intellect, put your trust in Jesus, for secretly in your heart He says: "Fear not, my child Jacob, the least of Israel; fear not, you worm Israel, I will protect you." If God is for us, what evil one is against us? For He has blessed the pure of heart and given the commandments; and so Jesus, who alone is truly pure, in a divine way readily enters into hearts that are pure and dwells in them. Therefore, as Paul counsels, let us ceaselessly exercise our intellect in devotion. For devotion uproots the seeds sown by the devil and is the path of the intelligence.

When the heart has acquired stillness it will perceive the heights and depths of knowledge; and the ear of the still intellect will be made to hear marvelous things from God.

Read: Psalm 1:2

APRIL 8

A PRECISE TRUTH

MARTYN LLOYD-JONES | 1961

David Martyn Lloyd-Jones (1899-1981) was a Welsh Protestant minister, preacher, and medical doctor.

The greatest danger confronting the Christian church at this moment is the failure to understand the necessity of a precise, clear knowledge of the truth. We are living in an age that is anti-theological, anti-doctrinal, and dislikes propositions and exact knowledge. It is a lazy age in every respect, an age that wants entertainment and dislikes effort. The principle is "something for nothing." This is particularly true in the realm of the Christian church.

This tendency shows itself in many ways, one of which says that Christianity is something so wonderful that it cannot be defined. You experience it, but if you try to analyze it, then you destroy it. Another says that Christianity is an attitude, a view of life. But what exactly is it? Well, you do not know, but that does not matter. You have got it! That is the great thing and you feel much happier and better than you did before.

Another asks what does it matter what people believe as long as they are Christ-like: generous and ready to help others? That is what makes people Christians. Yet this is the most subtle of all: the tendency to estimate whether people are Christians, not by what they actually say about their beliefs, but by what you feel about them. Though they may deny the very essence of Christianity, if I like them, if I can relate to them, then that is what counts.

So what do we say about this modern tendency? First, that Christians are mistaking natural qualities, a cultural veneer, for true Christian grace. It seems we are no longer capable of differentiating between the two. "What a gracious man he is," they say. They really mean: "He never criticizes and agrees with everybody and everything." I know of nothing more dangerous than that.

The Apostle's case was always this: there is only one gospel. Any departure from it is a lie. So this modern idea which puts personality, niceness, or "what I feel," before exact definitions and truth, is a denial of the whole of New Testament teaching.

READ: PHILIPPIANS 1:27

APRIL 9

ACCORDING TO THEIR WORKS

CLAUDIUS | 9TH CENTURY

Claudius of Turin (d. 827) was the Catholic bishop of Turin from 817 until his death.

We know, according to the Evangelist, that the words of the Lord were not understood, when he spoke to Peter, "You are Peter, and on this rock I will build my church, and . . . I will give you the keys of the kingdom of heaven" (Matthew 16:18-19 NIV). Because of these words spoken by the Lord, the race of ignorant men, having disregarded the understanding of all spiritual things, wish to go to Rome in order to acquire eternal life.

He who understands the keys of the kingdom of heaven as given above does not require that the intercession of the blessed Peter be limited to one locale. If we subtly consider the proper meaning of the words of the Lord, it was not said by him, "Whatever you loose in heaven will be loosed on earth, and whatever you bind in heaven will be held bound on earth." From this it is known that the ministry is granted to the overseers of the church only as long as they are on pilgrimage in the mortal body.

You object against me that the apostolic lord is upset with me—you also say that you are displeased with me. You said this of Paschal, bishop of the Roman church, who has since left this present life. A man is said to be apostolic who is guardian of the apostle or who exercises the office of an apostle. Surely a man should not be called apostolic who simply sits on the apostolic throne, but who carries out the office. The Lord said about those who hold a place, but do not carry out the office, "The scribes and the Pharisees sit upon the chair of Moses. All things therefore whatsoever they shall say to you, observe and do; but according to their works do not. For they say, and do not" (see Matthew 23:2-3).

READ: 2 CORINTHIANS 11:15

APRIL 10
A CRY TO PRAYER
BONAVENTURE | 13TH CENTURY

Bonaventure (1221-1274) was an Italian medieval scholastic theologian and philosopher and a cardinal bishop of Albano.

"Blessed are they that wash their robes in the blood of the Lamb, that they may have a right to the Tree of Life and may enter in by the gates into the City"; as if he were to say that one cannot enter into the heavenly Jerusalem through contemplation unless one enter through the blood of the Lamb as through a gate. For one is not disposed to contemplation which leads to mental elevation, unless one be with Daniel, a man of desires. But desires are kindled in us in two ways: by the cry of prayer, which makes one groan with the murmuring of one's heart, and by a flash of apprehension by which the mind turns most directly and intensely to the rays of light.

Therefore to the cry of prayer through Christ crucified, by Whose blood we are purged of the filth of vice, do I first invite the reader, lest perchance he should believe that it suffices to read without unction, speculate without devotion, investigate without wonder, examine without exultation, work without piety, know without love, understand without humility, be zealous without divine grace, or see without wisdom divinely inspired. Therefore to those predisposed by divine grace, to the humble and the pious, to those filled with compunction and devotion, anointed with the oil of gladness, to the lovers of divine wisdom, inflamed with desire for it, to those wishing to give themselves over to praising God, to wondering over Him, and to delighting in Him, do I propose the following reflections, hinting that little or nothing is the outer mirror unless the mirror of the mind be clear and polished.

Stir yourself then, O man of God, you who previously resisted the pricks of conscience, before you raise your eyes to the rays of wisdom shining in that mirror, lest by chance you fall into the lower pit of shadows from the contemplation of those rays.

READ: PSALM 5:3

April 11

What Does It Mean?

Charles Sheldon | 1897

Charles Monroe Sheldon (1857-1946) was an American minister and leader of the Social Gospel movement.

I've tramped through this city for three days trying to find a job; and in all that time I've not had a word of sympathy or comfort except from your minister here, who said he was sorry for me and hoped I would find a job somewhere.

Of course, I understand you can't all go out of your way to hunt up jobs for other people like me. I'm not asking you to; but what is meant by following Jesus? Do you mean that you are suffering and denying yourselves and trying to save lost, suffering humanity just as I understand Jesus did? What do you mean by it?

I see the ragged edge of things a good deal. My wife died four months ago. I'm glad she is out of trouble. My little girl is staying with a printer's family until I find a job. Somehow I get puzzled when I see so many Christians living in luxury and remember how my wife died in a tenement in New York City, gasping for air and asking God to take the little girl too. Of course I don't expect you people can prevent everyone from dying of starvation, lack of proper nourishment, and tenement air, but what does following Jesus mean? A member of a church was the owner of the tenement where my wife died, and I have wondered if following Jesus all the way was true in his case.

It seems to me there's an awful lot of trouble in the world that somehow wouldn't exist if all the people who sing your songs went and lived them out. I suppose I don't understand. But what would Jesus do? It seems to me sometimes as if the people in the big churches have good clothes and nice houses to live in, and money to spend for luxuries, while the people outside the churches, thousands of them, I mean, die in tenements, and walk the streets for jobs, and grow up in misery and drunkenness and sin.

Read: Mark 8:34

April 12

What Love Is

Aphraates | 4th century

St. Aphraates lived during the early fourth century and was the first of the Syriac church fathers.

And it was thus that our Savior taught us diligently to manifest love. For first He perfected it in Himself, and then He taught those who heard Him. And He reconciled our enmity with His Father because He loved us, and He yielded up His innocence in the stead of the debtors, and the Good in place of the evil ones was put to shame, and the Rich in our behalf was made poor, and the Living died in behalf of the dead, and by His death made alive our death.

And the Son of the Lord of all took for our sake the form of a servant, and He to whom all things were subject subjected Himself that He might release us from the subjection of sin. And by His great love He gave a blessing to the poor in spirit, and He promised the peacemakers they should be called His brothers and sons of God; and He promised the humble that they should inherit the land of life; and He promised the mourners that by their supplications they would be comforted; and He promised to the hungry fullness in His kingdom; and to those who weep that they should rejoice in His promise; and He promised to the merciful that they should be shown mercy; and to these who are pure in heart He said that they should see God; and to those who are persecuted on account of His Name He promised a blessing and rest in His kingdom.

And He changed our nature of dust and made us the salt of truth, and He delivered us from being the prey of the serpent, and He called us the light of the world; and He delivered us from the power of death; and He made us good instead of evil, and pleasing instead of hateful; and He imparted to us the perfect man; and He brought forth good things from His treasures, and delivered us from him who brought forth evil things from the superfluities of his heart.

Read: Ephesians 5:1-2

APRIL 13

A CONSECRATED LIFE

THEODORE THE STUDITE | 9TH CENTURY

Theodore the Studite (759-826) was a Byzantine Greek monk and abbot of the
Stoudios monastery in Constantinople.

Do not acquire any of this world's goods, nor hoard up privately for yourself
to the value of one piece of silver. Be without distraction in heart and soul and
your thought for those in your care who have been entrusted to you by God, and
have become your spiritual sons and brothers. Do not obtain any slave nor use
in your private service or in that of the monastery over which you preside, or in
the fields, man who was made in the image of God. For you should yourself be
as a servant to the brethren like-minded with you, at least in intention, even if in
outward appearance you are reckoned to be master and teacher.

Use all care that all things in the brotherhood be common and not distributed,
and let nothing, not even a needle, belong to any one in particular. Let your body
and your spirit, to say nothing of your goods, be ever divided in equality of love
among all your spiritual children and brethren.

Do not go out often, nor range around, leaving your fold without necessity. For
even if you remain always there, it is hard to keep safe your human sheep, so apt
are they to stray and wander.

Do not have any choice or costly garment, except for priestly functions. But
follow the Fathers in being shod and clad in humility. Be not delicate in food, in
private expenditure, or in hospitality; for this belongs to the portion of those
who take their joy in the present life. Do not lay up money in your monastery;
but things of all kinds, beyond what is needed, give to the poor at the entrance
of your court; for so did the Holy Fathers. Do not keep a safe place, nor have a
care for wealth. But let all your care be the guardianship of souls.

READ: PSALM 50:5

A New Message

F. J. Huegel | 1957

F. J. Huegel (1889-1971) was converted while in college. He went into full-time ministry and served as a chaplain in World War I and as a missionary to Mexico for twenty-five years.

When one holds up the picture of the Christian life as set forth by the Apostles, and compares that with what today goes under the same name, one staggers. It is not my object to pick to pieces the modern Christian. I have no quarrel with the Church. I have been for ten years a missionary of the Cross, and have no thought of deserting the ranks. My only purpose in calling attention to our failure as Christians is to point the way to the victorious life in Christ for those who are conscious of their spiritual poverty, and "hunger and thirst after righteousness."

It is for the Christian who finds himself at the brink of despair, because of the gruesome picture he presents, when all the while he longs to faithfully reflect the Master's image, that I feel that I have a message. It is for the one whose thirst for the water of life, far from being quenched, consumes him, and leaves him sick with yearnings. It is to the one who is weary of hollow mockeries, sick of shams, who has become the victim of a secret self-loathing—one who feels that as a Christian he should be free from the power of sin, but is crushed by a sense of failure. It is to those who long to have their life, service, and preaching charged with the Spirit of the living God that I feel that I have a word which will not fail to usher in a new day.

The Christian is not called upon to strain over a role as an actor would agonize over lines poorly learned. The Christian life in the thought of God is infinitely more blessed and compelling. Exceeding great and precious promises are given us, "that by these ye might be partakers of the divine nature" (2 Peter 1:4 KJV). The Believer is grafted into the Trunk of the Eternal Godhead. "I am the vine, ye are the branches" (John 15:5 KJV).

READ: 2 TIMOTHY 1:9-10

IN SEARCH OF THE KING

HENRY VAN DYKE | 1896

Henry Jackson van Dyke (1852-1933) was an American author, educator, and clergyman.

The old man walked slowly towards the Damascus gate. Just beyond, a troop of soldiers came dragging a young girl with torn dress and disheveled hair. As the Magian looked at her with compassion, she broke free and threw herself at his feet.

"Have pity on me," she cried, "My father is dead, and I am seized for his debts to be sold as a slave. Save me from worse than death!"

Artaban trembled. It was the old conflict in his soul, which had come to him in the palm grove of Babylon and the cottage at Bethlehem—the conflict between the expectation of faith and the impulse of love. This was the third trial, the final and irrevocable choice.

Only one thing was sure—to rescue this helpless girl would be a true deed of love. He took the pearl from his bosom; never had it seemed so radiant. He laid it in the girl's hand. "Thy ransom, daughter!"

Suddenly, the sky darkened and tremors ran through the earth. The soldiers fled in terror, but Artaban and the girl crouched helplessly in the street.

What had he to fear? What had he to live for? He had given away the last remnant of his tribute for the King. The quest was over, and it had failed.

Once more the ground quivered. A heavy tile fell and struck the old man on the temple. He lay breathless and pale, blood trickling from his wound. As the girl bent over him, a small, still voice came through the twilight. She turned, but saw no one.

Then the old man's lips moved: "Not so, my Lord! I have looked for you for thirty-three years; but I have never seen your face, nor ministered to you, my King."

The sweet voice came again. Again the girl heard it, very faintly. But now it seemed she understood: "*Verily I say unto thee, inasmuch as thou hast done it unto one of the least of these, thou hast done it unto me.*"

Wonder and joy lighted the pale face of Artaban. One last breath of relief exhaled gently from his lips.

His journey was ended. His treasures were accepted. The Other Wise Man had found the King.

READ: 1 CORINTHIANS 13:2

APRIL 16

ON ANTONY THE GREAT

ATHANASIUS | 4TH CENTURY

Antony the Great (c. 251-356), also known as Saint Anthony, was a Christian saint from Egypt and a prominent leader among the Desert Fathers.

Monasticism had not yet been established, therefore all those who wanted to live a solitary life went and lived on the outskirts of the city. This was what St. Anthony did as he dwelt alone, worshipping and living an ascetic life.

The devil fought him there by afflicting him with boredom, laziness, and phantoms of women. He overcame the devil's snares by the power of the Lord Christ. After that, he resided in one of the tombs and closed the door on himself. Some of his friends used to bring him food. When the devil perceived his ascetic life and his intense worship, he was envious of him, and he beat him mercilessly, then left him unconscious. When his friends came to visit him and found him in this condition, they carried him to the church. After he somewhat recovered, he went back to the same place.

The devil again resumed his war against St. Anthony, only this time the phantoms were in the form of wild beasts, wolves, lions, snakes, and scorpions. But the saint would laugh at them scornfully and say, "If any of you have any authority over me, only one would have been sufficient to fight me." At his saying this, they disappeared as though in smoke, for God gave him the victory over the devils. He was always singing this psalm, "Let God arise, let his enemies be scattered: let them also that hate him flee before him" (Psalm 68:1 KJV).

During the time of persecution, he longed to become a martyr. But God preserved him all along, according to His will, for the benefit of many. His fame spread abroad and it reached Emperor Constantine. The Emperor wrote to him, offering him praise and asked him to pray for him. St. Anthony did not give it any heed, but the brethren told him, "Emperor Constantine loves the church," and so he wrote a letter blessing him, and praying for the peace and safety of the empire and the church.

READ: REVELATION 12:11

APRIL 17

THE HAND OF PROVIDENCE

JOHN FLAVEL | 1678

John Flavel (1627-1691) was an English Presbyterian clergyman.

Scripture gives us a fair and lovely prospect of Providence in its universal, effectual, beneficial, and encouraging influence upon the affairs and concerns of the saints. It not only has its hand in this or that, but in all that concerns them throughout their lives, from first to last. Not only the great and more important, but the most minute and ordinary affairs of our lives are transacted and managed by it. It touches all things that touch us.

Providence not only undertakes, but perfects what concerns us. It goes through with its designs, and accomplishes what it begins. No difficulty so clogs it, no cross accident falls in its way, but it carries its design through it. Its motions are irresistible and uncontrollable; He performs it for us. And all its products and issues are exceedingly *beneficial* to the saints. It performs all things for them.

For what are the works of Providence but the execution of God's decree and the fulfilling of His Word? Therefore, whatever Providence does concerning them, it must be "the performance of all things for them." And if so, how cheering, supporting, and encouraging must the consideration of these things be in a day of distress and trouble! What life and hope will it inspire when great pressures lie upon us!

O how ravishing and delectable a sight will it be to behold at one view the whole design of Providence, and the proper place and use of every single act, which we could not understand in this world! All the dark, intricate, puzzling providences at which we were sometimes so offended, and sometimes amazed, which we could neither reconcile with the promise nor with each other; which we so unjustly censured and bitterly bewailed, we shall then see to be to us as the difficult passage through the wilderness was to Israel, "the right way to a city of habitation" (Psalm 107:7 KJV).

READ: PSALM 37:23

A HIGHER PURPOSE

PHILLIPS BROOKS | 19TH CENTURY

Phillips Brooks (1835-1893) was an American clergyman and author who served briefly as Bishop of Massachusetts in the Episcopal Church.

The purpose and result of freedom is service. It sounds to us at first like a contradiction, like a paradox. Great truths very often present themselves to us in the first place as paradoxes, and it is only when we come to combine the two different terms of which they are composed and see how it is only by their meeting that the truth does reveal itself to us, that the truth does become known.

It is by this same truth that God frees our souls, not from service, not from duty, but into service and into duty, and he who makes mistakes the purpose of his freedom mistakes the character of his freedom. He who thinks that he is being released from the work, and not set free in order that he may accomplish that work, mistakes the Christ from whom the freedom comes, mistakes the condition into which his soul is invited to enter.

The freedom of a man simply consists in the larger opportunity to be and to do all that God makes him in His creation capable of being and doing, then certainly if man has been capable of service it is only by the entrance into service, by the acceptance of that life of service for which God has given man the capacity, that he enters into the fullness of his freedom and becomes the liberated child of God. When man is set free simply into the enjoyment of his own life, simply into the realization of his own existence, he has not attained the purposes of his freedom; he has not come to the purposes of his life.

READ: 1 PETER 2:15-17

April 19

A Bitter Lament

Andrew of Crete | 8th century

Saint Andrew of Crete (c. 650-c. 726), also known as Andrew of Jerusalem, was an eighth-century bishop, theologian, homilist, and hymnographer.

He is my Helper and Protector, and has become my salvation. This is my God and I will glorify Him. My father's God and I will exalt Him. For gloriously has He been glorified.

Have mercy on me, O God, have mercy on me.

Where shall I begin to lament the deeds of my wretched life? What first-fruit shall I offer, O Christ, for my present lamentation? But in Thy compassion grant me release from my falls.

Having rivaled the first-created Adam by my transgression, I realize that I am stripped naked of God and of the everlasting kingdom and bliss through my sins.

Alas, wretched soul! Why are you like the first Eve? For you have wickedly looked and been bitterly wounded, and you have touched the tree and rashly tasted the forbidden food.

Adam was rightly exiled from Eden for not keeping Thy one commandment, O Savior. But what shall I suffer who am always rejecting Thy living words?

Attend, O heaven, and I will speak; O earth, give ear to a voice repenting to God and singing praises to Him. Attend to me, O God my Savior, with Thy merciful eye, and accept my fervent confession.

I have sinned above all men; I alone have sinned against Thee. But as God have compassion, O Savior, on Thy creature.

I looked at the beauty of the tree, and my mind was seduced; and now I lie naked, and I am ashamed. All the demon-chiefs of the passions have plowed on my back, and long has their tyranny over me lasted.

Glory to the Father, and to the Son, and to the Holy Spirit.

To the Holy Trinity: I sing of Thee as one in three Persons, O God of all, the Father and the Son and the Holy Spirit.

Now and ever, and to the ages of ages. Amen.

Read: Romans 3:20-24

APRIL 20

IN HIS IMAGE

DOROTHY L. SAYERS | 1941

Dorothy Leigh Sayers (1893-1957) was a renowned English crime writer, poet, playwright, essayist, translator, and Christian humanist.

In the beginning God created. He made this and He made that and He saw that it was good. And He created man in His own image; in the image of God created He him; male and female created He them. The expression "in His own image" has occasioned a good deal of controversy. Only the most simple-minded people of any age or nation have supposed the image to be a physical one.

The "image," whatever the author may have meant by it, is something shared by male and female alike. Yet Christian doctrine and tradition, indeed, by language and picture, sets its face against all sexual symbolism for the divine fertility. Its Trinity is wholly masculine; as all language relating to Man as a species is masculine.

The Jews, keenly alive to the perils of pictorial metaphor, forbade the representation of the Person of God in graven images. Nevertheless, human nature and the nature of human language defeated them. No legislation could prevent the making of verbal pictures: God walks in the garden, He stretches out His arm, His voice shakes the cedars, for man is so made that he has no way to think except in pictures. But continually, the voice of warning has been raised: "God is a spirit"; "without body, parts or passions"; He is a pure being, "I AM THAT I AM."

Man, very obviously, is not a being of this kind; his body, parts, and passions are only too conspicuous in his make-up. How then can he be said to resemble God? We observe that in the passage leading up to the statement about man, he has given no detailed information about God. Looking at man, he sees in him something essentially divine, but when we turn back to see what he says about the original upon which the "image" of God was modeled, we find only the single assertion, "God created." The characteristic common to God and man is apparently that: the desire and the ability to make things.

READ: GENESIS 1:27

APRIL 21

A FAITHFUL FELLOWSHIP

GEORGE FOX | 17TH CENTURY

George Fox (1624-1691) was an English Dissenter and a founder of the Religious
Society of Friends, commonly known as the Quakers or Friends.

So, meet together all you who fear the Lord God,
And think upon his name,
His mercies endure forever;
His mercies are in temptations and troubles,
His mercies are in afflictions, in reproaches, and in scorns.
Therefore rejoice, you simple ones, who love simplicity,
And meet and wait together to receive strength and wisdom from the
    Lord God;
And in departing from sin and evil,
You will be able to speak to the praise of the Lord.
And meeting and waiting in his power, which you have received,
In it all to improve your measure that God has given you;
For you never improve your measure,
So long as you rely upon any visible thing without you;
But when you come alone to wait upon God,
Everyone shall have a reward according to your deserts,
And everyone your penny, who are called into the vineyard to labor.
Therefore be faithful to God, and mind that which is committed to you,
As faithful servants, laboring in love;
Some threshing, and some plowing, and some to keep the sheep.
He who can receive this let him.
And all watch over one another in the spirit of God.
So God Almighty bless, guide, and prosper you
Unto his kingdom, where there is no tribulation.
When your minds run into anything outwardly, without the power,
It covers and veils the pure in you.

READ: 1 JOHN 1:7

APRIL 22

WAIT ON THE LORD

F.B. MEYER | 1896

Frederick Brotherton Meyer (1847-1929) was a Baptist pastor, author, and evangelist.

Sometimes it looks as if we are bound to act. Everyone says we must do something; and, indeed, things seem to have reached so desperate a pitch that we must. Behind are the Egyptians, right and left are inaccessible precipices; before is the sea. It is not easy at such times to stand still and see the salvation of God; but we must. When Saul compelled himself, and offered sacrifice, because he thought that Samuel was too late in coming, he made the great mistake of his life.

God may delay to come in the guise of His Providence. There was delay when Jesus came walking on the sea in the early dawn, or hastened to raise Lazarus. There was delay when the angel sped to Peter's side on the night before his expected martyrdom. He stays long enough to test patience of faith, but not a moment behind the extreme hour of need. "The vision is yet for an appointed time, but at the end it shall speak, and shall not lie: though it tarry, wait for it; because it will surely come, it will not tarry" (Habakkuk 2:3 KJV).

It is very remarkable how God guides us by circumstances. At one moment the way may seem utterly blocked, and then shortly afterward some trivial incident occurs, which might not seem much to others, but which to the keen eye of faith speaks volumes. The circumstances of our daily life are to us an infallible indication of God's will, when they concur with the inward promptings of the Spirit and with the Word of God. So long as they are stationary, wait. When you must act, they will open, and a way will be made through oceans and rivers, wastes and rocks.

READ: ISAIAH 52:12

APRIL 23

LOVE OVERCOMES SIN

THE UNKNOWN MYSTIC | 14TH CENTURY

The Unknown Mystic, an anonymous English monk, wrote a medieval spiritual guidebook that focused on a mystical approach to Christian prayer, where God is not found through rote knowledge but through "blind love."

When our Lord said to Mary, "Thy sins be forgiven thee," it was not for her great sorrow, nor for the remembering of her sins, nor for her meekness that she had in the beholding of her wretchedness. Then why? Surely because she loved much.

Here may men see what a privy pressing of love may purchase of our Lord, before all other works that man may think. Although she might not have felt the deep hearty sorrow of her sins—for all her lifetime she had them with her wherever she went, as though it were a burden bound together and laid up fully in her heart—nevertheless, she had a more hearty sorrow and doleful desire; and languished, almost to the death, for lacking of love, than she had for any remembrance of her sins.

And yet she knew well, that she was a wretch, and that her sins had made a division between her and her God that she loved so much: and also that they were in great part the cause of her languishing sickness for lack of love. But did she come down from the height of desire into the deepness of her sinful life, and searched in the foul stinking dunghill of her sins; searching them up, one by one, sorrowing and weeping upon each? No, surely she did not. Why? Because God, by His grace, let her know within in her soul that she should never bring it about. For so might she sooner have raised in herself an ability to have oft sinned; rather than have purchased by that work any plain forgiveness.

Therefore she hung her love and longing in this cloud of unknowing, and learned to love what she might not see clearly in this life, yet could feel in sweetness of love in her affection. So much so, that she had little special remembrance, whether she had ever been a sinner or none.

READ: 1 PETER 4:8

APRIL 24

SPIRITUAL CONSOLATION

IGNATIUS | 1548

St. Ignatius of Loyola (1419-1556) was the founder of the Jesuits; his Spiritual Exercises *are gaining popularity with both lay people and non-Catholics.*

In the persons who go from mortal sin to mortal sin, the enemy is commonly used to propose to them apparent pleasures, making them imagine sensual delights and pleasures in order to hold them more and make them grow in their vices and sins. In these persons the good spirit uses the opposite method, pricking them and biting their consciences through the process of reason.

In the persons who are going on intensely cleansing their sins and rising from good to better in the service of God our Lord, it is the method contrary to that in the first Rule, for then it is the way of the evil spirit to bite, sadden, and put obstacles, disquieting with false reasons, that one may not go on; and it is proper to the good to give courage and strength, consolations, tears, inspirations, and quiet, putting away all obstacles, that one may go on in well doing.

I call it spiritual consolation when some interior movement in the soul is caused, through which the soul comes to be inflamed with love of its Creator and Lord; and when it can in consequence love no created thing on the face of the earth in itself, but in the Creator of them all. Likewise, when it sheds tears that move to love of its Lord, whether out of sorrow for one's sins, or for the Passion of Christ our Lord, or because of other things directly connected with His service and praise. Finally, I call consolation every increase of hope, faith, and charity, and all interior joy that calls and attracts to heavenly things and to the salvation of one's soul, quieting it and giving it peace in its Creator and Lord.

READ: GALATIANS 6:9

THE NICENO-CONSTANTINOPOLITAN CREED

FIRST COUNCIL OF CONSTANTINOPLE | 381

The Niceno-Constantinopolitan Creed is the second version of the creed commonly referred to as the Nicene Creed. Its origin is of some debate, though it has been argued that this creed originated not as an editing by the First Council of Constantinople of the original Nicene Creed, but as an independent creed (probably an older baptismal creed) modified to make it more like the Nicene Creed of 325 and attributed to the Council of 381 only later.

We believe in one God, the Father Almighty, Maker of heaven and earth, and of all things visible and invisible.

And in one Lord Jesus Christ, the only-begotten Son of God, begotten of the Father before all worlds (æons), Light of Light, very God of very God, begotten, not made, being of one substance with the Father;

by whom all things were made;

who for us men, and for our salvation, came down from heaven, and was incarnate by the Holy Ghost of the Virgin Mary, and was made man;

he was crucified for us under Pontius Pilate, and suffered, and was buried, and the third day he rose again, according to the Scriptures, and ascended into heaven, and sitteth on the right hand of the Father;

from thence he shall come again, with glory, to judge the quick and the dead;

whose kingdom shall have no end.

And in the Holy Ghost, the Lord and Giver of life, who proceedeth from the Father, who with the Father and the Son together is worshiped and glorified, who spake by the prophets.

In one holy catholic and apostolic Church, we acknowledge one baptism for the remission of sins; we look for the resurrection of the dead, and the life of the world to come.

Amen.

READ: PSALM 146:5-6

APRIL 26

PERFECT LOVE

SAMUEL BRENGLE | 20TH CENTURY

Samuel Logan Brengle (1860-1936) was a commissioner in the Salvation Army and a leading author, teacher, and preacher on the doctrine of holiness.

I shall never forget my joy, mingled with awe and wonder, when this dawned upon my consciousness. For several weeks I had been searching the Scriptures, ransacking my heart, humbling my soul, and crying to God almost day and night for a pure heart and the baptism with the Holy Ghost, when one glad, sweet day this text suddenly opened to my understanding: "If we confess our sins, he is faithful and just to forgive us our sins, and to cleanse us from all unrighteousness" (1 John 1:9 KJV); and I was enabled to believe without any doubt that the precious Blood cleansed my heart, even mine, from all sin.

Shortly after that, while reading the words of Jesus to Martha—"I am the resurrection, and the life: he that believeth in me, though he were dead, yet shall he live: And whosoever liveth and believeth in me shall never die" (John 11:25-26 KJV)—instantly my heart was melted like wax before fire; Jesus Christ was revealed to my spiritual consciousness, revealed in me, and my soul was filled with unutterable love.

Then one day, with amazement, I said to a friend: "This is the perfect love about which the Apostle John wrote but it is beyond all I dreamed of. This love thinks, wills, talks with me; corrects, instructs, and teaches me." And then I knew that God the Holy Ghost was in this love, and that this love was God, for "God is love."

Oh, the rapture mingled with reverential, holy fear to be indwelt by the Holy Ghost, to be a temple of the Living God! But we must not draw back from the experience through fear. All danger will be avoided by meekness and lowliness of heart; by humble, faithful service; by keeping an open, teachable spirit; in a word, by looking steadily unto Jesus, to whom the Holy Spirit continually points us; that we may walk in the steps of Him whose Blood purchases our pardon, and makes and keeps us clean.

READ: 1 JOHN 4:18

APRIL 27

ONLY THE CROSS

JESSIE PENN-LEWIS | 19TH CENTURY

Jessie Penn-Lewis (1861-1927) was a Welsh evangelical speaker and author of a number of Christian evangelical works.

What a gospel for the people! Let us give it to them. It is truly a gospel of glad tidings—the Cross the place of victory over sin as well as the place of reconciliation with God.

In every one of the epistles of Paul we find that he refers to the finished work of Christ at Calvary, in one aspect or another. Everything he says in all his letters revolves around the center of the Cross.

In Galatians especially, are so many references to the Cross, that the epistle might be called the Epistle of the Cross. The Apostle writes about himself, but what was true for Paul is true for us. "But as for me," says the Apostle, "far be it from me to boast, save only in the Cross of our Lord Jesus Christ; whereby the world is crucified unto me, and I unto the world" (see Galatians 6:14).

The believer's death with Christ upon His Cross therefore means being crucified to the world in all its aspects. Not to be a miserable, joyless person, but one filled with the joy and glory of another world. It is a delivering Cross—that liberates you to have the very foretaste of heaven in you, as already sharers of the power of the age to come. Let each one of us put in our claim for deliverance from the world, so that, as Christians, we do not pander to it, dress like it, act like it, and behave like it.

Note also that to experience this, it must be a real fellowship with Christ in His death. And those who have proved it know that this application of the Cross does actually cut you off from the "world," there is a "gulf" between you and the world, and you can see the people of the world on the other side. Thus looking at the world from the Cross, you can go to the world of mankind, 'sent' as Christ was sent, to reveal the heart of God, with His compassion of love and His spirit of sacrifice.

READ: GALATIANS 6:14-15

APRIL 28

BEARING WITNESS

BEDE | 731

Bede (c. 672-735), also referred to as Saint Bede, was a British monk, well-known author, and scholar. His most famous work, The Ecclesiastical History of England, *gained him the title "The Father of English History."*

In the year of our Lord 286, Diocletian reigned twenty years, and made Maximian his colleague in the empire. When an order was sent by Maximian that Carausius should be put to death, he possessed himself of Britain, and held it for the space of seven years. At length he was put to death by the treachery of his associate Allectus. The usurper held the island three years, and was then vanquished by Asclepiodotus, the captain of the Praetorian guards, who thus restored Britain to the Roman Empire.

Meanwhile, Diocletian in the east, and Maximian in the west, commanded the churches to be destroyed, and the Christians to be persecuted and slain. This persecution was the tenth since the reign of Nero and was more lasting and cruel than almost any before it. It was carried on incessantly for ten years, with burning of churches, outlawing of innocent persons, and the slaughter of martyrs. Finally, Britain also attained to the great glory of bearing faithful witness to God.

When the storm of persecution ceased, the faithful Christians who had hidden themselves in woods, deserts, and secret caves, came forth and rebuilt the churches which had been leveled to the ground, and celebrated festivals and performed their sacred rites with pure hearts and lips. This peace continued in the Christian churches of Britain until the time of the Arian madness, which, although it was exposed and condemned in the Council of Nicaea, nevertheless, the deadly poison of its evil spread to the churches in the islands, as well as to those of the rest of the world.

READ: 2 THESSALONIANS 1:2-5

APRIL 29

CLEAVING TO GOD

ALBERT THE GREAT | 13TH CENTURY

Albertus Magnus (c. 1206-1280), also known as Albert the Great and Albert of Cologne, was a Dominican friar and a bishop who achieved fame for his comprehensive knowledge of and advocacy for the peaceful coexistence of science and religion.

I have had the idea of writing something for myself on and about the state of complete and full abstraction from everything and of cleaving freely, confidently, nakedly, and firmly to God alone, especially since the goal of Christian perfection is the love by which we cleave to God.

Indeed the Lord God is Spirit, and those who worship him must worship in spirit and in truth; that is, understanding and desire, stripped of all images. This can be done best when a man is disengaged and removed from everything else. There, in the presence of Jesus Christ, the mind alone turns in security confidently to the Lord its God with its desire. In this way it pours itself forth into him in full sincerity with its whole heart and the yearning of its love, and is plunged, enlarged, set on fire, and dissolved into him.

Certainly, anyone who desires and aims to arrive at and remain in such a state must above all have eyes and senses closed and not be inwardly involved or worried about anything. Here he can commit himself and all that he has, individually and as a whole, to God's unfailing providence, in accordance with the words of Peter, cast all your care upon him (1 Peter 5:7), who can do everything.

This, after all, is the hidden heavenly treasure, none other than the pearl of great price. For what good does it do a religious man if he gains the whole world but suffers the loss of his soul? Or what is the benefit of his state of life, if he is without a life of spiritual humility and truth in which Christ abides through a faith created by love? This is what Luke means when he says the Kingdom of God (that is, Jesus Christ) is within you.

READ: DEUTERONOMY 10:20

APRIL 30

WOMANLY AMBITIONS

CATHERINE BOOTH | 1859

Catherine Booth (1829-1890) was the wife of the founder of The Salvation Army, William Booth. Because of her considerable influence, she was known as the "Army Mother."

The first and most common objection urged against the public exercises of women, is that they are unnatural and unfeminine. Many labor under a very great but common mistake—that of confounding nature with custom. Use, or custom, makes things appear to us natural which, in reality, are very unnatural; while, on the other hand, novelty and rarity make very natural things appear strange and contrary to nature.

Making allowance for the novelty of the thing, we cannot discover anything either unnatural or immodest in a Christian woman, becomingly attired, appearing on a platform or in a pulpit. By *nature* she seems fitted to grace either. God has given to woman a graceful form and attitude, winning manners, persuasive speech, and, above all, a finely-tuned emotional nature, all of which appear to us as eminently *natural* qualifications for public speaking.

We admit that the trammels of custom, the force of prejudice, and one-sided interpretations of Scripture, have hitherto almost excluded her from this sphere; but, before it is pronounced to be unnatural, it must be proved either that woman has not the *ability* to teach or to preach, or that as soon as she presumes to step on the platform or into the pulpit, she loses the delicacy and grace of the female character.

Who would dare charge the sainted Madame Guyon, Lady Maxwell, the talented mother of the Wesleys, Mrs. Fletcher, Mrs. Whiteman, or Miss Marsh with being unwomanly or ambitious? These ladies we know have won alike from friends and enemies the highest eulogies as to the devotedness, purity, and sweetness of their lives. Yet these were all more or less public women, every one of them expounding and exhorting from the Scriptures to mixed companies of men and women. Ambitious doubtless they were; but theirs was an ambition akin to His, who, for the "joy that was set before Him, endured the cross, despising the shame." Would that all the Lord's people had more of this ambition.

READ: ROMANS 10:13

MAY 1

LED BY THE SPIRIT

B. B. WARFIELD | 1903

Benjamin Breckinridge Warfield (1851-1921) was an American Presbyterian theologian and scholar who served as professor of theology at Princeton Seminary from 1887 to 1921.

There is certainly abundant reason why we should seek to learn what the Scriptures mean by "spiritual leading." There are few subjects so intimately related to the Christian life, of which Christians appear to have formed conceptions so inadequate—even positively erroneous. Many of the best Christians would shrink with something like distaste from affirming themselves to be "led by the Spirit of God." It is surely enough, however, to motivate us to search the Scriptures to learn what it is to be "led by the Spirit of God," to read the solemn words: "As many as are led by the Spirit of God, these are sons of God" (Romans 8:14). If this is true, surely it behooves all who believe themselves to be God's children to know what the leading of the Spirit is.

All who are led by the Spirit of God are the children of God; and if children, then heirs of God and joint heirs with Christ Jesus. Paul points us not to the victory of good over evil, but to the conflict of good with evil—not to the end, but to the process—as the proof of childship to God. Therefore the note of the passage is not one of fear and despair, but of hope and triumph: "If God be for us who can be against us?" (Romans 8:31 KJV). Let our hearts repeat this cry of victory today.

And as we repeat it, let us go onward, in hope and triumph, in our holy efforts. Let our weak knees be strengthened and new vigor enter our every nerve. The victory is assured. The Holy Spirit within us cannot fail us. The way may be rough; dangers, pitfalls are on every side. But the Holy Spirit is leading us. Surely, in that assurance, despite dangers and weakness, and panting chest and swimming head, we can find strength to go ever forward.

READ: ROMANS 8:14

May 2
Trust in His Name

Ralph Erskine | 18th century

Ralph Erskine (1685-1752) was a Scottish churchman and the brother of another prominent minister, Ebenezer Erskine.

Do you need wonders to be wrought for you? His name is Wonderful; look to him so to do, for his name's sake. Do you need counsel and direction? His name is the Counselor: cast yourself on him and his name for this. Have you mighty enemies to debate with? His name is the mighty God; seek that he may exert his power for his name's sake. Do you need his fatherly pity? His name is the everlasting Father; "As a father pitieth his children, so the LORD pitieth them that fear him" (Psalm 103:13 KJV).

Do you need peace external, internal, or eternal? His name is the Prince of Peace. Do you need healing? O sirs, his name is *Jehovah-Rophe*, the Lord the healer and physician; seek, for his name's sake, that he may heal all your diseases. Do you need pardon? His name is *Jehovah-Tsidkenu*, the Lord our righteousness; seek, for his name's sake, that he may be merciful to your unrighteousness. Do you need defense and protection? His name is *Jehovah-Nissi*, the Lord your banner. Seek for his name's sake, that his banner of love and grace may be spread over you. Do you need provision in extreme want? His name is *Jehovah-Jireh*, in the mount of the Lord it shall be seen, the Lord will provide.

Do you need his presence? His name is *Jehovah-Shammah*, the Lord is there: *Immanuel*, God with us. Do you need strength? His name is the Strength of Israel. Do you need comfort? His name is the Consolation of Israel. Do you need shelter? His name is the City of Refuge. Have you nothing and need all? His name is All in All. Sit down and devise names to your wants and needs, and you will find he has a name suitable thereunto; for your supply, he has wisdom to guide you; and power to keep you; mercy to pity you; truth to shield you; holiness to sanctify you; righteousness to justify you; grace to adorn you; and glory to crown you. Trust in his name, who saves for his name's sake.

Read: Psalm 48:10

M AY 3

LOVE CHRIST SINCERELY

THOMAS DOOLITTLE | 17TH CENTURY

Thomas Doolittle (c. 1632-1707) was an English nonconformist tutor, author, pastor, and popular preacher.

Love shows the true character of a man, according to the object which he loves more than anything else: for as is the love, so is the man. According to his love, so might you confidently designate the man. If he is a lover of honor, he is an ambitious man; a lover of pleasure, a sensual man; and if he chiefly love the world, he is a covetous man. If a man loves righteousness, he is a religious man; if the things above, a heavenly-minded man; and if he love Christ with a preeminent love, he is a sincere man: "Rightly do they love you" (Song of Solomon 1:4).

If Christ has our love, he has our all; and Christ never has what he deserves from us, till he has our love. True love withholds nothing from Christ, when it is sincerely set upon him. If we actually love him, he will have our time, and he will have our service, and he will have the use of all our resources, and gifts, and graces. Indeed, then he shall have our possessions, freedom, and our very lives, whenever he calls for them.

In the same way, when God loves any of us, he will withhold nothing from us that is good for us. He does not hold back his own only begotten Son. When Christ loves us, he gives us everything we need—his merits to justify us, his Spirit to sanctify us, his grace to adorn us, and his glory to crown us. Therefore, when any of us love Christ sincerely, we lay everything down at his feet, and give up all to be at his command and service: "And they loved not their lives unto the death" (Revelation 12:11 KJV).

READ: 1 PETER 3:15

MAY 4

IN GOD'S LOVE

JUDE 1 C. 80

Jude was the brother of Jesus, according to the New Testament. He is traditionally identified as the author of the Epistle of Jude, which is reckoned among the seven general epistles of the New Testament.

But, dear friends, remember what the apostles of our Lord Jesus Christ foretold. They said to you, "In the last times there will be scoffers who will follow their own ungodly desires." These are the people who divide you, who follow mere natural instincts and do not have the Spirit.

But you, dear friends, by building yourselves up in your most holy faith and praying in the Holy Spirit, keep yourselves in God's love as you wait for the mercy of our Lord Jesus Christ to bring you to eternal life.

Be merciful to those who doubt; save others by snatching them from the fire; to others show mercy, mixed with fear—hating even the clothing stained by corrupted flesh.

To him who is able to keep you from stumbling and to present you before his glorious presence without fault and with great joy—to the only God our Savior be glory, majesty, power and authority, through Jesus Christ our Lord, before all ages, now and forevermore! Amen.

READ: NEHEMIAH 1:5

May 5

The Common Prayer

Dwight L. Moody | 1873

Dwight Lyman Moody (1837-1899), also known as D. L. Moody, was an American evangelist and publisher who founded the Moody Church, the Moody Bible Institute, and Moody Publishers.

Those who have left the deepest impression on this sin-cursed earth have been men and women of prayer. You will find that *prayer* has been the mighty power that has moved not only God, but man.

Abraham was a man of prayer, and angels came down from heaven to converse with him.

Jacob's prayer was answered in the wonderful interview at Peniel, that resulted in his having such a mighty blessing, and in softening the heart of his brother Esau.

The child Samuel was given in answer to Hannah's prayer.

Elijah's prayer closed up the heavens for three years and six months, and he prayed again and the heavens gave rain.

The Apostle James tells us that the prophet Elijah was a man "subject to like passions as we are."

I am thankful that those men and women who were so mighty in prayer were just like ourselves. We are apt to think that those prophets and mighty men and women of old time were different from what we are. To be sure they lived in a much darker age, but they were of like passions with ourselves.

Read: James 5:16

MAY 6
A GOOD WORD

JOHANNES ERIUGENA | 9TH CENTURY

Johannes Scotus Eriugena (c. 815-c. 877) was an Irish theologian, neoplatonist philosopher, and poet. He is known for having translated and made commentaries upon the work of Pseudo-Dionysius.

All things were made through him, through God-the-Word himself. Through the very God-Word, all things were made. And what does "All things were made through him" (John 1:3 ASV) mean if not that, as the Word was born before all things from the Father, all things were made with him and by him?

For the generation of the Word from the Father is the very creation itself of all causes, together with the operation and effect of all that proceeds from them in kinds and species. Truly, all things were made from the generation of God-the-Word from God-the-beginning.

Hear, then, the divine and ineffable paradox—the unopenable secret, the invisible depth, the incomprehensible mystery! Through him, who was not made but begotten, all things were made but not begotten.

The beginning, the principle, from whom all things are is the Father; the beginning, the principle, through whom all things exist is the Son. The Father speaks his Word—the Father brings forth his Wisdom—and all things are made. The prophet said, "In wisdom hast thou made them all" (Psalm 104:24 KJV). And elsewhere, introducing the Father in person, the Father says, "My heart has brought forth." And what did his heart bring forth? He explains it himself: "I spoke a good Word." I speak a good Word, I bring forth a good Son. The Father's heart is his own substance, of which the Son's own substance was begotten.

READ: GENESIS 1:24-25

May 7

Knowledge without Power

Martyn Lloyd-Jones | 1961

David Martyn Lloyd-Jones (1899-1981) was a Welsh Protestant minister, preacher, and medical doctor.

Now this is a tragic misunderstanding that regards Christianity merely as one teaching among a number of other high, idealistic moral teachings; for example, those of Plato, Socrates, Aristotle, Seneca, and others. They add to their list of great teachers the name of "Jesus," and He generally comes somewhere about the center. Some rise superior to Him, others are esteemed His inferiors.

Christianity has been reduced to a moral, ethical code and teaching—a variant of the theme of "Goodness, Beauty, and Truth" to which we are to aspire. "Look to the example of Jesus," they say. Example of Jesus? I know of nothing that is so discouraging as the example of Jesus! I look at His moral stature, at His absolute perfection, and I feel that I am already condemned and hopeless. Imitation of Christ? It is the greatest nonsense that has ever been uttered! Imitation of Christ? I who cannot satisfy myself and my own demands, and other people still less—am I to imitate Christ?

It is not surprising that failure has resulted, and that people have left the Christian church; it is not surprising that we are faced with a moral collapse in this country, and in all countries, at the present time; for the non-Christian ethical teaching leaves it all to me, strengthless and powerless though I am.

But Christianity is no mere code of ethics. Our educationalists cannot turn to us and say, "Well now, you representatives of the Christian church. Do not be narrow-minded, but give us your help, we want to know what you think about sex, and many other factors in life." I answer that what is needed is not what I think about sex, but a power that will deliver a man from being mastered and controlled by it. It is not knowledge we need; it is power. And that is where your moral ethical systems break down and fail completely. They have no power to offer, none at all.

Read: Romans 1:16

May 8

One Man's Cruelty

Tacitus | 115

Publius (or Gaius) Cornelius Tactitus (56-117) was a senator and a historian of the Roman Empire. The surviving portions of his two major works—the Annals *and the* Histories—*span the history of the Roman Empire from the death of Augustus in 14 A.D. to the death of emperor Domitian in 96.*

Consequently, to get rid of the report, Nero fastened the guilt and inflicted the most exquisite tortures on a class hated for their abominations, called Christians by the populace. Christus, from whom the name had its origin, suffered the extreme penalty during the reign of Tiberius at the hands of one of our procurators, Pontius Pilatus, and a most mischievous superstition, thus checked for the moment, again broke out not only in Judea, the first source of the evil, but even in Rome, where all things hideous and shameful from every part of the world find their center and become popular.

Accordingly, an arrest was first made of all who pleaded guilty; then, upon their information, an immense multitude was convicted, not so much of the crime of firing the city, as of hatred against mankind. Mockery of every sort was added to their deaths. Covered with the skins of beasts, they were torn by dogs and perished, or were nailed to crosses, or were doomed to the flames and burnt, to serve as a nightly illumination, when daylight had expired.

Nero offered his gardens for the spectacle, and was exhibiting a show in the circus, while he mingled with the people in the dress of a charioteer or stood aloft on a car. Hence, even for criminals who deserved extreme and exemplary punishment, there arose a feeling of compassion; for it was not, as it seemed, for the public good, but to glut one man's cruelty, that they were being destroyed.

Read: Jeremiah 15:21

MAY 9

THE MURDER OF THOMAS BECKET

EDWARD GRIM | 12TH CENTURY

Thomas Becket (1118-1170), a saint of the Roman Catholic Church, was Archbishop of Canterbury from 1162 until his murder in 1170. Edward Grim, a monk, observed the attack on Becket from the safety of a hiding place near the altar.

The knights stormed the cathedral. "Absolve," they cried, "and restore to communion those whom you have excommunicated, and restore their powers to those whom you have suspended."

He answered, "There has been no satisfaction, and I will not absolve them."

"Then you shall die," they cried, "and receive what you deserve."

"I am ready," he replied, "to die for my Lord, that in my blood the Church may obtain liberty and peace."

Then they lay sacrilegious hands on him, pulling and dragging him that they may kill him outside the church, or carry him away a prisoner, as they afterwards confessed. But when he could not be forced away from the pillar, one of them pressed on him and clung to him more closely. Him he pushed off saying, "Touch me not, Reginald; you owe me fealty and subjection; you and your accomplices act like madmen."

The knight, fired with a terrible rage at this severe repulse, waved his sword over the sacred head. "No faith," he cried, "nor subjection do I owe you against my fealty to my lord the King."

Then the unconquered martyr seeing the hour at hand which should put an end to this miserable life, inclined his neck as one who prays and joining his hands he lifted them up. The wicked knight, fearing lest he should be rescued by the people and escape alive, leapt upon him suddenly and wounded this lamb on the head, cutting off the top of the crown which the sacred unction of the chrism had dedicated to God.

Then he received a second blow on the head but still stood firm. At the third blow he fell on his knees and elbows, offering himself a living victim, and saying in a low voice, "For the Name of Jesus and the protection of the Church I am ready to embrace death."

READ: PHILIPPIANS 1:21

MAY 10

LOVE AND WAR

LESLIE WEATHERHEAD | 1945

Leslie Dixon Weatherhead (1893-1976) was an English preacher, author, and theologian in the liberal Protestant tradition.

"Ye have heard that it hath been said, Thou shalt love thy neighbour, and hate thine enemy. But I say unto you, Love your enemies" (Matthew 5:43-44 KJV). That seems a formidable subject to discuss during wartime. You might even think it a dangerous subject and one likely to undermine the morale of our people. It might be easier to forget that Jesus ever said those words.

I should not be at all surprised if someone felt immediately cynical, saying in his heart, "Do you expect us to love the Gestapo? Are you seriously asking us to love those who run concentration camps, persecute the Jews, lock up little children in filthy railway cars and send them to unknown destinations, tearing them away from their parents? Have you already forgotten the Nazi atrocities, the inhuman brutality, and authentic records of bestiality? Do you suggest that on an eight-thousand-pound bomb we should tie a label, 'With love from Britain'?"

If anyone feels like that, I entirely understand. But since Jesus did say these words, and since it is sheer cowardice to put them in cold storage and drag them out again after the war, when perhaps it is easier to love the people of hostile nations, let us quietly think together about them, reminding ourselves of two important facts:

Love your enemies! Never let yourself hate! You may have a desperate task to break the evil which threatens the world, and the only way may be to fight and kill. But though we fight to the death, let us maintain unbroken goodwill and have the highest welfare of our enemies, as of the whole world, clearly in our minds, as the goal toward which we move. Those enemies also—possessed though they may be at present by evil demons—are the sons of the same Father who hates evil more than we do, but who loves all his children.

READ: LUKE 6:27-28

May 11

Impediments of the World

Augustine Baker | c. 1636

Augustine Baker (1575-1641) was a Benedictine mystic and an ascetic writer. He was one of the earliest members of the newly restored English Benedictine Congregation.

Now to what end did we come into religion, but only to avoid all these impediments in the world, which pull us away from attending to God and following His divine guidance? In this very point lies the difference between a secular and a religious state, that a secular person secularly minded, by reason of the noise, tumults, and unavoidable distractions, solicitudes, and temptations which are in the world, cannot without much ado find leisure to attend unto God and the gaining of His love even for a few minutes every day, or little oftener than the laws of the Church necessarily oblige him.

And all the directions that he is capable of in God's service must come from without, for by reason that his soul is so filled with images vain or sinful, and so agitated with impetuous affections and designs, he cannot recollect himself to hear God speaking in him. Whereas, a religious person professes his only business to be attending to God's internal voice, for which purpose he renounces all these impediments and distractions.

And the general, of all others most efficacious, means to remove all these impediments is, by abstraction and prayer in spirit, to aspire unto an habitual state of recollection and introversion; for such prayer, besides the virtue of impetration, by which God will be moved according to His so frequent and express promises to be a light to the meek and humble, hath also a direct virtue to procure this illumination, inasmuch as therein our souls see Him and nothing else, so that they have no other guide to follow but Him.

Read: Luke 12:31

May 12

Always Attentive

Salvian | 5th century

Salvian was a Christian writer of the fifth century, believed to be born at Cologne sometime between 400 and 405.

Speaking through the Sacred Books, the Divine Word says: "The eyes of the Lord are in every place, beholding the evil and the good." Here you find God present, looking upon us, his eyes watching us wherever we may be. If the Divine Word assures us that God observes the good and the wicked, it is expressly to prove that nothing escapes his watchful scrutiny.

For your fuller comprehension, hear the testimony of the Holy Spirit in another part of the Scriptures, when it says: "Behold, the eye of the Lord is upon them that fear him . . . to deliver their soul from death, and to keep them alive in famine" (Psalm 33:18-19 KJV). This is why God is said to watch over the just, that he may preserve and protect them. For the propitious oversight of his divinity is the safeguard of our mortal life. Elsewhere the Holy Spirit speaks in the same fashion: "The eyes of the Lord are upon the righteous, and his ears are open unto their cry" (Psalm 34:15 KJV).

See with what gentle kindness the Scripture says the Lord treats his people. For when it says the eyes of the Lord are on the righteous, his watchful love is shown; when it says that his ears are always open to their prayers, his readiness to hear is indicated. That his ears are always open to the prayers of the righteous proves not merely God's attention, but one might almost say his obedience. For how are the ears of the Lord open to the prayers of the righteous? How, except that he always hears, always hears clearly, always grants readily the pleas he has heard, bestows on men at once what he has clearly heard them ask? So the ears of our Lord are always ready to listen to the prayers of his saints, always attentive. How happy should we all be if we ourselves were as ready to hearken to God as he is to hear us!

Read: Psalm 61:1-2

MAY 13

WHO DO YOU SAY THAT I AM?

G. A. CHADWICK | 1896

George Alexander Chadwick (1840-1923) was a bishop and writer best known for his Bible expository.

"Who do men say that I am?" Jesus asked. The answer would tell of acceptance or rejection, the success or failure of His ministry, regarded in itself, and apart from ultimate issues unknown to mortals. From this point of view it had very plainly failed. At the beginning there was a clear hope that this was He that should come, the Son of David, the Holy One of God. But now the pitch of men's expectation was lowered. Some said John the Baptist, risen from the dead, as Herod feared; others spoke of Elijah, who was to come before the great and notable day of the Lord; in the sadness of His later days some had begun to see a resemblance to Jeremiah, lamenting the ruin of his nation; and others fancied a resemblance to various of the prophets.

Beyond this the apostles confessed that men were not known to go. Their enthusiasm had cooled, almost as rapidly as in the triumphal procession, where they who blessed both Him and "the kingdom that cometh," no sooner felt the chill of contact with the priestly faction, than their confession dwindled into "This is Jesus, the prophet of Nazareth." "But who say ye that I am?" (see Mark 8:29) He added; and it depended on the answer whether or not there would prove to be any solid foundation, any rock, on which to build His Church.

Much difference may be tolerated there, but on one subject there must be no hesitation: to make Him only a prophet among others, to honor Him even as the first among the teachers of mankind, is to empty His life of its meaning, His death of its efficacy, and His church of its authority. And yet the danger was real, as we may see by the fervent blessing which the right answer won. For it was no longer the bright morning of His career, when all bare Him witness and wondered; the noon was over now, and the evening shadows were heavy and lowering. To confess Him then was to have learned what flesh and blood could not reveal.

READ: MARK 8:27

MAY 14

TOUCHED BY DEVOTION

JOSEPH ADDISON | c. 1714

Joseph Addison (1672-1719) was an English essayist, poet, playwright, and politician.

It has been observed by some writers that man is more distinguished from the animal world by devotion than by reason, as several brute creatures display in their actions something like a faint glimmering of reason, though they betray, in no single circumstance of their behavior, any thing that bears the least affinity to devotion.

It is certain that the propensity of the mind to religious worship; the natural tendency of the soul to fly to some superior Being for succor in dangers and distresses; the gratitude to an invisible Superintendent, which arises in us upon receiving any extraordinary and unexpected good fortune; the acts of love and admiration with which the thoughts of men are so wonderfully transported, meditating upon the divine perfections; and the universal concurrence of all the nations under heaven in the great article of adoration plainly show that devotion or religious worship must be the effect of a tradition from some first founder of mankind, or that it is conformable to the natural light of reason, or that it proceeds from an instinct implanted in the soul itself.

For my part, I look upon all these to be the concurrent causes; but which ever of them shall be assigned as the principle of divine worship, it manifestly points to a Supreme Being as the first author of it. The most illiterate man who is touched with devotion, and uses frequent exercises of it, contracts a certain greatness of mind, mingled with a noble simplicity, that raises him above those of the same condition; and there is an indelible mark of goodness in those who sincerely possess it.

READ: JOHN 4:24

MAY 15

A PRAYER FOR AMERICA

PETER MARSHALL | 1944

Dr. Peter Marshall (1902-1949) was a Scottish-American preacher who twice served as chaplain of the United States Senate. He is most popularly remembered for the biography, A Man Called Peter.

May all of America come to understand that right-living alone exalts a nation, that only in Your will can peace and joy be found. But, Lord, this land cannot be righteous unless her people are righteous, and we, here gathered, are part of America. We know that the world cannot be changed until the hearts of men are changed. Our hearts need to be changed.

We therefore confess to You that:

Wrong ideas and sinful living have cut us off from You.

We have been greedy.

We have sought to hide behind barricades of selfishness; shackles have imprisoned the great heart of America.

We have tried to isolate ourselves from the bleeding wounds of a blundering world.

In our self-sufficiency we have sought not Your help.

We have disguised selfishness as patriotism; our arrogance has masqueraded as pride.

We have frittered away time and opportunities while the world bled.

Our ambitions have blinded us to opportunities.

We have bickered in factory and business, and sought to solve our differences only through self-interest.

Lord God, forgive us! By Your guidance and Your power may our land become God's own country, a nation contrite in heart, confessing her sins; a nation sensitive to injustice and wrong still in our midst.

Hear this our prayer and grant that we may confidently expect to see it answered in our time, through Jesus Christ, our Lord. Amen.

READ: 2 CHRONICLES 7:14

MAY 16

THE VICTORY OF TELEMACHUS

JOHN FOXE | 1559

John Foxe (1517-1587) was an English historian and martyrologist.

The combats began; the gladiators with nets tried to entangle those with swords, and when they succeeded, mercilessly stabbed their antagonists to death with the three-pronged spear. Many had been slain, and the people, madly excited by the desperate bravery of those who continued to fight, shouted their applause. But suddenly there was an interruption.

A robed figure appeared among the audience, and then boldly leaped down into the arena. Without hesitation, he advanced upon two gladiators engaged in a life-and-death struggle, and laying his hand upon one of them sternly reproved him for shedding innocent blood, and then, turning toward the thousands of angry faces around him, declared, "Do not requite God's mercy in turning away the swords of your enemies by murdering each other!"

Angry shouts drowned his voice: "This is no place for preaching! The customs of Rome must be observed! On, gladiators!" The gladiators would have again attacked each other, but the man stood between, trying in vain to be heard. "Sedition! Down with him!" was then the cry; and the gladiators at once stabbed him to death. Stones also rained down upon him from the furious people, and thus he perished, in the midst of the arena.

His dress showed him to be one of the hermits who vowed themselves to a holy life of prayer and self-denial, and who were revered by even the thoughtless and combat-loving Romans. He had come from the wilds of Asia on a pilgrimage, to visit the churches and keep his Christmas at Rome; they knew his name was Telemachus. His spirit had been stirred by the sight of thousands flocking to see men slaughter one another, and in his simple-hearted zeal he had tried to convince them of the cruelty and wickedness of their conduct.

He died, but not in vain. His work was accomplished at the moment he was struck down, for the shock of such a death before their eyes turned the hearts of the people; from the day Telemachus fell dead in the coliseum, no other fight of gladiators was ever held there.

READ: PROVERBS 15:9

May 17

Real Reconciliation

Desmond Tutu | 2004

The Most Reverend Dr. Desmond Mpilo Tutu (b. 1931) is a South African activist and Christian cleric who rose to worldwide fame during the 1980s as an opponent of apartheid.

For our nation to heal and become a more humane place, we had to embrace our enemies as well as our friends. The same is true the world over. True enduring peace—between countries, within a country, within a community, within a family—requires real reconciliation between former enemies and even between loved ones who have struggled with one another.

How could anyone really think that true reconciliation could avoid a proper confrontation? After a husband and wife or two friends have quarreled, if they merely seek to gloss over their differences or metaphorically paper over the cracks, they must not be surprised when they are soon at it again, perhaps more violently than before, because they have tried to heal their ailment lightly.

True reconciliation is based on forgiveness, and forgiveness is based on true confession, and confession is based on penitence, on contrition, on sorrow for what you have done. We know that when a husband and wife have quarreled, one of them must be ready to say the most difficult words in any language, "I'm sorry," and the other must be ready to forgive for there to be a future for them.

Forgiveness gives us the capacity to make a new start. That is the power, the rationale, of confession and forgiveness. It is to say, "I have fallen but I am not going to remain there. Please forgive me." And forgiveness is the grace by which you enable the other person to get up with dignity, to begin anew. Not to forgive leads to bitterness and hatred, which gnaw away at the vitals of one's being. Whether hatred is projected out or projected in, it is always corrosive of the human spirit.

In the act of forgiveness, we are declaring our faith in the future of a relationship and in the capacity of the wrongdoer to change. We are welcoming a chance to make a new beginning.

Read: Ephesians 4:32

MAY 18

MY HUMAN FRAILTY

LANCELOT ANDREWES | 17TH CENTURY

Lancelot Andrewes (1555-1626) was an English clergyman and scholar who held high positions in the Church of England during the reigns of Queen Elizabeth I and King James I.

Have mercy on me, Lord, for I am weak;
remember, Lord, how short my time is;
remember that I am but flesh,
a wind that passeth away, and cometh not again.
My days are as grass, as a flower of the field;
for the wind goeth over me, and I am gone,
and my place shall knave me no more.
I am dust and ashes, earth and grass,
flesh and breath, corruption and the worm,
a stranger upon the earth, dwelling in a house of clay,
few and evil my days, today, and not tomorrow,
in the morning, yet not until night,
in a body of sin, in a world of corruption,
of few days, and full of trouble,
coming up, and cut down like a flower,
and as a shadow, having no stay.
Remember this, O Lord, and suffer, remit;
what profit is there in my blood,
when I go down to the pit?
By the multitude of Thy mercies,
by the riches and excessive redundance of Thy pity;
by all that is dear to Thee, all that we should plead,
and before and beyond all things, by Thyself,
by Thyself; O Lord, and by Thy Christ.
Lord, have mercy upon me, the chief of sinners.

READ: 2 CORINTHIANS 12:9

MAY 19

ALIVE IN CHRIST

PAUL | C. 60

Paul the Apostle (c. 5 A.D.-c. 67) was one of the most influential early Christian missionaries. His writings formed a considerable portion of the New Testament.

Now if Christ is preached that he hath been raised from the dead, how say some among you that there is no resurrection of the dead? But if there is no resurrection of the dead, neither hath Christ been raised: and if Christ hath not been raised, then is our preaching vain, your faith also is vain.

Yea, we are found false witnesses of God; because we witnessed of God that he raised up Christ: whom he raised not up, if so be that the dead are not raised. For if the dead are not raised, neither hath Christ been raised: and if Christ hath not been raised, your faith is vain; ye are yet in your sins. Then they also that are fallen asleep in Christ have perished.

If we have only hoped in Christ in this life, we are of all men most pitiable. But now hath Christ been raised from the dead, the firstfruits of them that are asleep. For since by man came death, by man came also the resurrection of the dead.

For as in Adam all die, so also in Christ shall all be made alive. But each in his own order: Christ the firstfruits; then they that are Christ's, at his coming. Then cometh the end, when he shall deliver up the kingdom to God, even the Father; when he shall have abolished all rule and all authority and power. For he must reign, till he hath put all his enemies under his feet. The last enemy that shall be abolished is death. For, He put all things in subjection under his feet.

But when he saith, All things are put in subjection, it is evident that he is excepted who did subject all things unto him. And when all things have been subjected unto him, then shall the Son also himself be subjected to him that did subject all things unto him, that God may be all in all.

READ: JOHN 11:25

May 20

But for a Moment

Frances Havergal | 1879

Frances Ridley Havergal (1836-1879) was an English religious poet and hymn writer.

Look back through the history of the church in all ages, and mark how often a great work and mighty influence grew out of a mere moment in the life of one of God's servants; a mere moment, but overshadowed and filled with the fruitful power of the Spirit of God.

The moment may have been spent in uttering five words, but they have fed five thousand, or even five hundred thousand. The rapid speaker or the lonely thinker little guessed what use his Lord was making of that single moment. There was no room in it for even a thought of that. If that moment had not been, though perhaps unconsciously, "kept for Jesus," but had been otherwise occupied, what a harvest to His praise would have been missed!

The same thing is going on every day. It is generally a moment—either an opening or a culminating one—that really does the work. It is not so often a whole sermon, as a single short sentence in it that wings God's arrow to a heart. It is seldom a whole conversation that is the means of bringing about the desired result, but some sudden turn of thought or word, which comes with the electric touch of God's power. Sometimes it is less than that; only a look (and what is more momentary?) has been used by Him for the pulling down of strongholds.

Oh, how much we have missed by not placing them at his disposal! What might He not have done with the moments freighted with self or loaded with emptiness, which we have carelessly let drift by! Oh, what might have been if they had all been kept for Jesus! How He might have filled them with His light and life, enriching our own lives that have been impoverished by the waste, and using them in far-spreading blessing and power!

Read: Proverbs 3:6

MAY 21
ALL IN ALL
MEISTER ECKHART | 14TH CENTURY

Eckhart von Hochheim (c. 1260-1328), commonly known as Meister Eckhart, was a German theologian, philosopher, and mystic.

One ought to keep hold of God in everything and accustom his mind to retain God always among his feelings, thought, and loves. Take care how you think of God. As you think of him in church or closet, think of him everywhere. Take him with you among the crowds and turmoil of the alien world.

As I have said so often, speaking of uniformity, we do not mean that one should regard all deeds, places, and people as interchangeable. That would be a great mistake; for it is better to pray than to spin, and the church ranks above the street. You should, however, maintain the same mind, the same trust, and the same earnestness toward God in all your doings. Believe me, if you keep this kind of evenness, nothing can separate you from God-consciousness.

On the other hand, the person who is not conscious of God's presence, but who must always be going out to get him from this and that, who has to seek him by special methods, as by means of some activity, person, or place—such people have not attained God. It can easily happen that they are disturbed, for they have not God and they do not seek, think, and love only him, and therefore, not only will evil company be to them a stumbling block, but good company as well—not only the street, but the church; not only bad deeds and words, but good ones as well. The difficulty lies within the man, for whom God has not yet become everything. If God were everything, the man would get along well wherever he went and among whatever people, for he would possess God and no one could rob him or disturb his work.

READ: PSALM 1:2

May 22

A Morning Devotion

John Baillie | 1936

John Baillie (1886-1960) was a Scottish theologian, a minister of the Church of Scotland, professor at Edinburgh University, and brother of theologian Donald Macpherson Baillie.

Eternal Father of my soul, let my first thought today be of you, let my first impulse be to worship you, let my first spoken word be your name, let my first action be to kneel before you in prayer.

For your perfect wisdom and perfect goodness;

For the love wherewith you love mankind;

For the love wherewith you love me;

For the great and mysterious opportunity of my life;

For the indwelling of your Spirit in my heart;

For the sevenfold gifts of your Spirit;

I praise and worship you, O Lord.

Yet let me not, when this morning prayer is said, think my worship ended and spend the day in forgetfulness of you. Rather from these moments of quietness let light go forth, and joy, and power, that will remain with me through all the hours of the day;

Keeping me chaste in thought;

Keeping me temperate and truthful in speech;

Keeping me faithful and diligent in my work;

Keeping me humble in my estimation of myself;

Keeping me honorable and generous in my dealings with others;

Keeping me loyal to every hallowed memory of the past;

Keeping me mindful of my eternal destiny as a child of Thine.

O God, who has been the Refuge of my fathers through many generations, be my Refuge today in every time and circumstance of need. Be my Guide through all that is dark and doubtful. Be my Guard against all that threatens my spirit's welfare. Be my Strength in time of testing. Gladden my heart with your peace; through Jesus Christ my Lord. Amen.

Read: Psalm 143:8

MAY 23

AN ACCEPTABLE SACRIFICE

The Martyrdom of Polycarp | c. 160

The Martyrdom of Polycarp *is one of the very few eyewitness writings from the age of persecutions, detailing Polycarp's death at the hands of the Romans.*

When he had at last finished his prayer, the hour came for departure, and they set him on an ass, and led him into the city. And the police captain Herod and his father Niketas met him and sat by his side trying to persuade him, saying: "But what harm is it to say, 'Lord Caesar,' and to offer sacrifice, and be saved?"

At first he did not answer them, but when they continued he said: "I am not going to do what you counsel me." And they began to speak fiercely to him, and turned him out in such a hurry that he scraped his shin. He walked on quickly and was taken to the arena, while the uproar in the arena was so great that no one could even be heard.

Now when Polycarp entered into the arena there came a voice from heaven: "Be strong, Polycarp, and play the man." No one saw the speaker, but our friends who were there heard the voice. And next he was brought forward, and the Pro-Consul pressed him and said: "Take the oath and I will let you go, revile Christ." Polycarp said: "For eighty-six years have I been his servant, and he has done me no wrong—how can I blaspheme my King who saved me?"

So they did not nail him, but bound him, and he looked up to heaven and said: "O Lord God Almighty, Father of thy beloved and blessed Jesus Christ, through Whom we have received full knowledge of thee! I bless thee, that Thou hast granted me this day and hour, that I may share, among the number of the martyrs, in the cup of thy Christ. And may I, today, be received among them before Thee, as a rich and acceptable sacrifice. For this reason I also praise Thee for all things, I bless Thee, I glorify Thee through the everlasting and heavenly high Priest, Jesus Christ, through whom be glory to Thee with him and the Holy Spirit, both now and for the ages that are to come, Amen."

READ: PHILIPPIANS 2:17-18

MAY 24

AN INEXCUSABLE PERSECUTION

ANTON PRAETORIUS | 1598

Anton Praetorius (1560-1613) was a German Calvinist pastor who spoke out against the persecution of witches and against torture.

Who can describe all the horror of such prisons? I was always incensed when I saw them, my hair stands on end when I write about them; my heart seems nigh to bursting when I reflect that one human being, for the sake of a few sins (for are we not all unrighteous?), can torment another so brutally.

According to imperial law, "the prisons ought to be so constructed as to afford shelter and protection, and not to be a torment to the poor inmates. He who can preserve and protect a human being and does not do so is a murderer." But how much more woe to that man who not only causes offence, but leads another straight on the road to desperation and into the chamber of death! Isaiah says: "God looked that he should do judgment, and behold iniquity; and do justice, and behold a cry." Bethink you, you judges, God marks and hears and writes it in his tables.

To all the horrors of imprisonment is then added the barbarous torturing. I have something more to say to you judges. Take it in good part from me, for I mean it well. You are much too brutal, unjust, superstitious, scandalous, and tyrannical in your trials by torture. I am not well pleased to see that the rack is being used, for pious kings and judges among the first people of God did not use it, because it was introduced by heathen tyrants, because it is the mother of many and great lies, because it often does great bodily injury to men and women, and finally, because on account of it many people succumb to death without fair trial and sentence, yea even before they have been found guilty: tortured today, dead tomorrow.

You think, no doubt, you are doing right, and you drag in secular law and imperial ordinances and old custom to justify you. But human laws must give way to the ordinances of God, which teach that we may question, examine, take oaths from accused persons, but not torture them.

READ: LUKE 6:31-36

MAY 25

WHEREVER PRAYER IS MADE

ROBERT HAWKER | 1855

Robert Hawker (1753-1827) was a prominent vicar of the Anglican Church who was called the "Star of the West" for his superlative preaching that drew thousands.

"And on the Sabbath day we went out of the city to the riverside, where prayer was customarily made" (Acts 16:13). What, they had no church, no synagogue, no house of prayer, in all the city? Was it like another Athens, wholly given to idolatry? My soul, think of your privileges, and learn rightly to prize them, and use them to the glory of the great Giver. It was "on the Sabbath day." What a mercy to poor fallen man is the Sabbath. And yet what multitudes slight, despise, and never profit by it!

There is something very interesting in what the apostle here says of going out "by the riverside." Probably it was in the memory of the church, that in Babylon, where the people were captives, the Lord made the river Chebar famous for visions to one prophet, and Hiddekel to another. But, blessed be God! Though our land is so sinful, we are not given up to captivity; and while many of the nations around have their churches turned into stables, amidst the din and horrors of war, our candlestick is not yet removed out of its place.

Precious Jesus! Wherever prayer is commonly to be made by your people, let my soul delight to be found. Let me hear your voice inviting to communion: "Come with me from Lebanon, my spouse, with me from Lebanon." Yea, Lord, I would follow the Lamb wherever he goes. I would follow you to the assemblies of your people. I would wait to see the goings of my God and King in his sanctuary. I would have my whole soul athirst for you, as the hart for the cooling streams. And while I join your people in the great congregation, where prayer is habitually to be made, I pray your grace, and the influences of your blessed Spirit, to fire my soul with foretastes of that glorious assembly, which are keeping an eternal Sabbath above, where the everlasting praises of God and of the Lamb will engage and fill my raptured soul with joy unspeakable and full of glory to all eternity.

READ: PSALM 42:1

MAY 26

TRUE RELIGION

GIROLAMO SAVONAROLA | 1497

Girolamo Savonarola (1452-1498) was an Italian Dominican friar who vehemently preached against the moral corruption of the clergy in his time.

In order to connect what has already been laid down with what still remains to be said, it is necessary to acknowledge the existence on earth of some true religion, or form of Divine worship. Religion, or worship, signifies the due honor paid to God, as to the universal Principle, Ruler, and End of all things. Every effect turns naturally to its cause; submits itself to its cause, in order to become like to it; and, in a certain sense, invokes the protection of its cause. By acting thus, the effect is paying honor and worship to its cause.

Now, as man is the effect of God, there must be in his nature an instinct prompting him to turn to God, to become subject to Him, to resemble Him, and to invoke Him, in order from Him to obtain beatitude. As no natural inclination is given us in vain, these promptings must spring from religion; and they are proofs that some true form of Divine worship exists in the world.

It is clear that a natural tendency to religion is innate in the heart of man, from the fact that some form, though frequently an erroneous form, of Divine worship has existed through all generations. If, then, there be no possibility of satisfying this natural inclination, God has provided better for the needs of irrational creatures than for those of man.

It is the property of a cause to infuse its goodness and perfection into its effect, in order that this effect may, as far as is possible, resemble the cause. God, who is the Supreme Good and the First Cause of all things, desires, more earnestly than does any other cause, to infuse His goodness into man in order to bring him to beatitude; and, as the perfection of man consists in that interior homage whereby he subjects himself to God, it is clear that God cannot have made this interior homage impossible, and that, in other words, some true religion exists in the world.

READ: DEUTERONOMY 6:5

MAY 27

EVERYWHERE AND INESCAPABLE

G. CAMPBELL MORGAN | 1937

Reverend Doctor George Campbell Morgan (1863-1945) was an evangelist, preacher, and a leading Bible scholar.

God is the age-abiding, ever and everywhere present Fact, and men who forget Him are leaving out of their calculations the supreme quantity, and therefore their findings are inevitably doomed to be wrong. A science that forgets God is blind, seeing only that which is near, and at last boasting itself that it has no interest in anything that is far. The philosophy that excludes God is equally incomplete, and therefore incompetent.

Science starts with emptiness of mind, a perfectly proper attitude. Philosophy starts with a question, "What is truth?" a perfectly fair method of operation. But science proceeding to the discovery of the facts will inevitably finally touch God. The question is whether it will dare to call Him God when it finds Him. Philosophy attempting to account for things and to give us the true wisdom of life must take God into account. The question is whether it will ultimately do so or not.

The one fact from which there is no escape is the fact of God. God is not distanced from human life. In Him we live and move and have our being. God is not uninterested in human life. If the great revelation of these sacred writings is to be trusted, there is absolutely nothing in which God is not interested.

One human life perfectly poised toward God and adjusted toward His good and perfect will is a human life realized, fulfilled, and progressively glorious. A society, which the church of God ought to be, discovering His will, walking in the way of it, obedient to the light that ever shines more and more unto the perfect day, is a society within the boundaries of which there is no lonely soul, for when one weeps, all weep; when one laughs, all laugh. A nation seeking righteousness rather than revenue, eager to glorify God rather than to maintain its face in the world, is a nation great, secure, impregnable, mighty with essential might.

READ: ISAIAH 44:24

MAY 28

THE TRUTH WITHIN THE LIE

ANTONY | 4TH CENTURY

Antony the Great (c. 251-356), also known as Saint Anthony, was a Christian saint from Egypt and a prominent leader among the Desert Fathers.

Someone once knocked at my cell door. When I went outside, I saw someone who appeared huge and tall. I asked, "Who are you?" and he said, "I am Satan."

I said, "What are you doing here?"

He replied, "Why do the monks and all Christians censure me for no reason? Why do you torment me every hour?"

I said, "Why do you torment them?"

He replied, "I am not the one tormenting them. They disturb themselves, for I have become weak. Haven't they read that 'the enemy is finished, in perpetual ruin; their cities plowed under' (see Psalm 9:6)? I no longer have anything, no place, no weapon, no city. Everywhere there are Christians, even the desert is full of monks! They should mind their own business and stop censuring me for no reason!"

I was struck by the grace of the Lord and said to him, "You are a perpetual liar and never tell the truth, but this once, even if you did not mean to, you have told the truth. For when Christ came, he rendered you a weakling. He threw you down and left you defenseless."

When Satan heard the Savior's name, he could not endure it, for it scorched him. He then became invisible.

READ: ROMANS 16:20

MAY 29

AN IMMOVABLE ROCK

FREDERIC FARRAR | 1874

Frederic William Farrar (1831-1903) was a British preacher and author whose works, especially the Life of Christ, *were translated into many languages.*

The Byzantine Empire was preeminently the age of treachery. . . . The Asiatic churches had already perished. The Christian faith, planted in the dissolute cities of Asia Minor, had produced many fanatical ascetics, and a few illustrious theologians, but it had no renovating effect upon the people at large. It introduced among them a principle of interminable and implacable dissensions, but it scarcely tempered in any appreciable degree their luxury or their sensuality.

The apparent triumph of Christianity was in some sense, and for a time, its real defeat, the corruption of its simplicity, the defacement of its purest and loftiest beauty. Yet, however much the divine ideal might be obscured, it was never wholly lost. The sun was often clouded; but behind that veil of earthly mists, on the days which seemed most dark, it was there always, flaming in the zenith, and it could make the darkest clouds palpitate with light.

No age since Christ died was so utterly corrupt as not to produce some prophets and saints of God. These saints, these prophets, in age after age, were persecuted, were sawn asunder, were slain with the sword by kings and priests; but the next generation, which built their sepulchers, had, in part at least, profited by their lessons.

"The Church," said St. Chrysostom, "cannot be shaken. The more the world takes counsel against it, the more it increases; the waves are dissipated, the rock remains immovable."

READ: JUDE 1:17-25

MAY 30

IN DEFENSE OF REASON

GALILEO | 1615

Galileo Galilei (1564-1642), commonly known as Galileo, was an Italian physicist, mathematician, astronomer, and philosopher.

First they have endeavored to spread the opinion that such propositions in general are contrary to the Bible and are consequently damnable and heretical. They know that it is human nature to take up causes whereby a man may oppress his neighbor, no matter how unjustly, rather than those from which a man may receive some just encouragement. Hence they have had no trouble in finding men who would preach the damnability and heresy of the new doctrine from their very pulpits, thus doing impious and inconsiderate injury not only to that doctrine and its followers but to all mathematics and mathematicians in general.

Next, becoming bolder, they began scattering rumors among the people that before long this doctrine would be condemned by the supreme authority. In order to facilitate their designs, they seek so far as possible (at least among the common people) to make this opinion seem new and to belong to me alone. They pretend not to know that its author, or rather its restorer and confirmer, was Nicholas Copernicus; and that he was not only a Catholic, but a priest and a canon, highly esteemed by the church.

Now as to the false aspersions which they so unjustly seek to cast upon me, I have thought it necessary to justify myself, as these men make a shield of their hypocritical zeal for religion. They go about invoking the Bible, which they would use to their deceitful purposes. Contrary to the sense of the Bible and the intention of the holy Fathers, they would extend such authorities until even in purely physical matters—where faith is not involved—they would have us altogether abandon reason and the evidence of our senses in favor of some biblical passage, though under the surface meaning of its words this passage may contain a different sense. I hope to show that I proceed with much greater piety than they do, when I argue not against condemning this book, but against condemning it in the way they suggest— that is, without understanding it, weighing it, or so much as reading it.

READ: PROVERBS 14:6

MAY 31

PURSUED BY GOD

DONALD BARNHOUSE | 1950

Donald Grey Barnhouse (1895-1960) was an American preacher, pastor, theologian, writer, and radio pioneer who preached over the radio on a program known as "The Bible Study Hour."

The pursuing love of God is the greatest wonder of the spiritual universe. We leave God in the heat of our own self-desire and run from His will because we want so much to have our own way. We get to a crossroads and look back in pride, thinking that we have outdistanced Him. Just as we are about to congratulate ourselves on our achievement of self-enthronement, we feel a touch on our arm and turn in that direction to find Him there.

"My child," He says in great tenderness, "I love you; and when I saw you running away from all that is good, I pursued you through a shortcut that love knows well, and awaited you here at the crossroads." Once we have torn ourselves free from His grasp and rushed off again, we are sure, this time, that we have succeeded in escaping from Him.

But, once more, the touch of love is on our other sleeve and when we turn quickly we find that He is there, pleading with the eyes of love, and showing Himself once more to be the tender and faithful One, loving to the end. He will always say, "My child, my name and nature are Love, and I must act according to that which I am. So it is that I have pursued you, to tell you that when you are tired of your running and your wandering, I will be there to draw you to myself once more."

READ: MATTHEW 18:12

June 1

Whom He Rewards in Heaven

Odo of Cluny | 10th century

Saint Odo of Cluny (c. 878-942) was the second abbot of Cluny and is a saint of the Roman Catholic Church.

I marvel rather, that in this age of ours, when charity has almost entirely grown cold and the time of Antichrist is at hand, the miracles of the saints should not cease, but He is mindful of the promise that He makes by Jeremiah: "I will not turn away from doing good to my people" (see Jeremiah 32:40). And of this good that He has done the apostle bears witness, when he says that God, not leaving Himself in any age without a witness, in His kindness fills the hearts of men with joy. If, therefore, it pleases the divine goodness that He who did wonderful things for our fathers should be glorified also in our times, we ought by no means to be incredulous.

For it seems that the divine dispensation performs these things in our age and through a man of our time, because everything that the saints did or said in the past has been forgotten. And since, as in the days of Noah, a man of God was found who lived according to the law, God set him up as an example to those who saw him, that their hearts should be inspired to imitate one who was their neighbor and whom they saw to live a just and pious life. And let not the observance of the commandments of God seem hard or impossible, since it is seen to have been achieved by a layman of great position. For nothing more encourages mental cowardice than that the retribution of good or evil works that is to follow in the next life should not be meditated upon in the present. And against this Scripture warns us that in all our actions we should remember our last end.

God, therefore, exalts on earth in the sight of his contemporaries the servant whom He rewards in Heaven, so that by that which is done outwardly the contemners of God may see inwardly that God is not served in vain, but that as He Himself testifies, He will glorify those who glorify Him and bring down in shame those who despise Him.

Read: Hebrews 11:6

JUNE 2

ALWAYS ON GUARD

WILHELMUS À BRAKEL | 1700

Wilhelmus à Brakel (1635-1711) was a highly esteemed and influential minister in the Netherlands during the period of the Dutch Second Reformation.

The spiritual life is a precious and desirable treasure to the believer, far excelling the entire world and all that is in it. It has many enemies that lie in wait—not to be a partaker of it, but to destroy it. But the believer knows the value of this life, is desirous to preserve and increase it, takes care that it is not injured, and is always on guard against danger approaching from elsewhere. If he becomes aware of something, he is alert and stands ready with his weapons in hand to turn away the enemy, attacking all those who come too close.

Spiritual watchfulness first pertains to the spiritual influences of the Holy Spirit, such as light, comfort, and strength—whereby the spiritual life of the soul is strengthened. Secondly, watchfulness pertains to all that issues forth from the soul, such as thoughts, words, and deeds, lest the soul be injured by any sin. There is a striving that our entire conduct may be according to God's will, whereby spiritual life increases in strength. Time and again the Christian seeks counsel and asks, "Lord, what wilt Thou have me to do?" (Acts 9:6 KJV). He looks whether the way before him is safe and each time sets down his feet with caution, lest he step into a snare. He walks, so to speak, on his toes.

Thirdly, the person who is spiritually watchful also keeps an eye out for all that enters the soul, so that no enemy will sneak in to harm his spiritual life. The Christian knows his enemies—the devil, the world, and his flesh—and he knows their wickedness and their tireless activity. He is on guard against the world when it approaches him with flattery, threats, or persecutions, conquering all this by faith. He is on guard against his flesh, indwelling corruption, and the sin that so easily besets him. For this very reason he "closes the doors and the windows."

READ: 1 PETER 5:8-9

June 3
Prayer for Peace
Clement of Alexandria | c. 215

Titus Flavius Clemens (c. 150-c. 215), known as Clement of Alexandria, was a Christian theologian.

Be gracious, O Instructor, to us Thy children, Father, Charioteer of Israel, Son and Father, both in One, O Lord.

Grant to us who obey Thy precepts, that we may perfect the likeness of the image, and with all our power know Him who is the good God and not a harsh judge.

And do Thou Thyself cause that all of us who have our conversation in Thy peace, who have been translated into Thy commonwealth, having sailed tranquilly over the billows of sin;

May be wafted in calm by Thy Holy Spirit, by the ineffable wisdom, by night and day to the perfect day.

And giving thanks may praise, and praising thank the Alone Father and Son, Son and Father, the Son, Instructor and Teacher, with the Holy Spirit;

All in One, in whom is all, for whom all is One, for whom is eternity, whose members we all are, whose glory the aeons are; for the All-good, All-lovely, All-wise, All-just One.

To whom be glory both now and for ever. Amen.

Read: Philippians 4:9

THE MERCIES OF GOD

WILLIAM SANGSTER | c. 1961

William Sangster (1900-1960) was a gifted British preacher, evangelist, and teacher. After serving in the Army in World War I, he felt the call of God on his life to preach, and with his wife, Margaret, served Methodist charges in Wales, Liverpool, Scarborough, and Leeds.

If, as the Bible teaches, "the steps of a good man are ordered by the LORD," a mature Christian will thank God even in trouble, the heaviest and most desolating trouble, that, though God did not "lead" him into sickness, he is not deserted in it; that, though he cannot see it as yet, he has faith to believe that somewhere there is mercy at the heart of it, or good that can come out of it; that it is, indeed, only another of the "all things" that still "work together for good to them that love God" (Romans 8:28 KJV).

The prayer of thanksgiving at such a time may indeed be what the Scriptures call a "sacrifice of thanksgiving"; a thanksgiving that almost has blood upon it; an adoring venture of faith—believing in defiance of the God-denying look of things. But the mature will be able to offer even that, not easily but definitely. And the sacrifice of thanksgiving will be precious in God's sight.

Thank God that those times which strain faith so hard come only occasionally in life. For the most part we travel a sunlit road, and when we are unaware of the love of God it is often because we have not looked for it. To see the evidence of God's mercies you have only to look.

READ: 1 THESSALONIANS 5:16-18

June 5

Virtues Evangelized

Susanna Wesley | 1734

Susanna Wesley (1669-1742) was the mother of John and Charles Wesley. Although she never preached a sermon, published a book, or founded a church, she is known as the Mother of Methodism, in no small part because of her influence upon the lives of her sons.

If we could indeed do honor to our Savior, we should take all fitting occasions to make men observe the excellence and perfection of the moral virtues taught by Christ and his apostles, far surpassing all that was pretended to by the very best of the heathen philosophers. All their morality was defective in principle and direction, was intended only to regulate the outward actions, but never reached the heart, or at the highest it looked no farther than the temporal happiness of mankind.

But moral virtues evangelized, or improved into Christian duties, have partly a view to promote the good of human society here, but chiefly to qualify the observers of them for a much more blessed and more enduring society hereafter. I cannot stay to enlarge on this vast subject, nor indeed (considering whom I write to) is it needful. Yet one thing I cannot forbear adding, which may carry some weight with his admirers, and that is, the very wise and just reply which Mr. Locke made to one that desired him to draw up a system of morals. "Did the world," says he, "want a rule, I confess there could be no work so necessary, nor so commendable. But the gospel contains so perfect a body of ethics that reason may be excused from that enquiry, since she may find man's duty clearer and easier in Revelation than in herself."

That you may continue steadfast in the faith and increase more and more in the knowledge and love of God, and of his Son, Jesus Christ! That holiness, simplicity, and purity (which are different words signifying the same thing) may recommend you to the favor of God Incarnate! That his Spirit may dwell in you, and keep you still (as now) under a sense of God's blissful presence, is the hearty prayer of, dear son,

Your affectionate mother, and most faithful friend,

Susanna Wesley

Read: 2 Peter 3:18

ONENESS IN CHRIST

GARDNER C. TAYLOR | 1974

Dr. Gardner Calvin Taylor (b. 1918) is an American preacher, known as the "dean of American preaching." Taylor was a close friend and mentor to Martin Luther King Jr. and played a prominent role in the religious leadership of the civil rights movement.

We who name the name of Jesus as Lord proclaim that in his spirit is the way to the world's long-hoped-for Zion of peace. He has plumbed the depths of our universe and come aloft bearing in his spirit the way to peace, the only way honored by the very structure of our universe.

It was his faith that a band of committed men and women, partakers of his spirit and consecrated to his will, would be a saving leaven in the world loaf. At a certain point in his ministry, he waited for the return of his disciples he had sent out. When they reported to him their success, his word was "I saw Satan fall from heaven like lightning"—as if their experiences ratified a deep conviction of his.

Men aflame with his purposes can storm the ramparts of this world's disharmonies, can bring a new earth wherein dwelleth righteousness and peace. Our world's greatest need is men and women in every land, of every kindred and every language, committed to our oneness in Christ that is deeper than any national difference—our common faith leaping iron curtains, bridging oceans, uniting continents, abolishing borders, bringing to pass that anguished prayer fashioned in his spirit: "Holy Father, keep through thine own name those whom thou has given me, that they may be one, even as we are" (John 17:11 KJV).

Enough men and women committed to a oneness in Christ can break the evil spell of our recurring slaughters, pull down flags of national pride, and raise the blood-stained banner of Calvary's kingdom in their stead. Deeper than all differences of nation or language or culture is our oneness in Christ who hath broken down the wall of partition. Committed Christians of every language, of every kindred, of every tribe shall make the earth hear the echo of heaven's theme.

READ: JOHN 17:23

June 7

Love Not the World

John | c. 90

John the Apostle (c. 6 A.D.-c. 100) was one of the twelve apostles of Jesus.

My little children, these things write I unto you that ye may not sin. And if any man sin, we have an Advocate with the Father, Jesus Christ the righteous: and he is the propitiation for our sins; and not for ours only, but also for the whole world. And hereby we know that we know him, if we keep his commandments.

He that saith, I know him, and keepeth not his commandments, is a liar, and the truth is not in him; but whoso keepeth his word, in him verily hath the love of God been perfected. Hereby we know that we are in him: he that saith he abideth in him ought himself also to walk even as he walked.

Beloved, no new commandment write I unto you, but an old commandment which ye had from the beginning: the old commandment is the word which ye heard. Again, a new commandment write I unto you, which thing is true in him and in you; because the darkness is passing away, and the true light already shineth. He that saith he is in the light and hateth his brother, is in the darkness even until now.

He that loveth his brother abideth in the light, and there is no occasion of stumbling in him. But he that hateth his brother is in the darkness, and walketh in the darkness, and knoweth not whither he goeth, because the darkness hath blinded his eyes.

I write unto you, my little children, because your sins are forgiven you for his name's sake. I have written unto you, little children, because ye know the Father. I have written unto you, fathers, because ye know him who is from the beginning. I have written unto you, young men, because ye are strong, and the word of God abideth in you, and ye have overcome the evil one. Love not the world, neither the things that are in the world. If any man love the world, the love of the Father is not in him.

Read: Deuteronomy 7:9

June 8

A True Hymn

George Herbert | 1633

George Herbert (1593-1633) was a Welsh-born English poet, orator, and Anglican priest who wrote religious poems throughout his life. He was noted for his unfailing care for his parishioners.

Joy, my Life, my Crown!
My heart was meaning all the day,
Somewhat it fain would say,
And still it runneth muttering up and down
With only this, my Joy, my Life, my Crown!
Yet slight not those few words;
If truly said, they may take part
Among the best in art:
The fineness which a hymn or psalm affords
Is, when the soul unto the lines accord.
He who craves all the mind,
And all the soul, and strength, and time,
If the words only rhyme,
Justly complains that somewhat is behind
To make His verse, or write a hymn in kind.
Whereas if the heart be moved,
Although the verse be somewhat scant,
God doth supply the want;
As when the heart says, sighing to be approved,
"O, could I love!" and stops, God writeth, "Loved."

Read: Psalm 23:5

June 9

A Love Like No Other

Sojourner Truth | 1850

Sojourner Truth (c. 1797-1883), born into slavery as Isabella Baumfree, was an African-American abolitionist and women's rights activist.

Sojourner Truth's mother talked to her of God. From these conversations, her mind drew the conclusion that God was a great man and, being located high in the sky, could see all that transpired on the earth. She believed he not only saw but also noted down all her actions in a great book.

She desired to talk to God, but her vileness utterly forbade it and she began to wish for someone to speak to God for her. Then a space seemed opening between her and God, and she felt that if someone who was worthy in the sight of heaven would but plead *for* her in their own name, and not let God know it came from *her*, who was so unworthy, God might grant it. At length a friend appeared to stand between herself and an insulted Deity; but who was this friend? "Who *are* you?" she exclaimed, as the vision brightened into a form distinct, beaming with the beauty of holiness, and radiant with love.

Her whole soul was in one deep prayer that this heavenly personage might be revealed to her and remain with her. At length, after bending both soul and body with the intensity of this desire, till breath and strength seemed failing and she could maintain her position no longer, an answer came to her, saying distinctly, "It is Jesus." "Yes," she responded, "it is *Jesus*."

Previously, she heard Jesus mentioned in reading or speaking but had received from what she heard no impression that he was any other than an eminent man, like a Washington or a Lafayette. Now he appeared to her so mild, so good, and so every way lovely, and he loved her so much! And, how strange that he had always loved her, and she had never known it! And how great a blessing he conferred, in that he should stand between her and God! And God was no longer a terror and a dread to her. In the light of her great happiness, the world was clad in new beauty, the very air sparkled as with diamonds and was redolent of heaven.

Read: 2 Thessalonians 2:16-17

THE PURPOSE OF PRAYER

JOHN CALVIN | 1536

John Calvin (1509-1564) was an influential French theologian and pastor during the Protestant Reformation. He was a principal figure in the development of the system of Christian theology later called Calvinism, and published the first edition of his seminal work, Institutes of the Christian Religion, *in 1536.*

Some ask if God needs us as advisers. After all, if he already knows about our problems and is wise enough to know what we need, why bother to pray?

Anyone who asks such questions does not understand why the Lord taught us to pray. It is not so much for his sake as for ours. Faithful people in the Bible were certain that God was merciful and kind. But the more they realized this, the more fervently they prayed. Elijah is one such example. He was confident that God would break a drought and send desperately needed rain. In his confidence he prayed anxiously with his face between his knees. In no way did he doubt God would send rain. He understood that it was his duty to lay his desires before God.

It is true that God is awake and watches over us continuously. Sometimes he will assist us even when we do not ask. But it is in our own best interest to pray constantly. When we do, we will begin to understand that it is God who is in charge. It will keep us free of evil desires because we will learn to place all our wishes in his sight. Most importantly, it will prepare us to understand that God is the giver, and we will be filled with genuine gratitude and thanksgiving.

READ: PHILIPPIANS 4:6

June 11
Bound by Love
Tertullian | c. 197 a.d.

Quintus Septimius Florens Tertullianus (c. 160-c. 220), anglicized as Tertullian, was a prolific early Christian author and apologist from Carthage in the Roman province of Africa. He has been called the "founder of Western theology."

The peculiarities of the Christian society have much positive good. We are a body knit together by a common religious profession, by unity of discipline, and by the bond of a common hope. We meet together as an assembly and congregation, that, offering up prayer to God as with united force, we may wrestle with Him in our supplications. This violence God delights in. We pray, too, for the emperors, for their ministers and for all in authority, for the welfare of the world, for the prevalence of peace, for the delay of the final consummation.

The tried men of our elders preside over us, obtaining that honor not by purchase, but by established character. There is no buying and selling of any sort in the things of God. Though we have our treasure chest, it is not made up of purchase money, as of a religion that has its price. On the monthly day, if he likes, each puts in a small donation; but only if it be his pleasure, and only if he be able: for there is no compulsion; all is voluntary.

These gifts are not taken thence and spent on feasts, and drinking bouts, and eating houses, but to support and bury poor people, to supply the wants of boys and girls destitute of means and parents, and of old persons confined now to the house; such, too, as have suffered shipwreck; and if there happen to be any in the mines, or banished to the islands, or shut up in the prisons, for nothing but their fidelity to the cause of God's church, they become the nurslings of their confession. But it is mainly the deeds of a love so noble that lead many to put a brand upon us. See, they say, how they love one another, for they themselves are animated by mutual hatred; how they are ready even to die for one another, for they themselves will sooner put to death.

Read: 1 Corinthians 12:12-13

JUNE 12

SHADES OF ANGER

JOHN TRAPP | 17TH CENTURY

John Trapp (1601-1669) was an English Anglican Bible commentator. His commentary is still read today and is often quoted by other religious writers.

He who would be angry without sin must not be angry at anything except sin. Our Savior was angry with Peter and angry with the Pharisees for the hardness of their hearts. Moses was filled with holy anger at the people over the golden calf. And God's blessing is upon every such good heart, who has such feeling and stomach for the things of God.

Equanimity in such circumstances would be no better than complacency or listlessness. "Do not I hate them, O LORD, that hate thee?" said David. "I hate them with perfect hatred: I count them mine enemies." (Psalm 139:21-22 KJV). This is the anger of zeal, found in Phinehas, Elijah, Elisha, and supremely and perfectly in our Savior. It should also have been found in Adam toward his wife, and in Eli toward his sons, and in Lot toward his servants.

Anger must have a good rise and a good end, observed Bucer; a good cause and a good outcome. The Lord condemns "whosoever is angry with his brother without a cause" (Matthew 5:22 KJV). It is no sin to be angry at sin, but when we are angry it is hard not to sin. Anger is a tender virtue, and through our ineptitude is easily corrupted and made dangerous.

There is, then, a just cause of anger, and there must be a just measure observed, so that our anger for sin does not rob us of the capacity either to pity the sinner (as our Savior in his anger did the obstinate Pharisees) or to pray for him (as Moses did for those idolaters of Exodus 32:31-32). Anger that is not thus contained is but a momentary madness.

READ: EPHESIANS 4:26

JUNE 13

FROM SUFFERING TO GLORY

JOHN WIMBER | 1991

John Richard Wimber (1934-1997) was a charismatic pastor and one of the founding leaders of the Vineyard Movement.

Jesus understood sickness as an enemy of men and women. Its source was evil and from Satan's kingdom. The deepest sickness is sin, and all other consequences of sin, including physical sickness and poverty, are subordinated to that. This does not mean that every sick person who is prayed for will be healed in this life; but it does mean that forgiveness of sins is available to all, and for many there will be physical healing. In the age to come, there will be complete healing of all who turn to Christ: the eradication of all disease, poverty, hatred, and sin.

But the fact remains that some type of suffering is a mark of the Christian life. Paul and other New Testament writers teach that suffering is prerequisite to glory. Paul writes in Romans 8:17, "If we are children [of God], then we are heirs—heirs of God and co-heirs with Christ, if indeed we share in his sufferings in order that we may also share in his glory" (NIV).

Very few Christians would argue that we should pray for persecution; we do pray for deliverance, protection, peace, and release from oppressors. Christianity is a religion of life and victory over the world, the flesh, and the devil; it is not a religion of death and suffering. Yet at the same time we know that God works through persecution and even triumphs through it. "The blood of the martyrs," wrote a third century bishop, "is the seed of the church" (see Revelation 6:9-11).

The same argument may be made about sickness. Christians do not pray for sickness; we are called to pray for healing. Yet at the same time we know that God works through our sicknesses. My point is quite simple: just because we recognize God works through evils does not mean we react passively to them. Further, whether or not someone believes sickness is included in our sharing in the sufferings of Christ, the general principle still applies: God can use illness, but we do not have to be passive about it.

READ: ROMANS 8:28

June 14

There Is Freedom

Richard Allen | c. 1830

Richard Allen (1760-1835) was a minister, writer, and founder of the African Methodist Episcopal Church, the first independent black denomination in the United States.

I was born in the year of our Lord 1760, on February 14th, a slave to Benjamin Chew, of Philadelphia. My mother and father and four children of us were sold into Delaware State, and I lived with him until I was upwards of twenty years of age, during which time I was awakened and brought to see myself poor, wretched, undone, and lost.

Shortly after I obtained mercy through the blood of Christ, I went rejoicing for several days and was happy in the Lord. But I was tempted to believe I was deceived and was constrained to seek the Lord afresh. One night I cried unto Him who delighteth to hear the prayers of a poor sinner; and all of a sudden my dungeon shook, my chains flew off, and glory to God, my soul was filled. Now my confidence was strengthened that the Lord had heard my prayers and pardoned all my sins. I was constrained to go from house to house, telling all what a dear Savior I had found.

My master was an unconverted man, but he was very tender and humane. Our neighbors, seeing that our master indulged us with the privilege of attending meeting, said that Stokeley's negros would soon ruin him. So my brother and myself determined that we would attend our master's business so that it should not be said that religion made us worse servants. At length our master said he was convinced that religion made slaves better, and often boasted of his slaves for their honesty and industry.

I asked him if I might ask the preachers to come and preach at his house. He being old and infirm, cheerfully agreed. At length Freeborn Garrettson preached from these words, "Thou art weighed in the balances, and art found wanting" (Daniel 5:27 KJV). My master believed himself to be one of that number, and after that he could not be satisfied to hold slaves, believing it to be wrong.

Read: Luke 4:18

JUNE 15

OF PRICELESS WORTH

HENRY VENN | 18TH CENTURY

Henry Venn (1725-1797) was an English evangelical minister and one of the founders of the Clapham Sect, a small but influential evangelical group within the Anglican Church.

It is evident that man is endued with an active principle, entirely distinct from his body. For while his body is chained down to a spot of earth, his soul can soar and move freely in contemplation; can reflect, and with variety almost infinite, can compare the numberless objects which present themselves before it. When his body has attained maturity and perfect strength, his soul arrives not to a state of perfection, but goes on increasing in wisdom and knowledge; and when the body is feeble or sinks into decay, the soul is often full of vigor, or feels grief and anguish all its own.

To demonstrate the excellency of the soul is of great importance: because all that is comprehended under the word *religion*, respects the soul. And many precepts in the book of God must be resisted as unreasonable or unnecessary, if the salvation of the soul be not considered as the greatest good man can attain; the ruin of it, the greatest evil he can suffer.

What can be imagined more grand than the account of its creation? Look up to the heavens; immensely high, immeasurably wide as they are, God only spoke, and instantly, with all their host, they had their being. But, behold! Before the human soul is formed, a council of the Eternal Trinity is held. God said, "Let us make man in our own image, after our own likeness" (see Genesis 1:26). He formed man's soul, with its moral faculties and powers: a sinless, immortal transcript of himself.

To deface this image, and ruin a creature which the love of God had so highly exalted, was an attempt equal to the detestable malice Satan bore against God and against the favorite work of his hand. But no sooner did the devil, by his accursed subtlety, bring on the soul an injury, tending to its utter destruction, than the most high God, by the method used to recover it, declared a second time still more loudly the exceeding greatness of its worth.

READ: MATTHEW 13:45-46

June 16

A Celebration for the Ages

Isidore | 7th century

Saint Isidore of Seville (c. 560-636) served as archbishop of Seville for more than three decades and is considered "the last scholar of the ancient world."

The term *pasch* is not Greek but Hebrew, and it derives not from "suffering," but from the Hebrew word *pasch*, meaning "passover," because at that time the people of God passed over out of Egypt. Whence the Gospel says, "Jesus knowing that his hour was come, that he should pass out of this world to the Father" (see John 13:1).

Easter Eve is held as a continuous vigil because of the coming of our King, so that the time of his resurrection might find us not sleeping but vigilant. The reason for this night's vigil is twofold: it is because on that night he then received life, although he suffered death, or because at the same hour at which he was resurrected he will afterwards come for the Judgment.

We celebrate Easter Day in that manner not only to call to mind the death and resurrection of Christ, but also to ponder the other things that are attested concerning him, with regard to the meaning of the sacraments. This is for the sake of the beginning of a new life and for the sake of the new person whom we are commanded to put on, taking off the old, purging out "the old leaven" that we may be "a new dough . . . for Christ our *pasch* is sacrificed" (see 1 Corinthians 5:7).

Therefore, because of this newness of life the first month of the new things (i.e., the new crops; see Exodus 23:15) in the months of the year is mystically attributed to the paschal celebration. Indeed that Easter Day is celebrated on a day of the third week signifies that in the whole time of the world, which is accomplished in seven periods of days, this holy event has now opened up the third age. For the first age is before the Mosaic law, the second under the law, and third under grace. It is also because of these three ages of the world that the resurrection of the Lord is on the third day.

Read: Ephesians 2:7

JUNE 17

THE BURDEN OF PERSECUTION

NICHOLAS OF CUSA | 1453

Nicholas of Cusa (1401-1464) was a German philosopher, theologian, jurist, mathematician, astronomer, and cardinal of the Catholic Church.

After the brutal deeds recently committed by the Turkish ruler at Constantinople were reported to a certain man, who had once seen the sites of those regions, he was inflamed by a zeal for God, and implored the Creator of all things that in his mercy he restrain the persecution, raging more than ever because of different religious rites.

After several days—perhaps because of long-continued meditation—a vision was revealed to this zealous man. From it he concluded that of a few wise men familiar with the differences observed in religions throughout the world, a single easy harmony could be found and through it a lasting peace established by appropriate and true means.

For he was caught up to a certain intellectual height where, as if among those who had departed from life, an examination of this question was thus held in a council of the highest with the Almighty presiding. The King of heaven and earth stated that the sad news of the groans of the oppressed had been brought to him from this world's realm: because of religion many take up arms against each other and either force men to renounce their long-practiced tradition or inflict death on them. There were many bearers of these lamentations from all the earth, and the King ordered that they be present in the full assembly of the saints.

Then one leader, in the name of all these envoys, said: "O Lord, King of the universe, what does every creature have that you have not given it? But a great multitude cannot exist without considerable diversity and almost everyone is forced to lead a life burdened with sorrows and to live under the subjection of the rulers who reign over them. Therefore, come to our aid you who alone are able. For you, almighty God, who are invisible to every mind, are able to show yourself as visible to whom you will and in the way in which you can be grasped. Therefore, do not hide yourself any longer, O Lord; be merciful and show your face, and all peoples will be saved."

READ: JOHN 17:3

THE WORK OF THE CREATOR

STEPHEN CHARNOCK | 17TH CENTURY

Stephen Charnock (1628-1680) was an English Puritan Presbyterian clergyman.

God is the great spring and author of our recovery; for he was principally engaged in the whole undertaking and effecting of our redemption and reconciliation by Christ. God was the first mover in those acts whereby the first foundation stone was laid and the building reared. All was begun by his order, and managed by his direction and influence.

The story of the creation seems to intimate some other work to be done in the world by God besides that work of creation which God the Father made at that time. Thrice repeated, he rested from that work which he had made; he made no more of that kind and nature. But a rest he could not find; he rested from it, but not in it; for he foresaw how soon he should be disturbed by the entrance of sin. A work there was remaining wherein he intended to bring forth the glory of his divine excellency which yet lay hid.

He would no less have a hand in the second creation of all things by Christ than he had in the first, since a greater glory was to redound to him as reconciling than as creating, by how much it is more excellent to give man a happy being than to give man a bare being. As man was made to declare the glory of Christ, so is Christ formed to declare the glory of God. As all influences the members receive in point of direction and motion are from the head, so all the influences Christ had were from God, as the head directing and moving him. As the head counsels what the members act, so God counsels what Christ acts. God brings forth this Mediator as his divine image, and diffuses all his perfections in and through him before the eyes of men, and thought it a work too worthy to be contrived by any but himself, and transacted by any but his Son. God only sent him to make it, and called him back to himself as soon as ever he had finished it.

READ: JOHN 1:18

JUNE 19

LAYING THE FOUNDATION

JAMES GIBBONS | C. 1917

James Gibbons (1834-1921) was a cardinal of the Roman Catholic Church, only the second American to receive that distinction.

In this country, the citizen happily enjoys the largest liberty. But the wider the liberty, the more efficient should be the safeguards to prevent it from being abused and degenerating into license. The ship that is destined to sail on a rough sea and before strong winds, should be well ballasted. To keep the social planet within its proper orbit, the centripetal force of religion should counterbalance the centrifugal motion of free thought.

The only effectual way to preserve the blessings of civil freedom within legitimate bounds, is to inculcate in the mind of youth while at school, the virtues of truth, justice, honesty, temperance, self-denial, and those other fundamental duties comprised in the Christian code of morals.

The catechetical instructions given once a week in our Sunday schools, though productive of very beneficial results, are insufficient to supply the religious wants of our children. They should, as far as possible, breathe every day a healthy religious atmosphere in those schools in which not only is their mind enlightened, but the seeds of faith, piety, and sound morality are nourished and invigorated. By what principle of justice can you fill their mind with earthly knowledge for several hours each day, while their heart, which requires far more cultivation, must be content with the paltry allowance of a few weekly lessons?

Nor am I unmindful of the blessed influence of a home education, and especially of a mother's tutelage. As she is her child's first instructor, her lessons are the most deep and lasting. The intimate knowledge she has acquired of her child's character by constant intercourse, the tender love subsisting between them, and the unbounded confidence placed in her by her pupil, impart to her instructions a force and conviction which no other teacher can hope to win.

READ: PROVERBS 22:6

June 20
To Truly See God
Charles Kingsley | 19th century

Charles Kingsley (1819-1875) was an English preacher, writer, and champion for social change. He once wrote that false religion was "the opiate of the people." Karl Marx seized upon the phrase and famously labeled all religion by the title.

If any man wishes to see God truly and fully, with the eyes of his soul: if any man wishes for that beatific vision of God; that perfect sight of God's perfect goodness; then must that man go, and sit down at the foot of Christ's cross, and look steadfastly upon him who hangs thereon. And there he will see what the wisest and best among the heathen, among all who are not Christian men, never have seen, and cannot see unto this day, however much they may feel (and some of them, thank God, do feel) that God is the Eternal Goodness, and must be loved accordingly.

On the cross, the Father justified himself to man; yea, glorified himself in the glory of his crucified Son. On the cross God proved himself to be perfectly just, perfectly good, perfectly generous, perfectly glorious, beyond all that man could ever have dared to conceive or dream. That God must be good, the wise heathens knew; but that God was so utterly good that he could stoop to suffer, to die, for men and by men: that they never dreamed.

That was the mystery of God's love, which was hid in Christ from the foundation of the world, and which was revealed at last upon the cross of Calvary by him who prayed for his murderers, "Father, forgive them; for they know not what they do" (Luke 23:34 KJV). That truly blessed sight of a Savior-God, who did not disdain to die the meanest and the most fearful of deaths, that came home at once, and has come home ever since, to all hearts which had left in them any love and respect for goodness, and melted them with the fire of divine love; as God grant it may melt yours, this day, and henceforth forever.

Read: John 20:14-18

June 21

An Effective Witness

John Chrysostom | 387

John Chrysostom (c. 344-407) was an important early church father who was known for his eloquence in preaching and public speaking, as well as his denunciation of abuse of authority by both ecclesiastical and political leaders.

Let us show forth then a new kind of life. Let us make earth heaven; let us hereby show the Greeks of how great blessings they are deprived. For when they behold in us good conversation, they will look upon the very face of the kingdom of heaven.

Yea, when they see us gentle, pure from wrath, from evil desire, from envy, from covetousness, rightly fulfilling all our other duties, they will say, "If the Christians are become angels here, what will they be after their departure hence? If where they are strangers they shine so bright, how great will they become when they shall have won their native land!"

Thus they too will be reformed, and the world of godliness "will have free course," not less than in the apostles' times. For if they, being twelve, converted entire cities and countries; were we all to become teachers by our careful conduct, imagine how high our cause will be exalted. For not even a dead man raised so powerfully attracts the Greek, as a person practicing self-denial. At that indeed he will be amazed, but by this he will be profited. That is done, and is passed away; but this abides, and is constant culture to his soul.

Read: Matthew 5:16

JUNE 22

A MIGHTY FORTRESS

MARTIN LUTHER | 1527

Martin Luther (1483–1546) was a German priest and professor of theology who initiated the Protestant Reformation.

A mighty fortress is our God, a bulwark never failing;
Our helper he, amid the flood of mortal ills prevailing.
For still our ancient foe doth seek to work us woe;
His craft and power are great; and, armed with cruel hate,
On earth is not his equal.
Did we in our own strength confide, our striving would be losing—
Were not the right man on our side, the man of God's own choosing.
Dost ask who that may be? Christ Jesus, it is he,
Lord Sabaoth his name, from age to age the same,
And he must win the battle.
And though this world, with devils filled, should threaten to undo us;
We will not fear, for God hath willed His truth to triumph through us.
The prince of darkness grim—we tremble not for him;
His rage we can endure, for lo! His doom is sure,
One little word shall fell him.
That word above all earthly powers—no thanks to them—abideth;
The Spirit and the gifts are ours through him who with us sideth.
Let goods and kindred go, this mortal life also;
The body they may kill: God's truth abideth still,
His kingdom is forever.

READ: 2 SAMUEL 22:2-3

THE AUTHORITY OF GOD

BILLY GRAHAM | 2010

William Franklin "Billy" Graham (b. 1918) is an American evangelist. Graham has preached the gospel in person to more people than any other person in history.

Now, Satan will do everything he can to divert us from the message of Scripture, but we must stand firm. God has spoken, and we must be faithful to that message. When Jesus was upon the earth, He held His crowds spellbound. He talked to the leaders of His day, and He spoke as one having authority, and He absolutely shook them by the great authority with which He spoke, because it was the authority of God the Father.

The great prophets of the past also spoke with authority, and their secret is traceable to the fact that they believed their message, and they would say time after time, "Thus saith the Lord." Or, "The Word of the Lord came unto me saying."

Today, if you want to be used of God, if you want people to turn from false messiahs and listen to you, if you want to turn people from darkness unto light and from the power of Satan unto God, you and I must speak, we must work, and we must live with that authority that our Lord Himself had. The world longs for authority and certainty; it is weary of theological floundering and uncertainty; nothing is gained psychologically or spiritually by casting aspersions on the light.

Our generation, especially in the West, occupied itself with criticism of the Scriptures and all too soon found itself questioning divine revelation. Don't make that mistake. Take the Bible as God's holy Word.

READ: LUKE 10:19

June 24

In Need of a Savior

John Stott | 1958

John Robert Walmsley Stott (1921-2011) was an Anglican clergyman who was noted as a leader of the worldwide evangelical movement.

It is by the Spirit of Christ that we can be changed so that we become more like Christ, as we continue to maintain our focus on him. Yes, we have our part to play, in turning from what we know to be wrong, in the exercise of faith and discipline. But making us holy is essentially the work of the Holy Spirit.

William Temple used to illustrate the point in this way: It is no good giving me a play like *Hamlet* or *King Lear*, and telling me to write a new play just like it. Shakespeare could do it; I can't. And it is no good showing me a life like the life of Jesus and telling me to live a life just like it. Jesus could do it; I can't. But if the genius of Shakespeare could come and live inside me, I would then be able to write plays like he did. And if the Spirit of Jesus would come and live inside me, I would then be able to live a life like he did.

This is the open secret of how to live as a Christian. It is not about us struggling in vain to become more like Jesus, but about allowing him, by the power of the Spirit, to come and change us from the inside. Once again we see that to have him as our example is not enough; we need him as our Savior.

Read: Ephesians 2:22

JUNE 25

GOD WILL CONQUER

FYODOR DOSTOYEVSKY | 1880

Fyodor Dostoyevsky (1821-1881) was a Russian writer of realist fiction and essays. He is best known for his novels Crime and Punishment, The Idiot, *and* The Brothers Karamazov—*a spiritual drama that enters deeply into the ethical debates of God, free will, and morality.*

He jumped up in a frenzy, flung off the towel, and fell to pacing up and down the room again. Alyosha recalled what he had just said. "I seem to be sleeping awake . . . I walk, I speak, I see, but I am asleep."

It seemed to be just like that now. Alyosha did not leave him. The thought passed through his mind to run for a doctor, but he was afraid to leave his brother alone: there was no one to whom he could leave him. By degrees Ivan lost consciousness completely at last. He still went on talking, talking incessantly, but quite incoherently, and even articulated his words with difficulty.

Suddenly he staggered violently; but Alyosha was in time to support him. Ivan let him lead him to his bed. Alyosha undressed him somehow and put him to bed. He sat watching over him for another two hours. The sick man slept soundly, without stirring, breathing softly and evenly. Alyosha took a pillow and lay down on the sofa, without undressing.

As he fell asleep he prayed for Mitya and Ivan. He began to understand Ivan's illness. "The anguish of a proud determination. An earnest conscience!" God, in Whom he disbelieved, and His truth were gaining mastery over his heart, which still refused to submit. "Yes," the thought floated through Alyosha's head as it lay on the pillow, "yes, if Smerdyakov is dead, no one will believe Ivan's evidence; but he will go and give it." Alyosha smiled softly. "God will conquer!" he thought.

"He will either rise up in the light of truth, or . . . he'll perish in hate, revenging on himself and on everyone his having served the cause he does not believe in," Alyosha added bitterly, and again he prayed for Ivan.

READ: REVELATION 6:2

JUNE 26

IMPENDING EVILS

SIR THOMAS MORE | 16TH CENTURY

Sir Thomas More (1478-1535) was an English lawyer, social philosopher, author,
statesman, and notable Renaissance humanist. He was an opponent of the Protestant
Reformation, believing that it would throw society into chaos.

Remember that the Evangelists, in predicting that kingdom, announce a
dreadful advent! And that, according to the received opinion of the church,
wars, persecutions, and calamities of every kind, the triumph of evil, and the
coming of Antichrist are to be looked for, before the promises made by the
prophets shall be fulfilled.

Consider this also, that the speedy fulfillment of those promises has been the
ruling fancy of the most dangerous of all madmen, from John of Leyden and his
frantic followers, down to the saints of Cromwell's army, Venner and his Fifth-
Monarchy men, the fanatics of the Cevennes, and the blockheads of your own
days, who beheld with complacency the crimes of the French Revolutionists, and
the progress of Bonaparte towards the subjugation of Europe, as events tending
to bring about the prophecies; and, under the same besotted persuasion, are
ready at this time to co-operate with the miscreants who trade in blasphemy
and treason!

But you who neither seek to deceive others nor yourself, you who are neither
insane nor insincere, you surely do not expect that the millennium is to be
brought about by the triumph of what are called liberal opinions; nor by
enabling the whole of the lower classes to read the incentives to vice, impiety,
and rebellion which are prepared for them by an unlicensed press; nor by
Sunday schools, and religious tract societies; nor by the portentous bibliolatry of
the age! And if you adhere to the letter of the Scriptures, methinks the thought
of that consummation for which you look, might serve rather for consolation
under the prospect of impending evils, than for a hope upon which the mind can
rest in security with a calm and contented delight.

READ: REVELATION 12:10

June 27

Alas! and Did My Savior Bleed

Isaac Watts | 1707

Isaac Watts (1674-1748) was an English hymn writer, theologian, and logician.
He was a prolific writer, credited with some 750 hymns, many of which have been
translated into other languages and remain in active use today.

Alas! and did my Savior bleed
And did my Sovereign die?
Would He devote that sacred head
For sinners such as I?
Was it for crimes that I had done
He groaned upon the tree?
Amazing pity! grace unknown!
And love beyond degree!
Well might the sun in darkness hide
And shut his glories in,
When Christ, the mighty Maker died,
For man the creature's sin. Thus might I hide my blushing face
While His dear cross appears,
Dissolve my heart in thankfulness,
And melt my eyes to tears.
But drops of grief can ne'er repay
The debt of love I owe:
Here, Lord, I give my self away
'Tis all that I can do.
At the cross, at the cross where I first saw the light,
And the burden of my heart rolled away,
It was there by faith I received my sight,
And now I am happy all the day!

Read: 1 Corinthians 1:18

JUNE 28

THE ALPHA AND OMEGA

JOHN | c. 105

Saint John of Patmos is the author of the book of Revelation in the New Testament.
While in exile on the Greek island of Patmos, John wrote to the seven Christian
churches in Asia to relate two visions he experienced.

Then I saw "a new heaven and a new earth," for the first heaven and the first
earth had passed away, and there was no longer any sea. I saw the Holy City,
the new Jerusalem, coming down out of heaven from God, prepared as a bride
beautifully dressed for her husband. And I heard a loud voice from the throne
saying, "Look! God's dwelling place is now among the people, and he will dwell
with them. They will be his people, and God himself will be with them and be
their God. 'He will wipe every tear from their eyes. There will be no more death'
or mourning or crying or pain, for the old order of things has passed away."

He who was seated on the throne said, "I am making everything new!" Then he
said, "Write this down, for these words are trustworthy and true."

He said to me: "It is done. I am the Alpha and the Omega, the Beginning and
the End. To the thirsty I will give water without cost from the spring of the water
of life. Those who are victorious will inherit all this, and I will be their God
and they will be my children. But the cowardly, the unbelieving, the vile, the
murderers, the sexually immoral, those who practice magic arts, the idolaters
and all liars—they will be consigned to the fiery lake of burning sulfur. This is
the second death."

READ: ISAIAH 46:10

JUNE 29
A DECLARATION OF THANKS
CHARLESTOWN, MASSACHUSETTS | 1676

On June 20, 1676, the governing council of Charlestown, Massachusetts, held a meeting to determine how best to express thanks for the good fortune that had seen their community securely established. By unanimous vote they instructed Edward Rawson, the clerk, to proclaim June 29 as a day of thanksgiving, our nation's first.

The Holy God having by a long and continual series of His afflictive dispensations in and by the present war with the heathen natives of this land, written and brought to pass bitter things against his own covenant people in this wilderness, yet so that we evidently discern that in the midst of His judgments He hath remembered mercy, having remembered His footstool in the day of His sore displeasure against us for our sins, with many singular intimations of His fatherly compassion and regard; preserving many of our towns from desolation threatened, and attempted by the Enemy, and giving us especially of late with many of our confederates many signal advantages against them, without such disadvantage to ourselves as formerly we have been sensible of, if it be the Lord's mercy that we are not consumed, it certainly bespeaks our positive thankfulness, when our enemies are in any measure disappointed or destroyed; and fearing the Lord should take notice under so many intimations of His returning mercy, we should be found an insensible people, as not standing before Him with thanksgiving, as well as lading Him with our complaints in the time of pressing afflictions.

The Council has determined to appoint and set apart the 29th day of this June, as a day of solemn thanksgiving and praise to God for His goodness and favor, many particulars of which mercy might be instanced, but we doubt not those who are sensible of God's afflictions, have been as diligent to espy Him returning to us; and that the Lord may behold us as a people offering praise and thereby glorifying Him; the Council doth commend it to the respective ministers, elders and people of this jurisdiction; solemnly and seriously to keep the same beseeching that being persuaded by the mercies of God we may all, even this whole people offer up our bodies and souls as a living and acceptable service unto God by Jesus Christ.

READ: PSALM 100:4

June 30

Until It Hurts

Mother Teresa | 1994

Mother Teresa (1910-1997), born Agnes Gonxha Bojaxhiu, was a Catholic nun of Albanian ethnicity and Indian citizenship who founded the Missionaries of Charity in Calcutta, India, in 1950.

We are reminded that Jesus came to bring the good news to the poor, when He said: "Peace I leave with you, My peace I give unto you" (John 14:27 KJV). He came not to give the peace of the world which is only that we don't bother each other. He came to give the peace of heart which comes from loving—from doing good to others.

Jesus gave His life to love us and He tells us that we also have to give whatever it takes to do good to one another. And in the Gospel Jesus says very clearly: "Love . . . as I have loved you" (John 15:12 KJV). Jesus died on the Cross because that is what it took for Him to do good to us—to save us from our selfishness in sin. He gave up everything to do the Father's will to show us that we too must be willing to give up everything to do God's will. If we are not willing to give whatever it takes to do good to one another, sin is still in us. That is why we too must give to each other until it hurts.

It is not enough to say: "I love God," but I also have to love my neighbor. St. John says that you are a liar if you say you love God and you don't love your neighbor. How can you love God whom you do not see, if you do not love your neighbor whom you see, whom you touch, with whom you live?

And so it is very important for us to realize that love, to be true, has to hurt. I must be willing to give whatever it takes not to harm other people and, in fact, to do good to them. This requires that I be willing to give until it hurts. Otherwise, there is no true love in me and I bring injustice, not peace, to those around me.

READ: MARK 10:21

July 1

No Room in the Inn

Horace Bushnell | 1864

Horace Bushnell (1802-1876) was an American Congregationalist theologian, author, and pastor.

If the carpenter and his wife are in a plight, people as humble as they can well enough take the stable, when there is nothing better to be had. So it was, and perhaps it was more fitting to be so; for the great Messiah's errand allows no expectation of patronage, even for his infancy. He comes into the world and finds it preoccupied.

A marvelous great world it is, and there is room in it for many things: for wealth, ambition, pride, pleasure, trade, society, dissipation, powers, kingdoms, armies and their wars; but for him there is the smallest room possible: room in the stable—but not in the inn. There he begins to breathe, and at that point introduces himself into his human life as a resident of our world—the greatest and most blessed event, humble as the guise of it may be, that has ever transpired among mortals.

If it be a wonder to men's eyes and ears, a wonder even to science itself, when the flaming air-stone pitches into our world, as a stranger newly arrived out of parts unknown in the sky, what shall we think of the more transcendent fact, that the Eternal Son of God is born into the world; that proceeding forth from the Father, not being of our system or sphere, not of the world, he has come as a Holy Thing into it—God manifest in the flesh, the Word made flesh, closeted in humanity, there to abide and work until he has restored the race itself to God!

Nor is this wonderful annunciation any less welcome, or any less worthy to be celebrated by the hallelujahs of angels and men, that the glorious visitant begins to breathe in a stall. Was there not a certain propriety in such a beginning, considered as the first chapter and symbol of his whole history, as the Savior and Redeemer of mankind? This brings us to the impressive fact that Jesus could not find room in the world then, and has never yet been able to find it.

Read: Luke 2:7

July 2
Slaying the Flesh
Thomas Fuller | c. 1665

Thomas Fuller (1608-1661) was an English churchman and historian. He is remembered for his writings, particularly Worthies of England, *published after his death.*

I read, in the Revelation, of a beast, one of whose heads was, as it were, wounded to death. I expected in the next verse that the beast should die, as the most probable consequence, considering:

1. It was not a scratch, but a wound.

2. Not a wound in a fleshy part, or limbs of the body, but in the very head, the throne of reason.

3. No light wound, but in outward apparition (having no other probe but St. John's eyes to search it), it seemed deadly.

But mark what immediately follows: his deadly wound was healed. Who would have suspected this inference from these premises? But is this not the lively emblem of my natural corruption?

Sometimes I conceived that, by God's grace, I have conquered and killed, subdued and slain, maimed and mortified, the deeds of the flesh: never more shall I be molested or buffeted with such a bosom sin: when, alas! The next moment, the news is that it is revived and recovered.

Thus tenches, though grievously gashed, presently plaster themselves whole by that slimy and unctuous humor they have in them; and thus the inherent balsam of badness quickly cures my corruption, not a scar to be seen. I perceive I shall never finally kill it, till first I be dead myself.

Read: Colossians 3:1-11

JULY 3

A PERILOUS TASK

JEROME | 383

Jerome (c. 340-420) was an early Christian priest, apologist, translator, and interpreter. He is known for his translation of the Bible into Latin (the Vulgate).

You urge me to revise the old Latin version, and, as it were, to sit in judgment on the copies of the Scriptures which are now scattered throughout the whole world; and you would have me decide which of them agree with the Greek original. The labor is one of love, but at the same time, both perilous and presumptuous; for in judging others I must be content to be judged by all; and how can I dare to change the language of the world in its hoary old age, and carry it back to the early days of its infancy?

If we are to pin our faith to the Latin texts, it is for our opponents to tell us which; for there are almost as many forms of texts as there are copies. If, on the other hand, we are to glean the truth from a comparison of many, why not go back to the original Greek and correct the mistakes introduced by inaccurate translators, and the blundering alterations of confident but ignorant critics, and, further, all that has been inserted or changed by copyists more asleep than awake?

I am not discussing the Old Testament, which was turned into Greek by the seventy elders, but the New Testament. This was undoubtedly composed in Greek, with the exception of the work of Matthew the Apostle, who was the first to commit to writing the Gospel of Christ, and who published his work in Judea in Hebrew characters. We must confess that as we have it in our language it is marked by discrepancies, and now that the stream is distributed into different channels, we must go back to the fountainhead.

I therefore promise in this short preface the four Gospels only, which are to be taken in the following order: Matthew, Mark, Luke, and John. But I have used my pen with some restraint, and while I have corrected only such passages as seemed to convey a different meaning, I have allowed the rest to remain as they are.

READ: REVELATION 22:18-19

July 4

A Man of Principle

James Allen | c. 1910

James Allen (1864-1912) was a British philosophical writer known for his inspirational books and poetry, and known as a pioneer of the self-help movement.

The man that stands upon a principle is the same calm, dauntless, self-possessed man under all circumstances. When the hour of trial comes, and he has to decide between his personal comforts and Truth, he gives up his comforts and remains firm. Even the prospect of torture and death cannot alter or deter him.

The man of self regards the loss of his wealth, his comforts, or his life as the greatest calamities which can befall him. The man of principle looks upon these incidents as comparatively insignificant and not to be weighed with loss of character, or loss of Truth. To desert Truth is, to him, the only happening which can really be called a calamity.

It is the hour of crisis which decides who are the minions of darkness and who the children of Light. It is the epoch of threatening disaster, ruin, and persecution which divides the sheep from the goats and reveals to the reverential gaze of succeeding ages the men and women of power.

It is easy for a man, so long as he is left in the enjoyment of his possessions, to persuade himself that he believes in and adheres to the principles of Peace, Brotherhood, and Universal Love; but if, when his enjoyments are threatened, or he imagines they are threatened, he begins to clamor loudly for war, he shows that he believes in and stands upon, not Peace, Brotherhood, and Love, but strife, selfishness, and hatred.

He who does not desert his principles when threatened with the loss of every earthly thing, even to the loss of reputation and life, is the man of power; is the man whose every word and work endures; is the man whom the afterworld honors, reveres, and worships. Rather than desert that principle of Divine Love on which he rested and in which all his trust was placed, Jesus endured the utmost extremity of agony and deprivation; and today the world prostrates itself at his pierced feet in rapt adoration.

Read: Philippians 2:15-16

July 5

A Holy Union

John of Ruysbroeck | 14th century

The Blessed John of Ruysbroeck (c. 1293-1381) was one of the Flemish mystics.

When God thought the time had come, and had mercy on the suffering of His beloved, He sent His Only Begotten Son to earth, in a fair chamber, in a glorious temple; that is, in the body of the Virgin Mary.

There He was married to this bride, our nature, and He united her with His own person through the most pure blood of this noble Virgin. The priest who married the bride was the Holy Ghost; the angel Gabriel brought the offer; the glorious Virgin gave her consent.

Thus Christ, our faithful Bridegroom, united our nature with His person; and He has sought us in strange countries, and taught us heavenly customs and perfect faithfulness, and has labored for us and fought as our champion against the adversary. And He has broken open our prison, and won the victory, and by His death slain our death; and He has redeemed us by His blood, and made us free through His living waters of baptism, and enriched us with His sacraments and with His gifts: that we might go out (as He says) with all the virtues, to meet Him in the house of glory and to enjoy Him without end in eternity.

Read: Philippians 2:5-11

July 6

Holy, Holy, Holy!

Reginald Heber | c. 1809

Reginald Heber (1783-1826) was the Church of England's Bishop of Calcutta, who is remembered primarily as a hymn writer.

Holy, holy, holy! Lord God Almighty!
Early in the morning our song shall rise to Thee;
Holy, holy, holy, merciful and mighty!
God in three Persons, blessed Trinity!
Holy, holy, holy! All the saints adore Thee,
Casting down their golden crowns around the glassy sea;
Cherubim and seraphim falling down before Thee,
Who was, and is, and evermore shall be.
Holy, holy, holy! Though the darkness hide Thee,
Though the eye of sinful man Thy glory may not see;
Only Thou art holy; there is none beside Thee,
Perfect in pow'r, in love, and purity.
Holy, holy, holy! Lord God Almighty!
All Thy works shall praise Thy Name, in earth, and sky, and sea;
Holy, holy, holy; merciful and mighty!
God in three Persons, blessed Trinity!

Read: Isaiah 6:1-3

July 7
A Wise Leader
Sir Thomas More | 16th Century

Sir Thomas More (1478-1535) was an English lawyer, social philosopher, author, statesman, and notable Renaissance humanist. He opposed the Protestant Reformation on the basis that it would throw society into chaos.

Machiavelli is always sagacious, but the tree of knowledge of which he had gathered grew not in Paradise; it had a bitter root, and the fruit savors thereof, even to deadliness. He believed men to be so malignant by nature that they always act malevolently from choice, and never well except by compulsion—a devilish doctrine, to be accounted for rather than excused by the circumstances of his age and country. For he lived in a land where intellect was highly cultivated and morals thoroughly corrupted.

The rule of policy as well as of private morals is to be found in the gospel; and a religious sense of duty toward God and man is the first thing needful in a statesman: herein he has an unerring guide when knowledge fails him, and experience affords no light. This, with a clear head and a single heart, will carry him through all difficulties; and the just confidence which, having these, he will then have in himself, will obtain for him the confidence of the nation.

In every nation, indeed, which is conscious of its strength, the minister who takes the highest tone will invariably be the most popular; let him uphold, even haughtily, the character of his country, and the heart and voice of the people will be with him. But haughtiness implies always something that is hollow: the tone of a wise minister will be firm but calm.

In all cases he will do that which is lawful and right, holding this for a certain truth, that in politics the straight path is the sure one! Such a minister will hope for the best, and expect the best; by acting openly, steadily, and bravely, he will act always for the best; and so acting, be the issue what it may, he will never dishonor himself or his country, nor fall under the "sharp judgment" of which they that are in "high places" are in danger.

Read: 1 Samuel 2:35

July 8

Well Known to God

Ralph Sockman | 1946

Ralph Washington Sockman (1889-1970) was an author and the senior pastor of Christ Church (United Methodist) in New York City. He gained considerable prominence in the United States as the featured speaker on the weekly NBC radio program, "National Radio Pulpit."

But the psalmist was talking about something more than such a self-starting and self-sustained belief in oneself. Listen to him: "Wait on the Lord: be of good courage, and he shall strengthen thine heart" (Psalm 27:14 kjv). Ah, that is something more than the cocksureness of self-reliance. That is something more than a success complex built up by a business tycoon through repeated triumphs over competitors. It is not the self-intoxication of a Napoleon or a Hitler. No, the psalmist was counseling a courage rooted in soil deeper than his own subconscious mind. He was saying that when we wait on the Lord, God strengthens our hearts with the feeling that he believes in us, and that begets a belief in ourselves.

Such was the feeling which sustained the Pilgrim Fathers in their stormy voyage across the Atlantic to the bleak shores of wintry New England. When their feet landed on Plymouth Rock, their leader is reported to have repeated the words of St. Paul: "As unknown, and *yet* well known; as dying, and behold we live" (2 Corinthians 6:9). Those Pilgrim Fathers did not believe in themselves because of any great deeds they had done of themselves. They were unknown to men, but well known to God. They felt that God had his eye on them, that God believed in them. That is what made them believe in themselves and their cause. That helped to make them brave.

People spend so much time discussing whether they can believe in God. Why not reverse the question and ask whether we are the kind of persons in whom God can believe? That is the point to start from in getting a grip on God.

Read: Psalm 27:11-14

JULY 9
LOVING GOD AND NEIGHBOR
EUCHERIUS | C. 448

Saint Eucherius (c. 380-c. 449) was a high-born and high-ranking ecclesiastic in the Christian Church of Gaul.

Jerusalem and Zion are the church or the soul; in the psalm: praise the Lord, Jerusalem. And to be noted: because everyone generally comes together in the church, this can also refer to the soul.

The sons of Zion and the sons of Jerusalem are the sons of the church; in the psalm: let the sons of Zion rejoice in the king.

The tabernacle is the body of the Lord or the church; in the psalm: his tent (tabernacle) is pitched in the sun.

The ark is the flesh of the Lord or the hearts of the saints; in the psalm: you are the ark of my sanctification. The same is the church in which those who will be saved are hidden; in Genesis: only Noah and those with him in the ark remained.

The stone tablets are two, I think, because of the two testaments or because of the two teachings about loving God and neighbor; in Exodus: and the Lord said to Moses, "Carve two stone tablets."

The law is divine teaching; in the psalm: the law of the Lord is pure.

The agreement is a compact of divine grace with man; in the psalm: I did not see them obeying the pact.

The testament is a confirmation of divine will; in the prophet: and I will confirm the testament with the house of Judah.

Circumcision is the finishing off of vices; in the apostle: you were circumcised with a circumcision not done by hands in the finishing off of the flesh of the body.

The horn is strength or the kingdom; in Kings: and he raised high the horn of His Christ.

Purple is the type of those martyred through bloodshed; in Exodus: all, who saw with the heart, in the beginning brought to God gold, silver, copper, hyacinth, purple, scarlet, goats' hair, and linen. Scarlet is the same, or the ardor of charity or the remembrance of the cross.

READ: MATTHEW 22:38-40

July 10
THE PURSUIT OF HAPPINESS
KARL WUTTKE | 1873

Karl Friedrich Adolf Wuttke (1819-1870) was a German Protestant theologian and professor from Breslau.

"Love is the fulfilling of the law" (Romans 13:10 KJV); in this formula the Christian idea of the moral motive is very definitely expressed; love leads to the fulfillment of the law; it is the rich fullness in which all law is included. Without love there is no morality; and where love is, there morality is truly free, for love develops itself into all forms of the moral. Hence Christ sums up the whole law in the one precept of love to God and to our neighbor; "This is the love of God, that we keep his commandments" (1 John 5:3 KJV); love is not and cannot be a mere inert feeling, but it is active, it produces that which its subject loves—brings about the full and free harmony of the person and his life with God.

Whoever assigns any other motive for morality than love, knows nothing of the moral. But love tends by its essential nature to a unity of the diverse—seeks not its own mere isolated being. Mere self-love to the exclusion of love to others is not love at all, but only immoral self-seeking; it is indeed a motive to action, but to anti-moral action. There is no form of moral activity conceivable which would not be an expression of love. The moral love of the divine is also hatred against that which is ungodly.

The formula "Blessed is he that," and other similar ones, are very frequently given as an encouragement to moral obedience; but also Christ himself and the apostles expressly present such a motive: "Do this and thou shalt live"; but neither the Old nor the New Testament separate this striving for happiness from the love to God and our neighbor in which, in fact, both Covenants find the true motive to moral action. There is, in reality, no essential antagonism between love and the striving after happiness; but the latter is directly implied in the former, and is, in the nature of the case, inseparable from it. Christianity knows no other happiness than love to God in the consciousness of being loved by him.

READ: MATTHEW 5:1-11

July 11

The Historical and Allegorical

Boëthius | c. 523

Anicius Manlius Severinus Boëthius (c. 480-524) was a Christian philosopher of the early sixth century.

The divine nature then, abiding from all eternity and unto all eternity without any change, by the exercise of a will known only to Himself, determined of Himself to form the world, and brought it into being when it was absolutely naught; but by His Word He brought forth the heavens, and created the earth so that He might make natures worthy of a place in heaven, and also fit earthly things to earth.

But although in heaven all things are beautiful and arranged in due order, yet one part of the heavenly creation, seeking more than nature and the Author of Nature had granted them, was cast forth from its heavenly habitation; and because the Creator did not wish the role of the angels, that is of the heavenly city whose citizens the angels are, to be diminished, He formed man out of the earth and breathed into him the breath of life. He endowed him with reason, He adorned him with freedom of choice and established him in the joys of Paradise, making covenant beforehand that if he would remain without sin He would add him and his offspring to the angelic hosts; so that as the higher nature had fallen low through the curse of pride, the lower substance might ascend on high through the blessing of humility.

But the father of envy, loathe that mankind should climb to the place where he himself deserved not to remain, put temptation before them and laid them open to punishment for disobedience, promising man also the gift of Godhead, the arrogant attempt to seize which had caused his own fall.

All this was revealed by God to His servant Moses, whom He vouchsafed to teach the creation and origin of man, as the books written by him declare. For the divine authority is always conveyed in one of the following ways—the historical, which simply announces facts; the allegorical, whence historical matter is excluded; or else the two combined, history and allegory conspiring to establish it. All this is abundantly evident to pious hearers and steadfast believers.

READ: GENESIS 1:26-31

July 12

Longing for Freedom

Hannah Hurnard | 1955

Hannah Hurnard (1905-1990) was a Christian author, born in Colchester, England, to Quaker parents, who is best known for her allegory Hinds' Feet on High Places.

She lifted her eyes and looked across the Valley and the river to the lovely sunset-lighted peaks of the mountains, then cried out in desperate longing, "Oh, if only I could escape from the Valley of Humiliation altogether and go to the High Places, completely out of reach of all the Fearings and my other relatives!"

No sooner were these words uttered when to her complete astonishment the Shepherd answered, "I have waited a long time to hear you make that suggestion, Much-Afraid. It would indeed be best for you to leave the Valley for the High Places, and I will very willingly take you there myself. The lower slopes of those mountains on the other side of the river are the border-land of my Father's Kingdom, the Realm of Love. No Fears of any kind are able to live there because 'perfect love casteth out fear and everything that torments.'"

Much-Afraid stared at him in amazement. "Go to the High Places," she exclaimed, "and live there? Oh, if only I could! For months past the longing has never left me. I think of it day and night, but it is not possible. I could never get there. I am too lame." She looked down at her malformed feet as she spoke, and her eyes again filled with tears and despair and self-pity. "These mountains are so steep and dangerous. I have been told that only the hinds and the deer can move on them safely."

"It is quite true that the way up to the High Places is both difficult and dangerous," said the Shepherd. "It has to be, so that nothing which is an enemy of Love can make the ascent and invade the Kingdom. The inhabitants of the High Places do need 'hinds' feet.' I have them myself," he added with a smile. "But, Much-Afraid, I could make yours like hinds' feet also, and set you upon the High Places."

Read: 2 Samuel 22:33-35

July 13

The Secret Place

Albert the Great | 13th Century

Albertus Magnus (c. 1206-1280), also known as Albert the Great and Albert of Cologne, was a Dominican friar and a bishop who achieved fame for his comprehensive knowledge of and advocacy for the peaceful coexistence of science and religion.

Since indeed the Lord God is Spirit, and those who worship him must worship in spirit and in truth, in other words, by knowledge and love, that is, understanding and desire, stripped of all images. This is what is referred to in Matthew 6:6: "When you pray, enter into your inner chamber," that is, your inner heart; "and having closed the door," that is, of your senses, and there with a pure heart and a clear conscience, and with faith unfeigned; "pray to your Father," in spirit and in truth, "in secret."

This can be done best when a man is disengaged and removed from everything else, and completely recollected within himself. There, in the presence of Jesus Christ, with everything, in general and individually, excluded and wiped out, the mind alone turns in security confidently to the Lord its God with its desire. In this way it pours itself forth into him in full sincerity with its whole heart and the yearning of its love, in the most inward part of all its faculties, and is plunged, enlarged, set on fire and dissolved into him.

Certainly, anyone who desires and aims to arrive at and remain in such a state must needs above all have eyes and senses closed and not be inwardly involved or worried about anything, nor concerned or occupied with anything, but should completely reject all such things as irrelevant, harmful, and dangerous. Then he should withdraw himself totally within himself and not pay any attention to any object entering the mind except Jesus Christ, the wounded one, alone. Here he can commit himself and all that he has, individually and as a whole, promptly, securely, and without discussion, to God's unwearying providence, in accordance with the words of Peter, *cast all your care upon him* (see 1 Peter 5:7), who can do everything.

Read: John 4:21-24

July 14
The Smallest Things
Adam Clarke | 19th Century

Adam Clarke (1760-1832) was a British Methodist theologian and scholar who is primarily remembered for his commentary on the Bible that took him forty years to complete.

Nothing escapes his merciful notice, not even the smallest things, of which he may be said to be only the Creator and Preserver; how much less those of whom he is the Father and Savior! There is not a circumstance in our life or an occurrence in our business that God will not make subservient to our salvation, if we have a simple heart and teachable spirit. Nothing is more astonishing than the care and concern of God for his followers. The least circumstances of their life are regulated, not merely by the general providence which extends to all things, but by a particular providence, which fits and directs all things to the design of their salvation, causing them all to cooperate for their present and eternal good.

"If God be for us, who can be against us?" (Romans 8:31 kjv). He who is infinitely wise has undertaken to direct us; he who is infinitely powerful has undertaken to protect us; he who is infinitely good has undertaken to save us. What cunning, strength, or malice can prevail against his wisdom, power, and goodness? None. Therefore we are safe who love God, and not only shall we sustain no essential damage by the persecutions of ungodly men, but even these things work together for our good.

The person whom Christ terms "happy" is one who is not under the influence of fate or chance, but is governed by an all-wise providence, having every step directed to the attainment of immortal glory, being transformed by the power into the likeness of the ever blessed God. The belief in an all-wise, all-directing providence is a powerful support during the most grievous accidents of life. Let man, who is made for God and eternity, learn from a flower of the field how low the care of Providence stoops.

Read: Matthew 6:25-34

FROM DARKNESS TO LIGHT

MIGUEL DE MOLINOS | 1675

Miguel de Molinos (c. 1628-1697) was a priest and the chief apostle of the religious revival known as Quietism.

When God had a mind to instruct his own captain, Moses, and give him the two tablets of the Law, written in stone, he called him up to the mountain, at what time God being there with him, the mount was darkened and environed with thick clouds, Moses standing idle, not knowing what to think or say. Seven days later God commanded Moses to come up to the top of the mountain, where he showed him his glory, and filled him with great consolation.

So in the beginning, when God intends after an extraordinary manner, to guide the soul into the school of the Divine and loving notices of the internal Law, he makes it go with darkness, and dryness, that he may bring it near to himself, because the Divine majesty knows very well, that it is not by the means of one's one ratiocination, or industry, that a soul draws near to him, and understands the Divine documents; but rather by silent and humble resignation.

The patriarch Noah gave a great instance of this; who after he had been by all men reckoned a fool, floating in the middle of a raging sea, wherewith the whole world was overflowed, without sails and oars; and environed with wild beasts, that were shut up in the ark, walked by faith alone, not knowing nor understanding what God had a mind to do with him.

What most concerns thee, oh redeemed soul, is patience, not to desist from the prayer thou art about, though thou cannot enlarge in discourse. Walk with firm faith and a holy silence, dying in thy self, with all thy natural industry, trusting that God, who is he who is and changes not, neither can err, intends nothing but thy good. It is clear that he who is at dying, must needs feel it, but how well is time employed, when the soul is dead, dumb, and resigned in the presence of God, there without any clutter or distraction, to receive the Divine influences.

READ: HEBREWS 12:1-2

THE RECKONING

R. G. LEE | 1957

R. G. Lee (1886-1978) was an American Southern Baptist preacher and pastor who served an unprecedented three terms as president of the Southern Baptist Convention.

I introduce to you Ahab, the vile human toad who squatted upon the throne of his nation—the worst of Israel's kings. King Ahab had command of a nation's wealth and a nation's army, but he had no command of his lusts and appetites. Ahab wore rich robes, but he had a sinning and wicked heart beneath them. He ate the finest food the world could supply—but he had a starved soul. He lived in palaces sumptuous within and without, yet he tormented himself for one bit of land more. Ahab was a king with a throne and a crown and a scepter, yet he lived nearly all of his life under the thumb of a wicked woman—a tool in her hands.

The Bible tells us: "But there was none like unto Ahab, which did sell himself to work wickedness in the sight of the LORD, whom Jezebel his wife stirred up. . . . And Ahab did more to provoke the LORD God of Israel to anger than all the kings of Israel that were before him" (1 Kings 21:25; 16:33 KJV).

When I see Ahab fall in his chariot and the dogs eating Jezebel by the walls of Jezreel, I say, as the Scripture says: "O that thou hadst hearkened to my commandments! then had thy peace been as a river, and thy righteousness as the waves of the sea" (Isaiah 48:18 KJV). "Payday—Someday!" God said it—and it was done! From this we learn the power and certainty of God in carrying out His own retributive providence, that men might know that His justice slumbers not. Even though the mill of God grinds slowly, it grinds to powder.

The only way I know for any man or woman on earth to escape the sinner's payday on earth and the sinner's hell beyond—is through Christ Jesus, who took the sinner's place upon the cross, becoming for all sinners all that God must judge, that sinners through faith in Christ Jesus might become all that God cannot judge.

READ: 1 KINGS 16:33

THE LIFE OF JOHN

JACOBUS DE VORAGINE | 13TH CENTURY

Jacobus de Voragine (c. 1230-1298) was an Italian church writer and archbishop of Genoa. He was the author of The Golden Legend, *one of the most popular religious works of the Middle Ages.*

Saint John the apostle and evangelist was son of Zebedee, who had married the third sister of our Lady to wife, and who was brother to St. James of Galicia. This said John signified as much as the grace of God, and well might he have such a name, for he had of our Lord four graces above the other apostles.

The first is that he was beloved of our Lord. The second was, that our Lord kept to him his virginity like as St. Jerome said, for he was at his wedding, and he abode a clean virgin. The third is that our Lord made him to have much great revelation and knowledge of his divinity, and of the finishing of the world, like as it appeared in the beginnings of his evangel, and in the Apocalypse. The fourth grace is that our Lord committed to him especially the keeping of his sweet mother.

He was, after the ascension of our Lord, in Jerusalem with the apostles and others, and after they were, by the ordinance of the Holy Ghost, confirmed in the Christian faith by the universal world, St. John came into Greece, where he conversed with and converted many people and founded many churches in the Christian faith as well by miracles as by doctrine.

Saint Jerome said of this glorious apostle St. John, that, when he was so old, so feeble, and so unmighty that his disciples sustained and bare him in going to church, and as of times he rested, he said to his disciples: Fair children, love ye together, and each of you love the other. And then his disciples demanded why he said such words to them so often. He answered to them and said: "Our Lord had so commanded, and whomsoever accomplished well this commandment it should suffice him for to be saved."

READ: JOHN 21:20-25

JULY 18

REVELATION

GUSTAV OEHLER | 1884

Gustav Friedrich Oehler (1812-1872) was a German theologian, professor, and pastor.

The biblical idea of revelation has its root in the idea of creation. Revelation is the development of the relation in which God has placed Himself to the world in bringing it into existence. The basis of revelation is laid in the fact that the world was called into existence by the word of God, and was animated by His Spirit. The production of different classes of beings advances by design, and reaches its goal only when God has created man in His own image.

In this progression the foundation of revelation is laid. For revelation is, in general, God's witness and communication of Himself to the world for the realization of the end of creation, and for the reestablishment of the full communion of man with God. After the tearing asunder through sin of the bond of the original communion of man with God, God testifies, partly in nature and the historical guidance of mankind, and partly in each one's conscience, of His power, goodness, and justice, and thus draws man to seek God.

The outer and inner forms of this universal revelation stand in a continual relation of reciprocity, since man's inward experience of the divine testimony is awakened through the objective outward witness of God; but this outward witness is first understood by the inward. Yet the personal communion of man with God, as demanded by his ideal constitution, is not recovered by means of the general revelation.

READ: MATTHEW 16:13-17

July 19

The Finished Work of Faith

Stephen Charnock | 17th century

Stephen Charnock (1628-1680) was an English Puritan Presbyterian clergyman. He served as chaplain to Henry Cromwell in Ireland, and later, though prevented from public ministry, continued to study and minister in England.

The blood of Christ does not perfectly cleanse us here from sin, in regard of the sense of it. Some sparks of the fiery law will sometimes flash in our consciences, and the peace of the gospel be put under a veil. The smiles of God's countenance seem to be changed into frowns, and the blood of Christ appears as if it ran low. Evidences may be blurred and guilt revived. Satan may accuse, and conscience knows not how to answer him. There will be moments of unbelief, distrusts of God, and misty steams from the miry lake of nature. But it has laid a perfect foundation, and the top stone of a full sense and comfort will be laid at last.

Peace shall be as an illustrious sunshine without a cloud, a triumphant breaking out of love, without any arrows of wrath sticking fast in the conscience; a sweet calm, without any whisper of a blustering tempest; the guilt of sin shall be forever wiped out of the conscience, as well as blotted out of God's book. The accuser shall no more accuse us, either to God or ourselves; no new indictment shall be formed by him at the bar of conscience; nay, conscience itself shall be forever purged, and sing an uninterrupted *requiem*, and hymn of peace, and shall not hiss the least accusation of a crime.

As God's justice shall read nothing for condemnation, so conscience shall read nothing for accusation. The blood of Christ will be perfect in the effects of it. As it rent the veil between God and us, it will rend the veil between conscience and us. As Christ said when he was giving up his spirit, "It is finished," it is then a believer may say his fears are finished, when he is breathing forth his soul into the arms of his sacrificed Savior. The soul shall be without fault before the throne of God.

Read: Hebrews 9:23-28

|ULY 20

WITH FEAR AND TREMBLING

A.T. ROBERTSON | 1954

*Archibald Thomas Robertson (1863-1934) was an American biblical scholar,
theologian, professor, and author.*

People today do not tremble much in the presence of God and most have little
sense of fear. Jonathan Edwards' great sermon on "Sinners in the Hands of an
Angry God" finds little echo today. We live in a light-hearted and complacent
age. The Puritans went too far to one extreme, but we are going too much to the
other. We all need a fresh sense of solemn responsibility to Almighty God.

The Pharisees held to both divine sovereignty and human free agency as
most modern Christians do in varying degrees, to be sure. Paul seems to see no
contradiction between them, as Jesus did not. All our modern efforts to explain
the harmony between these two necessary doctrines fail, but we must hold them
both true nevertheless. God must be supreme to be God at all. Man must be free
to be man at all.

But Paul gives the divine sovereignty as the reason or ground for the human
free agency. He exhorts the Philippians to work out their own salvation with fear
and trembling precisely because God works in them both the willing and the
doing for His good pleasure. We can at least feel that the working of God's will
has provided the whole plan of salvation in which we are included and at which
we are at work. We toil in the sphere of God's will. But we are conscious also that
our own wills have free play in this sphere. God presses His will upon ours. We
feel the impact of the divine energy upon our wills, which are thereby quickened
into activity.

A child can grasp this, and rest upon it. A boy of four said joyfully to his
mother, "When we do anything, it's really God doing it." So then in one sense
God does it all. We were dead in trespasses and sins till God's Spirit touched us
and we leaped to life in Christ. This is the mystery of grace. God plants in our
souls the germ of spiritual life and He does not let it die. His Spirit broods over
us and energizes us to grow and work out what God has worked in us.

READ: PHILIPPIANS 2:11-13

JULY 21

SAVE YOURSELVES

LUKE | C. 62

Luke the Evangelist was an early Christian writer who the church fathers such as
Jerome and Eusebius said was the author of the Gospel of Luke and the Acts of the
Apostles. He is considered one of the Four Evangelists.

Then Peter stood up with the Eleven, raised his voice and addressed the crowd:
"Fellow Jews and all of you who live in Jerusalem, let me explain this to you;
listen carefully to what I say.

"I can tell you confidently that the patriarch David died and was buried,
and his tomb is here to this day. But he was a prophet and knew that God had
promised him on oath that he would place one of his descendants on his throne.
Seeing what was to come, he spoke of the resurrection of the Messiah, that he
was not abandoned to the realm of the dead, nor did his body see decay. God
has raised this Jesus to life, and we are all witnesses of it. Exalted to the right
hand of God, he has received from the Father the promised Holy Spirit and has
poured out what you now see and hear.

"For David did not ascend to heaven, and yet he said, 'The Lord said to my
Lord: "Sit at my right hand until I make your enemies a footstool for your feet."'
Therefore let all Israel be assured of this: God has made this Jesus, whom you
crucified, both Lord and Messiah."

When the people heard this, they were cut to the heart and said to Peter and
the other apostles, "Brothers, what shall we do?"

Peter replied, "Repent and be baptized, every one of you, in the name of Jesus
Christ for the forgiveness of your sins. And you will receive the gift of the Holy
Spirit. The promise is for you and your children and for all who are far off—for
all whom the Lord our God will call."

With many other words he warned them; and he pleaded with them, "Save
yourselves from this corrupt generation." Those who accepted his message were
baptized, and about three thousand were added to their number that day.

READ: ACTS 2

July 22

Whosoever Will

Jacobus Arminius | 16th century

Jacobus Arminius (1560-1609) is the Latinized name of Jakob Hermanszoon, a Dutch theologian and professor during the Protestant Reformation period, whose views became the basis of Arminianism and the Dutch Remonstrant movement.

This doctrine inverts the order of the Gospel of Jesus Christ. For in the Gospel, God requires repentance and faith on the part of man, by promising to him life everlasting, if he consents to become a convert and a believer.

But it is stated in this decree of Predestination, that it is God's absolute will to bestow salvation on certain particular men, and that he willed at the same time absolutely to give those very individuals repentance and faith, by means of an irresistible force, because it was his will and pleasure to save them. By this decree of Predestination it is also taught that God wills not to confer on certain individual men that grace which is necessary for conversion and faith because he has absolutely decreed their condemnation.

The Gospel says, "God so loved the world, that he gave his only begotten Son, that whosoever believeth in him should . . . have everlasting life" (John 3:16 KJV). But this doctrine declares: "God so loved those whom he had absolutely elected to eternal life, as to give his son to them alone, and by an irresistible force to produce within them faith on him." To embrace the whole in few words, the Gospel says, "fulfill the command, and you shall obtain the promise; believe, and you shall live." But this doctrine says, "Since it is my will to give you life, it is therefore my will to give you faith."

I disapprove. This decree, by which God decreed to save and damn certain particular persons, has its foundation in the foreknowledge of God, by which he knew from all eternity those individuals who would, through his grace, believe and persevere; and, by which foreknowledge, he likewise knew those who would not.

Read: John 3:16-17

July 23

At Work in Our World

Harvey Cox | 2010

Harvey Gallagher Cox Jr. (b. 1929) is a preeminent American theologian, scholar, and author who became widely known with the publication of The Secular City *in 1965.*

What does the future hold for religion, and for Christianity in particular? Most important, though often unnoticed, is a profound change in the elemental nature of religiousness. The resurgence of religion was not foreseen. On the contrary, not many decades ago thoughtful writers were confidently predicting its imminent demise. Science, literacy, and more education would soon dispel the miasma of superstition and obscurantism. Religion would either disappear completely or survive in family rituals, quaint folk festivals, and exotic references in literature, art, and music. Religion, we were assured, would certainly never again sway politics or shape culture. But the soothsayers were wrong. Instead of disappearing, religion—for good or ill—is now exhibiting a new vitality all around the world and making its weight widely felt in the corridors of power.

Not only has religion reemerged as an influential dimension of twenty-first-century life; what it means to be "religious" is shifting significantly from what it meant as little as a half century ago. Since religions interact with each other in a global culture, this tremor is shaking virtually all of them, but it is especially evident in Christianity, which in the past fifty years has entered into its most momentous transformation since its transition in the fourth century from what had begun as a tiny Jewish sect into the religious ideology of the Roman Empire.

Scholars of religion refer to the current metamorphosis in religiousness with phrases like the "move to horizontal transcendence" or the "turn to the immanent." But it would be more accurate to think of it as the rediscovery of the sacred in the immanent, the spiritual within the secular. More people seem to recognize that it is our everyday world, not some other one, that, in the words of the poet Gerard Manley Hopkins, "is charged with the grandeur of God."

Read: Acts 2:14-21

JULY 24
THE SCIENCE OF FAITH
CHARLES HODGE | 1873

Charles Hodge (1797-1878) was a Presbyterian theologian, a leading exponent of historical Calvinism, and the principal of Princeton Theological Seminary between 1851 and 1878.

In every department the man of science is assumed to understand the laws by which the facts of experience are determined; so that he not only knows the past, but can predict the future. The astronomer can foretell the relative position of the heavenly bodies for centuries to come. The chemist can tell with certainty what will be the effect of certain chemical combinations.

If, therefore, theology be a science, it must include something more than a mere knowledge of facts. It must embrace an exhibition of the internal relation of those facts, one to another, and each to all. It must be able to show that if one be admitted, others cannot be denied.

God does not teach men astronomy or chemistry, but He gives them the facts out of which those sciences are constructed. Neither does He teach us systematic theology, but He gives us in the Bible the truths which, properly understood and arranged, constitute the science of theology. As the facts of nature are all related and determined by physical laws, so the facts of the Bible are all related and determined by the nature of God and of His creatures.

And as He wills that men should study His works and discover their wonderful organic relation and harmonious combination, so it is His will that we should study His Word, and learn that, like the stars, its truths are not isolated points, but systems, cycles, and epicycles, in unending harmony and grandeur. Besides all this, although the Scriptures do not contain a system of theology as a whole, we have, in the Epistles of the New Testament, portions of that system wrought out to our hands. These are our authority and guide.

READ: 2 TIMOTHY 2:14-16

July 25

In Search of the Kingdom

Henry Suso | 14th century

Henry Suso (c. 1300-1366), also called Amandus, was a German mystic.

Even as the soul of Christ had to descend into hell, before it ascended into heaven, so must the soul of man. And mark how this comes to pass. When a man truly perceives and considers who and what he is, and finds himself wholly base and wicked, and unworthy of all the consolation and kindness that he ever received, either from God or from the creatures, he falls into such a profound abasement and contempt for himself, that he thinks himself unworthy to walk upon the earth.

And therefore he will not and dare not desire any consolation or release, either from God or any creature; and he does not lament for his condemnation and punishment, for they are right and just, and in accordance with God's will. Nothing grieves him but his own guilt and wickedness; for this reason he is heavy and troubled.

This is the meaning of true repentance for sin. And the man who in this life enters into this hell, enters afterwards into the kingdom of heaven, and has a foretaste of that which exceeds all the delights and happiness which he has ever had, or could have, from the things of time. But while a man is in this hell, no one can comfort him, neither God, nor the creatures. Of this condition it has been written, "Let me die, let me perish! I live without hope; from within and from without I am condemned, let no man pray for my deliverance."

Now God has not forsaken man, while he is in this hell, but He is laying His hand upon him, that he may desire nothing but the eternal Good only. When, therefore, the man cares for and seeks and desires the eternal Good and nothing else, and seeks not himself, nor his own things, but the glory of God only, he is made to partake of every kind of joy, blessedness, peace, rest, and comfort, and from that time forward is in the kingdom of God.

Read: Colossians 3:15-17

July 26

Blessed Is

Matthew | c. 84

Matthew the Evangelist was a first-century Galilean tax collector who was chosen by Jesus of Nazareth to be one of the twelve disciples.

Now when Jesus saw the crowds, he went up on a mountainside and sat down. His disciples came to him, and he began to teach them. He said:

"Blessed are the poor in spirit,
for theirs is the kingdom of heaven.
Blessed are those who mourn,
for they will be comforted.
Blessed are the meek,
for they will inherit the earth.
Blessed are those who hunger and thirst for righteousness,
for they will be filled.
Blessed are the merciful,
for they will be shown mercy.
Blessed are the pure in heart,
for they will see God.
Blessed are the peacemakers,
for they will be called children of God.
Blessed are those who are persecuted because of righteousness,
for theirs is the kingdom of heaven.

"Blessed are you when people insult you, persecute you and falsely say all kinds of evil against you because of me. Rejoice and be glad, because great is your reward in heaven, for in the same way they persecuted the prophets who were before you."

Read: Matthew 5

July 27
The Mark of the Believer
Francis Schaeffer | 1970

Francis August Schaeffer (1912-1984) was an American evangelical Christian theologian, philosopher, and Presbyterian pastor.

Through the centuries men have displayed many different symbols to show that they are Christians. They have worn marks in the lapels of their coats, hung chains about their necks, even had special haircuts. Of course, there is nothing wrong with any of this, if one feels it is his calling. But there is a much better sign—one that has not been used just as a matter of expediency on some special occasion or in some specific era. It is a universal mark that is to last through all the ages of the church till Jesus comes back.

What is this mark?

At the close of his ministry, Jesus looks forward to his death on the cross, the open tomb, and the ascension. Knowing that he is about to leave, Jesus prepares his disciples for what is to come. It is here that he makes clear what will be the distinguishing mark of the Christian:

"A new command I give you: Love one another. As I have loved you, so you must love one another. By this all men will know that you are my disciples, if you love one another" (John 13:34-35 NIV).

This passage reveals the mark that Jesus gives to label a Christian, not just in one era or in one locality, but at all times and all places until Jesus returns.

Notice that what he says here is not a description of a fact. It is a command which includes a condition: "By this all men will know that you are my disciples, *if* you love one another" (John 13:35 NIV). An *if* is involved. If you obey, you will wear the badge Christ gave. But since this is a command, it can be violated.

The point is that it is possible to be a Christian without showing the mark, but if we expect non-Christians to know that we are Christians, we must show the mark.

Read: John 13:35

JULY 28

A PICTURE OF HOLINESS

JOHN RYLE | 1879

John Charles Ryle (1816-1900) was the first Anglican bishop of Liverpool.

Holiness is *the habit of being of one mind with God,* according as we find His mind described in Scripture. It is the habit of agreeing in God's judgment—hating what He hates—loving what He loves—and measuring everything in this world by the standard of His Word. He who most entirely agrees with God, he is the most holy man.

A holy man will *endeavor to shun every known sin, and to keep every known commandment.* He will have a decided bent of mind toward God, a hearty desire to do His will—a greater fear of displeasing Him than of displeasing the world, and a love of all His ways. He will feel what David felt when he said, "I esteem all Thy precepts concerning all things to be right, and I hate every false way."

A holy man will *strive to be like our Lord Jesus Christ.* He will not only live the life of faith in Him, and draw from Him all his daily peace and strength, but he will also labor to have the mind that was in Him, and to be "conformed to His image." It will be his aim to bear with and forgive others, even as Christ forgave us—to be unselfish, even as Christ pleased not Himself—to walk in love, even as Christ loved us—to be lowly minded and humble, even as Christ made Himself of no reputation and humbled Himself.

He will remember that Christ was a faithful witness for the truth—that He came not to do His own will—that He would continually deny Himself in order to minister to others—that He was full of love and compassion for sinners—that He was bold and uncompromising in denouncing sin—that He sought not the praise of men, when He might have had it. These things a holy man will try to remember. By them he will endeavor to shape his course in life, asking himself the question, "What would Christ have said and done, if He were in my place?"

READ: EPHESIANS 5:1-3

JULY 29

DISCIPLINE

GEORGE HERBERT | 1633

George Herbert (1593-1633) was a Welsh-born English poet, orator, and Anglican
priest who wrote religious poems throughout his life. He was noted for his unfailing care
for his parishioners.

Throw away thy rod,
Throw away thy wrath:
O my God,
Take the gentle path.

For my heart's desire
Unto thine is bent:
I aspire
To a full consent.

Nor a word or look
I affect to own,
But by book,
And thy book alone.

Though I fail, I weep:
Though I halt in pace,
Yet I creep
To the throne of grace.

Then let wrath remove;
Love will do the deed:
For with love
Stone hearts will bleed.

Love is swift of foot;
Love's a man of war,
And can shoot,
And can hit from afar.

Who can scape his bow?
That which wrought on thee,
Brought thee low,
Needs must work on me.

Throw away thy rod;
Though man frailties hath,
Thou art God:
Throw away thy wrath.

READ: PSALM 136:1-3

July 30

Jesus and the Kingdom

Jürgen Moltmann | 1993

Jürgen Moltmann (b. 1926) is a German Reformed theologian.

Anyone who gets involved with Jesus gets involved with the kingdom of God. This is an inescapable fact, for Jesus' own concern was, and is, God's kingdom. Anyone who looks for God and asks about the kingdom in which "righteousness and peace kiss each another" (Psalm 85:10 NIV) should look at Jesus and enter into the things that happened in his presence and that still happen today in his Spirit. That is obviously and palpably true, for who is Jesus? Simply the kingdom of God in person.

The two belong inseparably together: Jesus and the kingdom of God—the kingdom of God and Jesus. Jesus brings God's kingdom to us human beings in his own unique way and guides us into the breadth and beauty of the kingdom. And God's kingdom makes Jesus the Christ, the savior and deliverer for us all. So if we want to learn what that mysterious "kingdom of God" really is, we have to look at Jesus. And if we want to understand who Jesus really is, we have to experience the kingdom of God.

If we open the New Testament, we find that it doesn't give a definition of the kingdom of God at all. Jesus never explicitly explained "the concept" of the kingdom. "Jesus assumes that what the term means is familiar," says a recent church memorandum in Germany. So one might perhaps think; but it is not in fact true. Jesus provided us with no old or new "concept" of the kingdom of God at all. He brought God's kingdom himself. That is something very different. It is one thing to define the proper concepts about life, and quite another to live rightly. It is one thing to learn a concept of happiness, and another to be happy. And so it is one thing to reduce the kingdom of God to a definition, and quite another to experience it, to feel it, to see it, and to taste it.

READ: MARK 1:15

J U L Y   31

More Than a Religion

Paul Tillich | 1955

Paul Johannes Tillich (1886-1965) was a German-American theologian and philosopher, and one of the most influential Protestant theologians of the twentieth century.

If I were asked to sum up the Christian message for our time, I would say with Paul: It is the message of a "New Creation." We belong to the Old Creation, and the demand made upon us by Christianity is that we also participate in the New Creation. We have known ourselves in our old being, and we shall ask ourselves in this hour whether we also have experienced something of the New Being in ourselves.

What is this New Being? Paul answers first by saying what it is not. It is neither circumcision nor uncircumcision, he says. For Paul and for the readers of this letter, this meant something very definite. It meant that neither to be a Jew nor a pagan is ultimately important; that only one thing counts—namely, the union with Him in whom the New Reality is present.

We read something of the New Creation in Paul's second letter to the Corinthians: "If any one is in Christ, he is a new creature: the old state of things has passed away; a new state of things has come into existence" (2 Corinthians 5:17 Weymouth). Christianity is the message of the New Creation, the New Being, the New Reality, which has appeared with the appearance of Jesus, who for this reason is called the Christ, the Messiah, the selected and anointed one who brings the new state of things.

Circumcision or uncircumcision—what does that mean for us? It can also mean something very definite, but at the same time something very universal. It means that no religion as such produces the New Being. In the words of Paul, we can say: "No religion matters—only a new state of things." Let us think about this striking assertion. What it says first and foremost is that Christianity is more than a religion; it is the message of a New Creation.

Read: 2 Corinthians 5:17-21

August 1

Take up the Cross

Maria Skobtsova | c. 1937

Maria Skobtsova (1891-1945), known as Mother Maria, was a Russian noblewoman, poet, nun, and member of the French Resistance during World War II. She was sent to Ravensbruck concentration camp, where she took the place of a Jewish woman who was going to be sent to the gas chamber, and died in her place.

The meaning and significance of the cross are inexhaustible. The cross of Christ is the eternal tree of life, the invincible force, the union of heaven and earth, the instrument of a shameful death. But how should our crosses resemble the one cross of the Son of Man? For even on Golgotha there stood not one, but three crosses: the cross of the God-man and the crosses of the two thieves.

Are these two crosses not symbols, as it were, of all human crosses, and does it not depend on us which one we choose? For us the way of the cross is unavoidable in any case; we can only choose to freely follow either the way of the blaspheming thief and perish, or the way of the one who called upon Christ and be with Him today in paradise.

What is most essential, most determining in the image of the cross is the necessity of freely and voluntarily accepting it and taking it up. Christ freely, voluntarily took upon Himself the sins of the world, and raised them up on the cross, and thereby redeemed them and defeated hell and death. In taking the cross on his shoulders, man renounces everything—and that means that he ceases to be part of this whole natural world. He ceases to submit to its natural laws, which free the human soul from responsibility.

Natural laws not only free one from responsibility, they also deprive one of freedom. Indeed, what sort of responsibility is it, if I act as the invincible laws of my nature dictate, and where is the freedom, if I am entirely under the law? And so the Son of Man showed his brothers in the flesh a supernatural path of freedom and responsibility. The free path to Golgotha—that is the true imitation of Christ.

Read: Luke 9:22-24

August 2

My Begotten Son

The Gospel of the Hebrews | 2nd century

The Gospel of the Hebrews, sometimes called the Hebrew Gospel, is a lost gospel preserved in fragments within the writings of the church fathers. This non-canonical gospel gives an account of the life and ministry of Jesus of Nazareth, and was believed by early Christian Nazarenes and Ebionites to be the original version of Matthew.

When Christ wished to come upon the earth to men, the good Father summoned a mighty power in heaven, which was called Michael, and entrusted Christ to the care thereof. And the power came into the world and it was called Mary, and Christ was in her womb seven months.

And it came to pass when the Lord was come up out of the water, the whole fount of the Holy Spirit descended upon him and rested on him and said to him: My son, in all the prophets was I waiting for thee that thou should come and I might rest in thee. For thou art my rest; thou art my first-begotten Son that reigneth for ever.

He that marvels shall reign, and he that has reigned shall rest.

He that seeks will not rest until he finds; and he that has found shall marvel; and he that has marveled shall reign; and he that has reigned shall rest.

And never be ye joyful, save when ye behold your brother with love.

And when the Lord had given the linen cloth to the servant of the priest, he went to James and appeared to him. For James had sworn that he would not eat bread from that hour in which he had drunk the cup of the Lord until he should see him risen from among them that sleep. And shortly thereafter the Lord said: Bring a table and bread! And immediately it added: he took the bread, blessed it and brake it and gave it to James the Just and said to him: My brother, eat thy bread, for the Son of man is risen from among them that sleep.

Read: Matthew 27:52-54

AUGUST 3

IN SERVICE OF HIS GREATNESS

MOSES AMYRAUT | 1660

Moses Amyraut (1596-1664) was a French Protestant theologian and metaphysician. He is most noted for his modifications to Calvinist theology regarding the nature of Christ's atonement.

I assert that all the service mortals are able to render to the Supreme Being is reducible to these four principal points; first, Adoration of his excellent nature above all other Beings in the Universe; next, Assurance in his goodness, with expectation of assistance from him in exigencies. Thirdly, the expressing of Thankfulness for benefits already received, and lastly, the embracing and practice of Virtue, in the conduct of life, out of regard and obedience to him.

As to the trust and dependence upon his goodness, the most devout nations have always with good reason esteemed it a principal part of his honor and of his service. For if there be anything that can challenge veneration in the world, it is the power to do good; if any thing love and commendation, it is the will to put that power in use.

Wherefore, whatever is venerable and praiseworthy in the inclinations of men must be in a degree infinitely more eminent in the Deity, as well because of the infinite perfection of his being, as in that he is the force from whence all other things derive the perfections they own; of necessity these two properties are to be found in him: one, that he takes pleasure to expand himself in acts of goodness towards his creatures, and particularly toward mankind, in whom his image is resplendent; the other, that his power to do good is incapable of circumscription.

READ: 1 THESSALONIANS 5:17-19

August 4

An Absolute Claim

Walter Martin | 1965

Walter Ralston Martin (1928-1989) was an American evangelical minister, author, and Christian apologist who founded the Christian Research Institute in 1960.

I must dissent from the view that "all roads that lead to God are good" and believe instead the words of our Lord, "I am the way, the truth, and the life: no man cometh unto the Father, but by me" (John 14:6 KJV). It should be carefully noted that Jesus did not say, "I am one of many equally good ways," or "I am a better way than the others, I am an aspect of truth; I am a fragment of the life." Instead, His claim was absolute, and allegiance to Him, as the Savior of the world, was to take precedence over all the claims of men and religions.

Christ pointed out that the false prophets would come and the history of the heresies of the first five centuries of the Christian church bear out the accuracy of His predictions. Christ further taught that the fruits of the false prophets would also be apparent, and that the church would be able to detect them readily. Let us never forget that "fruits" from a corrupt tree can also be doctrinal, as well as ethical and moral. A person may be ethically and morally "good" by human standards, but if he sets his face against Jesus Christ as Lord and Savior, and rejects Him, his fruit is corrupt, and he is to be rejected as counterfeit.

The apostle John understood this when he wrote, "They went out from us, but they were not of us; for if they had been of us, they would no doubt have continued with us: but they went out, that they might be made manifest that they were not all of us" (1 John 2:19 KJV) The Bible, then, does speak of false prophets, false christs, false apostles, and "deceitful workers, transforming themselves into the apostles of Christ. And no marvel; for Satan himself is transformed into an angel of light. Therefore it is no great thing if his ministers also be transformed as the ministers of righteousness; whose end shall be according to their works" (2 Corinthians 11:13-15 KJV).

Read: John 14:5-7

AUGUST 5

A BETTER CHARTER

EBENEZER ERSKINE | 1746

Ebenezer Erskine (1680-1754) was a Scottish minister whose actions led to the establishment of the Secession Church, formed of dissenters from the Church of Scotland.

Sin robbed us of our title and charter to eternal life; whenever the covenant of works was broken, our charter was gone. But Christ restores a better charter, even the covenant of grace; he himself is "given for a covenant to the people," and is the Alpha and Omega of the covenant; all the promises and blessings of it are "in him yea and amen."

The covenant of works was a frail covenant, a slippery security; but the covenant of grace, and the charter granted to us in Christ, is a lasting charter: "The mountains shall depart, and the hills be removed; but my kindness shall not depart from thee, neither shall the covenant of my peace be removed, saith the LORD that hath mercy on thee" (Isaiah 54:10 KJV).

In short, Christ restores beauty and order again to the whole creation. Whenever man sinned, there fell such a dead weight upon the creation, that the whole of it was like to crumble to its original chaos; but the thing that prevented it was the Son of God bought this earth as a theatre on which his love to sinners might be displayed; therefore he will uphold the theatre till the scene be acted; and when it is acted, he will commit it to the flames.

There is a word to that purpose, "I will preserve thee, and give thee for a covenant of the people, to establish the earth, to cause to inherit the desolate heritages" (Isaiah 49:8). The theatre of this earth was giving way under the weight of the wrath of God; but Christ, being given as a covenant of the people, upholds the earth and all things by the word of his power.

READ: ROMANS 8:18-25

A GLIMPSE AT THE WORLD OF THE EARLY CHURCH

PHILO | C. 50

Philo (20 B.C.-50 A.D.), known also as Philo of Alexandria and Philo the Jew, was a Hellenistic Jewish biblical philosopher born in Alexandria.

For who—when he saw Gaius, after the death of Tiberius Caesar, assuming the sovereignty of the whole world in a condition free from all sedition, and regulated by and obedient to admirable laws, and adapted to unanimity and harmony in all its parts, east and west, south and north; so that they all partook of and enjoyed one common universal peace—could fail to marvel at and be amazed at his extraordinary and unspeakable good fortune, since he had thus succeeded to a ready-made inheritance of all good things.

From the rising to the setting sun, all the land in short on this side of the ocean and beyond the ocean, at which all the Roman people and all Italy rejoiced, and even all the Asiatic and European nations. For accordingly now there was nothing else to be seen in any city, but altars, and victims, and sacrifices, and men clothed in white garments and wearing cheerful countenances, and festivals, and assemblies, and musical contests, and horse races, and revels, and feasts lasting the whole night long, and holidays, and every kind of pleasure addressed to every one of the senses.

But in the eighth month a severe disease attacked Gaius who had changed the manner of his living which was a little while before, while Tiberius was alive, very simple and on that account more wholesome than one of great sumptuousness and luxury; for he began to indulge in abundance of strong wine and eating of rich dishes, and in the abundant license of insatiable desires and great insolence, and in the unseasonable use of hot baths, and emetics, and then again in winebibbing and drunkenness, and returning gluttony, and in lust after boys and women, and in everything else which tends to destroy both soul and body, and all the bonds which unite and strengthen the two; for the rewards of temperance are health and strength, and the wages of intemperance are weakness and disease which bring a man near to death.

READ: EPHESIANS 5:10-12

August 7

Persevere

Polycarp | 154

Polycarp was Bishop of Smyrna (located in modern-day Turkey). He was a student of Ignatius and was martyred in 155.

Be compassionate, merciful to all, bringing back those that have wandered from the faith, caring for all the weak, neglecting neither widow nor orphan nor poor, but always providing for that which is good before God and man. Refrain from wrath, favoritism of the rich, hasty and unfair judgment, greed and love of money. Be slow to believe evil of others and judge them—because we all owe the debt of sin.

If we pray that the Lord forgive us, we also ought to forgive, for we stand before the eyes of the Lord and of God, and we must all appear before the judgment seat of Christ, and each must give an account of himself. So let us serve him with fear and all reverence, as He himself commanded us, and as did the Apostles, who brought us the Gospel, and the Prophets who foretold the coming of our Lord. Let us be zealous for good, refraining from offence, from the false brethren, and from those who bear the name of the Lord in hypocrisy, who deceive empty-minded men.

Let us then persevere unceasingly in our hope, and in the pledge of our righteousness, that is in Christ Jesus, who bore our sins in His own body on the tree, who did no sin, neither was guile found in his mouth. But for our sakes, that we might live in him, he endured all things. Let us then be imitators of his endurance, and if we suffer for his name's sake let us glorify Him. For this is the example which He gave us in himself, and this is what we have believed.

Read: Galatians 6:9-10

August 8

The Work of the Master

A. B. Bruce | 1870

Alexander Balmain Bruce (1831-1899) was a Scottish minister and theologian.

"Follow me," said Jesus, "and I will make you fishers of men" (Matthew 4:19 KJV). These words show that the great Founder of the faith desired not only to have disciples, but those who would make disciples of others: to cast the net of divine truth into the sea of the world, and to land on the shores of the divine kingdom a great multitude of believing souls. Both from His words and actions we can see that He attached supreme importance to that part of His work which consisted in training the twelve, as if it had been the principal part of His own earthly ministry. And such, in one sense, it really was.

The careful, painstaking education of the disciples guaranteed that the Teacher's influence on the world should be permanent. We may say that, but for the twelve, the doctrine, the works, and the image of Jesus might have perished from human remembrance, nothing remaining but a vague mythical tradition, of no historical value and of little practical influence.

Those on whom so much depended required very extraordinary qualifications. They must be superior to all conventional notions of human and divine dignity, capable of glorying in the cross of Christ, and willing to bear a cross themselves. The apostolic character, in short, must combine freedom of conscience, enlargement of heart, enlightenment of mind, and all in the superlative degree.

The humble fishermen of Galilee had much to learn; so much, that the time of their apprenticeship seems all too short. They were indeed godly men, showing the sincerity of their piety by forsaking all for their Master's sake. But at the time of their call they were exceedingly ignorant, narrow-minded, and superstitious, full of Jewish prejudices, misconceptions, and animosities. They had much to unlearn of what was bad, as well as much to learn of what was good, and they were slow both to learn and to unlearn. Men of good honest heart, the soil of their spiritual nature was fitted to produce an abundant harvest; but it needed much laborious tillage before it would yield its fruit.

Read: Mark 1:16-18

August 9

If

Amy Carmichael | 1940

Amy Wilson Carmichael (1867-1951) was a Protestant Christan missionary in India, who opened an orphanage and founded a mission in Dohnavur.

IF . . . I have not compassion on my fellow servant, even as my Lord had pity on me, then I know nothing of Calvary love.

IF . . . I belittle those whom I am called to serve; if I adopt a superior attitude, forgetting "Who made thee to differ? and what hast thou that thou hast not received?" then I know nothing of Calvary love.

IF . . . I can enjoy a joke at the expense of another; if I can in any way slight another in conversation, or even in thought, then I know nothing of Calvary love.

IF . . . I can write an unkind letter, speak an unkind word, think an unkind thought without grief and shame, then I know nothing of Calvary love.

IF . . . I do not forget about such a trifle as personal success, so that it never crosses my mind, or if it does, is never given a moment's room there; if the cup of spiritual flattery tastes sweet to me, then I know nothing of Calvary love.

IF . . . in the fellowship of service I seek to attach a friend to myself, so that others are caused to feel unwanted; if my friendships do not draw others deeper in, but are ungenerous, then I know nothing of Calvary love.

IF . . . I slip into the place that can be filled by Christ alone, making myself the first necessity to a soul instead of leading it to fasten upon Him, then I know nothing of Calvary love.

IF . . . the burdens of others are not my burdens too, and their joys mine, then I know nothing of Calvary love.

IF . . . when an answer I did not expect comes to a prayer which I believed I truly meant, I shrink back from it; if the burden my Lord asks me to bear is not the burden of my heart's choice, and I fret inwardly and do not welcome His will, then I know nothing of Calvary love.

Read: 1 Corinthians 13:1-3

August 10

Adultery and Divorce

Asterius | 4th century

Saint Asterius of Amasea (c. 350-c. 410) was first a lawyer and then a bishop
of Amasea.

This law of self-control is not ordained by God for women alone, but for
men also. But they who give heed to secular lawgivers, and leave to men the
unrestricted license of adultery, while they are stern judges and teachers of the
sanctity of women, are themselves shamelessly licentious. Healers of others,
according to the proverb, they are yet themselves full of sores.

If any one upbraids them with these offenses, they offer a subtle and playful
defense. For men, they say, even if they approach many women, do their own
heart no harm; but women, if they sin, introduce alien heirs into their houses
and families. But let the sophistical inventors of this frivolous justification of
their conduct know that they themselves are overturning other hearths and
homes. For the women with whom they associate are surely the daughters or
wives of somebody.

If the wretch is a father, let him think on the feelings of a father who has been
thus disappointed; if a husband, let him imagine himself the injured man.
For usually it is well that each one judge the affairs of another as he wishes
another to judge his own. And if any, heeding the law of the Romans, consider
fornication permissible, they make a dreadful mistake, not knowing that God
lays down law in one way, while men make statutes in another.

Listen to Moses, as he proclaims the will of God, and utters bitter
condemnation against fornicators. Listen to Paul when he says: "Fornicators and
adulterers God will judge" (Hebrews 13:4 KJV). Other teachers will not be able to
save you in the time of retribution but, trembling and filled with consternation,
they shall melt away. Let those, therefore, whose purpose it is to live with the
very purest wives, make their own manner of life a model for their spouses, in
order that they may maintain in the home a worthy rivalry in virtue.

Read: Ephesians 5:22-28

August 11

For the Journey

Desiderius Erasmus | 1531

Desiderius Erasmus Roterodamus (1466-1536) was a Dutch Renaissance humanist,
Catholic priest, and theologian.

To one that is about to begin any business:

May it prove happy and prosperous for the public good. May God prosper
what you are about. God bless your labors. God bless your endeavors. I pray that
by God's assistance you may happily finish what you have begun. May Christ in
Heaven prosper what is under your hand. May what you have begun end happily.
May what you are set about end happily.

You are about a good work; I wish you a good end of it, and that propitious
Heaven may favor your pious undertakings. Christ give prosperity to your
enterprise. May what you have undertaken prosper. I heartily beg of Almighty
God that this design may be as successful as it is honorable. May the affair so
happily begun, more happily end. I wish you a good journey to Italy, and a
better return.

I pray God that, this journey being happily performed, we may in a short
time have the opportunity of congratulating you upon your happy return. May
it be your good fortune to make a good voyage thither and back again. May
your journey be pleasant, but your return more pleasant. I wish this journey
may succeed according to your heart's desire. May you set sail with promising
presages. I wish this journey may succeed according to both our wishes.

I wish this bargain may be for the good and advantage of us both: a happy
match to us all. The blessed Jesus God keep thee. Kind heaven return you safe.
God keep thee who art one half of my life. I wish you a safe return. I wish that
this New Year may begin happily, go on more happily, and end most happily
to you, and that you may have many of them, and every year happier than
the other.

Read: Deuteronomy 28:12

August 12

Of Fire and Tongues

Donald Gee | 1949

Donald Gee (1891-1966) was an English Pentecostal Bible teacher who wrote the book Wind and Flame, *the story of Pentecostalism in Europe during the twentieth century.*

The Pentecostal movement shares with most sections of the Holiness movement, and some others in the church, the conviction that the baptism in the Holy Spirit, which occurred on the Day of Pentecost as recorded in Acts 2, remains as a separate individual experience possible for all Christians, irrespective of time or place.

The dispensational significance of the gift of the Holy Spirit on the Day of Pentecost is fully recognized; but there were also subsequent repetitions of that blessing. Moreover, for the individual recipient of the baptism in the Spirit it is subsequent to, and distinct from, regeneration, as in the case of Saul of Tarsus, three days after his conversion. Our Lord Himself received the fullness of the Spirit as a separate and distinct enduement of power when He "was about thirty years of age" (see Luke 3:22-23).

The New Testament is clear that the gift of the Spirit in the beginning was invariably witnessed to by some physical manifestation—something others could "see and hear" (Acts 2:33). The most usual and most persistent manifestation was speaking with tongues. In order to safeguard the vital point that the baptism in the Holy Spirit ought to be regarded by Christians as a perfectly definite experience and spiritual crisis for the individual, the Pentecostal movement has consistently taught that speaking with tongues is the scriptural initial evidence of that baptism. This challenging doctrine has proved to be the most provocative feature in the testimony. Sometimes it may not have been presented wisely or well, but Pentecostal people feel that God has entrusted them with this testimony on that point.

Summed up broadly, the distinctive testimony of the Pentecostal movement within the church is to the abiding possibility and importance of the supernatural element in Christian life and service, particularly as contained in the manifestation of the Spirit. The real value of such a witness and such a faith would seem to be beyond question, whatever divergence of view may exist upon details.

Read: Acts 2:1-4

August 13

Into All the World

William Carey | 1792

William Carey (1761-1834) was an English Baptist missionary and minister, known as the "Father of Modern Missions."

That God's kingdom may come, and his will be done on earth as it is in heaven, it becomes us not only to express our desires of that event by words, but to use every lawful method to spread the knowledge of his name. In order to do this, it is necessary that we should become acquainted with the religious state of the world; and an inclination to conscientious activity therein would form one of the strongest proofs that we are the subjects of grace and partakers of that spirit of universal benevolence and genuine philanthropy, which appears so eminent in the character of God himself.

Sin was introduced among the children of men by the fall of Adam and has ever since been spreading its baneful influence. By changing its appearance to suit the circumstances of the times, it has grown up in ten thousand forms and constantly counteracted the will and designs of God. Yet God repeatedly made known his intention to prevail finally over the power of the devil, to destroy all his works, and set up God's own kingdom and extend it as universally as Satan extended his.

It was for this purpose that the Messiah came and died, that God might be just, and the justifier of all that should believe in him. He sent forth the disciples to preach the good tidings to every creature, and to endeavor by all possible methods to bring a lost world to God. They went forth according to their divine commission, and wonderful success attended their labors.

Since the apostolic age many other attempts to spread the gospel have been made, which have been considerably successful, notwithstanding which a very considerable part of mankind are still involved in all the darkness of heathenism. Some attempts are still underway, but they are inconsiderable in comparison with what might be done if the whole body of Christians entered heartily into the spirit of the divine command on this subject. Some think little about, others are unacquainted with, the state of the world, and others love their wealth better than the souls of their fellow creatures.

Read: Mark 16:15-20

AUGUST 14
MERE LOGIC
GORDON CLARK | 1965

Gordon Haddon Clark (1902-1985) was an American philosopher, scholar, and theologian.

"Mere human logic." This phrase seems to be increasing in its use among evangelical speakers and writers. Unfortunately, if followed with consistency, Christianity becomes impossible either to understand or to be coherent. Review all that has been presented here. Then consider: reason, revelation, and logic make up the very fabric of language communication, and there is no other form of communication! Also, who structured human language—God Himself! "Mere human logic" is God's design for human language and communication. To call it "mere" is to deprecate God. He does not create "mere"; He creates great and glorious. Reason, revelation, and logic are great and glorious!

At least one origin of this claim seems to be several systematic theology texts. These theologians seem to have the right intent to take a solid stand for the omniscience of God and the infinite extent to which His mind and understanding exceeds that of man. I have no quarrel with giving God His highest glory in wisdom. However, He has created us in His own image. God chose language and its necessary structure for communication. He pushes His people to understand as much as they are able with His special revelation as the basis and limiting factor for knowledge and truth (Romans 12:2; Colossians 1:9, 2:2). "The secret *things belong* to the LORD our God, but those *things which are* revealed *belong* to us and to our children forever, that *we* may do all the words of this law," (Deuteronomy 29:29). By this statement, an incredible amount of knowledge is needed to be able to obey Him! By this statement, also, an entire system of ethics is named ("this law"). So, "mere human logic" should be changed to "the great logic of God is His image in man."

READ: DEUTERONOMY 29:29

August 15

FOLLOW ONLY CHRIST

JOHN WYCLIFFE | 14TH CENTURY

John Wycliffe (c. 1328-1384), also known as Wycliffe John, was an English theologian, lay preacher, translator, reformist, and university teacher. He is considered the founder of the Lollard movement, a precursor to the Protestant Reformation.

I suppose over this that the gospel of Christ be heart of the corps of God's law; for I believe that Jesus Christ, who gave in his own person this gospel, is very God and very man, and by this heart passes all other laws.

And of this gospel I take as true that Christ for the time that he walked here was the poorest man of all, both in spirit and in having; for Christ says that he had nought for to rest his head on. And Paul says that he was made needy for our love. And more poor might no man be, neither bodily nor in spirit. And thus Christ put from him all manner of worldly lordship. For the gospel of John tells us that when they would have made Christ king, he fled and hid himself from them, for he would have none of such worldly highness.

And over this I believe that no man should follow the Pope, nor any saint that is in heaven, except inasmuch as he follows Christ. For John and James erred when they coveted worldly highness; and Peter and Paul sinned also when they denied and blasphemed Christ; but men should not follow them in this, for then they went from Jesus Christ.

And this I take as wholesome counsel, that the Pope leave his worldly lordship to worldly lords, as Christ gave them—and move speedily all his clerks to do so. For thus did Christ, and taught thus his disciples, till the fiend had blinded this world.

READ: LUKE 18:28-30

August 16

Of Holy Happiness

Thomas Aquinas | c. 1270

Thomas Aquinas (1225-1274) was an Italian Dominican priest and, along with Augustine, the most influential Christian philosopher and theologian through the Middle Ages.

Now man's happiness is twofold. One is proportionate to human nature, a happiness, to wit, which man can obtain by means of his natural principles. The other is a happiness surpassing man's nature, and which man can obtain by the power of God alone, by a kind of participation of the Godhead, about which it is written that by Christ we are made "partakers of the divine nature" (2 Peter 1:4).

And because such happiness surpasses the capacity of human nature, man's natural principles which enable him to act well according to his capacity do not suffice to direct man to this same happiness. Hence it is necessary for man to receive from God some additional principles, whereby he may be directed to supernatural happiness, even as he is directed to his connatural end by means of his natural principles, albeit not without divine assistance. Such like principles are called theological virtues: first, because their object is God, inasmuch as they direct us aright to God; secondly, because they are infused in us by God alone; thirdly, because these virtues are not made known to us, save by divine revelation, contained in Holy Writ.

These virtues are called divine, not as though God were virtuous by reason of them, but because by them God makes us virtuous, and directs us to Himself. Hence they are not exemplar but exemplate virtues. The reason and will are naturally directed to God, inasmuch as He is the beginning and end of nature, but in proportion to nature. But the reason and will, according to their nature, are not sufficiently directed to Him in so far as He is the object of supernatural happiness.

Read: 2 Peter 1:3-4

August 17
In Search of Revival
R. A. Torrey | 1903

Reuben Archer Torrey (1856-1928) was an American evangelist, pastor, educator, and writer.

The history of the church of Jesus Christ on earth has been largely a history of revivals. When you read many of the church histories that have been written the impression that you naturally get is that the history of the church of Jesus Christ here on earth has been largely a history of misunderstandings, disputes, doctrinal differences, and bitter conflicts; but, if you will study the history of the living church, you will find it has been largely a history of revivals.

Humanly speaking, the church of Jesus Christ owes its very existence today to revivals. Time and time again the church has seemed to be on the verge of utter shipwreck; but just then God has sent a great revival and saved it. And if you will study the history of revivals you will find that every real revival in the church has been the result of prayer. There have been revivals without much preaching; there have been revivals with absolutely no organization; but there has never been a mighty revival without mighty praying.

That is what we need more than anything else today, in our own land and in all lands—a mighty outpouring of the Spirit of God. The most fundamental trouble with most of our present-day so-called revivals is that they are man-made and not God-sent. They are worked up (I almost said faked up) by man's cunningly devised machinery—not prayed down. Oh, for an old-time revival, a revival that is really and not spuriously of the Pentecostal pattern. But let us not merely sigh for it; let us cry for it, cry to God, cry long and cry loud if need be, and then it will surely come.

Read: Zechariah 2:10-13

The Spread of "Superstition"

Pliny the Younger | 2nd Century

Gaius Plinius Caecilius Secundus (61-c. 112), better known as Pliny the Younger, was a lawyer, author, and magistrate of Ancient Rome.

I have never participated in trials of Christians. I therefore do not know what offenses it is the practice to punish or investigate, and to what extent. And I have been not a little hesitant as to whether there should be any distinction on account of age or no difference between the very young and the more mature; whether pardon is to be granted for repentance, or, if a man has once been a Christian, it does him no good to have ceased to be one; whether the name itself, even without offenses, or only the offenses associated with the name are to be punished.

Meanwhile, in the case of those who were denounced to me as Christians, I have observed the following procedure: I interrogated these as to whether they were Christians; those who confessed I interrogated a second and a third time, threatening them with punishment; those who persisted I ordered executed. For I had no doubt that, whatever the nature of their creed, stubbornness and inflexible obstinacy surely deserve to be punished. There were others possessed of the same folly; but because they were Roman citizens, I signed an order for them to be transferred to Rome.

These Christians asserted, however, that the sum and substance of their fault or error had been that they were accustomed to meet on a fixed day before dawn and sing responsively a hymn to Christ as to a god, and to bind themselves by oath, not to some crime, but not to commit fraud, theft, or adultery, not falsify their trust, nor to refuse to return a trust when called upon to do so. Accordingly, I judged it all the more necessary to find out what the truth was by torturing two female slaves who were called deaconesses. But I discovered nothing else but depraved, excessive superstition.

I therefore hastened to consult you. For the contagion of this superstition has spread not only to the cities but also to the villages and farms. But it seems possible to check and cure it.

Read: Acts 11:19-24

AUGUST 19

NO DISTANCE IN PRAYER

HUDSON TAYLOR | 1894

James Hudson Taylor (1832-1905) was a British Protestant Christian missionary who served fifty-one years in China and founded the China Inland Mission.

Let me tell you how God answered the prayers of my dear mother for my conversion.

In the afternoon I looked through my father's library to find some book with which to while away the unoccupied hours. Nothing attracting me, I turned over a little basket of pamphlets and selected from among them a gospel tract which looked interesting, saying to myself, "There will be a story at the beginning, and a sermon or moral at the close: I will take the former and leave the latter for those who like it."

I sat down to read the little book in an utterly unconcerned state of mind, believing indeed that if there were any salvation, it was not for me. Little did I know at the same time what was going on in the heart of my dear mother, seventy or eighty miles away.

She arose from the table where she was dining, with an intense yearning for the conversion of her boy. She went to her room and turned the key in the door, resolving not to leave that spot until her prayers were answered. Hour after hour did she plead for me, until at length she could pray no longer, but was constrained to praise God for that which His Spirit taught her had already been accomplished—the conversion of her only son.

I, in the meantime, while reading this little tract was struck with the sentence, "The finished work of Christ." What was finished? Then it came to my mind, "If the whole work of salvation was finished and the whole debt paid, what is there left for me to do?" And with this dawned the joyful conviction, as light flashed into my soul by the Holy Spirit, that there was nothing in the world to be done but to fall down on one's knees and, accepting this Savior and His salvation, to praise Him forevermore.

Thus while my dear mother was praising God on her knees in her chamber, I was praising Him in the old warehouse.

READ: JAMES 5:16

August 20

They That Wait

Matthew Henry | 1706

Matthew Henry (1662-1714) was an English Presbyterian minister and commentator on the Bible who is best known for his Exposition of the Old and New Testaments, *which provides an exhaustive, verse-by-verse study of the Bible.*

Those who deal with God will find it is not in vain to trust in Him; for, one, He is good to those who do so. He is good to all; His tender mercies are over all his works; all His creatures taste of His goodness. But He is in a particular manner good to those who wait for Him, to the soul that seeks Him.

Note, while trouble is prolonged, and deliverance is deferred, we must patiently wait for God and his gracious returns to us. While we wait for Him by faith, we must seek Him by prayer; our souls must seek Him, else we do not seek so as to find. Our seeking will help to keep up our waiting. To those who thus wait and seek, God will be gracious. He will show them His marvelous loving-kindness.

Two, those who do so will find it good for them. It is good (it is our duty, and will be our unspeakable comfort and satisfaction) to hope and quietly wait for the salvation of the Lord; to hope that it will come, though the difficulties that lie in the way of it seem insupportable, to wait till it does come, though it be long delayed; and while we wait, to be quiet and silent, not quarreling with God, nor making ourselves uneasy, but acquiescing in the divine disposals. If we call to mind, "Father, thy will be done," we may have hope that all will end well at last.

Read: Jeremiah 14:22

August 21

In Search of a Better Faith

George Buttrick | 1948

George A. Buttrick (1892-1980) was a British Presbyterian minister, author, scholar, theologian, teacher, and university professor.

A magazine editor, who has both chance and desire to keep his finger on the public pulse, tells of a comment made by a member of his staff. It was spoken, not as from reporter to editor, but man to man in half confession: "There's a vague change. People want to believe something. But what? They look at the church, then look away again—it is not there. What can a man believe?"

Actually the change is not in the fact that "people want to believe something," for human nature has always harbored that want. However much people may want to question and know, far more eagerly they want to believe. Faith is as instinctive as breathing; skepticism at long last is an affront. People not only want to believe; they do believe—something or someone. If they do not believe in God, they try to believe in success or in themselves. When faith in Christ is thwarted or shelved, faith does not cease; as well might a man resolve not to breathe. No, he then sets his faith on gadgets or Hitler or scientism.

Modern man, while repudiating the "sentimentalism" of religious belief, may have sold out to a vast fiction; perhaps he worships his own arguments as the final test of truth. So the "change" indicated by the reporter is not in the fact that "people want to believe something," for that basic want can never change, but in the fact that people are growing tired of modern nostrums and are searching for a better faith.

Read: Romans 3:20-26

THE ROAD TO THE KINGDOM

SAINT BENEDICT | 6TH CENTURY

Saint Benedict of Nursia (480-547) is a Christian saint, often called the founder of Western Christian monasticism. His main achievement is his Rule, *containing precepts for his monks, which became one of the most influential religious rules in Western Christendom.*

My son, pay attention to what the master says. Listen with the ear of your heart. Welcome this advice and carry it out diligently. It comes from a father who loves you. You have drifted away from him through sloth and disobedience. Diligent obedience will bring you back. This message from me is for you if you are ready to abandon your own will, once and for all, and fight for the true King, Christ the Lord, with the strong, noble weapons of obedience.

We plan to establish a school for the Lord's service. We want nothing harsh, nothing burdensome in its regulations. The common good, however, may prompt us to a bit of strictness, to amend faults and preserve love. Don't be intimidated and run off the road leading to salvation, for it is bound to be narrow at the outset. But as we move along in this way of life and in faith, we shall soon be running on the road of God's commandments, our hearts bubbling over with the unspeakable joy of love. Never swerving from his instructions and faithfully following his teaching in the monastery all the days of our life, we shall patiently share in the sufferings of Christ, that we may be found worthy to share in his kingdom.

READ: MATTHEW 7:14

AUGUST 23

EVIDENCE OF MERCY

THOMAS SHEPARD ｜ 17TH CENTURY

Thomas Shepard (1605-1649) was an English minister who emigrated in 1635 to the Massachusetts Colony, where he was regarded as one of the foremost Puritan ministers of his day.

But you will say, "To what end should I perform good works, if I can not be saved by them?" First, to carry you to the Lord Jesus, the only Savior. He only is able to save (not good works) all that come unto God by him. Secondly, use good works as evidences of God's everlasting love to you when you be in Christ; for the graces and duties of God's people, although they be not causes, yet they be tokens and pledges of salvation to one in Christ: they do not save a man, but accompany and follow such a man as shall be saved.

Good works, therefore, being evidences and pledges of salvation, use them to that end, and make much of them therefore. Should a man that has a fair evidence for his lordship, because he did not purchase his lordship, therefore cast it away? No, because it is an evidence to assure him that it is his own; and so, to defend him against all such as seek to take it from him, he will carefully preserve the same. So, because good works do not save you, will you cast them away? No, for they are evidences (if you are in Christ) that the Lord and mercy are your own.

Christ shed his blood that he might purchase unto himself a people zealous of good works, not to save our souls by them, but to honor him. O, let not the blood of Christ be shed in vain! Grace and good works are a Christian's crown; it is sin only that makes a man base. Now, shall a king cast away his crown, because he bought not his kingdom by it? No; because it is his ornament and glory to wear it when he is made a king. So I say to you, it is better that Christ should be honored than your soul saved; and, therefore, perform good works, because they honor the Lord Jesus Christ.

READ: MATTHEW 5:16

AUGUST 24

SHOULD CHRISTIANITY FAIL . . .

J. B. PHILLIPS | 1952

John Bertram Phillips (1906-1982) was an English Bible translator, writer, and clergyman.

The diagnosis of the world's sickness is that the power to love has been wrongly directed. It has either been turned in upon itself or given to the wrong things. The outward symptoms and results of this misdirection are plainly obvious (at least in other people) in what we call "sin" or "selfishness."

The drastic "conversion" which God-become-Man called for is the reversal of the wrong attitude, the deliberate giving of the whole power to love, first to God, and then to other people. Without this reversal He spoke quite bluntly of a world doomed to destruction.

Critics often complain that if the world is in its present state after nineteen centuries of Christianity, then it cannot be a very good religion. They make two ridiculous mistakes. In the first place, Christianity—the real thing—has never been accepted on a large scale and has therefore never been in a position to control "the state of the world," though its influence has been far from negligible. And in the second place, they misunderstand the nature of Christianity. It is not to be judged by its success or failure to reform the world which rejects it. If it failed *where it is accepted* there might be grounds for complaint, but it does not so fail. It is a revelation of the true way of living, the way to know God, the way to live a life of eternal quality, and is not to be regarded as a handy social instrument for reducing juvenile delinquency or the divorce rate.

Any "religion," provided it is accepted by the majority of people, can exert that sort of restrictive pressure. The religion of Jesus Christ changes people (if they are willing to pay the price of being changed) so that they quite naturally live as "sons and daughters of God," and of course they exert an excellent influence on the community. But if real Christianity fails, it fails for the same reasons that Christ failed—and any condemnation rightly falls on the world which rejects both Him and it.

READ: JOHN 12:44-48

AUGUST 25

THE PRAYER OF THE RIGHTEOUS

ORIGEN | 233

Origen (c. 185-254) was an early Christian African scholar and theologian, and one of the most distinguished writers of the early church.

I think I ought to say something about the subjects of prayer. It seems to me that four subjects, which I have found here and there throughout the Scriptures, may be outlined, and that everyone should form his prayer accordingly.

The subjects are these: At the beginning and preamble of the prayer, so far as possible, God is to be glorified, through Christ glorified together with him, in the Holy Spirit hymned together with him. And next in order after this each one must offer general thanksgiving including blessings bestowed on many besides himself, together with those he has personally obtained from God.

After thanksgiving, it seems to me that he ought to accuse himself bitterly before God of his own sins, and then ask God, first for healing that he may be delivered from the habit that causes him to sin, and secondly for forgiveness of the past. After confession, it seems to me that in the fourth place he should add his request for great and heavenly things, his own and general, and also for his family and his dearest. And finally, having begun by glorifying God, it is fitting to conclude and bring the prayer to an end by glorifying him, hymning and glorifying the Father of the universe through Jesus Christ in the Holy Spirit, "to whom be the glory for ever."

READ: LUKE 11:1-4

August 26

Living Stones

Adam Clarke | 1826

Adam Clarke (1760-1832) was a British Methodist theologian and biblical scholar. He is primarily remembered for writing a commentary on the Bible, which took him forty years to complete and was a primary Methodist theological resource for 200 years.

Many talk much, and indeed well, of what Christ has done for us; but how little is spoken of what he is to do *in* us! He was incarnated, suffered, died, and rose again from the dead; ascended to heaven, and there appears in the presence of God for us. These were all saving, atoning, and mediating acts for us; that he might reconcile us to God; that he might blot out our sin; that he might purge our consciences from dead works; that he might bind the strong man armed—take away the armor in which he trusted, wash the polluted heart, destroy every foul and abominable desire, all tormenting and unholy tempers; that he might make the heart his throne, fill the soul with his light, power, and life; and, in a word, "destroy the works of the devil."

These are done in us; without which we cannot be saved unto eternal life. But these acts done in us are consequent on the acts done for us: for had he not been incarnated, suffered, and died in our stead, we could not receive either pardon or holiness; and did he not cleanse and purify our hearts, we could not enter into the place where all is purity: for the beatific vision is given only to them who are purified from all unrighteousness, for it is written, "Blessed are the pure in heart: for they shall see God" (Matthew 5:8 KJV).

Nothing is purified by death—nothing in the grave; nothing in heaven. The living stones of the temple, like those of that at Jerusalem, are hewn, squared, and cut here, in the church militant, to prepare them to enter into the composition of the church triumphant. This perfection is the restoration of man to the state of holiness from which he fell, by creating him anew in Christ Jesus, and restoring to him that image and likeness of God which he has lost.

Read: Hebrews 10:10-17

August 27

A Little Drop of Grace

Johannes Tauler | 14th century

Johannes Tauler (c. 1300-1361) was a German mystic theologian.

All works which men and all creatures can ever work, even to the end of the world, without the grace of God—all of them together, however great they may be, are an absolute nothing, as compared with the smallest work which God has worked in men by His grace. As much as God is better than all His creatures, so much better are His works than all the works, or wisdom, or designs, which all men could devise.

Even the smallest drop of grace is better than all earthly riches that are beneath the sun. Yea, a drop of grace is more noble than all angels and all souls, and all the natural things that God has made. And yet grace is given more richly by God to the soul than any earthly gift. It is given more richly than brooks of water, than the breath of the air, than the brightness of the sun; for spiritual things are far finer and nobler than earthly things.

The whole Trinity—Father, Son, and Holy Ghost—gives grace to the soul, and flows immediately into it; even the highest angel, in spite of his great nobility, cannot do this. Grace looses us from the snares of many temptations; it relieves us from the heavy burden of worldly cares, and carries the spirit up to heaven, the land of spirits. It kills the worm of conscience, which makes sins alive. Grace is a very powerful thing. The man to whom cometh but a little drop of the light of grace, to him all that is not God becomes as bitter as gall upon the tongue.

Read: 2 Corinthians 12:9

AUGUST 28

NOT BY WORKS

W. A. CRISWELL | 1963

Wallie Amos Criswell (1909-2002) was an American pastor and author, twice elected president of the Southern Baptist Convention, and described by many as one of the twentieth century's greatest expository preachers.

"Blessed are they that wash their robes," that trust in Jesus, that look in faith to Him, asking Him for forgiveness and mercy. John didn't write, "Blessed are they that do good and that pay their debts and that are honest, and that are virtuous, and that are clean, and that obey the commandments." All of these things we do because of what God has done for us.

But we don't do those things in order to find forgiveness of sin and a right of entrance into the city of God. All the good works we do are out of hearts of love and gratitude for what God has done for us, but no man earns his way by doing these good things, by being baptized, by joining the church, by observing the Lord's Supper, by being an honest and an upright citizen. No man earns his way into Heaven by doing good works.

While Paul and Barnabas were preaching that a man could be saved by trusting Jesus, the sect of the Pharisees that belonged to the church at Jerusalem, who had been converted and baptized, but were still legalists, came down to Antioch and said, "You can't be saved. Why, you heathen, you came right out of idolatry into the faith of Jesus. You can't be saved. You've got to keep the Law of Moses."

Centuries later, while Martin Luther, a monk, was climbing on his knees up the Sancta Scala, the so-called sacred stairway in Rome, supposed to be the stairway that Jesus walked up when he went into Pilate's judgment hall—halfway up he suddenly stopped. There came a ringing verse out of Habakkuk, and Romans, and Galatians, and Hebrews that struck a fire in his soul. The verse was this: "The just, those that are justified by God, shall live by faith and not by works" (see Habakkuk 2:4; Romans 1:17; Galatians 3:11; and Hebrews 10:38 KJV).

READ: EPHESIANS 2:8-9

AUGUST 29

LEARN GLADLY

HUGH | 12TH CENTURY

Hugh of Saint Victor (c. 1096-1141) was appointed a canon of the Victorine canons around the turn of the twelfth century and quickly made a name for himself for being a very well-read and educated person.

The prudent scholar, therefore, hears everyone freely, reads everything, and rejects no book, no person, no doctrine. He seeks from all indifferently what he sees is lacking in himself; he considers not how much he may know, but how much he may not know. Hence the Platonic saying: "I prefer to learn modestly from another, rather than shamelessly to thrust forward my own knowledge." Why are you ashamed to learn and not ashamed to be ignorant? This is more shameful that that. Or why do you strive for the heights, when you are lying in the depths?

Consider rather what your powers are strong enough to bear. He advances most suitably who proceeds in an orderly way. When some desire to make a great leap, they fall into the abyss. Do not, therefore, hasten too fast, and thus you will more quickly achieve wisdom. Learn gladly from everyone what you do not know, since humility can make yours that which nature made the possession of someone else. You will be wiser than everyone, if you will learn from everyone. Those who receive from everyone are richer than anyone.

Finally, hold no knowledge cheap, since all knowledge is good. If there is time, scorn no writing, or at least read it, since if you gain nothing, you will lose nothing, especially as in my estimation there is no book which does not set forth something to be desired. If it is treated in an appropriate place and order, there is none which does not have something special, which the diligent reader has found nowhere else. The rarer it is, the more gratefully it should be enjoyed. Yet there is nothing good which is not made better.

READ: 2 PETER 1:5-8

August 30
Who Shall Separate Us?
Paul | c. 56

Paul the Apostle, (c. 5 A.D.-c. 67) also called the apostle Paul, Saul of Tarsus, and Saint Paul, was one of the most influential early Christian missionaries. His writings formed a considerable portion of the New Testament.

What, then, shall we say in response to these things? If God is for us, who can be against us? He who did not spare his own Son, but gave him up for us all—how will he not also, along with him, graciously give us all things?

Who will bring any charge against those whom God has chosen? It is God who justifies. Who then is the one who condemns? No one. Christ Jesus who died—more than that, who was raised to life—is at the right hand of God and is also interceding for us.

Who shall separate us from the love of Christ? Shall trouble or hardship or persecution or famine or nakedness or danger or sword? As it is written: "For your sake we face death all day long; we are considered as sheep to be slaughtered."

No, in all these things we are more than conquerors through him who loved us. For I am convinced that neither death nor life, neither angels nor demons, neither the present nor the future, nor any powers, neither height nor depth, nor anything else in all creation, will be able to separate us from the love of God that is in Christ Jesus our Lord.

Read: John 10:27-30

AUGUST 31

NEW LIFE FOR DRY BONES

ROBERT MCCHEYNE | 19TH CENTURY

Robert Murray McCheyne (1813–1843) was a minister in the Church of Scotland from 1835 to 1843, until his early death during an epidemic of typhus.

These bones were dead, dry, spiritless, lifeless, without flesh, without ears to hear; and yet God says: "Prophesy upon these bones, and say unto them, O ye dry bones, hear the word of the LORD." And while he prophesied "there was a noise, and behold a shaking, and the bones came together, bone to his bone. And when I beheld, lo, the sinews and the flesh came up upon them, and the skin covered them above" (see Ezekiel 37:4-8 KJV).

The effects produced by the prophesying of Ezekiel to the dry bones were very remarkable. The bones came together, bone to his bone; the flesh, the sinews, the skin came up upon them, and covered them; but still there was no breath in them—they were as dead as ever. And, oh! how like this is to the effects which often follow on the preaching of the Word.

How often are people outwardly reformed! Instead of Sabbath breaking, there is Sabbath observance; instead of drunkenness, sobriety—the form of godliness, but none of the power. The bones, sinews, flesh, and skin of godliness, but none of the living breath of godliness. Ah! my friends, is not this just the way with our congregations at this day? Abundance of head knowledge, but where is the lowly heart that loves the Savior? Abundance of orthodoxy and argument, but where is the simple faith in the Lord Jesus, and love to all the saints?

Does not the Savior say, when he looks down on our churches: "There is no breath in them"? Oh! Then, brethren, let us, one and all, give heed to the second command to the prophet: "Prophesy unto the Spirit, son of man; say, Come from the four winds, O Spirit, and breathe upon these slain, that they may live. So I prophesied as he commanded, and the breath came into them, and they lived, and stood up upon their feet, an exceeding great army" (see Ezekiel 37:9-10).

READ: MATTHEW 24:31

September 1

No Retreat

George Kulp | 20th century

George Brubaker Kulp (1845-1939) was an American preacher, pastor, soldier, and author who was known for his fiery, no-nonsense style.

A Christian is one who reproduces the life of Christ, and that only is Christianity which produces the work of Christ. You do not alter a thing, or the nature of it, because you put a label on it. Christianity must prove itself. It must prove by its works that it is of God. The Church itself must prove its right to exist, and it does it only as it manifests the spirit of Christ, and reproduces His works. Men are asking that the Church today do as it did in the days of the apostles.

We need what they had, we want what they had; that when the critic and the opposer shall find fault with the work we are doing, they will not be able to do it successfully, because the man stands in our midst who has been blessed, aye, and lifted up, a new creature in Christ Jesus. I have a very firm conviction that any preacher, any church, any denomination that comes to the end of the year and then makes a report like this, "We have held our own," causes hell to have a jubilee. The orders are, "Forward, March." We are never to camp twice in the same place. Get so far along each day that you can never see the ashes of your last campfire.

We have no business standing still. We need, we must have, trophies every day to prove that we belong to Christ. The people are crying out, "Oh, for the days of the Fathers." Hear God's Word, "Say not that the former days were better than these, for thou inquirest not wisely concerning this" (see Ecclesiastes 7:10). Today as ever in the past, faith is the victory. That is true, or God is not. Today we ought to be better able to take the journey that Abraham took.

Read: Acts 4:20

SEPTEMBER 2

A LAST WILL AND TESTAMENT

FRANCIS OF ASSISI | 1226

Saint Francis of Assisi (c. 1181-1226), one of the most venerated religious figures in history, was an Italian Catholic friar and preacher who founded the Franciscan Order.

While I was still in my sins, it seemed to me bitterly unpleasant to see lepers, but the Lord led me among them and gave me pity for them. And when I left them, that which had been bitter to me was turned into sweetness of soul and body.

And the Lord gave me such faith in churches that I knelt in simplicity and said, "We adore thee, most holy Lord Jesus Christ, and all thy churches which are in the world, and we bless thee because thou hast redeemed the world through thy holy cross."

And afterward, the Lord gave me brothers, and no one showed me what I ought to do, but the Lord himself revealed to me that I ought to live according to the form of the holy gospel, and I caused it to be written in a few simple words. And the pope confirmed the rule. And those who came to adopt this life gave all they had to the poor.

And I labored with my hands, and I wish all my brothers to engage in some honest work. And those who do not know how, shall learn; not because of the desire to receive wages for their labor, but to set a good example and to escape idleness.

And the brothers shall not say that this is another rule, because it is only a reminder, an admonition, an exhortation, and my testament, which I, your poor brother, Franciscus, make for you, that we wholly observe the rule which we have promised to the Lord.

And whoever shall observe them shall be filled in heaven with the blessing of the most high heavenly Father, and in the earth he shall be filled with the benedictions of His Son, with the most holy Spirit, and with all the virtues of heaven and of all the saints. And I, your poor brother and servant, Franciscus, as far as I can, confirm to you, within and without, that most holy benediction. Amen.

READ: ROMANS 12:1

SEPTEMBER 3

CHRISTIANITY AND CIVILIZATION

RICHARD NIEBUHR | 1951

Helmut Richard Niebuhr (1894-1962) was an American author, theologian, and scholar, and one of the most important Christian theological-ethicists of the twentieth century.

A many-sided debate about the relations of Christianity and civilization is being carried on in our time. Historians and theologians, statesmen and churchmen, Christians and anti-Christians participate in it. It is carried on publicly by opposing parties and privately in the conflicts of conscience. Sometimes it is concentrated on special issues, such as those of the place of Christian faith in general education or of Christian ethics in economic life. Sometimes it deals with broad questions of the church's responsibility for social order or of the need for a new separation of Christ's followers from the world.

When it seems that the issue has been clearly defined as lying between the exponents of a Christian civilization and the non-Christian defenders of a wholly secularized society, new perplexities arise as devoted believers seem to form a common cause with secularists; for instance, calling for the elimination of religion from public education, or for the Christian support of apparently anti-Christian political movements.

In this situation it is helpful to remember that the question of Christianity and civilization is by no means a new one; that Christian perplexity in this area has been perennial, and that the problem has been an enduring one through all the Christian centuries. It is helpful also to recall that the repeated struggles of Christians with this problem have yielded no single Christian answer, but only a series of typical answers which together, for faith, represent phases of the strategy of the militant church in the world.

In attempting to set forth typical Christian answers to the problem of Christ and culture and in so doing contribute to the mutual understanding of variant and often conflicting Christian groups, we must acknowledge the conviction that Christ as living Lord is answering the question in the totality of history and life in a fashion which transcends the wisdom of all his interpreters, yet employs their partial insights and their necessary conflicts.

READ: ISAIAH 55:8-9

SEPTEMBER 4

WORTHY OF DESIRE

BASIL THE GREAT | 4TH CENTURY

Basil of Caesarea (330-379), also called Saint Basil the Great, was the bishop of Caesarea Mazaca in Cappadocia. He was an influential fourth-century Christian theologian and monastic known for his care of the poor and underprivileged.

We Christians hold that this human life is not a supremely precious thing, nor do we recognize anything as unconditionally a blessing which benefits us in this life only. Neither pride of ancestry, nor bodily strength, nor beauty, nor greatness, nor the esteem of all men, nor kingly authority, nor, indeed, whatever of human affairs may be called great, do we consider worthy of desire or the possessors of them as objects of envy; but we place our hopes upon the things which are beyond, and in preparation for the life eternal do all things that we do. Accordingly, whatever helps us toward this we say that we must love and follow after with all our might, but those things which have no bearing upon it should be held as naught.

Into the life eternal the Holy Scriptures lead us, which teach us through divine words. But so long as our immaturity forbids our understanding their deep thought, we exercise our spiritual perceptions upon profane writings, which are not altogether different, and in which we perceive the truth as it were in shadows and in mirrors. Thus we imitate those who perform the exercises of military practice, for they acquire skill in gymnastics and in dancing, and then in battle reap the reward of their training.

We must believe that the greatest of all battles lies before us, in preparation for which we must do and suffer all things to gain power. Consequently we must be conversant with poets, with historians, with orators, indeed with all men who may further our soul's salvation. Just as dyers prepare the cloth before they apply the dye, be it purple or any other color, so indeed must we also, if we would preserve indelible the idea of the true virtue, become first initiated in the pagan lore, then at length give special heed to the sacred and divine teachings, even as we first accustom ourselves to the sun's reflection in the water, and then become able to turn our eyes upon the very sun itself.

READ: MATTHEW 13:44

When Innocent Blood Cries Out

John Woolman | 1754

John Woolman (1720-1772) was an American itinerant Quaker preacher who traveled throughout the American colonies, advocating against conscription, military taxation, and particularly slavery.

Where blood has been shed unrighteously, and remains unatoned for, the cry thereof is very piercing. Under the humbling dispensations of divine Providence, this cry has deeply affected my heart, and I feel a concern to open, as I may be enabled, that which lies heavy on my mind. He who of old heard the groans of the children of Israel under the hard taskmasters in Egypt, I trust has looked down from His holy habitation on the miseries of these deeply oppressed people.

The unoffending aged and infirm made to labor too hard, kept on a diet less comfortable than their weak state requires, and exposed to great difficulties under hard-hearted men, to whose sufferings I have been a witness. Innocent youth taken by violence from their native land, from their friends and acquaintances; put on board ships with hearts laden with sorrow; exposed to great hardships at sea; placed under people, where their lives have been attended with great provocation to anger and revenge.

With the condition of these youth, my mind has often been affected, as with the afflictions of my children, and in a feeling of the misery of these people, and of that great offense which is ministered to them, my tears have often poured out before the Lord.

That Holy Spirit which affected my heart when I was a youth, I trust is often felt by the Negroes in their native land, inclining their minds to that which is righteous, and had the professed followers of Christ in all their conduct toward them manifested a disposition answerable to the pure principle in their hearts, how might the Holy Name have been honored among the Gentiles. But in the present state of things, how contrary is this practice to that meek Spirit, in which our Savior laid down His life for us, that all the ends of the Earth might know salvation in His name.

Read: Jeremiah 22:3

SEPTEMBER 6
THE LIVING HOPE
J. I. PACKER | 1973

James Innell Packer (b. 1926) is a British-born Canadian theologian in the low-church Anglican and Reformed traditions. He is considered one of the most influential evangelicals in North America.

Suppose that Jesus, having died on the cross, had stayed dead. Suppose that, like Socrates or Confucius, he was now no more than a beautiful memory. Would it matter? We should still have his example and teaching; wouldn't that be enough? Enough for what?

Not for Christianity. Had Jesus not risen, but stayed dead, the bottom would drop out of Christianity, for four things would then be true.

First, to quote Paul, "if Christ has not been raised, your faith is futile; you are still in your sins" (1 Corinthians 15:17 NIV).

Second, there is then no hope for our rising either; we must expect to stay dead too.

Third, if Jesus Christ is not risen, then he is not reigning and will not return and every single item in the Apostles' Creed after "suffered and was buried" will have to be struck out.

Fourth, Christianity cannot be what the first Christians thought it was—fellowship with a living Lord who is identical with the Jesus of the Gospels. The Jesus of the Gospels can still be your hero, but he cannot be your Savior. . . .

Jesus' resurrection marked Jesus out as Son of God (Romans 1:4); it vindicated his righteousness (John 16:10); it demonstrated victory over death (Acts 2:24); it guaranteed the believer's forgiveness and justification (1 Corinthians 15:17; Romans 4:25); and it brings him into the reality of resurrection life now (Romans 6:4).

Marvelous!

You could speak of Jesus' rising as the most hopeful—hope-full—thing that has ever happened, and you would be right!

READ: MARK 16:6

S E P T E M B E R   7

THE HOLY SPIRIT AT WORK

AUGUSTINE | 5TH CENTURY

Augustine (354-430) was bishop of Hippo Regius and one of the most important figures in the development of Western Christianity. After his conversion, Augustine developed his own approach to philosophy and theology, accommodating a variety of methods and perspectives.

If you wish to have the Holy Spirit, mark this well, my brethren. Our spirit by which man is a living being is called the soul, . . . so you see what the soul does in the body. It gives life to all the members; it sees through the eyes, it hears through the ears, it smells through the nostrils, it talks through the tongue, it works through the hands, it walks through the feet; it is present at one and the same time to all the members so that they may live; to each it gives life, to each it assigns its duty.

The eye does not hear, nor the ear see, nor the tongue see, nor does the ear or eye talk; but yet it lives, the ear lives, the tongue lives; their duties are diverse, life they share in common. So is the church of God: in some saints she works miracles, in other saints she preaches the truth, in others she protects virginity, in yet others she preserves conjugal chastity, in some she does one thing, in others another; all do that which is severally proper to them, but all share life in an equal degree.

Now what the soul is to the body of man, that the Holy Spirit is in the body of Christ, which is the church. The Holy Spirit does that in the whole church, which the soul does in all the members of a single body. . . . If therefore you wish to live by the Holy Spirit, hold fast to charity, love truth, long for unity, so that you may attain to eternity.

READ: COLOSSIANS 3:14-16

A HIGHER CALLING

DANIEL STEELE | 1875

Daniel Steele (1824-1914) was a Methodist Episcopal pastor and professor and the first great Bible scholar and theologian of the Holiness movement.

My brother or sister in Christ Jesus: permit an older soldier to offer a few words of advice to a new recruit in the army of the Lord. An ancient writer has wisely said that there have been from the beginning two orders of Christians. The one lives a harmless life, doing many good works, abstaining from gross evils, and attending the ordinances of God, but waging no downright earnest warfare against the world, nor making strenuous efforts for the promotion of Christ's kingdom, nor aiming at special spiritual excellence, but at the average attainments of their neighbors.

The other class of Christians not only abstains from every form of vice, but they are zealous of every kind of good works. They attend all the ordinances of God. They use all diligence to attain the whole mind that was in Christ, and to walk in the very footsteps of their beloved Master. They unhesitatingly trample on every pleasure which disqualifies for the highest usefulness. They deny themselves, not only of indulgences expressly forbidden, but of those which by experience they have found to diminish their enjoyment of God. They take up their cross daily.

They are not Quietists, ever lingering in secret places delighting in the ecstasies of enraptured devotion; they go forth from the closet, as Moses came from the mount of God, with faces radiant with the divine glory. Men tremble before them as Satan in *Paradise Lost*, when he first saw the sinless pair in Eden "trembled to behold how awful goodness is."

Next to the power of Jesus, the living Head, these earnest believers preserve and perpetuate the Church from age to age. The secret of their strength is that they, by the guidance of the Spirit, found the King's highway up the summit of Christian holiness. They strove, they agonized to plant their feet on that sunlit height. They have left the first principles of the doctrine of Christ and have gone on to perfection.

READ: JAMES 2:24

SEPTEMBER 9

SUBMISSION TO HIS WILL

HUGH BINNING | 1650

Hugh Binning (1627-1653) was a Scottish philosopher, and regent and professor of philosophy at the University of Glasgow.

There is nothing wherein I know Christians more deficient than in this point of submission, which I take to be one of the greatest and sweetest, though hardest duties of a Christian. It is hardly to be found among men—a real subjection of our spirits to His goodwill and pleasure. There is nothing so much blessed in Scripture as waiting on Him, as yielding to Him to be disposed upon: "Blessed are all they that wait on Him."

Pride is the greatest opposite, and He opposes Himself most to that, for it is in its own nature most derogatory to the highness and majesty of God, which is His very glory. Therefore submission is most acceptable to Him, when the soul yields itself and its will to Him. He condescends far more to it; He cannot be an enemy to such a soul. Submission to His Majesty's pleasure, is the very bowing down of the soul willingly to anything He does or commands—whatever yoke He puts on, of duty or suffering, to take it on willingly, without answering again, which is the great sin condemned in servants; to put the mouth in the dust, and to keep silence, simply because He does it.

There is submission indeed—silence of mind and mouth—a restraint put upon the spirit to think nothing grudgingly of Him for anything He does. Your impatience cannot help you, but hurt you; quiet and silent stooping makes it easy in itself and brings in more help beside, even divine help. Learn to obey Him simply because He commands, and by this means you shall in due time have more sweet peace and real gain, though you intend it not. Commit your way wholly to Him, and let Him do what He pleases. Be not anxious in that, but be diligent, and you shall only gain by it; besides, the honor redounds to Him.

READ: JOB 22:21

September 10
Sanctified by the Spirit
Abraham Kuyper | 1900

Abraham Kuyper (1837-1920) was a Dutch politician, journalist, statesman, and theologian. He founded the Anti-Revolutionary Party and was prime minister of the Netherlands from 1901-1905.

It should be emphasized that sanctification does not imply human efforts and exertions to supplement Christ's work, but it is the additional grace of supernaturally creating a holy disposition in the saint. Sin imparts pollution, i.e., there can be no sin without begetting sin. Sin generates sin; it is always the mother of sin. If this sin-begetting process were not stopped in our hearts, sin's chain would remain unbroken, link upon link, and only sin would be the result.

But this is not the divine purpose. God wills that men should see our good works and glorify the Father which is in heaven. Therefore God has prepared good works that we should walk in them. But if the stain of sin were to work in us without any interruption, not one of us could ever do a single good work. Light would never shine in the children of light, and there would be no occasion to glorify the Father in heaven.

Good works wrought in us by the Holy Spirit independently of us cannot offer such occasion. His works are always holy; there is nothing surprising in that. But when He causes holy works to proceed from us in such a way that they are truly our own, then there is occasion for praise. Then men will ask in surprise, "Who wrought this in them?" and looking up, will glorify the Father.

The indwelling Spirit is the actual Worker. He performs it in all the saints, not partly, but wholly, both in life and in death, or in the hour of death alone. The latter applies to elect children, to idiots and insane persons, and to persons converted on their deathbed. In all others He performs it during their lifetime and in the hour of their departure.

Read: 1 Corinthians 6:11

SEPTEMBER 11

NOT OF THE WORLD

JACQUES DE VITRY | 13TH CENTURY

Jacques de Vitry (c. 1160-1240) was a French theologian, chronicler, and cardinal from 1229-1240.

For some time I was at the Papal Court (of Pope Honorius III at Perugia), where I saw much that distressed me. Everybody was so preoccupied with secular and temporal matters, pertaining to kings and kingdoms, to disputes and lawsuits, that one could hardly speak of spiritual things.

One solace, however, I have found in these parts. Great numbers of men and women, many of them worldly and wealthy, have forsaken everything for Christ and abandoned the world. They are called Brothers Minor, and the Pope and the Cardinals hold them in great esteem. They do not trouble at all about temporal things but strive every day with fervent longing and vehement zeal to save souls which are in danger, detaching them from the world and guiding them. Already by the grace of God they have reaped a rich harvest, gaining many souls.

They live according to the tenets of the primitive church, of which it is written, "the multitude of them that believed were of one heart and of one soul" (Acts 4:32 KJV). In daytime they go out into the towns and villages, so as to harvest souls by active work; at night they return to the hermitage or some solitary retreat and practice meditation.

The women enclose themselves in various hospices near the towns; they accept no gifts, but live by the work of their hands. It distresses and perturbs them when clerics and laymen honor them more than they desire.

The men of the order meet once a year with great spiritual gain, at an appointed place, so that they can rejoice in God and eat together, take counsel with good men and promulgate their holy institutions, which are confirmed by the Pope. Then they disperse again for a year and go to Lombardy, Tuscany, Apulia, and Sicily. Even the Pope's secretary, Brother Nicolas, a holy and religious man, left the court so as to join them, but he was called back by the Pope, to whom he is indispensable.

READ: 2 CORINTHIANS 6:16-18

THE CHRIST INVASION

DAVID BURRELL | 19TH CENTURY

David James Burrell (1844-1926) was an American professor, writer, preacher, and pastor of the Marble Collegiate Church in New York City, the oldest continuing Protestant congregation in the United States.

The Incarnation was an invasion. God crossed the border into the territory of Earthly Power. No trumpets were heard, no roar of artillery disturbed the quiet of the early morning. A mother sat crooning to an Infant in her arms. That was all; but it was the first note of the onset. What could be more helpless than the pink, dimpled hand that lay upon that mother's breast? Yet that hand was destined to cut the sinews of Roman supremacy and change the currents of history through the ages.

We do not see the Child and the Emperor come face to face until the Child has grown to manhood. His ministry is under way. He has gone up and down among the villages preaching, working wonders, troubling the corrupt times. He enters Jerusalem at length and begins to preach. Herod, desirous of making an end of his influence, presumes to threaten him. But Jesus sees through the shallow device of the intriguing court. Observe his calm disdain: "Behold I cast out devils and do cures today and tomorrow, and the third day I shall be perfected. I must walk today and tomorrow and the day following; for it cannot be that a prophet shall perish out of Jerusalem" (see Luke 13:32-33). And the work goes on.

It is the story of the centuries. "Let loose the lions!" cries Caesar. "We will make an end of the Nazarene and his religion!" But the blood of the martyrs is ever the seed of the Church. So runs the Parable of Progress: "The kingdom of heaven is like to a grain of mustard seed, which a man took and sowed in his field: which indeed is the least of all seeds: but when it is grown, it is the greatest among herbs, and becometh a tree" (Matthew 13:31-32 KJV).

READ: MATTHEW 2:7-8

September 13

From Your Abundance

Gregory Palamas | 14th century

Gregory Palamas (1296-1359) was a monk of Mount Athos in Greece and later the archbishop of Thessaloniki.

If you fail to notice your suffering brothers—that is, Christ's brothers—and refuse to share your abundant food, shelter, clothing, and care with the needy, if you withhold your surplus rather than attend to their needs, then listen carefully and groan; indeed, it is we ourselves who should listen and groan—I who speak these things stand accused. My conscience testifies that I am not entirely free of passion. While some may shiver and go without, I eat well and am nicely clothed.

But even more to be mourned are those with treasures beyond their daily needs who cling to them, even seek to expand their holdings. Though commanded to love their neighbor as themselves, they have not loved their neighbor even as much as they have loved dust—for it is gold and silver that they have loved, and what are gold and silver but dust?

Read: 2 Corinthians 9:7-9

September 14

Above Fear

Ephrem | 4th century

Ephrem the Syrian (c. 306-373) was a Syriac and a prolific Syriac-language hymnographer and theologian who wrote a wide variety of hymns, poems, and sermons in verse, as well as prose biblical exegesis.

Whoever is steeped in love like a child is above fear; and whoever is timorously subject to fear, vain terror always tortures him. It helps athletes too in a competition to be above fear through the encouragement of a good hope, and not to fall under the sickly apprehensions which result from a timorous habit of thought. Athletes perhaps (might) well fear because the victor is crowned and the loser suffers shame, for they do not divide the victory between the two of them.

But not only upon us weak ones does the constraint of fear fall, but even upon the heroes and valiant themselves. Nor have I said this in order to find comfort for our folly, but that we might remind thy wisdom. For when Peter despised fear and was wishing to walk upon the waters, yet he was nigh to sinking on account of fear which fell upon him; and the fear which was weaker than he on dry land, when it came among the waves into a place in which it was strengthened became powerful against him and overcame him.

From this it is possible to learn that when any one of all the desires in us is associated with an evil habit which helps it, then that desire acquires power and conquers us. For fear and love were weighed in the midst of the sea as in a balance, and fear turned the scale and won; and that Simon whose faith was lacking and rose in the balance was himself nigh to sinking in the midst of the sea.

If, therefore, Peter was afraid of the waves, though the Lord of the waves was holding his hand, how much more should weak ones fear the waves of controversy, which are much stronger than the waves of the sea! For in the waves of the sea (only) bodies are drowned, but in the waves of investigation minds sink or are rescued.

Read: Matthew 14:25-32

A MATCHLESS LOVE

THOMAS BROOKS | 17TH CENTURY

Thomas Brooks (1608-1680) was an English nonconformist Puritan preacher and author.

Let us admire and wonder at the love of Jesus Christ to poor sinners: that Christ should rather die for us, than for the angels. They were creatures of a more noble lineage, and in all probability might have brought greater revenues of glory to God; yet that Christ should pass by those golden vessels, and make us vessels of glory—oh, what amazing and astonishing love is this! This is the envy of devils and the admiration of angels and saints.

The angels were more honorable and excellent creatures than we. They were celestial spirits; we of earthly bodies, dust and ashes. They were immediate attendants upon God in his private chamber; we but servants in the lower house of this world, further removed from his glorious presence. Their office was to sing songs of praise to God in the heavenly paradise; ours to dress the garden of Eden, which was but an earthly paradise. They sinned but once, and but in thought, as is commonly believed; but Adam sinned in thought by lusting, in deed by tasting, and in word by excusing. Why did not Christ suffer for their sins, as well as for ours? Why not for theirs, rather than ours? We ask this question, not as being curious to search thy secret counsels, O Lord, but that we may be the more swallowed up in the admiration of the "breadth, and length, and depth, and height . . . [of] the love of Christ, which passeth knowledge"(Ephesians 3:18-19 KJV).

The apostle, being in a holy admiration of Christ's love, affirms it to surpass knowledge (Ephesians 3:18-19); that God, who is the eternal Being, should love man when he had scarce a being (Proverbs 8:30-31). Oh, such was Christ's transcendent love, that man's extreme misery could not abate it. The wretchedness of man's condition did but heighten the holy flame of Christ's love. Heaven, through its glory, could not contain him, such was his perfect matchless love to fallen man. That Christ's love should extend to the ungodly, to sinners, to enemies that were in arms of rebellion against him, is the highest improvement of love.

READ. EPHESIANS 3.1/-19

SEPTEMBER 16

WHY DO YOU TARRY?

CLARENCE E. MACARTNEY | 1948

Clarence Edward Noble Macartney (1879-1957) was a prominent conservative Presbyterian pastor and author.

Why tarriest thou? That seems a strange question for a man like Paul, who was the embodiment of energy, conviction, and decision. Whatever he did, he did with all his might. But since this question was asked him by God through His messenger, Ananias, it would appear that after his extraordinary experience at the Gates of Damascus, where he was smitten to the ground by the heavenly light and heard a voice saying, "Saul, Saul, why persecutest thou me?" Paul was still delaying to act upon the knowledge that had been given him and had not yet confessed the name of Jesus.

When he came to the house of Judas, Ananias, conquering the natural fears that he felt at meeting this bloody persecutor of the Christians, put his hand on him and said, "Brother Saul, receive thy sight." When Paul's eyes were opened, Ananias said, "The God of our fathers hath chosen thee, that thou shouldest know his will, and see that Just One, and shouldest hear the voice of his mouth. For thou shalt be his witness unto all men of what thou hast seen and heard. And now why tarriest thou? arise, and be baptized, and wash away thy sins, calling on the name of the Lord" (Acts 22:13-16 KJV). Then Paul no longer tarried. He confessed his faith in that Jesus whom he had persecuted and blasphemed, was baptized into the faith of Christ, and went forth to preach His everlasting Gospel.

"Why tarriest thou?" Here is a question which speaks to every man who is in a wrong way or in the grip of an evil habit. If he knows it to be evil and dangerous, and conscience, fear, or his better nature has spoken to his soul, telling him to come out of this evil way and to break the chains of this evil habit, then the strange thing is that a man should tarry. Yet nothing could be more apparent than that men do tarry. They delay to make the move, to take the step that will deliver them and set them free.

READ: ACTS 22:12-16

SEPTEMBER 17

THE CHRISTIAN

WILLIAM COWPER | 18TH CENTURY

William Cowper (1731-1800) was an English poet and hymnodist. One of the most popular poets of his time, Cowper changed the direction of eighteenth-century poetry by writing of everyday life and scenes of the English countryside.

Honor and happiness unite
To make the Christian's name a praise;
How fair the scene, how clear the light,
That fills the remnant of His days!
A kingly character He bears,
No change His priestly office knows;
Unfading is the crown He wears,
His joys can never reach a close.
Adorn'd with glory from on high,
Salvation shines upon His face;
His robe is of the ethereal dye,
His steps are dignity and grace.
Inferior honors He disdains,
Nor stoops to take applause from earth;
The King of kings Himself maintains
The expenses of His heavenly birth.
The noblest creature seen below,
Ordain'd to fill a throne above;
God gives him all He can bestow,
His kingdom of eternal love!
My soul is ravished at the thought!
Methinks from earth I see Him rise!
Angels congratulate His lot,
And shout Him welcome to the skies.

READ: ROMANS 8:17

WHEN HE COMES IN GLORY

TERTULLIAN | C. 210

Quintus Septimius Florens Tertullianus (c. 160-c. 220), anglicized as Tertullian, was a prolific early Christian author and apologist from Carthage in the Roman province of Africa. He has been called the "founder of Western theology."

But what a spectacle is that fast-approaching advent of our Lord, now highly exalted, now a triumphant One! What that exultation of the angelic hosts! What the glory of the rising saints! What the kingdom of the just thereafter! What the city New Jerusalem! Yes, and there are other sights: that last day of judgment, when the world hoary with age, and all its many products, shall be consumed in one great flame!

How vast a spectacle then bursts upon the eye! What there excites my admiration? Which sight gives me joy and exultation as I see so many illustrious monarchs, whose reception into the heavens was publicly announced, groaning now in the lowest darkness with great Jove himself; governors of provinces, too, who persecuted the Christian name, in fires more fierce than those with which in the days of their pride they raged against the followers of Christ.

What world's wise men besides, the very philosophers, in fact, who were wont to assure their followers that either they had no souls, or that they would never return to the bodies which at death they had left, now covered with shame before the poor deluded ones, as one fire consumes them!

"This," I shall say, "this is that carpenter's son, that Sabbath-breaker, that Samaritan, and devil-possessed! This is He whom you purchased from Judas! This is He whom you struck with reed and fist, contemptuously spat upon, and gave gall and vinegar to drink! This is He whom His disciples secretly stole away, that it might be said He had risen again!"

And yet even now we in a measure have them by faith in the picturings of imagination. But what are the things which eye has not seen, ear has not heard, and which have not so much as dimly dawned upon the human heart? Whatever they are, they are nobler, I believe, than circus, and both theatres, and every racecourse.

READ: MATTHEW 25:31

SEPTEMBER 19

WHAT IS FAITH?

GEORGE MÜLLER | 19TH CENTURY

Born as Georg Ferdinand Müller (1805-1898), he was a Christian evangelist and the director of the Ashley Down orphanage in Bristol, England. Müller established 117 schools that provided a Christian education to more than 120,000 children, many of them orphans.

What is Faith? In the simplest manner in which I am able to express it, I answer: Faith is the assurance that the thing which God has said in His Word is true, and that God will act according to what He has said in His Word. This assurance, this reliance on God's Word, this confidence is Faith.

No Impressions Are to Be Taken in Connection with Faith. Impressions have neither one thing nor the other to do with faith. Faith has to do with the Word of God. It is not impressions, strong or weak, which will make any difference. We have to do with the written Word and not ourselves or our impressions.

Probabilities Are Not to Be Taken into Account. Many people are willing to believe regarding those things that seem probable to them. Faith has nothing to do with probabilities. The province of Faith begins where probabilities cease and sight and sense fail. A great many of God's children are cast down and lament their want of Faith. They write to me and say that they have no impressions, no feeling, they see no probability that the thing they wish will come to pass. Appearances are not to be taken into account. The question is whether God has spoken it in His Word.

And now, beloved Christian friends, you are in great need to ask yourselves whether you are in the habit of thus confiding, in your inmost soul, in what God has said, and whether you are in earnest in seeking to find whether the thing you want is in accordance with what He has said in His Word.

READ: HEBREWS 11:1

WITH HIS GRACE

JAN VAN RUYSBROECK | 14TH CENTURY

Jan van Ruysbroeck (1293-1381) was a Flemish mystic. He founded a congregation in Groenendaal, and his writings were widely circulated during his lifetime, influencing an entire generation of Christian mystics.

First, we feel God in His grace; and when we apprehend this, we cannot remain idle. For like as the sun, by its splendor and its heat, enlightens and gladdens and makes fruitful the whole world, so God does to us through His grace: He enlightens and gladdens and makes fruitful all men who desire to obey Him.

If, however, we would feel God within us, and have the fire of His love ever more burning within us, we must, of our own free will, help to kindle it in four ways: We must abide within ourselves, united with the fire through inwardness. And we must go forth from ourselves towards all good men with loyalty and brotherly love. And we must go beneath ourselves in penance, betaking ourselves to all good works, and resisting our inordinate lusts. And we must ascend above ourselves with the flame of this fire, through devotion, and thanksgiving, and praise, and fervent prayer, and must ever cleave to God with an upright intention and with sensible love.

And thereby God continues to dwell in us with His grace; for in these four ways is comprehended every exercise which we can do with the reason, and in some wise, but without this exercise no one can please God. He who is most perfect in this exercise, is nearest to God. And therefore it is needful for all men; and above it none can rise save the contemplative men. And thus, in this first way, we feel God within us through His grace, if we wish to belong to Him.

READ: EPHESIANS 3:14-19

A Call for Prophets

Leonard Ravenhill | 1955

Leonard Ravenhill (1907-1994) was an English Christian evangelist and best-selling author who focused on the subjects of prayer and revival. He is best known for his books and sermons, which challenged the modern church to compare itself to the early Christian church as chronicled in the book of Acts.

There is a terrible vacuum in evangelical Christianity today. The missing person in our ranks is the prophet. The man with a terrible earnestness. The man totally otherworldly. The man rejected by other men, even other good men, because they consider him too austere, too severely committed, too negative and unsociable.

Let him be as plain as John the Baptist.

Let him for a season be a voice crying in the wilderness of modern theology and stagnant "churchianity."

Let him be as selfless as Paul the apostle.

Let him, too, say and live, "This ONE thing I do."

Let him reject ecclesiastical favors.

Let him be self-abasing, non-self-seeking, non-self-projecting, non-self-righteous, non-self-glorying, non-self-promoting.

Let him say nothing that will draw men to himself, but only that which will move men to God.

Let him come daily from the throne room of a holy God, the place where he has received the order of the day.

Let him, under God, unstop the ears of the millions who are deaf through the clatter of shekels milked from this hour of material mesmerism.

Let him cry with a voice this century has not heard because he has seen a vision no man in this century has seen. God send us this Moses to lead us from the wilderness of crass materialism, where the rattlesnakes of lust bite us and where enlightened men, totally blind spiritually, lead us to an ever-nearing Armageddon.

God have mercy! Send us PROPHETS!

Read: Jeremiah 35:15

S EPTEMBER 22

AWAKE MY SOUL

THOMAS KEN | 17TH CENTURY

Thomas Ken (1637-1711) was one of the fathers of modern English hymnology and an English cleric who was considered the most eminent of the English non-juring bishops.

Awake, my soul, and with the sun
Thy daily stage of duty run;
Shake off dull sloth, and joyful rise,
To pay thy morning sacrifice.

Thy precious time misspent, redeem,
Each present day thy last esteem,
Improve thy talent with due care;
For the great day thyself prepare.

By influence of the Light divine
Let thy own light to others shine.
Reflect all Heaven's propitious ways
In ardent love, and cheerful praise.

In conversation be sincere;
Keep conscience as the noontide clear;
Think how all seeing God thy ways
And all thy secret thoughts surveys.

Wake, and lift up thyself; my heart,
And with the angels bear thy part,
Who all night long unwearied sing
High praise to the eternal King.

All praise to Thee, who safe has kept
And hast refreshed me while I slept,
Grant, Lord, when I from death shall wake
I may of endless light partake.

READ: PSALM 57:8-11

SEPTEMBER 23

SOUND THE CALL

BILLY GRAHAM | 2010

William Franklin "Billy" Graham (b. 1918) is an American evangelist. It is said that Graham has preached the gospel in person to more people than any other person in history.

We Christians are holding the light, and we're to let it shine. It may seem but a twinkling candle in the world of darkness, but it is our business to let it shine. We're striking with a hammer, and the blows may seem only to jar our own hands as we strike, but we'll keep on hammering at the hearts of people. We're using a sword, and at first it may seem that we are getting nowhere, but God the Holy Spirit will use it.

We have won hearts and souls, and we must keep standing and crying out, "Come, all you who are thirsty, come to the waters," (Isaiah 55:1 NIV). Amid the spiraling forces of revolution, materialism, and nihilism, the world needs to hear that clear, loud, authoritative Word of the living God. God says, "If the trumpet does not sound a clear call, who will get ready for battle?" (1 Corinthians 14:8 NIV). This is an hour when we ought to declare the Word of God to a generation that some people feel may be the last generation.

You have the greatest challenge, the greatest opportunity, and the greatest responsibility of any generation in history. And as those early disciples brought the Gospel two thousand years ago, so we in the twenty-first century are to carry the Gospel and the Word of God in this generation. I believe that Jesus Christ is coming soon. I do not know when. We're told not to speculate on dates, but it seems to me that all the prophecies that the Lord left us are coming to a climax at this moment in history. For the Lord said, "And this gospel of the kingdom will be preached in the whole world . . . and then the end will come" (Matthew 24:14 NIV).

READ: MATTHEW 5:15-16

September 24

An Account of Jesus

Josephus | 93

Josephus (37-c. 100) also known as Titus Flavius Josephus, was a first-century Roman-Jewish historian and hagiographer of priestly and royal ancestry who recorded Jewish history with special emphasis on the First Jewish-Roman War, which resulted in the destruction of Jerusalem in 70 A.D.

Now there was about this time Jesus, a wise man, if it be lawful to call him a man; for he was a doer of wonderful works, a teacher of such men as receive the truth with pleasure. He drew over to him both many of the Jews and many of the Gentiles. He was Christ.

And when Pilate, at the suggestion of the principal men among us, had condemned him to the cross, those that loved him at the first did not forsake him; for he appeared to them alive again the third day, as the divine prophets had foretold these and ten thousand other wonderful things concerning him.

And the tribe of Christians, so named for him, are not extinct at this day.

Read: Luke 18:31

A BEAUTIFUL NAME

DE WITT TALMAGE | 19TH CENTURY

Thomas De Witt Talmage (1832-1902) was an American preacher, reformer, and clergyman. He was one of the most prominent religious leaders in the United States during the nineteenth century.

You may have noticed that it is impossible to dissociate a name from the person who has the name. So there are names that are to me repulsive—I do not want to hear them at all—while those very names are attractive to you. Why the difference? It is because I happen to know persons by those names who are cross, sour, snappish, and unfriendly; while the persons you know by those names are pleasant and attractive.

As we cannot dissociate a name from the person who holds the name, that consideration makes Christ's name so unspeakably beautiful. No sooner is it pronounced in your presence than you think of Bethlehem and Gethsemane and Golgotha. You see the loving face, hear the tender voice, feel the gentle touch. You see Jesus, the One who, though banqueting with heavenly hierarchies, came down to breakfast on the fish that rough men had just hauled out of Gennesaret; Jesus, the One who, though the clouds are the dust of His feet, walked on the road to Emmaus.

Just as soon as that name is pronounced in your presence, you think of how the Shining One gave back the centurion's daughter, how He helped the blind man to the sunlight, how He made the cripple's crutches useless, how He looked down into the babe's laughing eyes and, as the little one struggled to go to Him, flung out His arms around him, impressed a loving kiss on his brow and said, "Of such is the kingdom of heaven."

What a beautiful name—Jesus! It stands for love, for patience, for kindness, for forbearance, for self-sacrifice, for magnanimity. It is aromatic with all odors and accordant with all harmonies.

READ: PHILIPPIANS 2:9-11

OF FEAR AND TREMBLING

W. A. CRISWELL | 1963

Wallie Amos Criswell (1909-2002) was an American Southern Baptist pastor and author, described as one of the twentieth century's greatest expository preachers.

Wherever the apostle Paul went, people turned to the Lord, they were saved, they were baptized, they were organized into churches. Around the Mediterranean world he planted the gospel of the Son of God.

In 2 Corinthians chapter 5, verse 11, he writes: "Knowing therefore the terror of the Lord, we persuade men" (KJV). That's the great basic foundational truth, revelation, startling fact upon which the apostle based the gospel that he preached was this: that it is a dreadful thing and a fearful thing to fall into the hands of the living God.

Now I do not know a truth, a revelation, a fact that is more scorned or scoffed at or belittled or ridiculed than this first one with which Paul begins. "Why there's nothing to be afraid of before God. There's no judgment awaiting the unforgiven sinner. There is no condemnation in perdition and hell. There's no day of reckoning before God."

That is a modern theology, and that is a modern preaching; but it is not the preaching of the Bible, and certainly it is not the preaching of the apostle Paul. He begins with the great foundational revelation: there is such a thing as the terror of the Lord. The Old Testament proverb said, "The beginning of wisdom is"— what? "The fear of the Lord" (see Psalm 110:10; Proverbs 9:10). The beginning of wisdom is the fear of the Lord, for a man to tremble in the presence of the great God Almighty. Could I paraphrase that? "The beginning of salvation is the fear of the Lord."

READ: HEBREWS 10:29-31

SEPTEMBER 27

THE GOD OF MY HEART

WILLIAM LAW | 1754

William Law (1686-1761) was an English cleric and author whose theological writings deeply influenced the chief actors in the great evangelical revival.

The God of patience, meekness, and love is the one God of my heart. The whole bent and desire of my soul is to seek for all my salvation in and through the merits and mediation of the meek, humble, patient, resigned, suffering Lamb of God. He alone has power to bring forth the blessed birth of these heavenly virtues in my soul. He is the bread of God, that came down from heaven, of which the soul must eat, or perish and pine in everlasting hunger.

What a comfort it is to think that this Lamb of God, Son of the Father, light of the world, who is the glory of heaven and joy of angels, is as near to us—is truly in the presence of us—as He is in the presence of heaven; and that not a thought, look, and desire of our heart that presses toward Him, longing to catch, as it were, one small spark of His heavenly nature, is as sure of finding Him, touching Him, and drawing power from Him as the woman who was healed by longing but to touch the border of His garment.

This doctrine also makes me quite weary and ashamed of all my own natural tempers, as so many marks of the beast upon me; every whisper of my soul that stirs up impatience, uneasiness, resentment, pride, and wrath within me, shall be rejected with a "Get thee behind me, Satan," for it has its whole nature from him. For to give up all resentment of every kind, and on every occasion to sink down into the humility of meekness under all contrariety, contradiction, and injustice, always turning the other cheek to the smiter, however haughty, is the best of all prayers, the surest of all means to have nothing but Christ living and working in you, as the Lamb of God, that taketh away every sin that ever had power over your soul.

READ: ISAIAH 25:1

SEPTEMBER 28

A CALL FOR UNITY

IGNATIUS | 117

Ignatius was the third bishop of Antioch and a student of the apostle John. He was martyred in Rome in approximately 108 and wrote a series of letters to churches and individuals on his journey.

If anyone is not inside the sanctuary, he lacks God's bread. And if the prayer of one or two has great avail, how much more that of the bishop and the total Church. He who fails to join in your worship shows his arrogance by the very fact of becoming a schismatic. It is written, moreover, "God resists the proud." Let us, then, heartily avoid resisting the bishop so that we may be subject to God.

The more anyone sees the bishop modestly silent, the more he should revere him. For everyone the Master of the house sends on his business, we ought to receive as the One who sent him. It is clear, then, that we should regard the bishop as the Lord himself. Indeed, Onesimus spoke very highly of your godly conduct, that you were all living by the truth and harboring no sectarianism. Nay, you heed nobody beyond what he has to say truthfully about Jesus Christ.

I believed, then, that I saw your whole congregation in these people I have mentioned, and I loved you all. Hence I urge you to aim to do everything in godly agreement. Let the bishop preside in God's place, and the presbyters take the place of the apostolic council, and let the deacons (my special favorites) be entrusted with the ministry of Jesus Christ who was with the Father from eternity and appeared at the end of the world.

For when you obey the bishop as if he were Jesus Christ, you are (as I see it) living not in a merely human fashion but in Jesus Christ's way, who for our sakes suffered death that you might believe in his death and so escape dying yourselves. It is essential, therefore, to act in no way without the bishop, just as you are doing.

READ: EPHESIANS 4:3-6

KINGDOM RESPONSIBILITY

HUGH LATIMER | 16TH CENTURY

Hugh Latimer (c. 1487-1555) was a Fellow of Clare College, Cambridge, the Bishop of Worcester before the Reformation, and later Church of England chaplain to King Edward VI. In 1555, during the reign of Queen Mary, he was burned at the stake, becoming one of the three Oxford Martyrs of Anglicanism.

Here is a question for the rich. How is it that you happen to be rich? Is it because God has blessed you? By what means did you receive this blessing? Is it through prayer? You prayed for riches and God gave you riches? Very well.

But answer another question. What do others, who are not rich, seek in prayer? Do they not pray the same way you do? If everyone prays for riches, then it must be that your riches are not the result of your own prayers only, but also of others who have helped you pray. It follows that since you did not receive your riches through your own prayers alone, but through the prayers of the poor, then you are obligated to relieve poverty in any way you can.

Why does God give some a hundred and another thousands and some nothing at all? Here is the meaning. The rich are to distribute riches among the poor. Those who are rich are God's officers, God's treasurers. "It is God, not we, who makes things grow" (see 1 Corinthians 3:6).

READ: 1 TIMOTHY 6:17-19

SEPTEMBER 30

A CHRISTIAN WORLDVIEW

JAMES ORR | 1886

James Orr (1844-1913) was a Scottish Presbyterian minister and professor of church history and theology.

I now give what I consider the Christian view of the world to be.

I. First, then, the Christian view affirms the existence of a personal, ethical, self-revealing God—a system of theism, opposed to all other systems.

II. The Christian view affirms the creation of the world by God, His immanent presence in it, His transcendence over it, and His holy and wise government of it.

III. The Christian view affirms the spiritual nature and dignity of man—his creation in the divine image, and destination to bear the likeness of God in a perfected relation of sonship.

IV. The Christian view involves a fall as the presupposition of its doctrine of redemption; whereas the "modern" view of the world affirms that the so-called fall was in reality a rise, and denies by consequence the need of redemption.

V. The Christian view affirms the historical self-revelation of God to the patriarchs and in the line of Israel, and a gracious purpose of God for the salvation of the world, centering in Jesus Christ, His Son.

VI. The Christian view affirms that Jesus Christ was not mere man, but the eternal Son of God—a truly divine person—who is to be worshipped.

VII. The Christian view affirms the redemption of the world through a great act of atonement, to be appropriated by faith, and availing for all who do not willfully withstand and reject its grace.

VIII. The Christian view affirms that the historical aim of Christ's work was the founding of a Kingdom of God on earth, which includes not only the spiritual salvation of individuals, but a new order of society.

IX. Finally, the Christian view affirms that history has a goal, and that the present order of things will be terminated by the appearance of the Son of Man for judgment, the resurrection of the dead, and the final separation of righteous and wicked.

READ: JOHN 3:16-21

OCTOBER 1

PAYING THE PRICE

GEORGE W. TRUETT | 1915

George Washington Truett (1867-1944) was a Southern Baptist preacher, minister, and writer. One of the most significant voices of his era, he was invited by President Woodrow Wilson to address the Allied forces in Europe and gave a particularly memorable speech supporting freedom of religion on the steps of the U.S. Capitol in 1920.

The reason why so many people get so little out of their religion is because they put so little into it. If men want to see Jesus, see Him to the deepest joy of their hearts, and from Him have the noblest victories in their lives, then, for all this, they must pay the requisite price.

Paul paid such price. Gladly did he suffer the loss of all things: home, kindred, inheritance, comforts, country, life itself, that he might have the excellency of the knowledge of Christ Jesus, his Lord. Do you wonder that he had visions and revelations which could not be put into speech? Do you wonder that his letters abound in doxologies, as he contemplates the unfolding glory of his Lord? Paul paid the price for his glorious visions of Jesus.

Here, then, is the vital question for us. Will we pay the price to see Jesus as we need to see Him, as He would have us see Him? Are we willing to live for Him, to put Him first, to do His will, be what it may, lead where it will? Right here is the supreme battle of the Christian life. It is the battle between Christ and self. The self-centered life will not see Jesus, and must surely fail. The Christ-centered life will mount higher and higher in its visions of Jesus, and will more and more exult in the victory that overcomes the world.

READ: MATTHEW 19:29

OCTOBER 2

THE CONQUEROR COMES

EDWARD GRIFFIN | 19TH CENTURY

Edward Dorr Griffin (1770-1837) was an American preacher, pastor, educator, and a cofounder of the American Bible Society.

While tyrants are wading to power through the blood of slaughtered armies, and marching to the music of a nation's groans, there is a Conqueror of a far different sort. He too has his arrows and his two-edged sword, and "goes forth conquering and to conquer"; but his track is not marked with desolation and woe. His coming is not proclaimed by the cries of widows and orphans. Mercy is his banner, and with him marches salvation. He wounds only to heal, and kills only to make alive. "On his head" are "many crowns," and his name is called, "The Word of God" (see Revelation 19:12-13).

Fall down at the feet of this divine Conqueror, submit to his empire, and risk your eternal all upon his mediation. If you refuse, you should know that he has other arrows with which to reach your heart. "God shall shoot at [you] with an arrow; suddenly shall [you] be wounded," (Psalm 64:7 KJV). Those that will not have this King to reign over them, shall be brought forth and slain before him. He will reign till all his enemies are made his footstool.

His first coming, with all the kindness that attended it, was foretold in terms terrible to the wicked. And that coming which is yet in the future, is predicted in alarming language: "Why is Your apparel red, and Your garments like one who treads in the winepress? 'I have trodden the winepress alone, and from the peoples no one was with Me. For I have trodden them in My anger, and trampled them in My fury; their blood is sprinkled upon My garments, and I have stained all My robes. For the day of vengeance is in My heart, and the year of My redeemed has come'" (Isaiah 63:2-4).

Terrible things are to be accomplished upon the wicked, which will cause men's hearts to fail for fear. Therefore, seek the arrows of his love before the time comes for the arrows of his wrath. Run to the shelter of the Savior before you wish for the shelter of the rocks. May you be a trophy of his grace and rejoice in the day of his coming.

READ: PSALM 45:3-6

October 3

Purifying Fire

Catherine of Genoa | 15th century

Saint Catherine of Genoa (1447-1510) was an Italian Catholic saint and mystic, admired for her work among the sick and the poor.

The Spirit now obliged Humanity to take another step, requiring great submission of mind and body. She was directed to live in the hospital and devote herself to the service of the sick, as though she were a servant, hardly daring to speak and obedient to all that was imposed upon her. But she said to the Spirit:

"If you wish me to perform these works, give me the power to do them. I refuse none of them, but they must be done with some love, or they will be done poorly." Accordingly, she was granted some interest in her work; and in these employments, and in great poverty, the Spirit left her for many years.

When the Spirit had disciplined Humanity by such trials and humiliations, until she was able to look not only without disgust upon things which at first she naturally loathed, but also willingly busied herself with whatever was most offensive, she was put to another trial, being placed as superior in charge of this hospital, that it might be seen if her humanity would anywhere discover itself, by reason of this promotion.

She was tried by the Spirit in this way for many years, yet also aided and directed by him. And she remained in that love which was secretly increasing as Humanity was destroyed, for as she became rid of Self Love, did she become possessed by Pure Love, which penetrated and filled her proportionately as she became dead to self.

And thus this soul, burning with Pure Love, melted in that divine flame, and as this continually increased, the soul was always consuming with love; therefore she completed all her duties with eagerness, never resting, that she might forget the flame that devoured her more and more. She never could speak of this to anyone, but she talked of it to herself, unheard by others. The Spirit, having now taken possession of her, said: "I will no longer call her a human creature, so entirely do I behold God in her, and with nothing human remaining."

Read: Zechariah 13:9

OCTOBER 4
GOD'S GREATEST WORK
THOMAS BOSTON | 18TH CENTURY

Thomas Boston (1676-1732) was a Scottish minister and schoolmaster.

O the love of God to poor sinners of mankind! The greatest work that God ever did was for their salvation. He made the world for man and gave it to him, and the visible heavens, too. Yes, the highest heavens He also made for them and gives to them in His Son. But He did a greater work than all these when He did this miracle of the incarnation of His own Son and gave Him, an incarnate Redeemer, to them. How worthy are they to perish who will not be saved when God has wrought this greatest miracle to save them?

What unaccountable stupidity is it in men not to consider, admire, and be swallowed up in contemplation of this miracle; and not to be in deepest love with this miraculous personage given to them? Ah! Have we not all been careless, unmoved spectators of this miracle? How many have never spent a few minutes in the consideration and admiration of Him? Have you not gazed upon and wondered at some trifle more than at this greatest of the works of God? Have you not been more deeply in love with some person or thing for its shadowy excellencies than with this miraculous person?

Be exhorted, then, to give this wonderful One your heart. "My son, give me thine heart" (Proverbs 23:26 KJV). Make Him the choice of your soul. Take Him for your portion as One who is the best of portions. Let your soul solemnly consent to the offer of the gospel.

Part with all for Him, as the wise merchant who sold all that he had and bought the one pearl of great price. Give up your lusts and your idols; renounce the devil, the world, and the flesh, resting on Christ for all for time and eternity.

Dwell in the contemplation of His matchless excellencies. Let it be the substance of your religion to love Him, to admire Him, to be swallowed up in His love. And let love for Him set your soul moving in all holy obedience.

READ: PSALM 115:16

OCTOBER 5

THE WAY TO REVIVAL

JOSEPH PARKER | 19TH CENTURY

Joseph Parker (1830-1902) was an English pastor, preacher, and author known for his dramatic style.

Out of a true knowledge of sin will come a true appreciation of Jesus Christ as the Savior. Apart from this, he will be a strange teacher; with it, he will be the Redeemer for whom our hearts have unconsciously longed when they have felt the soreness and agony of sin. We could sum up the Christian creed in a sentence, yet that sentence contains more than all the libraries in the world. The faith which bears us up above all temptation and all controversy, the faith in which we destroy the power of the world and soar into the brightness of eternal day, is this: I believe in Jesus Christ, the Son of God!

The heart hungers for him, our sin cries out for his mercy, our sorrow yearns for his coming, and when he does come he speaks just the word that the soul needs. He understands us; he knows us altogether. He can get down into the low, dark pit into which sin has thrown us. He destroys the devil, and puts within us the Holy Ghost. He so fills us with life that death no longer has any terror with which to cause us fear.

His word is the best witness of its own power; it touches life at every point. It is most precious when most needed. It follows us in our wanderings and bids us return. It is always pure, noble, unselfish, unworldly; it gives us a staff for the journey, a sword for the battle, a shelter from the storm, and in the last darkening hour it gives us the triumph of immortality.

Only the liberated slave can know the joy of freedom; only the recovered leper can appreciate fully the blessing of health. It is so with our true Christian living: it cannot be judged by the rules of carnal criticism. The only solid basis of a genuine revival of religion is the need of being distinct and positive in our faith. Let us know what we believe. Let us be able to say with sureness and thankfulness what is the Rock on which we stand.

READ: PSALM 85:6

OCTOBER 6
AN OPEN WINDOW
MAX LUCADO | 1996

Max Lucado (b. 1955) is a best-selling author and minister in San Antonio, Texas.

Imagine yourself in a dark room. Windows closed. Curtains drawn. Shutters shut. In the darkness it's hard to believe there's daylight beyond the drapes. So you grope and try to feel your way across the floor. You take a step, disoriented and unsure where you're headed. Progress is slow and the journey painful. Stubbed toes, bruised shins, broken vases. It's hard to walk in a dark place.

Harder still to walk in a dark world. But many try. And, as a result, many are wounded in the effort: tripping over problems, bumping into one another in the shadows, ramming into walls.

But occasionally one of us makes a discovery. Reaching through the blackness, a hand finds curtains and a window latch. "Hey, everybody! The walls have windows!" The drapes are pulled back and the window opened. The sun floods into the room. What was dark is now bright. What was opaque is now clear. What was stale is now fresh. With the light comes a peace, a power, a desire to move closer to the light, and a confidence to step forward. Our timid steps are replaced by a certainty to our walk. A certainty to move through the corridors of life, opening one window after another to illuminate. What a difference! And all it took was one small gesture of opening curtains and raising the window.

Prayer does the same thing for us. Prayer is the window that God has placed in the walls of our world. Leave it shut and the world is a cold, dark house. But throw back the curtains and see his light. Open the window and hear his voice. Open the window of prayer and invoke the presence of God in your world.

READ: JAMES 5:16

OCTOBER 7

THE PERSUASION OF TRUTH

ATHENAGORAS | C. 180

Athenagoras of Athens (c. 133-190) was a Christian apologist and philosopher of the second century.

If I go minutely into the particulars of our doctrine, let it not surprise you. It is that you may not be carried away by the popular and irrational opinion, but may have the truth clearly before you.

What, then, are those teachings in which we are brought up? "I say unto you, Love your enemies; bless them that curse you; pray for them that persecute you; that ye may be the sons of your Father who is in heaven, who causes His sun to rise on the evil and the good, and sends rain on the just and the unjust" (see Matthew 5:44-45).

Allow me here to lift up my voice boldly in loud and audible outcry, pleading as I do before philosophic princes. For who of those that reduce syllogisms, and clear up ambiguities, and explain etymologies; or of those who teach homonyms and synonyms, and predicaments and axioms, and what is the subject and what the predicate, and who promise their disciples by these and such like instructions to make them happy: who of them have so purged their souls as, instead of hating their enemies, to love them; and, instead of speaking ill of those who have reviled them (to abstain from which is of itself an evidence of no mean forbearance), to bless them; and to pray for those who plot against their lives?

On the contrary, they never cease with evil intent to search out skillfully the secrets of their art, and are ever bent on working some ill, making the art of words and not the exhibition of deeds their business and profession. But among us you will find uneducated persons, and artisans, and old women, who, if they are unable in words to prove the benefit of our doctrine, yet by their deeds exhibit the benefit arising from their persuasion of its truth: they do not rehearse speeches, but exhibit good works; when struck, they do not strike again; when robbed, they do not go to law; they give to those that ask of them, and love their neighbors as themselves.

READ: 1 TIMOTHY 4:6-10

OCTOBER 8

HUMBLE ADORATION

LOUIS DE BLOIS | 16TH CENTURY

Louis de Blois (1506-1566), also known as Blosius, was a Flemish mystical writer and abbot of Liessies Abbey in Hainaut.

Thee, Father unbegotten; Thee, only-begotten Son; Thee, Holy Ghost, the Comforter; One, almighty, everlasting, and unchangeable God, Creator of heaven and earth, and of all things visible and invisible, I beseechingly adore. I praise Thee, oh blessed Trinity, ever at rest in Thy glorious light. I commend both my soul and body to Thy most tender care. I commit myself wholly to Thy will. To Thee be honor and glory. Amen.

Oh Heavenly Father, my Lord and my God, have mercy upon me a most worthless sinner, have mercy upon all men. In full reparation for all my iniquities and failings, and for the sins of the whole world, I offer unto Thee Thy beloved Son, Jesus Christ, in union with that excessive love which caused Thee to send Him to us as our Savior. I offer unto Thee His most holy incarnation, life, passion, and death. I offer Thee His most wonderful virtues, and whatsoever He did and suffered for our sakes. I offer Thee His labors, His travails, His torments, and precious blood. Keep me, Oh most merciful Father, by this Thy Son, in the power of the Holy Ghost. Be present with all miserable sinners, and of Thy mercy bring them back into the way of salvation. Grant unto all the living pardon and grace, and to the faithful departed, rest and everlasting light. Amen.

Oh Holy Spirit, most sweet Comforter, I beseech Thee, come and glide into my heart. Wash me over and over, and cleanse me thoroughly from all sin. Look on my soul, wash its filth, heal its wounds, bend its stiffness, warm its chill, guide its waywardness. Make me truly humble and resigned that I may please Thee; and ever rest upon me. Oh most blessed Light of all loveliness, be Thou shed on me! Kindle within me the fire of Thy burning love. Teach me, my Lord. Guide and protect me in all things. Strengthen my spirit; secure me in a right faith, unswerving hope, and sincere and perfect charity. Grant that I may always do Thy most gracious will. Amen.

READ: PSALM 51:2

OCTOBER 9

CLEANING THE TEMPLE

JOHN CHAPMAN | 19TH CENTURY

John Wilbur Chapman (1859-1918) was an American Presbyterian evangelist.

An old minister once said to me, "I wish that people were as much afraid of imperfection as of perfection." But we may forsake every known sin, and still be very imperfect in God's sight, for God beholds sin where we are blind to it. It is not a question as to whether I can keep from sinning or not—I know that I cannot; but the question is as to whether Jesus Christ can keep me. Who am I that I should limit the power of the Almighty? Has He not told us in Jude that He is able to keep us from stumbling? Is anything too hard for the Lord?

You are the temple of God, and the Spirit dwells in you, so that if you want Him to fill you, the first thing to do is to get the temple clean. God does not require golden vessels, or silver vessels, but He must have clean vessels. In the days of Hezekiah, when the temple was filled with things that had no place there, it had to be cleansed before God would manifest Himself there. Again, when the court was filled with moneychangers, Jesus had to drive them out with the scourge. Too many of us have allowed ourselves to be soiled by contact with the world. We may not be grossly inconsistent, yet many times we have lost our power.

We have been told that if we would be filled with the Spirit, we must weep, pray, agonize; but it is all to no purpose. One minister said to me: "I believe this filling is only for a few elect persons." Another said: "I have fulfilled every command of God, and still I am not filled." Brethren, the thing to do is to stop agonizing and just get down before God and say: "Search me, O God, and know my heart: try me, and know my thoughts: and see if there be any wicked way in me" (Psalm 139:23-24a KJV). Then ask Him to take it away. When you have become cleansed and set right, then God will be ready to fill you.

READ: 1 CORINTHIANS 3:16

OCTOBER 10

WHEN CHRIST COMES

CYRUS SCOFIELD | 1897

Cyrus Ingerson Scofield (1843-1921) was an American theologian, minister, and writer whose annotated study Bible is still a popular resource today.

Among the last words of comfort and exhortation given by our Lord to His perplexed and sorrowing disciples before His sacrifice on the cross were these: "Let not your heart be troubled: ye believe in God, believe also in me. In my Father's house are many mansions: if it were not so, I would have told you. I go to prepare a place for you. And if I go and prepare a place for you, I will come again, and receive you unto myself; that where I am, there ye may be also" (John 14:1-3 KJV).

Here the Lord speaks of His coming again in precisely the same terms as of His departure. The latter was, we know, personal and bodily. If we say that the former is impersonal and "spiritual," surely to such a forced interpretation of simple language we ought to be constrained only by the most imperative and unqualified Scripture elsewhere. But no such passages exist. We are not left to doubt upon this vital point, nor to draw conclusions of reason, however irresistible.

"Beloved, now are we the sons of God, and it doth not yet appear what we shall be: but we know that, when he shall appear, we shall be like him; for we shall see him as he is" (1 John 3:2 KJV). For this "blessed hope" we are taught to "watch" (Mark 13:33, 35, 37 KJV; Matthew 24:42; 25:13 KJV), "wait" (1 Thessalonians 1:10 KJV), and be "ready" (Matthew 24:44 KJV).

The Scripture makes it abundantly clear that the second coming will be personal and bodily. Therefore it does not mean the death of the believer, nor the destruction of Jerusalem, nor the descent of the Holy Spirit at Pentecost, nor the gradual diffusion of Christianity, but that it is the "blessed hope" of the church, the time when sleeping saints will be raised, and, together with saints then living, caught up to meet the Lord—the time when we who are now the sons of God will be like Him and when faithful saints will be rewarded for works of faith, for His name's sake.

READ: 1 THESSALONIANS 4:16-17

October 11

How to Spend the Day with God

Richard Baxter | 1671

Richard Baxter (1615-1691) was an English Puritan and considered a leading theologian of his day.

Sleep: Measure the time of your sleep appropriately so that you do not waste precious morning hours sluggishly in your bed. Let the time of your sleep be matched to your health and labor, and not to slothful pleasure.

First Thoughts: Let God have your first awaking thoughts; lift up your hearts to Him reverently and thankfully and cast yourself upon Him for the day which follows.

Prayer: Let prayer by yourself alone (or with your partner) take place before the collective prayer of the family. If possible let it be first, before any work of the day.

Family Worship: Let family worship be performed consistently and at a time when it is most likely for the family to be free of interruptions.

Diligence in Your Calling: Follow the tasks of your calling carefully and diligently: you will further the putting to death of all the fleshly lusts that are fed by ease and idleness.

Redeeming the Time: Place a high value upon your time, being more careful of not losing it than you would of losing your money. Do not let worthless recreations, idle talk, unprofitable company, or sleep rob you of precious time.

Eating and Drinking: Eat and drink with moderation and thankfulness for health, not for unprofitable pleasure. Never please your appetite in food or drink when it is prone to be detrimental to your health.

Prevailing Sin: If any temptation prevails against you and you fall into any sins or habitual failures, immediately lament it and confess it to God; repent quickly whatever the cost.

Closing the Day: Before returning to sleep, it is wise and necessary to review the events of the day, so that you may be thankful for all the special mercies and humbled for all your sins.

Read: Psalm 91:1-2

OCTOBER 12

THE WORK OF TRUTH

JOHN A. BROADUS | 19TH CENTURY

John A. Broadus (1827-1895) was an American scholar and academic, considered by some to be the father of American expository preaching.

"Sanctify them through thy truth: thy word is truth" (John 17:17 kjv). You will see he does not merely pray that they may be kept from evil, but that they may be made holy. Here is a common misconception about the service of Jesus Christ, the idea that it is merely a negative thing; that he proposes merely to keep us from doing evil, to keep us from doing harm. Some people think all there is in religion is to try to avoid doing harm, when Jesus goes on to pray that they may be made holy.

Piety is not merely a negative thing. The ten commandments, I know, are all in negative form, "thou shalt not." Even so, Christianity reveals that this is but one side, and that the other side, the nobler and more glorious side, is that we must not merely try to keep from doing wrong, but try to do right. Jesus does not simply pray that we may be kept from evil, but that we may be made holy. You should desire to be holy! Jesus wishes that for you, and therefore he prays, "Make them holy—make them holy through thy truth: thy word is truth."

It is truth that makes men holy. Earth's unholiness began with a lie that man believed and then went headlong into ruin. Truth is the medicine for the soul's disease. Nobody is ever made holy except through truth. The truth, even though it may be contaminated with error, may yet through God's blessing accomplish its healing, saving, sanctifying work. But it is only the truth that does the work.

I wish to offer you practical counsel. I offer it as the result of a good deal of observation and of my own efforts, amid a thousand infirmities and shortcomings, to lead a better life. My counsel is this: regard the Bible more than you have been accustomed to do, as that which we are to use as the means of becoming holy. Regard the Bible as the great means of making you better, of making you good. Use the Bible for that purpose.

READ: JOHN 17:17

OCTOBER 13

BE EVEN MORE DILIGENT

IGNATIUS | 108

Ignatius was the third bishop of Antioch and a student of the apostle John. He was martyred in Rome in approximately 108 and wrote a series of letters to churches and individuals on his journey.

Be even wiser and more diligent than you already are—wise as the serpent in all things and gentle as the dove. You are made of flesh and spirit. You must address the matters that appear before your eyes. But as a spiritual being, yearn even more for the invisible things. Pray that you will be shown what matters most; that you will lack nothing, and abound in every spiritual gift. You are needed for this time, for this season, just as a pilot needs winds or a storm-tossed mariner needs a safe haven. As God uses you, you will experience Him most deeply.

Be sober, ready to compete as God's athlete. The prize is incorruption and life eternal. But you are already convinced of that truth. Don't lose heart over teachers that seem eloquent and plausible to followers, yet clearly teach bad doctrine. Stand as firm as an anvil when it is hammered. Even great athletes receive blows before they are victorious. But bottom line, endure all things for God's sake—after all, He endures us.

Be even more diligent than you already are. Await Him that is above every season, the Eternal, the Invisible, who became visible for our sake. Await Him who is unchangeable and steadfast, who suffered and endured in all ways for our sake.

Don't neglect the widows. Be their protector even as the Lord is. Let nothing be done in the church without your consent; don't do anything without the consent of God, as indeed has been your commitment. Stand firm.

Hold church meetings more frequently—and greet everyone by name. Don't look down on slaves, whether male or female. Whether they become free or remain a slave, encourage them to serve others even more faithfully to the glory of God, that they may glorify God and receive their ultimate freedom from Him.

READ: 1 TIMOTHY 1:15-16

October 14

Whosoever Will

Harry Ironside | 20th century

Harry A. Ironside (1876-1951) was a Canadian-American Bible teacher, preacher, theologian, pastor, and author.

When the Lord Jesus, in the days of His earthly ministry, sent forth the twelve apostles to go throughout the land of Israel heralding His word, He evidently commanded them to emphasize the same message that John the Baptist preached and which He Himself proclaimed; for we are told in Mark 6:12 that "they went out, and preached that men should repent" (KJV).

After His atoning death and glorious resurrection, when He commissioned the eleven to go out into all the world and make known His gospel among all nations, we find Him again stressing the same solemn truth. The rending of the veil had ended the old dispensation; His triumph over death introduced the new one; but the call for men to repent was unrepealed. The gospel of the grace of God did not set this to one side, nor ignore it in the slightest degree. Men must still be called upon to change their attitude toward God and the sin question if they would receive forgiveness of sins. True, forgiveness is by faith, but there can be no faith without repentance, and no repentance without faith.

Scripture clearly teaches that God is sovereign and "worketh all things after the counsel of his own will" (Ephesians 1:11 KJV). It just as plainly shows us that man is a responsible creature, who has the power of choice and is called upon by the Lord to exercise that power and to turn to Him. "Turn ye, turn ye . . . for why will ye die?" "Choose you this day whom ye will serve." "Whosoever will, let him take the water of life freely." To those who refused His testimony the Savior sadly said, "Ye will not come to me, that ye might have life" (Ezekiel 33:11; Joshua 24:15; Revelation 22:17; John 5:40 KJV).

The truth of God's electing grace does not come into conflict with that of man's responsibility. Mr. Moody used to say in his downright, sensible, matter-of-fact manner, "The elect are the whosoever wills; the non-elect are the whosoever won'ts." What theologian could put it more clearly?

Read: Joshua 24:15

THE SWEET AND THE BITTER

BROTHER LAWRENCE | 1692

Brother Lawrence of the Resurrection (1614-1691) served as a lay brother in a Carmelite monastery in Paris. His letters were published after his death under the title The Practice of the Presence of God.

God knows best what we need, and all that He does is for our good. If we knew how much He loves us, we would always be prepared to receive equally and without preference the sweet or the bitter that comes from His hand; we would be pleased with anything that comes from Him.

Let all our efforts be to know God, for the more we get to know Him, the more we will desire to know Him even more. And as knowledge is commonly the measure of the depth of love, the deeper and more extensive our knowledge of Him grows, the greater will be our love for Him. I would remind you; if your love of God is great you will love Him equally in pains and pleasures.

Don't entertain yourself with the trifles of life. Do not seek to love God for any of the favors and comforts He brings you—even if those favors are good and noble. Such blessings, great or small, don't bring us close to Him. Only faith can do that. So don't seek Him for what you'll get but seek Him in faith. It is rude and worthy of blame if we ignore God because we are distracted by acquiring the trifles of life. This isn't what pleases God. Beware lest your pursuit of comforts and possessions will cost you terribly.

Simply and earnestly be devoted to Him. Get rid of distractions from your heart; let Him possess even your desires. If you want to ask for any favor from God, ask Him to give you even greater devotion to Him. Do your best in this area and you will soon discover a change of heart; you will begin to aspire for the heart of God, not possessions and comforts.

READ: LUKE 12:22-31

OCTOBER 16

TO SEE HIM CLEARLY

CHARLES FINNEY | 1843

*Charles Grandison Finney (1792-1875) was a prominent preacher during the Second
Great Awakening. His influence was so substantial that he has been called the "Father
of Modern Revivalism."*

So many have exceedingly narrow, partial, and obscure views of God; so
one-sided and distorted, that it is like anything else more than like God. Perhaps
Moses was somewhat in this condition. He had seen God in the burning bush,
he had heard his voice, he had been the rod of Jehovah's wrath on wicked
Egypt, he had stood on Sinai and seen God in fire and smoke and lightning,
but he could not be satisfied—still he must know more. Moses asked for new
revelations continually.

Many know God only as a lawgiver and judge. They understand his law, and
they cower in terror and fear; that is all they know of God. Others know nothing
of him but what they call his mercy and love; nothing of justice, and holiness,
and righteous indignation against sin. Now eventually Moses trusted firmly and
unwaveringly in God's truth. God had shown him his truth, and Moses never
forgot it.

It is vastly important that men should have a just and symmetrical view of
God's character; for where the revelation is partial, they show a want of balance
in their character. If they have not seen the justice and holiness of God, they
will have no awareness of the guilt of sin, of its deserving punishment, of God's
infinite hatred of it. They can have no proper sense of the condition of sinners;
no compassion, no ardent zeal, no burning love for them.

If men do not have a revelation of the mercy and love and compassion of God,
they will have very little confidence to pray for sinners; instead of laying hold of
God, even in the most desperate cases, they slacken and give up in despair. So
of all his attributes; if men have not sought and obtained a just view of God's
character, they will be like their views of God—ill-proportioned and unbalanced
in their own character.

READ: JOHN 14:8-11

OCTOBER 17

NEVER STOP MEETING

THE EPISTLE TO THE HEBREWS | C. 84

The Epistle to the Hebrews is one of the books in the New Testament, but its author is unknown. The central thought of the entire epistle is the doctrine of the Person of Christ and his role as mediator between God and humanity.

Therefore, brothers and sisters, since we have confidence to enter the Most Holy Place by the blood of Jesus, by a new and living way opened for us through the curtain, that is, his body, and since we have a great priest over the house of God, let us draw near to God with a sincere heart and with the full assurance that faith brings, having our hearts sprinkled to cleanse us from a guilty conscience and having our bodies washed with pure water. Let us hold unswervingly to the hope we profess, for he who promised is faithful. And let us consider how we may spur one another on toward love and good deeds, not giving up meeting together, as some are in the habit of doing, but encouraging one another—and all the more as you see the Day approaching.

You need to persevere so that when you have done the will of God, you will receive what he has promised. For, "In just a little while, he who is coming will come and will not delay." And, "But my righteous one will live by faith. And I take no pleasure in the one who shrinks back." But we do not belong to those who shrink back and are destroyed, but to those who have faith and are saved.

READ: 1 THESSALONIANS 5:11

October 18

The Dying Christian to His Soul

Alexander Pope | 18th century

Alexander Pope (1688-1744) was an eighteenth-century English poet, best known for his satirical verse and for his translation of Homer.

Vital spark of heav'nly flame!
Quit, O quit this mortal frame:
Trembling, hoping, ling'ring, flying,
O the pain, the bliss of dying!
Cease, fond Nature, cease thy strife,
And let me languish into life.

Hark! they whisper; angels say,
Sister Spirit, come away!
What is this absorbs me quite?
Steals my senses, shuts my sight,
Drowns my spirits, draws my breath?
Tell me, my soul, can this be death?

The world recedes; it disappears!
Heav'n opens on my eyes! my ears
With sounds seraphic ring!
Lend, lend your wings! I mount! I fly!
O Grave! where is thy victory?
O Death! where is thy sting?

Read: 1 Corinthians 15:54-55

OCTOBER 19

A LASTING HUMILITY

JOHN CASSIAN | 5TH CENTURY

John Cassian (c. 360-435), also known as John the Ascetic or John Cassian the Roman, was a Christian theologian who is known both as one of the Scythian monks and one of the Desert Fathers.

And so, if we wish in very deed and truth to attain to the crown of virtues, we ought to listen to those teachers and guides who, not dreaming with pompous declamations, but learning by act and experience, are able to teach us as well, and direct us likewise, and show us the road by which we may arrive at it by a most sure pathway; and who also testify that they have themselves reached it by faith rather than by any merits of their efforts.

And further, the purity of heart that they have acquired has taught them this above all; to recognize more and more that they are burdened with sin (for their compunction for their faults increases day by day in proportion as their purity of soul advances), and to sigh continually from the bottom of their heart because they see that they cannot possibly avoid the spots and blemishes of those faults which are ingrained in them through the countless triflings of the thoughts.

And therefore they declared that they looked for the reward of the future life, not from the merits of their works, but from the mercy of the Lord, taking no credit to themselves for their great circumspection of heart in comparison with others, since they ascribed this not to their own exertions, but to divine grace; and without flattering themselves on account of the carelessness of those who are cold, and worse than they themselves are, they rather aimed at a lasting humility by fixing their gaze on those whom they knew to be really free from sin and already in the enjoyment of eternal bliss in the kingdom of heaven, and so by this consideration they avoided the downfall of pride, and at the same time always saw both what they were aiming at and what they had to grieve over: as they knew that they could not attain that purity of heart for which they yearned while weighed down by the burden of flesh.

READ: PSALM 51:10-12

OCTOBER 20

WHAT GOD HAS DONE

KARL BARTH | 1933

Karl Barth (1886-1968) was a Swiss Reformed theologian who is believed to be one of the most important Christian thinkers of the twentieth century. Pope Pius XII described him as the most important theologian since Thomas Aquinas.

We will gladly let anyone tell us about the love of God; we rejoice when it is ardently proclaimed to us. But do we not see that all this is meaningless patter if we are not at the same time shocked as by a crash of lightning with a sense of the depth of our lost condition to which the love of God had to stoop?

We do not like to see that we are deeply imprisoned, and that we absolutely cannot in any way help ourselves; that it is true, we are a people who live in the shadow and darkness of death; that this is true, and is proclaimed to us in, with, and under the word "resurrection"—oh, that is for us the bitter, unacceptable, and unendurable truth which stirs us to rebellion. That is the darkness in the clear word "resurrection."

Oh, yes, we gladly allow it to be proclaimed to us, but that it is *God's* victory, and that this victory is contrary to our wishes, and comes as a result of our impotent helplessness—this is what we do not care to hear at all. "Ye were dead in your sins and trespasses, in which ye walked according to the course of this world. But God, who is rich in mercy, has made us alive with Christ" (see Ephesians 2:1-5). If only we could take the words "God has made us alive," without that word "but" which precedes it, and which so emphatically refers to our being dead in our sins!

Nevertheless, it must be seen and understood that in the midst of life, even in blooming and healthy life, there is a yawning chasm, a deep pit that cannot be filled by any art or power of man. Only one word is sufficient to cover this chasm, to fill this pit, and that is the word "resurrection"—"Jesus is victor!"

READ: PSALM 66:1-5

OCTOBER 21

ULFILAS AND THE CONVERSION OF THE GOTHS

SOCRATES | 4TH CENTURY

Ulfilas (c. 310-383), a bishop, missionary, and Bible translator, was a Goth who spent time inside the Roman Empire at the peak of the Arian controversy. He was ordained a bishop by Eusebius of Nicomedia and returned to his people to work as a missionary.

The barbarians dwelling beyond the Danube, who are called Goths, having been engaged in a civil war among themselves, were divided into two parties; of one of these Fritigernus was the leader, of the other Athanaric. When Athanaric had obtained an evident advantage over his rival, Fritigernus had recourse to the Romans and implored their assistance against his adversary. When these things were reported to the Emperor Valens, he ordered the troops garrisoned in Thrace to assist those barbarians against the barbarians fighting against them.

They won a complete victory over Athanaric beyond the Danube, totally routing the enemy. This was the reason why many of the barbarians became Christians; for Fritigernus, to show his gratitude to the Emperor for the kindness shown him, embraced the religion of the Emperor, and urged those under him to do the same. Therefore it is that even to this present time so many of the Goths are infected with the religion of Arianism, because the emperors at that time gave themselves to that faith.

Ulfilas, the bishop of the Goths at that time, invented the Gothic letters and, translating the Holy Scriptures into their own language, undertook to instruct these barbarians in the divine oracles. But when Ulfilas taught the Christian religion not only to the subjects of Fritigernus but to the subjects of Athanaric also, Athanaric, regarding this as a violation of the privileges of the religion of his ancestors, subjected many of the Christians to severe punishments, so that many of the Arian Goths of that time became martyrs. Arius, indeed, failing to refute the opinion of Sabellius the Libyan, fell from the true faith and asserted that the Son of God was a new god; but the barbarians, embracing Christianity with greater simplicity, despised this present life for the faith of Christ.

READ: ISAIAH 55:10 11

OCTOBER 22

LOVE EVERLASTING

THOMAS DOOLITTLE | 17TH CENTURY

Thomas Doolittle (c. 1632-1707) was an English nonconformist tutor, author, pastor, and popular preacher.

Love is the everlasting grace that will continue in use and increase, even when other graces will have ceased. Some graces are particularly suited to our present state of imperfection in this world. At the present time, we live by faith, repent and mourn for sin, live in hope of the glory which will be revealed, and wait until we possess the mansions above.

We patiently wait for all the good that is promised to us, but not yet conferred upon us. However, in the future faith will be turned into sight, hope into enjoyment, desires into gratification, and waiting into possession. When this happens, we will believe no more, hope no more, desire no more, and wait no more. But even then we will continue in love—indeed, we will love more than ever, more abundantly, perfectly, and continually, without pause or alteration. We will love eternally. One reason why love is considered the greatest of the three Christian virtues, is that it will last the longest. "And now abide faith, hope, love, these three; but the greatest of these *is* love" (1 Corinthians 13:13).

So it is that those who love Christ sincerely here, will love him perfectly hereafter, and be forever blessed in that love. But those who do not love him in this world, cannot love him in the next. For the lack of such love, they shall be accursed forever.

READ: 1 CORINTHIANS 13:8-13

OCTOBER 23

A PURE RELIGION

JAMES | 60

James the Just (d. 62) was the brother of Jesus and the author of the New Testament Epistle of James. He was an important leader of the Christian movement in Jerusalem in the decades after Jesus' death.

My dear brothers and sisters, take note of this: Everyone should be quick to listen, slow to speak and slow to become angry, because human anger does not produce the righteousness that God desires. Therefore, get rid of all moral filth and the evil that is so prevalent and humbly accept the word planted in you, which can save you.

Do not merely listen to the word, and so deceive yourselves. Do what it says. Anyone who listens to the word but does not do what it says is like someone who looks at his face in a mirror and, after looking at himself, goes away and immediately forgets what he looks like. But whoever looks intently into the perfect law that gives freedom, and continues in it—not forgetting what they have heard, but doing it—they will be blessed in what they do.

Those who consider themselves religious and yet do not keep a tight rein on their tongues deceive themselves, and their religion is worthless. Religion that God our Father accepts as pure and faultless is this: to look after orphans and widows in their distress and to keep oneself from being polluted by the world.

READ: MICAH 6:8

OCTOBER 24

FAITHFUL IN WAITING

ANDREW MURRAY | 1910

Andrew Murray (1828-1917) was a South African writer, teacher, and Christian pastor. The son of a Reformed Church missionary sent from Scotland to South Africa, Murray considered missions to be "the chief end of the church."

Waiting on God in heaven, and waiting for His Son from heaven—these two God has joined together, and no man may put them asunder. The Father who in His own time will reveal His Son from heaven, is the God who, as we wait on Him, prepares us for the revelation of His Son. The present life and the coming glory are inseparably connected in God and in us.

There is sometimes a danger of separating them. It is always easier to be engaged with the religion of the past or the future than to be faithful in the religion of today. As we look to what God has done in the past, or will do in time to come, the personal claim of present duty and present submission to His working may be escaped. There is such a danger of our being so occupied with the things that are coming more than with Him who is to come.

If you are waiting for Christ's coming, be sure that you wait on God now. The hope of that glorious appearing will strengthen you in waiting upon God for what He is to do in you now: the same omnipotent love that is to reveal that glory is working in you even now to fit you for it.

"The blessed hope and the appearing of the glory of our great God and Savior Jesus Christ" (see Titus 2:13) is one of the great bonds of union given to God's Church throughout the ages. "He shall come to be glorified in His saints, and to be marvelled at in all them that believed" (2 Thessalonians 1:10 ASV). Then we shall all meet, and the unity of the body of Christ will be seen in its divine glory. It will be the triumph of divine love.

READ: HABAKKUK 2:3

O C T O B E R   25

THINKING ONLY OF HIM

MADAME GUYON | C. 1720

*Jeanne-Marie Bouvier de la Motte-Guyon (1648-1717) was a French mystic who was
considered a heretic by church authorities and imprisoned from 1695 to 1703 after
publishing the book* A Short and Easy Method of Prayer.

We must begin to abandon and give up our whole existence to God, from the
strong conviction that the events of every moment result from his immediate
will and permission, and are just what our present condition requires. This
conviction will make us content with everything and cause us to regard all that
happens from God's perspective.

But, dearly beloved, you who sincerely wish to give yourselves up to God, I
implore you, that after having once made the donation, you do not take yourself
back again; remember, a gift once presented, is no longer at the disposal of
the giver.

Abandonment is the casting off of all selfish care that we may be fully at God's
disposal. All Christians are exhorted to abandonment; for it is said, "Take no
thought for the morrow; for your Heavenly Father knoweth that ye have need of
all these things" (see Matthew 6:32-34). "In all thy ways acknowledge him, and
he shall direct thy paths" (Proverbs 3:6 KJV). "Commit thy way unto the LORD;
trust also in Him and He will bring it to pass" (see Psalm 37:5).

Our abandonment, then, should be in respect to both external and internal
things, an absolute release of all our concerns into the hands of God, forgetting
ourselves and thinking only of Him; by which the heart will remain always
disengaged, free, and at peace.

It is practiced by continually surrendering our own will to the higher will of
God; renouncing every private inclination as soon as it arises, however good it
may appear; resigning ourselves in all things, whether for soul or body, for time
or eternity; forgetting the past, leaving the future to Providence, and devoting
the present to God. Surrender yourselves then to be led and disposed of just as
God pleases.

READ: MATTHEW 10:39

October 26

Peace and Unity

Justin Martyr | 160

Justin Martyr, born in Palestine, was an early Christian apologist (defender of the faith) and was executed in Rome under the Emperor Marcus Aurelius around 165.

Who then among you is noble-minded? Who compassionate? Who full of love? Let him declare, "If on my account subversion and disagreement and schisms have arisen in the church, I will depart, I will go away wherever you ask, and I will do whatever the majority commands; only let the flock of Christ live in peace under the authority of the church leaders."

Whoever acts in a way to build peace shall gain great glory in the Lord; and every church and place will welcome him with open arms. For, "the earth is the LORD's, and the fulness thereof" (Psalm 24:1 KJV). If you would live a godly life that is without regret and the need for repentance, never stop creating peace and unity in the flock.

Let us also pray for those who have fallen into any sin, that meekness and humility may be given to them, so that they may submit, not unto us, but to the will of God. For in this way they shall secure a fruitful and perfect remembrance from us, with sympathy for them, both in our prayers to God, and our mention of them to the saints.

Let us receive correction, beloved. And we should not feel displeased on this account. Those exhortations by which we challenge and encourage one another are both good in and of themselves, but they are highly profitable most of all in how they unite us to the will of God. For the holy Word says: "The LORD hath severely chastened me, yet hath not given me over to death" (see Psalm 118:18); and "For whom the Lord loveth he chasteneth, and scourgeth every son whom he receiveth" (Hebrews 12:6 KJV).

Read: John 17:20-23

OCTOBER 27

WILL YOU GO BACK WITH US OR NOT?

JOHN BUNYAN | 1678

John Bunyan's classic Christian allegory The Pilgrim's Progress *is considered the first novel in the English language. Bunyan (1628-1688) wrote this during an imprisonment for holding religious services outside the auspices of the Church of England.*

I saw a man clothed with rags, standing with his face turned from his own house, a book in his hand, and a great burden upon his back. I saw him open the book and read from it; and as he read he wept and trembled, finally crying out: "What shall I do?"

Distressed, he went home and told his wife that their city would be burnt with fire from heaven, and all would perish, unless they could find a way of escape. His relatives tried, without avail, to rid him of his fears.

Later I saw Christian—for this was the man's name—walking in the fields, still reading his book. Again he burst out crying: "What shall I do to be saved?" I looked and saw a man named Evangelist come up to him and ask: "Why do you cry?"

Christian told him and Evangelist said: "If this is your fear, why are you just standing here?"

"Because I don't know where to go," Christian answered.

Then Evangelist gave him a scroll with these words written on it: "Flee from the wrath to come." The man read it, looked at Evangelist and asked, "Where must I run?" Evangelist pointed beyond a very wide field and asked: "Do you see the wicket-gate?" "No," the man answered. "Do you see the distant shining light?" "I think I do," Christian answered.

Then said Evangelist: "Keep that light in your eye and go directly there. Then you'll see the gate. Knock and you will be told what you must do."

The man began to run. He hadn't got far when his wife and children and neighbors cried out to him to return. But the man ran on. Two of his neighbors, Obstinate and Pliable, resolved to bring him back by force. When they caught him, he told them that if they died in the City of Destruction, they would sink lower than the grave. He asked them to read in his book. Obstinate cried: "Away with your book! Will you go back with us or not?"

READ: LUKE 9:57-62

OCTOBER 28

IF YOU WERE TO DIE TODAY

THOMAS À KEMPIS | 1475

Thomas à Kempis (1380-1471) was a late medieval monk and the author of The Imitation of Christ, *one of the best-known and beloved books on devotion.*

Very soon your life here will end; consider, then, what may be in store for you elsewhere. Today we live; tomorrow we die and are quickly forgotten. Oh, the dullness and hardness of a heart which looks only to the present instead of preparing for that which is to come!

Therefore, in every deed and every thought, act as though you were to die this very day. If you are not prepared today, how will you be prepared tomorrow? Tomorrow is an uncertain day; how do you know you will have a tomorrow?

What good is it to live a long life if we change in that life so little? Indeed, a long life does not always benefit us, but on the contrary, frequently adds to our guilt. Many count up the years they have spent in religion but find their lives made little holier. Blessed is he who keeps the moment of death ever before his eyes and prepares for it every day.

Happy and prudent is he who tries now in life to be what he wants to be found in death. Perfect contempt of the world, a lively desire to advance in virtue, a love for discipline, the works of penance, readiness to obey, self-denial, and the endurance of every hardship for the love of Christ, these will give a man great expectations of a happy death.

See, then, the great danger from which you can free yourself and the great fear from which you can be saved, if only you will always be wary and mindful of death. Try to live now in such a manner that at the moment of death you may be glad rather than fearful. Learn to die to the world now, that then you may begin to live with Christ. Learn to spurn all things now, that then you may freely go to Him.

READ: PHILIPPIANS 1:20-21

October 29

The Devotion of Hearing

Oswald Chambers | 1927

Oswald Chambers (1874-1917) was a Scottish minister and teacher best known for the devotional classic My Utmost for His Highest, *which his wife compiled after his death.*

"Speak; for thy servant heareth" (1 Samuel 3:10 KJV). Because I have listened definitely to one thing from God, it does not follow that I will listen to everything He says. The way in which I show God that I neither love nor respect Him is by the stubbornness of my heart and mind to hear what He says. If I love my friend, I intuitively detect what he wants. Jesus says, "Ye are my friends" (John 15:14 KJV).

Have I disobeyed some command of my Lord's this week? If I had realized that it was a command of Jesus, I would not consciously have disobeyed it; but most of us show such disrespect to God that we do not even hear what He says. It is as if He never has spoken.

The destiny of my spiritual life is such identification with Jesus Christ that I always hear God, and I know that God always hears me (John 11:41). If I am united with Jesus Christ, I hear God, by the devotion of hearing all the time. A lily, or a tree, or a servant of God, may convey God's message to me. What hinders me from hearing is that I am taken up with other things. It is not that I will not hear God, but I am not devoted in the right place. I am devoted to things, to service, to convictions, and God may say what He likes but I do not hear Him.

The child-like attitude of faith is always ready to say, "Speak, Lord, for Thy servant heareth." If I have not cultivated this devotion of hearing, I can only hear God's voice at certain times; at other times I am distracted and consumed by other things—things which I say I must do, but that make me deaf to Him. Then I am not living with child-like faith.

Have you heard God's voice today?

Read: John 10:27

OCTOBER 30

THE WAY OF LIFE

FROM THE *Didache* | 125

The Didache, *an early second-century writing, was the very first catechism of the Christian church. It describes itself as "the teaching of the Lord to Gentiles by the Twelve Apostles."*

There are two Ways—Life and Death, and there is a great difference between the two. The Way of Life is this: First, thou shalt love the God who made you, and secondly, love your neighbor as yourself.

Don't do anything to anyone else that you wouldn't want done to yourself. Bless those that curse you and pray for your enemies. For what credit is it to you if you love those that love you? Do not even the heathen do the same? But for your part, love those that hate you, and you will have no enemies.

Do not refuse anyone that comes to you in need; for it is the Father's will that we give freely to all. But be cautious in what you receive from others. If you receive charity under the pressure of need, you are innocent. But if you accept charity when you have no need, you will be judged.

My children, flee from evil people. Don't be arrogant and prideful, for pride leads to murder. Don't be jealous or pick fights or let your emotions rule you; these, too, are causes of murder. Don't dwell on lustful thoughts, for lust leads to sexual immorality. Don't speak with crude and profane words; don't let your eyes dwell on someone else's spouse; these are the causes of adultery.

Don't pay attention to omens, or play around with spells, astrology, or magic; this leads to idol worship. Don't be a liar, for lying leads to theft. Don't be a lover of money, nor vain and self-promoting, for these things cause you to steal as well. Don't be a grumbler; don't be stubborn or dwell on evil, for these are sources of blasphemy.

Be long-suffering, merciful, and guileless. Don't exalt yourself, nor let your soul be presumptuous. Walk with righteous and humble men. If an accident befalls you, be assured nothing happens without God.

READ: JOHN 14:6

OCTOBER 31
DEATH HAS NO POWER
JOHN MILTON | 1667

John Milton (1608-1674) was a scholarly writer and poet who served as an official to Oliver Cromwell during a time of religious flux and political upheaval in the British Commonwealth.

The Law of God exact he shall fulfill
Both by obedience and by love, though love
Alone fulfill the Law; thy punishment
He shall endure by coming in the Flesh
To a reproachful life and cursed death,
Proclaiming Life to all who shall believe
In his redemption, and that his obedience
Imputed becomes theirs by Faith, his merits
To save them, not thir own, though legal works.
For this he shall live hated, be blasphem'd,
Seis'd on by force, judg'd, and to death condemnd
A shameful and accurst, nailed to the Cross
By his own Nation, slaine for bringing Life;
But to the Cross he nailes thy Enemies,
The Law that is against thee, and the sins
Of all mankinde, with him there crucifi'd,
Never to hurt them more who rightly trust
In this his satisfaction; so he dies,
But soon revives, Death over him no power
Shall long usurp; ere the third dawning light
Return, the stars of morn shall see him rise
Out of his grave, fresh as the dawning light.

READ: HOSEA 13:14

November 1

What Christ Has Done

Charles Haddon Spurgeon | 1860

Charles Haddon (C. H.) Spurgeon (1834–1892) was a British Particular Baptist minister who is known as the "Prince of Preachers."

Whom do you think Christ came to carry on His shoulders to Heaven? Those that can walk there themselves? No, let them trudge their weary way. If they think they can go to Heaven with their good works let them do so. One of two things: either you must be saved without deserving to be saved—saved by the works of Another—or else you must keep the whole Law and so inherit Heaven of your own right and patent. If, then, you are willing to come to Christ—just as you are without any preparation, simply as a sinner—then Christ has made atonement for you. Your guilt is put away—God accepts you—you are a pardoned man. You may go out at yonder door and say in your heart, "Therefore being justified by faith, we have peace with God through our Lord Jesus Christ. . . . And not only so, but we also joy in God through our Lord Jesus Christ, by whom we have now received the atonement" (Romans 5:1, 11 KJV).

As for holiness and good works, these shall come afterwards. Having believed in Christ, His Spirit shall be given and you shall be zealous for good works. While the legalist is talking about them, you shall do them. What you could not do before, you shall do now. When you have given up all trust in yourself you shall become holy and pure and the Spirit of God shall enter into you and shall renew you. You shall be kept by the power of God till, without spot, or wrinkle, or any such thing you shall be presented before your Father's face saved— saved eternally.

Read: Mark 2:17

November 2

Willing to Give

Smith Wigglesworth | 1937

Smith Wigglesworth (1859-1947) was born in Yorkshire, England, and was known as the "Apostle of Faith." He traveled the world as a Pentecostal evangelist, holding healing services.

All the Word is wonderful. This blessed Book brings such life and health and peace, and such abundance that we should never be poor any more. I want to show you how rich you may be, that in everything you can be enriched in Christ Jesus. He has abundance of grace for you and the gift of righteousness, and through His abundant grace all things are possible.

The Lord Jesus is always wanting to show forth His grace and love in order to draw us to Himself. God is willing to do things, to manifest His Word, and let us know in measure the mind of our God in this day and hour. There are many needy ones, many afflicted ones, but I do not think any present are half as bad as the leper we read of in Matthew 8. You may be suffering, but God will show forth His perfect cleansing, His perfect healing, if you have a living faith in Christ. He is a wonderful Jesus.

This leper must have been told about Jesus. How much is missed because people are not constantly telling what Jesus will do today. Probably someone had said, "Jesus can heal you." And so he was filled with expectation as he saw the Lord coming down the mountainside. Lepers were shut out as unclean and so it would have been very difficult for him to get near because of the crowd that surrounded Jesus. But as He came down from the mount He met this poor leper. Oh, this terrible disease! There was no help for him humanly speaking, but nothing is too hard for Jesus. The man cried, "Lord, if thou wilt, thou canst make me clean" (Matthew 8:2 KJV).

Was Jesus willing? You will never find Jesus missing an opportunity of doing good. The trouble is we do not come to Him, we do not ask Him for what He is more than willing to give.

Read: Matthew 7:7-11

NOVEMBER 3

A GLORIOUS CHANGE

GEORGE WHITEFIELD | 1760

*George Whitefield (1714-1770) was an Anglican evangelist and a key figure of the
Great Awakening. He drew great crowds and media coverage everywhere he traveled.*

To produce this glorious change, this new creation, the glorious Jesus left his
Father's bosom. For this he led a persecuted life; for this he died an ignominious
and accursed death; for this he rose again; and for this he now sits at the right
hand of his Father. All the precepts of his gospel, all his ordinances, all his
providences, whether of an afflictive or prosperous nature, all divine revelation
from the beginning to the end, all center in these two points: to show us how we
are fallen; and to complete a glorious and blessed change in our souls.

Others that were once as far from the kingdom of God as you are have been
partakers of this blessedness. What a wretched creature was Mary Magdalene.
And yet out of her Jesus Christ cast seven devils. Not only that, he appeared to
her first after he rose from the dead, and she became, as it were, an apostle to the
very apostles.

What a covetous creature was Zaccheus. He was a griping, cheating publican;
and yet, perhaps, in one quarter of an hour's time, his heart is enlarged, and he
was made quite willing to give half of his goods to feed the poor.

And to mention one more, what a cruel person was Paul. He was a persecutor,
a blasphemer, injurious; one that breathed out threats against the disciples of
the Lord, and made havoc of the church of Christ. And yet what a wonderful
turn did he meet with, as he was journeying to Damascus. From a persecutor,
he became a preacher; was afterwards made a spiritual father to thousands, and
now probably sits nearest the Lord Jesus Christ in glory. And why all this? That
he might be made an example to them that should hereafter believe.

O then believe, repent; I beseech you, believe the gospel. Indeed, it is glad
tidings, even tidings of great joy.

READ: JEREMIAH 18:1-6

NOVEMBER 4
THE WHOLE SOUL
JOHN CALVIN | 1560

John Calvin (1509-1564) was born into a wealthy family in Noyon, France. His father wanted him to pursue theology, but he studied law at the University of Paris. Never formally ordained, once he converted to Protestantism, his life was given to ministry.

Scripture not only directs us to seek to know God, the author of life; but after showing us how far we have fallen from our true origin, also sets Christ before us as a model—of which our lives should reflect. What do you possibly need beyond this? If the Lord adopts us as his children on the condition that our lives are a representation of Christ, unless we dedicate and devote ourselves to righteousness, we not only betray and rebel against our Creator, but also reject the Savior himself.

Since God revealed himself to us as a Father, we would be ungrateful if we did not live as his sons. Since Christ purified us by his blood, we would be foolish to be defiled with new pollution. Since he ingrafted us into his body, we, who are his members, should anxiously avoid contracting any stain or taint. Since he who is our head ascended to heaven, we should give up our attachment to the things of this world and with our whole soul aspire to heaven. These, I say, are the surest foundations of a well-regulated life.

But what of those who have nothing of Christ, yet call themselves Christians? How dare they boast of this sacred name! The Apostle Paul denies that any man truly knows Christ who has not learned to put off "the old man which grows corrupt according to the deceitful lusts . . . and . . . put on the new man which was created according to God, in true righteousness and holiness" (Ephesians 4: 22, 24). They are guilty then, of pretending a knowledge of Christ, with whatever eloquence they may speak of the Gospel.

Doctrine is not a matter of words, but of life; is not gained by intellectual pursuits, but is received only when it possesses the whole soul and finds its place in the inmost recesses of the heart.

READ: LUKE 8:15

NOVEMBER 5

THE DARKNESS OF DOUBT VANISHED

AUGUSTINE | 398

Augustine (354-430) was bishop of Hippo Regius and one of the most important figures in the development of Western Christianity. After his conversion, Augustine developed his own approach to philosophy and theology, accommodating a variety of methods and perspectives.

When a deep consideration from the secret bottom of my soul had drawn together and heaped up all my misery in the sight of my heart; there arose a mighty storm, bringing a mighty shower of tears. I threw myself down aimlessly under a certain fig tree, giving full vent to my tears. And, not in these words, yet to this purpose, I said, "O Lord, how long? How long, Lord, wilt Thou be angry forever? Remember not my former iniquities" (see Psalm 79:5, 8) for I felt that I was held by them. I sent up these sorrowful words: "How long, how long? Tomorrow? Why not now? Why is there not this hour an end to my uncleanness?"

So was I speaking and weeping in the most bitter contrition of my heart, when, suddenly I heard from a neighboring house a child's voice, chanting and repeating, "Take up and read; Take up and read." Instantly, my countenance altered. I wondered whether children were likely to play and sing such words— and thought not. So checking the torrent of my tears, I arose, interpreting it to be no other than a command from God to open the book, and read the first chapter I should find.

Eagerly I retrieved the volume of the Apostle, and in silence read that section on which my eyes first fell: "Let us walk properly, as in the day, not in revelry and drunkenness, not in lewdness and lust, not in strife and envy. But put on the Lord Jesus Christ, and make no provision for the flesh, to *fulfill its* lusts" (Romans 13:13-14). No further would I read; nor did I need to—for instantly, by a light as it were of serenity infused into my heart, all the darkness of doubt vanished away.

READ: PSALM 13:1-6

NOVEMBER 6

WHATEVER YOUR SITUATION

ST. FRANCIS DE SALES | 1619

Francis de Sales (1567-1622) was bishop of Geneva and was an accomplished preacher known for his writings on the topics of spiritual direction and spiritual formation.

When God made all things, he commanded the plants to bring forth fruit each according to its own kind. He has likewise commanded Christians, who are the living plants of his church, to bring forth the fruits of devotion, each one in accord with his character, his station, and his calling.

Devotion must be practiced in different ways by the nobleman and the working man; the servant and the prince; the widow, the unmarried girl, and the married woman. Tell me whether it is proper for a bishop to want to lead a solitary life; or for married people to have no concern about their income; or for a working man to spend his whole day in church like a priest? Is not this sort of devotion ridiculous, unorganized, and intolerable? Yet this absurd error occurs very frequently; but in no way does true devotion destroy anything at all. On the contrary, it perfects and fulfills all things. In fact if it ever works against anyone's legitimate station and calling, then it is very definitely false devotion.

The bee collects honey from flowers in such a way as to do the least damage to them, and he leaves them whole and fresh, just as he found them. True devotion does still better. Not only does it not injure any sort of calling or occupation, it even embellishes and enhances it. Through devotion your family cares become more peaceful, mutual love between husband and wife becomes more sincere, our service becomes more faithful, and our work, no matter what it is, becomes more pleasant and agreeable.

It is therefore an error and even a heresy to wish to exclude the exercise of devotion from military divisions, from the artisans' shops, from the courts of princes, from family households. In whatever situations we happen to be, we can and we must aspire to the life of perfection.

READ: COLOSSIANS 4:2

NOVEMBER 7

TO ACCOMPLISH THY WILL

FRANÇOIS FÉNELON | 1725

François de Salignac de la Mothe-Fénelon (1651-1715) was a French Roman Catholic theologian, poet, and writer.

Lord, I know not what I ought to ask of Thee; only you know what I need. You love me better than I know how to love myself.

O Father! I dare not ask for either crosses or consolations; I simply present myself before Thee, I open my heart to Thee.

Behold my needs, which I know not myself; see and do according to thy tender mercy. Smite, or heal; depress me, or raise me up. I adore all thy purposes without knowing them. I offer myself in sacrifice; I yield myself to Thee. I have no other desire than to accomplish thy will.

People cannot become perfect simply by hearing or reading about perfection. The chief thing is not to listen to myself, but to listen silently to God; to renounce all vanity and apply myself to real virtues; to talk little and to do much, without caring to be seen. He will teach me much more than all the most experienced persons and all the most spiritual books. I already know much more of good than I practice. Rather than gain more knowledge, I have a much greater need to put into practice that which I have already acquired.

The remedy for wandering thoughts and indifference is to set apart regular times for reading and prayer; to become involved in outward matters only when it is necessary; and to soften the hardness of your judgment, restrain your temper, and humble your mind, rather than to uphold your opinion, even when it is right.

"Learn of me," Jesus Christ says to us, "for I am meek and lowly in heart; and ye shall find rest unto your souls" (Matthew 11:29 KJV). Be sure that the grace, inward peace, and the blessing of the Holy Spirit will be with you, if you maintain gentleness and humility amid all your trials and difficulties.

READ: MATTHEW 11:29

NOVEMBER 8

WALKING BY FAITH

HANNAH WHITALL SMITH | 1875

Hannah Tatum Whitall Smith (1832-1911) was born in Philadelphia to a long line of influential Quakers. She was a lay speaker and author in the Holiness movement and an active supporter of women's suffrage and temperance.

The Lord deals with each of us differently, yet a personal consecration to God must be made by everyone who is seeking a clean heart—a covenant that we will be wholly and forever His.

This I did intellectually, with a heart full of hardness and darkness, unbelief and sin. I laid all upon the altar, a living sacrifice, to the best of my ability. And after I rose from my knees, I was painfully aware that there was no change in my feelings. But I was sure that I had made an entire and eternal consecration of myself to God, with all sincerity and honesty of purpose.

I knew that I must believe God accepted me, and had come to dwell in my heart. I did not believe this, and yet I desired to do so. I knew that my heart was full of evil. I seemed to have no power to overcome pride or to repel evil thoughts, which I abhorred. Satan struggled hard to beat me back from the Rock of Ages, but thanks to God I finally discovered how to live in the moment, and then I found rest.

All I had to do was look to Jesus for grace and trust Him to cleanse my heart and keep me from sin at the present moment. I would not permit the adversary to trouble me about the past or future. I determined to be a child of Abraham and walk by naked faith in the Word of God, not by inward feelings and emotions. Since then the Lord has given me a steady victory over those sins that enslaved me. My feelings vary, but when I have feelings, I praise God, and I trust in His word; and when I am empty and my feelings are gone, I do the same. I have covenanted to walk by faith and not by feelings.

READ: 2 CORINTHIANS 5:7

November 9

Justified by Faith

Martin Luther | 1518

Martin Luther (1483-1546) was a German priest and professor of theology who initiated the Protestant Reformation. He strongly disputed the assertion that freedom from God's punishment of sin could be purchased with money. His refusal to retract his writings resulted in his excommunication by the pope and condemnation as an outlaw by the emperor.

Although the works of man always seem attractive and good, they are nevertheless likely to be mortal sins. Human works appear attractive outwardly, but within they are filthy, as Christ says concerning the Pharisees in Matthew 23:27. For they appear good and beautiful, yet God does not judge according to appearances but searches the minds and hearts. For without grace and faith it is impossible to have a pure heart.

He is not righteous who does much, but he who, without work, believes much in Christ. For the righteousness of God is not acquired by means of acts frequently repeated, as Aristotle taught, but it is imparted by faith, for "He who through faith is righteous shall live" (see Romans 1:17), and "Man believes with his heart and so is justified" (see Romans 10:10). Not that the righteous person does nothing, but his works do not make him righteous; rather his righteousness creates works. For grace and faith are infused without our works. After they have been imparted the works follow. Thus Romans 3:20 states, "No human being will be justified in His sight by works of the law," and, "For we hold that man is justified by faith apart from works of law" (see Romans 3:28). In other words, works contribute nothing to justification.

Therefore man knows that works which he does by such faith are not his but God's. For this reason he does not seek to become justified or glorified through them, but seeks God. His justification by faith in Christ is sufficient to him. Christ is his wisdom, righteousness, etc., that he himself may be Christ's vessel and instrument.

Read: Galatians 2:16

NOVEMBER 10
A VISION OF PARADISE
PAPIAS | 150

Papias of Hierappolis (68-155) was a bishop whose writings were cited widely in the early church, but which survive only in fragments.

The days will come in which vines shall grow, having each ten thousand branches, and in each branch ten thousand twigs, and in each true twig ten thousand shoots, and in every one of the shoots ten thousand clusters, and on every one of the clusters ten thousand grapes, and every grape when pressed will give five-and-twenty metretes of wine. And when any one of the saints shall lay hold of a cluster, another shall cry out, "I am a better cluster, take me; bless the Lord through me."

In like manner, a grain of wheat will produce ten thousand ears, and that every ear will have ten thousand grains, and every grain will yield ten pounds of clear, pure, fine flour. Apples and seeds and grass will produce in similar proportions. All animals will feed only on that which grows from the earth and will be at peace and harmony with one another and under the control of man.

The Lord said, "These, then, are the times mentioned by the prophet Isaiah: 'And the wolf shall lie, down with the lamb'" (see Isaiah 11:6).

As the elders say, then those who are deemed worthy of an abode in heaven shall go there, others shall enjoy the delights of Paradise, and others shall possess the splendor of the city; for everywhere the Savior will be seen, according as they shall be worthy who see Him.

READ: JOHN 15:5-8

November 11
The Obedience of One
John Wesley | 18th century

John Wesley (1703-1791) was educated at Oxford, where in 1729 he became the leader of a group of young men who would later go on to found the Methodist Church.

How frequent and bitter is the outcry against Adam for the mischief he not only brought upon himself, but entailed upon all his descendants! By one man's disobedience, we all were not only deprived of the favor of God, but also of His image, of all virtue, righteousness, and true holiness. Death entered the world with all its pain, sickness, and a whole train of unholy passions and tempers. "For all this we may thank Adam" has been echoed down from generation to generation.

Yet many have questioned God's mercy, if not also His justice, asking, "Did God not foresee that Adam would abuse his liberty? Did He not know the terrible consequences this would have on all his posterity? Why did He permit that disobedience? Was it not easy for the Almighty to have prevented it?" He certainly did foresee the whole. This cannot be denied.

But by the fall of Adam, mankind has gained a capacity of attaining more holiness and happiness on earth than would have been possible otherwise. For if Adam had not fallen, Christ would not have died. Nothing can be clearer than this, nothing more undeniable. Do you not see that this was the very ground of His coming into the world? Unless many had been made sinners by the disobedience of one, by the obedience of one many would not have been made righteous.

There could then have been no such thing as faith in God, loving the world, giving His only Son for us. There could have been no such thing as faith in the Son of God, loving us and giving Himself for us. There could have been no faith in the Spirit of God, renewing the image of God in our hearts and raising us from the death of sin unto the life of righteousness. Indeed, justification by faith would not exist; nor redemption in the blood of Christ.

Read: 1 Corinthians 15:20-22

November 12

Into the Light

Sir Walter Raleigh | 1618

Sir Walter Raleigh (1552-1618) was an English aristocrat, writer, poet, soldier,
courtier, spy, and explorer. Sentenced to death for alleged treason—which many
believed unnecessary and unjust—he delivered the following speech in the Old Palace
Yard at Westminster prior to his execution.

I thank my God heartily that He hath brought me into the light to die, and not
left me to die in the dark prison of the Tower, where I have suffered a great deal
of adversity and a long sickness; and I thank God that my fever hath not taken
me at this time, as I prayed God it might not.

But this I say: For a man to call God to witness to a falsehood at any time is a
grievous sin! And what shall we hope for at the Day of Judgment? But to call God
to witness to a falsehood at the time of death is far more grievous and impious,
and there is no hope for such a one. And what should I expect that am now going
to render an account of my faith? I do, therefore, call the Lord to witness, as I
hope to be saved, and as I hope to be seen in His kingdom. If I speak not truth, O
Lord, let me never come into thy glory!

But in this I speak now, what have I to do with kings? I have nothing to do with
them, neither do I fear them. I have now to do with God; therefore, as I hope to
be saved at the last day, I never spoke dishonorably, disloyally, nor dishonestly
of the king.

And now I entreat you all to join with me in prayer, that the great God of
Heaven, whom I have grievously offended, being a man full of all vanity, and
having lived a sinful life, in all sinful callings, having been a soldier, a captain,
a sea captain, and a courtier, which are all places of wickedness and vice; that
God, I say, would forgive me, cast away my sins from me, and receive me into
everlasting life. So I take my leave of you all, making my peace with God.

Read: Isaiah 50:10

NOVEMBER 13

FACING TEMPTATION

JOHN KNOX | 16TH CENTURY

*John Knox (c. 1510-1572) was a Scottish clergyman and a leader of the Protestant
Reformation who is considered the founder of the Presbyterian denomination
in Scotland.*

I am moved to address this in order that those who fall into diverse temptations
would not judge themselves to be less acceptable in God's presence. On the
contrary, having the way prepared to victory by Christ Jesus, they should not fear
the crafty assaults of that subtle serpent Satan; but with joy and bold courage, we
may assure ourselves of God's present favor, and of final victory, by the means of
Him who, for our safeguard and deliverance, entered in the battle and triumphed
over His adversary and all his raging fury.

That the Son of God was tempted gives instruction to us that temptations,
although they be ever so grievous and fearful, do not separate us from God's
favor and mercy, but rather declare the great graces of God to appertain to
us, which makes Satan to rage as a roaring lion. For against none does he so
fiercely fight as against those of whose hearts Christ has taken possession. The
Spirit that led Christ into the wilderness was not the devil, but the Holy Spirit
of God the Father. Likewise by the same Spirit He was strengthened and made
strong, and, finally, raised up from the dead. The Spirit of God, I say, led Christ
to the place of this battle, where He endured combat for the whole forty days
and nights.

Oh, what comfort ought the remembrance of these signs be to our hearts!
Christ Jesus hath fought our battle; He himself hath taken us into His care and
protection; however the devil may rage by temptations, be they spiritual or
physical, he is not able to bereave us out of the hand of the Almighty Son of
God. To Him be all glory for His mercies most abundantly poured upon us!

READ: MATTHEW 4:1-11

NOVEMBER 14

THE APOSTLES' CREED

2ND CENTURY

The Apostles' Creed, sometimes called the Symbol of the Apostles, is an early declaration of Christian belief. It is widely used by a number of Christian denominations for both liturgical and catechetical purposes, including Catholics, Lutherans, Anglicans, and Western Orthodoxy. It is also used by Presbyterians, Methodists, and Congregationalists.

I believe in God the Father Almighty,
Maker of heaven and earth:
And in Jesus Christ, His only Son our Lord,
Who was conceived by the Holy Ghost,
Born of the Virgin Mary,
Suffered under Pontius Pilate,
Was crucified, dead, and buried:
He descended into hell;
The third day he rose again from the dead;
He ascended into heaven,
And sitteth on the right hand of God the Father Almighty;
From thence He shall come to judge the quick and the dead.
I believe in the Holy Ghost;
The holy catholic church;
The communion of saints;
The forgiveness of sins;
The resurrection of the body,
And the life everlasting.
Amen.

READ: ACTS 2:44

NOVEMBER 15

THE ABUNDANCE OF PRAYER

E. M. BOUNDS | 1913

Edward McKendree Bounds (1835-1913) was an American minister. A practicing lawyer, Bounds felt called to ministry and was ordained in the Methodist Church. He would serve as a chaplain during the Civil War, and later as a pastor during the rebuilding effort.

Prayer is a solemn service due to God, an adoration, a worship; the presenting of some desire, the expression of some need to Him, who, as a Father, finds His greatest pleasure in relieving the wants and granting the desires of His children. Prayer is the outstretched arms of the child for the Father's help. Prayer is the child's cry calling to the Father's ear, the Father's heart, and to the Father's ability; which the Father is to hear, the Father is to feel, and which the Father is to relieve. Prayer is the seeking of God's great and greatest good, which will not come if we do not pray.

Prayer is an ardent and believing cry to God for some specific thing. God's rule is to answer by giving the specific thing asked for. With it may come much of other gifts and graces. But even they come because God hears and answers prayer.

We follow the plain letter and spirit of the Bible when we affirm that God answers prayer, and answers by giving us the very things we desire, and that the withholding of that which we desire and the giving of something else is not the rule, but rare and exceptional. When His children cry for bread, He gives them bread.

Prayer is no petty invention of man, a fancied relief for fancied ills. Prayer is the contact of a living soul with God. Prayer fills man's emptiness with God's fullness. It fills man's poverty with God's riches. It puts away man's weakness with God's strength. It banishes man's littleness with God's greatness. Prayer is God's plan to supply man's great and continuous need with God's great and continuous abundance.

READ: 1 THESSALONIANS 5:17

NOVEMBER 16

IMITATE CHRIST

PAUL | 61

The following selection from Philippians is often referred to as the Kenosis Passage, which comes from the Greek term meaning "to empty." Many scholars believe that when Paul wrote this letter he inserted verses 6 and 7, having gleaned them from a hymn that was sung in the earliest Christian worship services.

Therefore if there is any encouragement in Christ, if there is any consolation of love, if there is any fellowship of the Spirit, if any affection and compassion, make my joy complete by being of the same mind, maintaining the same love, united in spirit, intent on one purpose.

Do nothing from selfishness or empty conceit, but with humility of mind regard one another as more important than yourselves; do not merely look out for your own personal interests, but also for the interests of others. Have this attitude in yourselves which was also in Christ Jesus, who, although He existed in the form of God, did not regard equality with God a thing to be grasped, but emptied Himself, taking the form of a bond-servant, and being made in the likeness of men.

Being found in appearance as a man, He humbled Himself by becoming obedient to the point of death, even death on a cross.

For this reason also, God highly exalted Him, and bestowed on Him the name which is above every name, so that at the name of Jesus every knee will bow, of those who are in heaven and on earth and under the earth, and that every tongue will confess that Jesus Christ is Lord, to the glory of God the Father.

READ: 1 PETER 4:1-2

NOVEMBER 17

THE PRICE OF GRACE

DIETRICH BONHOEFFER | 1937

Dietrich Bonhoeffer (1906-1945) was a German pastor, theologian, and martyr. His involvement in plans of the Abwehr to assassinate Adolf Hitler led to his arrest in April 1943 and his subsequent execution by hanging in April 1945, just twenty-three days before the Nazi surrender.

Cheap grace is the grace we bestow on ourselves. Cheap grace is the preaching of forgiveness without requiring repentance, baptism without church discipline, Communion without confession. . . . Cheap grace is grace without discipleship, grace without the cross, grace without Jesus Christ, living and incarnate.

Costly grace is the treasure hidden in the field; for the sake of it a man will gladly go and sell all that he has. It is the pearl of great price, which to buy, the merchant will sell all his goods. It is the kingly rule of Christ, for whose sake a man will pluck out the eye that causes him to stumble; it is the call of Jesus Christ at which the disciple leaves his nets and follows him.

Costly grace is the gospel which must be sought again and again and again, the gift which must be asked for, the door at which a man must knock. Such grace is costly because it calls us to follow, and it is grace because it calls us to follow Jesus Christ. It is costly because it costs a man his life, and it is grace because it gives a man the only true life. It is costly because it condemns sin, and grace because it justifies the sinner. Above all, it is costly because it cost God the life of his Son: "Ye were bought at a price," and what has cost God much cannot be cheap for us. Above all, it is grace because God did not reckon his Son too dear a price to pay for our life, but delivered him up for us. Costly grace is the Incarnation of God.

To endure the cross is not tragedy; it is the suffering which is the fruit of an exclusive allegiance to Jesus Christ. When Christ calls a man, he bids him come and die.

READ: 1 CORINTHIANS 6:19-20

November 18

The Treasure of Heaven

Anthony the Great | 4th century

Anthony the Great (c. 251-356), also known as Antony the Great, was born in Cooma near Herakleopolis, Magna, in lower Egypt to wealthy landowner parents. He was a Christian saint and a prominent leader among the Desert Fathers.

Wherefore, children, let us not faint nor deem that the time is long, or that we are doing something great, for "the sufferings of this present time are not worthy to be compared with the glory which shall be revealed in us" (Romans 8:18). Nor let us think, as we look at the world, that we have renounced anything of much consequence, for the whole earth is very small compared with all of heaven.

Even if we were lords of all the earth and gave it all up, it would never be worthy of comparison with the kingdom of heaven. For as a man should despise a copper drachma in order to gain a hundred drachmas of gold; so if a man were lord of all the earth and were to renounce it, that which he gives up is little, and he receives a hundredfold. But if not even the whole earth is equal in value to the heavens, then he who has given up a few acres leaves as it were nothing; and even if he has given up a house or much gold he ought not to boast nor be low-spirited.

Further, we should consider that even if we do not relinquish them for virtue's sake, still when we die we shall leave them behind. Why then should we not give them up for virtue's sake, that we may inherit a kingdom? Therefore let the desire for possessions take hold of no one, for what gain is it to acquire these things which we cannot take with us? Why not rather get those things which we can take away—prudence, justice, temperance, courage, understanding, love, kindness to the poor, faith in Christ, freedom from wrath, hospitality? If we possess these, we shall find them of great value in preparing for us a welcome there in the land of the meek-hearted.

Read: Matthew 6:20

November 19
A Hunger for the Supernatural
Friedrich Schleiermacher | 19th Century

Friedrich Daniel Ernst Schleiermacher (1768-1834) was a German theologian and philosopher whose work forms part of the foundation of the modern field of hermeneutics. Because of his profound impact on subsequent Christian thought, he is often called the "Father of Modern Liberal Theology."

Man is born with a religious capacity as with every other. If only his sense for the profoundest depths of his own nature is not crushed out, if only all fellowship between himself and the Primal Source is not quite shut off, religion would, after its own fashion, infallibly be developed. But in our time, alas! That is exactly what, in very large measure, does happen.

Who hinders the prosperity of religion? Not you, not the doubters and scoffers. Even though you were all of one mind to have no religion, you would not disturb Nature in her purpose of producing piety from the depths of the soul, for your influence could only later find prepared soil. Nor, as is supposed, do the immoral most hinder the prosperity of religion, for it is quite a different power to which their endeavors are opposed. But the discreet and practical men of today are, in the present state of the world, the enemies of religion, and their great preponderance is the cause why it plays such a poor and insignificant role, for from tender childhood they maltreat man, crushing out his higher aspirations.

With great reverence I regard the longing of young minds for the marvelous and supernatural. Joyfully taking in the motley show of things, they seek at the same time something else to set over against it. They search everywhere for something surpassing the accustomed phenomena and the light play of life. However many earthly objects are presented for their knowing, there seems still another sense unnourished. That is the first stirrings of religion.

Read: Luke 11:9

November 20

Love Your Enemy

Martin Luther King Jr. | 1957

Martin Luther King Jr. (1929-1968) was an American clergyman, activist, and prominent leader in the African-American civil rights movement.

"But I say unto you, Love your enemies, bless them that curse you, do good to them that hate you, and pray for them which despitefully use you . . . that ye may be the children of your Father which is in heaven" (Matthew 5:44-45 KJV).

Certainly these are great words, lifted to cosmic proportions. And over the centuries, many have argued that this is an extremely difficult command, going so far as to say that it just isn't possible; that this is just additional proof that Jesus was an impractical idealist who never quite came down to earth. But far from being an impractical idealist, Jesus has become the practical realist. Far from being the pious injunction of a utopian dreamer, this command is an absolute necessity for the survival of our civilization. Yes, it is love that will save our world and our civilization, love even for enemies.

Now let me hasten to say that Jesus realized that it's hard to love your enemies. He realized that it was painfully, pressingly hard. But Jesus was very serious when he gave this command; he wasn't playing. We have the Christian and moral responsibility to seek to discover the meaning of these words, and to discover how and why we should live by this command.

It is significant that Jesus does not say, "Like your enemy." Like is a sentimental, affectionate thing. There are many people that I find it difficult to like. I don't like what they say. I don't like their attitudes. I don't like some of the things they're doing. I don't like them. But Jesus says love them. And love is greater than like.

Love is understanding, redemptive goodwill for all men, because God loves them. You refuse to do anything that will defeat an individual, because you have *agape* in your soul. And you come to the point that you love the individual who does the evil deed, while hating the deed that the person does. This is what Jesus means when he says, "Love your enemy."

Read: Matthew 5:43-45

November 21

Truly God and Truly Man

The Confession of Chalcedon | 451

The Confession of Chalcedon, also known as the Doctrine of Hypostatic Union, was adopted at the first of seven ecumenical councils and is accepted by Eastern Orthodox, Catholic, and many Protestant churches.

We, then, following the holy Fathers, all with one consent, teach people to confess one and the same Son, our Lord Jesus Christ, the same perfect in Godhead and also perfect in manhood;

Truly God and truly man, of a reasonable rational soul and body;

Consubstantial co-essential with the Father according to the Godhead, and consubstantial with us according to the Manhood;

In all things like unto us, without sin;

Begotten before all ages of the Father according to the Godhead, and in these latter days, for us and for our salvation, born of the Virgin Mary, the Mother of God, according to the Manhood;

One and the same Christ, Son, Lord, only begotten, to be acknowledged in two natures, inconfusedly, unchangeably, indivisibly, inseparably;

The distinction of natures being by no means taken away by the union, but rather the property of each nature being preserved, and concurring in one Person and one Subsistence, not parted or divided into two persons, but one and the same Son, and only begotten God, the Word, the Lord Jesus Christ;

As the prophets from the beginning have declared concerning Him, and the Lord Jesus Christ Himself has taught us, and the Creed of the holy Fathers has handed down to us.

Read: Mark 15:39

November 22

Amazing Love

Charles Wesley | 1738

Charles Wesley (1707-1788) was an English leader of the Methodist movement and the younger brother of Anglican clergyman John Wesley. He is chiefly remembered for the many hymns he wrote.

And can it be that I should gain
An interest in the Savior's blood?
Died He for me, who caused His pain—
For me, who Him to death pursued?
Amazing love! How can it be,
That Thou, my God, shouldst die for me?
Amazing love! How can it be,
That Thou, my God, shouldst die for me?
He left His Father's throne above
So free, so infinite His grace—
Emptied Himself of all but love,
And bled for Adam's helpless race:
'Tis mercy all, immense and free,
For O my God, it found out me!
'Tis mercy all, immense and free,
For O my God, it found out me!
Long my imprisoned spirit lay,
Fast bound in sin and nature's night;
Thine eye diffused a quickening ray—
I woke, the dungeon flamed with light;
My chains fell off, my heart was free,
I rose, went forth, and followed Thee.
My chains fell off, my heart was free,
I rose, went forth, and followed Thee.

Read: 1 John 3:16

NOVEMBER 23

SHINE AS THE LEAST

DWIGHT L. MOODY | 1873

Dwight Lyman Moody (1837-1899), also known as D. L. Moody, was an American evangelist and publisher who founded the Moody Church, the Moody Bible Institute, and Moody Publishers.

God has no need of our strength or wisdom, but our ignorance and weakness; let us but give these to Him, and He can make use of us in winning souls.

"And they that be wise shall shine as the brightness of the firmament; and they that turn many to righteousness as the stars for ever and ever" (Daniel 12:3 KJV).

Now we all want to shine; but here God tells us who will shine forever—not statesmen or warriors, who shine only for a season; but namely those who win souls to Christ; even the little boy who persuades one to come to Christ.

Paul lists five things (1 Corinthians 1:27-29) that God makes use of: the weak, the foolish, the base, the despised, and those things which are not; in order that no flesh might glory in his sight. He can and will use us, when we are willing to be humble for Christ's sake; so with an ass's jawbone Samson slew his thousands, at the blowing of rams' horns the walls of Jericho fell. Let God work in His own way and with His own instruments; let us all rejoice that He should and get into the position in which God can use us.

There is much concern today over sins and deceptions, but I do not fear them half so much as that dead and cold formalism that has crept into the church of God. The unbelieving world, and these skeptics holding out their false lights, are watching you and me. Where one reads the Bible, a hundred read you and me: and if they find nothing in us, they set the whole thing aside as a myth.

He who has found his true work, winning souls to Christ, and does it, such is the happiest man. Job's circumstances changed when he began praying for his friends; so will all who work for others shine not only in heaven, but here and now.

READ: MATTHEW 5:14

NOVEMBER 24
FREE TO CHOOSE
MAX LUCADO | 1999

Max Lucado (b. 1955) is a best-selling author and minister in San Antonio, Texas.

The day is coming. In a few moments the stillness of the dawn will be exchanged for the noise of the day. For the next twelve hours I will be exposed to the day's demands. It is now that I must make a choice. Because of Calvary, I'm free to choose. And so I choose.

I CHOOSE LOVE . . . No occasion justifies hatred; no injustice warrants bitterness. I choose love. Today I will love God and what God loves.

I CHOOSE JOY . . . I will invite my God to be the God of circumstance. I will refuse to see any problem as anything less than an opportunity to see God.

I CHOOSE PEACE . . . I will live forgiven. I will forgive so that I may live.

I CHOOSE PATIENCE . . . I will overlook the inconveniences of the world. Instead of cursing the one who takes my place, I'll invite him to do so.

I CHOOSE KINDNESS . . . I will be kind to the poor, for they are alone. Kind to the rich, for they are afraid. And kind to the unkind, for such is how God has treated me.

I CHOOSE GOODNESS . . . I will go without a dollar before I take a dishonest one. I will be overlooked before I will boast.

I CHOOSE FAITHFULNESS . . . Today I will keep my promises. My associates will not question my word. My wife will not question my love. And my children will never fear that their father will not come home.

I CHOOSE GENTLENESS . . . If I raise my voice may it be only in praise. If I clench my fist, may it be only in prayer. If I make a demand, may it be only of myself.

I CHOOSE SELF-CONTROL . . . I will be drunk only by joy. I will be impassioned only by my faith. I will be influenced only by God. I will be taught only by Christ.

Love, joy, peace, patience, kindness, goodness, faithfulness, gentleness, and self-control. To these I commit my day.

READ: DEUTERONOMY 30:19

NOVEMBER 25

FEAR GOD—NOT THE DEVIL

SHEPHERD OF HERMES | 150

Written in Rome in the mid-second century during a time of persecution, this wonderful piece of literature by an unknown author was a great encouragement to the early Christian church.

I listened to the teaching of the Shepherd and he taught me: Fear and honor the Lord, and keep His commandments. For if you keep the commandments of God, you will be powerful in everything you do. Your actions will stand out with distinction and not be judged negatively by anyone. In honoring the Lord, you will do all things well. This is the fear that you need to have for your salvation.

But don't fear the devil. As a child of God who is reverent to the Lord, you have dominion over the devil, for there is no real power in him. So under no circumstances let the deceiver who has no real power become an object of fear for you. Fear the One with the true power, a glorious power. It's common sense. All should despise the one with no real power. But, as a strong caution I would add, fear the deeds of the devil—doing them yourself—since they are wicked. But as long as you honor God, you will not do these deeds, but will refrain from them.

If you do not wish to do that which is evil, fear the Lord, and you will not do it. And if you wish to do that which is good, fear the Lord, and you will do it. The reverence of the Lord is strong, great, and glorious. This is the fear that makes you strong and enables you to live for Him, keeping His commandments. They will be alive to God.

I asked the Shepherd why those who obey God's commands should be considered "alive to God"? Because all creation does not keep His commandments. Only those who fear the Lord and keep His commandments have life with God; but as to those who keep not His commandments, there is no life in them.

READ: LUKE 12:4-5

NOVEMBER 26

A TRUE PRIVILEGE

DAVID LIVINGSTONE | 1857

David Livingstone (1813-1873) was a Scottish Congregationalist pioneer medical missionary and explorer in Africa. His meeting with H. M. Stanley gave rise to the popular quotation, "Dr. Livingstone, I presume?"

Great pains had been taken by my parents to instill the doctrines of Christianity into my mind, and I had no difficulty in understanding the theory of our free salvation by the atonement of our Savior. But it was at a later time that I really began to feel the necessity and value of a personal application of the provisions of that atonement to my own case.

The change was like what may be supposed would take place were it possible to cure a case of "color blindness." The perfect freeness with which the pardon of all our guilt is offered in God's book drew forth feelings of affectionate love for Him who bought us with his blood, and a sense of deep obligation to Him for His mercy has influenced my conduct ever since.

In the glow of love that Christianity inspires, I soon resolved to devote my life to the alleviation of human misery. My simple prayer was, "God, send me anywhere, only go with me. Lay any burden on me, only sustain me. And sever any tie in my heart except the tie that binds my heart to Yours."

People talk of the sacrifice I have made in spending so much of my life in Africa. Can we call a sacrifice that which is simply paid back as a small part of a great debt owed to our God, which we can never repay? Is it a sacrifice that brings its own blessed reward in healthful activity, the consciousness of doing good, peace of mind, and the bright hope of a glorious destiny hereafter? Away with the word in such a view and with such a thought! It is emphatically no sacrifice. Say rather it is a privilege.

READ: MARK 16:15

NOVEMBER 27
THE WRITTEN WORD

RICHARD BAXTER | 17TH CENTURY

Richard Baxter (1615–1691) was an English Puritan who was considered a leading theologian of his day.

Make careful choice of the books which you read: let the holy scriptures ever have the preeminence, and next to them, those solid, lively, heavenly treatises which best expound and apply the scriptures, and next, credible histories, especially of the church . . . but take heed of false teachers who would corrupt your understandings.

As there is a more excellent appearance of the Spirit of God in the holy Scripture than in any other book whatever, so it has more power and fitness to convey the Spirit, and make us spiritual, by imprinting itself upon our hearts. As there is more of God in it, so it will acquaint us more with God, and bring us nearer Him, and make the reader more reverent, serious, and holy. Let scripture be first and foremost in your hearts and hands and other books be used as subservient to it.

Holy writings are nothing but a preaching of the gospel to the eye, as the voice preaches it to the ear. Vocal preaching has preeminence in moving the emotions, and adapting easily to the state of the congregation that hears it. But books have the advantage in many other respects: every congregation cannot hear the most judicious or powerful preachers, but every single person may read the books of the most powerful and judicious. Books are available every day and hour; when we can hear sermons only on occasion, and at certain times. If sermons are forgotten, they are gone; but a book may be read over and over, till we remember it. Good books are a very great mercy to the world. Knowing this, the Holy Ghost chose the way of writing to preserve His doctrine and laws to the church, recognizing how easy and sure a way it is of keeping it safe for all generations, in comparison with mere verbal traditions.

READ: JOB 19:23-24

THE GLORY OF THE CROSS

A. B. SIMPSON | 1909

Albert Benjamin Simpson (1843-1919) was a Canadian preacher, theologian, and founder of the Christian and Missionary Alliance, an evangelical Protestant denomination with an emphasis on global evangelism.

The Apostle Paul, speaking of the cross, can only express himself in terms of the loftiest exultation, "God forbid that I should glory, save in the cross of our Lord Jesus Christ" (Galatians 6:14 KJV). The cross of Jesus Christ has exalted Christ Himself by giving the universe a manifestation not only of the wisdom and love of God found nowhere else, but especially of the self-sacrificing love of Christ Himself.

In human history there is something higher than wealth, power, or brilliant gifts of intellect. Grecian culture commemorates the heroes of Thermopylae above all the other records of their country. Rome gloried in the legend of Horatius far more than in the pomp and pageantry of Augustus and Hadrian. The fame of Lincoln and McKinley has been heightened by the tragic story of their martyrdom. And the annals of Christian biography are rich in the record of heroic sacrifice. But there is no heroism like the story of Calvary, and there is no glory that can ever be compared with the crimson of the cross and the crown of thorns.

When we think of those Jesus Christ has rescued from sin and despair, we can better understand the promise, "He shall see of the travail of his soul, and shall be satisfied" (Isaiah 53:11 KJV). This was "the joy that was set before him" for which He "endured the cross, despising the shame, and is set down at the right hand of the throne of God" (Hebrews 12:2 KJV). The day is coming which will make up for all His shame and sorrow, when He shall present to Himself His glorious bride, "not having spot, or wrinkle, or any such thing" (Ephesians 5:27 KJV), and He "shall be satisfied."

READ: GALATIANS 6:14

NOVEMBER 29
INSTRUMENTS IN HIS HAND
ISAAC PENINGTON | 1658

Isaac Penington (1616-1679) was one of the early members of the Religious Society of Friends, also known as the Quakers, whose insightful writings are still popular today.

We are a people in whom God has raised up the seed of his own life, and caused it to reign over the earthly part in ourselves. And we have met with the call of God, and what God has made us in Christ, we know to be truth; and when we testify of this to the world we speak truth, though the world, which knows not the truth, cannot hear our voice.

Now our work in the world is to hold forth the virtues of him that has called us; to live like God; not to own anything in the world which God does not own; to forget our country, our kindred, our father's house, and to live like persons of another country. We are not to do anything of ourselves, and which is pleasing to the old nature; but all our words, all our conversation, yes, every thought, is to become new. And walking faithfully thus with God, we have a reward now, and a crown in the end, which does and will surpass all the reproaches and hardships we meet with in the world.

We are also to be witnesses for God, and to propagate his life in the world; to be instruments in his hand, to bring others out of death and captivity into true life and liberty. We are to fight against the powers of darkness everywhere, as the Lord calls us forth. And this we are to do in his wisdom, according to his will, in his power, and in his love, sweetness, and meekness. We are not to take ways according to our own wisdom, but the Lord must go before. Nor may we make use of our own strength, but feel his arm in our weakness. We must be true to God, handling the sword skillfully and faithfully, judging and cutting down the transgressor in the power and authority of God. And when the meek, the lowly, the humble thing is reached and raised, then the true love, the sweetness, the tenderness, the meekness must go forth to that.

READ: 1 PETER 2:9

NOVEMBER 30

SATISFACTION OF THE SOUL

PHILLIPS BROOKS | 19TH CENTURY

Phillips Brooks (1835-1893) was an American priest and theologian. He was Abraham Lincoln's pastor and also wrote the Christmas carol "O Little Town of Bethlehem."

I see so many Christians who are not deeply, thoroughly satisfied with the Christ whom they have chosen. They have really chosen Him. They know there is a happiness in Him that wickedness cannot give, but this happiness lies so deep! They know that it is there, but they have not uncovered it yet—not all of it. But here lies the happiness of wickedness—all plain and open. It sparkles in the sunshine. Its laughter rings out on the air.

There are a great many good people who wish that wicked people did not seem so happy. It puzzles them. They know that they are happier, but somehow their happiness is not so palpable. It lies far off. It lies deep down. The eating and drinking and merriment bewilder and amaze the patient toiler after righteousness, who has given up everything else that he may win Christ. He is not able all at once to measure their success and see its value, and say ungrudgingly and pityingly: "Yes, that is the joy that belongs to that kind of life—the joy that I put behind me once for all when I chose Christ. They have their reward. Let me press forward, and every day a little more and more have mine."

What shall such a half-discontented Christian do? He does not dream of turning back and giving up his Master. He is only bewildered. All he must do is to stand firm. As he goes on, as he learns more of Christ, as he sees more of what it is to serve Him, he will leave all these half-regrets behind him. It will no more trouble him that lower ambitions find their lower rewards. It is the satisfaction of the soul in Christ that makes the injustices of this world seem all right and clear. We shall have it perfectly when we get to heaven, and we might have far more of it than we do have now.

READ: PSALM 107:9

DECEMBER 1

A DANGEROUS DOCTRINE

CHARLES JEFFERSON | 20TH CENTURY

Charles E. Jefferson (1860-1937) was an American preacher, pastor, and scholar.

There is nothing a man can do that will win him the favor of God. It is not possible for him to crawl into it, climb up to it, earn it, or buy it. A man has God's favor at the start before he has done a single thing, because man is God's child. Believe that God's favor is something to be earned either by sacrifices or by noble deeds and you have missed the glory of the message which the Son of God came to bring. Believe that you have been redeemed by what God has done in Christ, then go on and live as a redeemed man ought to live, with thanksgiving and joy.

But is not this dangerous doctrine? Indeed it is. There is nothing so dangerous in this world as liberty, except the lack of it. Wherever this doctrine of salvation by faith has been preached boldly and with passion, it has been wrested by men to their own destruction. In the sixteenth century, under the preaching of Luther, crowds of men and women seized upon this idea of liberty and used it for an occasion to the flesh. Law, they said, has passed completely away. For the redeemed soul there is no law at all. Whatever a Christian does is right.

But Paul says, "Brethren, you have been called unto liberty; only use not liberty for an occasion to the flesh, but through love be servants one to another" (see Galatians 5:13). Does he say servant? That is the word. Do servants and liberty go together? Most assuredly they do. Only those who are bound are free. This is one of the paradoxes of the gospel. If you would be free you must take the yoke. Stand fast in the liberty, brethren, wherewith Christ has set us free. Revere it. Fight for it. Keep it. Only do not use it for an occasion to the flesh. Look constantly unto Jesus, who was the freest man who ever walked our earth, and yet who walked it always as a slave. Always free he was, but yet always bound, bound by the life of God within him.

READ: MATTHEW 11:29

DECEMBER 2
A CONQUEROR WITH CHRIST
JOHN WESLEY | 1738

John Wesley (1701-1791), along with his brother Charles, was the father of the English Methodist movement. He preached a personal relationship with Jesus Christ.

In the evening I went very unwillingly to a society in Aldersgate Street, where one was reading Luther's preface to the Epistle to the Romans. About a quarter before nine, while he was describing the change that God works in the heart through faith in Christ, I felt my heart strangely warmed. I felt I did trust in Christ, Christ alone, for salvation; and an assurance was given me that He had taken away my sins, even mine, and saved me from the law of sin and death.

I began to pray with all my might for those who had in a most particular manner despitefully used and persecuted me. I then testified openly to all who were there what I now first felt in my heart. But it was not long before the enemy suggested, "This cannot be faith; for where is your joy?"

Then was I taught that peace and victory over sin are essential to faith in the Captain of our salvation; but that, as to the transfers of joy that usually attend the beginning of it, especially in those who have mourned deeply, God sometimes gives, and sometimes withholds them according to the counsels of His own will.

After my return home, I was much buffeted with temptations, but I cried out, and they fled away. They returned again and again. Each time I lifted up my eyes, and He "sent me help from his holy place." And in this I found the difference between my new life and my former one. I was striving, yes, fighting with all my might under the law, as well as under grace. But before I was sometimes, if not often conquered; now, I was always conqueror.

READ: ROMANS 8:37

DECEMBER 3

THE OPTIMISM OF FAITH

REINHOLD NIEBUHR | 1937

Karl Paul Reinhold Niebuhr (1892-1971) was an American theologian, author, and commentator on public affairs.

In the Jewish-Christian tradition this problem of pessimism and optimism is solved by faith in a transcendent God who is at once the creator of the world (source of its meaning) and judge of the world (i.e., goal of its perfection). It was this faith in a transcendent God that made it possible for Hebraic religion to escape both the parochial identification of God and the nation and the pantheistic identification of God and the imperfections of historical existence. It provided, in other words, for both the universalism and the perfectionism that are implied in every vital ethics.

It is interesting to note that the process of divorcing God from the nation was a matter of both spiritual insight and actual experience. If the early prophets had not said, as Amos, "Are ye not as children of the Ethiopians unto me . . .? saith the LORD" (Amos 9:7 KJV), faith in the God of Israel might have perished with the captivity of Judah. But it was the exile that brought this process to a triumphant conclusion. A second Isaiah could build on the spiritual insights of an Amos, and could declare a God who gave meaning to existence quite independent of the vicissitudes of a nation, which had been the chief source of all meaning to the pious Jew.

In the same manner, faith in a transcendent God made it possible to affirm confidence in a meaningful existence even though the world was full of sorrow and evil. Some of the sorrow and misery was attributed to human sin. It was because man sinned that thorns and thistles grew in his field and he was forced to earn his bread by the sweat of his brow. The myth of the fall may solve the problem of evil too easily by attributing all inadequacies of nature to the imperfections of man, but it contains one element of truth—that it reduces man's pride and presumption in judging the justice of the universe by making him conscious of his own sin and suggesting that at least some of what he suffers is a price of the freedom which makes it possible for him to sin.

READ: ROMANS 8:28

DECEMBER 4

A FEW GOOD MEN

ROBERT COLEMAN | 1963

Robert E. Coleman (b. 1928) is an American preacher, evangelist, scholar, and author whose books have been translated into more than 100 languages.

It all started by Jesus calling a few men to follow him. This revealed the direction his evangelistic strategy would take. His concern was not with programs to reach the multitudes, but with men whom the multitudes would follow. Remarkable as it may seem, Jesus started to gather these men before he ever organized an evangelistic campaign or even preached a sermon in public. Men were to be his method of winning the world to God.

Jesus' plan was to enlist men who could bear witness to his life and carry on his work after he returned to the Father. John and Andrew were the first to be invited as Jesus left the scene of the great revival of John the Baptist at Bethany beyond the Jordan. Andrew in turn brought his brother Peter. The next day Jesus found Philip on his way to Galilee, and Philip found Nathanael. There is no evidence of haste in the selection of these disciples, just determination. The particulars surrounding the call of each of the twelve are not recorded in the Gospels, but it is believed that they all occurred in the first year of the Lord's ministry.

By any standard of sophisticated culture then and now these men would surely be considered a rather ragged collection of souls. They were impulsive, temperamental, easily offended, and had all the prejudices of their environment. In short, these men were not the kind of group one would expect to win the world for Christ. Yet Jesus saw in these simple men the potential of leadership for the Kingdom. They were indeed "unlearned and ignorant" according to the world's standard, but they were teachable. Though often mistaken in their judgments and slow to comprehend spiritual things, they were honest men, willing to confess their need.

As it turned out, these few early converts of the Lord were destined to become the leaders of his church that was to go with the gospel to the whole world, and from the standpoint of his ultimate purpose, the significance of their lives would be felt throughout eternity. That's the only thing that counts.

READ: LUKE 6:13

DECEMBER 5

A BEAUTIFUL SOUND

KENNETH E. HAGIN | 1979

Kenneth Erwin Hagin (1917-2003) was an influential American Pentecostal preacher. He founded RHEMA Bible Training Center and is often referred to as the father of the Word of Faith movement.

What is that sound? What is that sound that I hear?

It's the sound of many feet—it's the sound of beautiful feet.

It's the sound of feet going forth with the good news.

Who are these that make this sound of tramp, tramp, tramp, as they go tramping along?

They are those chosen of the Lord, called of God, equipped by His Spirit.

They come from the very bosom of the Father; from the right hand of God.

For their Master, even the Lord Himself, as He ascended on High, gave gifts unto men.

And He gave some, apostles; and some, prophets; and some, evangelists; and some, pastors and teachers (Ephesians 4:11 KJV).

They come from the very throne of God—from the right hand of authority.

Where are they going?

They're going to the uttermost parts of the earth.

They're going where an empty hand is reaching out for help.

They're going where there is a hungry cry—

Hunger for the bread of this life and for the true Bread of life.

They're going around the world to tell the story, to proclaim the message,

To do the work that God called them to do.

READ: ISAIAH 52:7

DECEMBER 6

A SEA OF HUMANITY

WILLIAM BOOTH | 19TH CENTURY

William Booth (1829-1912) was an English Methodist preacher who founded the
Salvation Army.

On a recent journey, I had a vision of a dark and stormy ocean. Black clouds
hung heavily; vivid lightning flashed and loud thunder rolled, and the waves
rose, towered, and broke, only to rise again. In that ocean I saw myriads of
poor human beings shouting and shrieking, cursing and struggling; and as they
screamed, some sank to rise no more.

Out of this dark, angry ocean, a mighty rock rose up with its summit towering
high above the black clouds. And all around the base of this great rock was a vast
platform where a number of the poor struggling, drowning wretches continually
climbed out of the angry ocean. A few of those who were already safe on the
platform were helping those still in the angry waters reach the place of safety.

The occupants of that platform were divided into different sets or classes, and
they occupied themselves with different pleasures and employments. But only a
very few seemed to make it their business to get people out of the sea. Though
all of them had been rescued from the ocean, they did not seem to care about
the poor perishing ones who were struggling and drowning right before their
very eyes . . . many of whom were their own husbands and wives, brothers and
sisters, even their own children. Now this could not have been due to ignorance,
because they lived right there in full sight of it all and even talked about it
sometimes. Many even went regularly to hear lectures and sermons in which the
awful state of these poor drowning creatures was described.

But those on the platform to whom He called, who professed to love and
worship Him, were so taken up with their professions, money, and pleasures, their
families and circles, their religions and arguments about it, and their preparation
for going to the mainland, that they did not listen to the cry that came to them
from this wonderful being who had Himself gone down into the sea. If they heard,
they did not heed it. They did not care. And so the multitude went on right before
them struggling and shrieking and drowning in the darkness.

READ: JOHN 4:35

DECEMBER 7
A HOLY FAIRY TALE
J. R. R. TOLKIEN | 1938

John Ronald Reuel Tolkien (1892-1973) was an English writer, poet, scholar, and the
author of many works, including The Hobbit *and* The Lord of the Rings. *He was*
known for his Christian faith and the influence he had in C. S. Lewis's conversion.

The Gospels contain a fairy story, or a story of a larger kind which embraces
all the essence of fairy stories. They contain many marvels—peculiarly artistic,
beautiful, and moving: "mythical" in their perfect, self-contained significance.
This story begins and ends in joy. It has preeminently the "inner consistency of
reality." There is no tale ever told that men would rather find was true, and none
which so many skeptical men have accepted as true on its own merits. For the art
of it has the supremely convincing tone of primary art, that is, of creation. To
reject it leads either to sadness or to wrath.

It is not difficult to imagine the peculiar excitement and joy that one would
feel, if any particularly beautiful fairy story were found to be "primarily"
true. The joy would have exactly the same quality, if not the same degree, as
the joy which the "turn" in a fairy story gives. It looks forward (or backward:
the direction in this regard is unimportant) to the Great Eucatastrophe. The
Christian joy, the gloria, is of the same kind; but it is preeminently high and
joyous. But this story is supreme; and it is true. Art has been verified. God is
the Lord, of angels, and of men—and of elves. Legend and history have met
and fused.

But in God's kingdom the presence of the greatest does not depress the
small. Redeemed man is still man. Story, fantasy, still go on, and should go on.
The Christian has still to work, with mind as well as body, to suffer, hope, and
die; but he may now perceive that all his bents and faculties have a purpose,
which can be redeemed. All tales may come true; and yet, at the last, redeemed,
they may be as like and as unlike the forms that we give them as man, finally
redeemed, will be like and unlike the fallen that we know.

READ: LUKE 24:44

December 8

The Trinity

From The Athanasian Creed | 500

The Athanasian Creed is a Christian statement of belief, focusing on Trinitarian doctrine, that has been used by Christian churches since the sixth century. It is the first creed in which the equality of the three persons of the Trinity is explicitly stated, and differs from the other creeds in the inclusion of anathemas, or condemnations of those who disagree with the Creed.

We worship one God in Trinity, and Trinity in Unity; neither confounding the Persons; nor dividing the Essence. For there is one Person of the Father; another of the Son; and another of the Holy Ghost. But the Godhead of the Father, of the Son, and of the Holy Ghost is all one: the Glory equal, the Majesty coeternal. Such as the Father is, such is the Son, and such is the Holy Ghost. The Father uncreated, the Son uncreated, and the Holy Ghost uncreated. The Father unlimited, the Son unlimited, and the Holy Ghost unlimited. The Father eternal, the Son eternal, and the Holy Ghost eternal.

And yet they are not three eternals; but one eternal. As also there are not three uncreated, nor three infinites, but one uncreated, and one infinite. So likewise the Father is Almighty; the Son Almighty; and the Holy Ghost Almighty. And yet they are not three Almighties; but one Almighty. So the Father is God, the Son is God, and the Holy Ghost is God. And yet they are not three Gods, but one God. So likewise the Father is Lord, the Son Lord, and the Holy Ghost Lord. And yet not three Lords, but one Lord. For like as we are compelled by the Christian verity: to acknowledge every Person by himself to be both God and Lord; And in this Trinity none is before or after another; none is greater or less than another. But the whole three Persons are coeternal and coequal. So that in all things, as aforesaid, the Unity in Trinity and the Trinity in Unity is to be worshipped. He therefore that will be saved, let him thus think of the Trinity.

Read: John 4:23-24

DECEMBER 9
WORLDLY DEPENDENCIES
HENRI NOUWEN | 1981

Henri Jozef Machiel Nouwen (1932-1996) was a Dutch-born priest and writer who authored forty books about spirituality.

In general we are very busy people. Our days and weeks are filled with engagements, and our years filled with plans and projects. There is seldom a period in which we do not know what to do, and we do not even take the time and rest to wonder if any of the things we think, say, or do are *worth* thinking, saying, or doing.

How horrendously secular our lives tend to be. Why is this so? Why do we children of the light so easily become conspirators with the darkness? The answer is quite simple. Our identity, our sense of self, is at stake. Secularity is a way of being dependent on the responses of our milieu. The secular or false self is the self which is fabricated, as Thomas Merton says, by social compulsions.

"Compulsive" is indeed the best adjective for the false self. It points to the need for ongoing and increasing affirmation. Who am I? I am the one who is liked, praised, admired, disliked, hated, or despised. Whether I am a pianist, a businessman, or a minister, what matters is how I am perceived by my world. If being busy is a good thing, then I must be busy. If having money is a sign of real freedom, then I must claim my money. If knowing many people proves my importance, I will have to make the necessary contacts. The compulsion manifests itself in the lurking fear of failing and the steady urge to prevent this by gathering more of the same—more work, more money, more friends.

These very compulsions are at the basis of the two main enemies of the spiritual life: anger and greed. They are the inner side of a secular life, the sour fruits of our worldly dependencies. When my sense of self depends on what others say of me, anger is a quite natural reaction to a critical word. And when my sense of self depends on what I can acquire, greed flares up when my desires are frustrated. Thus greed and anger are brother and sister of a false self fabricated by the social compulsions of an unredeemed world.

READ: ROMANS 13:12

DECEMBER 10

THE LAW OF LOVE

PHILIPP MELANCHTHON | 1531

Philipp Melanchthon (1497-1560), born Philipp Schwartzerdt, was a German Protestant Reformer, theologian, and a collaborator with Martin Luther.

It is written in Jeremiah 31:33, "I will put my law in their inward parts, and write it in their hearts" (KJV). And in Romans 3:31, Paul says, "Do we, then, make void the law through faith? God forbid: yea, we establish the law" (KJV). And Christ says in Matthew 19:17, "If thou wilt enter into life, keep the commandments" (KJV). These and similar sentences testify that the Law ought to be begun in us, and should be kept by us more and more.

Furthermore, we speak not of rituals, but of that Law which gives commandment concerning the movements of the heart. Because faith brings the Holy Ghost, and produces a new life in our hearts, it is necessary that it should produce spiritual movements in our hearts. And what these movements are, the prophet shows, when he says: "I will put my law in their inward parts, and write it in their hearts" (Jeremiah 31:33 KJV). Therefore, when we have been justified by faith and regenerated, we begin to fear and love God, to pray to Him, to expect aid from Him, to give thanks and praise Him, and to obey Him in afflictions. We begin also to love our neighbors, because our hearts have spiritual and holy movements [there is now, through the Spirit of Christ, a new heart, mind, and spirit within].

These things cannot occur until we have been justified by faith, and, regenerated, we receive the Holy Ghost. First, because the Law cannot be kept without the knowledge of Christ; and likewise the Law cannot be kept without the Holy Ghost. But the Holy Ghost is received by faith, according to the declaration of Paul in Galatians 3:14: "That we might receive the promise of the Spirit through faith" (KJV).

READ: JOHN 14:15-17

DECEMBER 11

NO ROOM FOR IDLENESS

JEREMY TAYLOR | 1650

Jeremy Taylor (1613-1667) was an English minister and writer known for his poetic style.

God has given to each man a short time here on earth, and yet upon this short time eternity depends. For this reason, for every hour of our life (as persons capable of laws, and knowing good from evil) we must give account to the great Judge of men and angels. And this is what our blessed Savior told us, that we must account for every idle word; not meaning that every word which is not intended for edification, or is less prudent, shall be reckoned for a sin; but that the time which we spend in our idle talking and unprofitable discourse; that time which might and ought to have been employed to spiritual and useful purposes—that is to be accounted for.

For we must remember that we have a great work to do—many enemies to conquer, many evils to prevent, much danger to run through, many difficulties to be mastered, many necessities to serve; and much good to do—many children to provide for, many poor to relieve, many diseases to cure; besides our private and our public cares, and duties of the world, which necessity and the providence of God have adopted into the family of religion.

God has given every man work enough to do, that there should be no room for idleness; and yet has ordered the world, so that there is room for devotion. He that has the fewest businesses of the world is called upon to spend more time in the dressing of the soil; and he that has the most affairs may order them so that they shall be a service of God; while at certain periods, they are blessed with prayers and actions of religion, and all day long are hallowed by a holy intention. Idleness is the greatest prodigality in the world; it throws away that which is invaluable in respect of its present use, and irreparable when it is past, and which no power of art or nature can recover.

READ: MATTHEW 12:36

DECEMBER 12

GRASPING FOR POWER

EUGENE PETERSON | 2006

Eugene H. Peterson (b. 1932) is perhaps best known for his best-selling paraphrase of the Bible, The Message. *He has written many other books on spirituality and pastoral ministry.*

While the magi approached the birth of Jesus with reverential awe, Herod, hearing the news, was full of dread. It is possible to fashion values and goals so defiant of God that any rumor of his reality shakes our foundation.

But Herod, impressive and fearful to his contemporaries, looks merely ridiculous to us. His secret, lying intrigues are useless before the ingenuous, unarmed invasion of history in Jesus at Bethlehem. His threat, which seems so ominous, is scarcely more than a pretext for accomplishing God's will. The flight into Egypt, retracing the ancient route of redemption, is part of a finely wrought salvation history.

The slaughtered children participate in the messianic birth pangs: Christ enters a world flailing in rebellion. Herod, in a tantrum, hysterically tries to hold on to his kingdom. The voice in Ramah reverberates in history's echo chambers and gets louder every year.

Lord, I see that Herod is real enough: he opens scenes, he triggers sequences, but he doesn't cause anything. Evil can't. Only you, God, cause, and what you cause is salvation, through Jesus, my Lord and Savior. Amen.

READ: MATTHEW 2:16

December 13

A Personal God

E. Stanley Jones | 1942

E. Stanley Jones (1884–1973) was a Methodist minister and theologian perhaps best known for his humanitarian efforts in India.

A little boy stood before the picture of his absent father, and then turned to his mother and wistfully said, "I wish father would step out of the picture."

This little boy expressed the deepest yearning of the human heart. We who have gazed upon the picture of God in nature are grateful, but not satisfied. We want our Father to step out of the impersonal picture and meet us as a person. "The impersonal laid no hold on my heart," says Tulsi Das, the great poet of India. It never does, for the human heart is personal and wants a personal response.

"Why won't principles do? Why do we need a personal God?" someone asks. Well, suppose you go to a child crying for its mother and say, "Don't cry, little child; I'm giving to you the principle of motherhood." Would the tears dry and the face light up? Hardly. The child would brush aside your principle of motherhood and cry for its mother. We all want, not a principle nor a picture, but a person.

The Father *has* stepped out of the picture. The Word *has* become flesh. That is the meaning of Christmas. Jesus is Immanuel—God with us. He is the personal approach from the unseen. We almost gasp as the picture steps out of the frame. We did not dare dream God was like Christ. But He is. Just as I analyze chemically the tiny sunbeam and discover in it the chemical make-up of the vast sun, so I look at the character and life of Jesus, and I know what God's character is like. He is Christ-like.

"You have an advantage," said Dr. Hu Shih, the father of the renaissance movement in China, "in that all the ideas in Christianity have become embodied in a person." Yes, and the further advantage of our faith is this: The Christmas word must become flesh in me. I too must become the word made flesh. I must be a miniature Christmas.

Read: 1 John 3:2

DECEMBER 14

A GLORIOUS MYSTERY

JOHN YOUNG | 1857

John Young (1805-1881) was an English theologian and pastor.

The doctrine of incarnation is simply true. It is the darkness, but it is also the glory of the spiritual history of mankind. It is the central fact in the scheme of moral providence, its unity, harmony, and fountain of power. It is the realization of the highest purposes of God, the discovery of the depth of his wisdom, love, and might. "The Word was made flesh, and dwelt among us, (and we beheld his glory, the glory as of the only begotten of the Father,) full of grace and truth" (John 1:14 KJV).

Having reached this conclusion, a flood of light is reflected back on the Christian records; and many of their announcements, before scarcely credible, become luminous and consistent. These records are separated at once and forever from all mythologies, whether of Egypt, India, Greece, or Rome. *Their* foundation is not fable, but fact—a fact, profoundly mysterious, indeed, but also incomparably glorious. The combination of mystery and glory at the very basis, and on the very threshold of the Gospels, not only prepares the mind for all the peculiarities of their structure, but demands, and even necessitates, discoveries in harmony with this primal characteristic.

If Jesus is the incarnation of divinity, it is no longer hard to believe that both his entrance into the world and his departure from it were supernatural. So far from being anomalous, this is altogether necessary and natural. Anything else would not have been in keeping with the history. His resurrection and his ascension to heaven are transparencies as pure as his miraculous birth. It was essential that, having lain in the grave and "tasted death for every man," he should rise again and pass into the skies. Thus has he become a glorious prophecy and type of the destiny of all good, which, though struggling hard with evil, and often seemingly overborne, shall ultimately exhibit and assert its indestructible vitality—a prophecy and type of the destiny of all the good, who, though despised, persecuted, and slain, shall rise again unhurt, emancipated, and glorified, to immortal life.

READ: 1 TIMOTHY 3:16

DECEMBER 15

CHRISTMAS EVERYWHERE

PHILLIPS BROOKS | 1903

*Phillips Brooks (1835-1893) was an American priest and theologian. He was Abraham
Lincoln's pastor and also wrote the Christmas carol "O Little Town of Bethlehem."*

Everywhere, everywhere, Christmas tonight!
Christmas in lands of the fir tree and pine,
Christmas in lands of the palm tree and vine,
Christmas where snow peaks stand solemn and white,
Christmas where cornfields stand sunny and bright.
Everywhere, everywhere, Christmas tonight!
For the Christ-child who comes is the Master of all;
No palace too great, no cottage too small.
The Angels who welcome Him sing from the height,
"In the city of David, a King in His might."
Everywhere, everywhere, Christmas tonight.
Then let every heart keep its Christmas within,
Christ's pity for sorrow, Christ's hatred for sin,
Christ's care for the weakest, Christ's courage for right,
Christ's dread for darkness, Christ's love of the light,
Everywhere, everywhere, Christmas tonight!
So the stars of the midnight which compass us round
Shall see a strange glory, and hear a sweet sound,
And cry, "Look! the earth is aflame with delight,
O sons of the morning, rejoice at the sight."
Everywhere, everywhere, Christmas tonight.

READ: LUKE 2:13-14

DECEMBER 16

THE GRAND MIRACLE

C. S. LEWIS | 1947

C. S. Lewis (1898–1963) is possibly the most respected Christian writer of the twentieth century. He wrote more than thirty books, including The Chronicles of Narnia *and* Mere Christianity.

The central miracle asserted by Christians is the incarnation. They say that God became man. Every other miracle prepares for this, or exhibits this, or results from this. Just as every natural event is the manifestation at a particular place and moment of nature's total character, so every particular Christian miracle manifests at a particular place and moment the character and significance of the incarnation. There is no question in Christianity of arbitrary interferences just scattered about. It relates not a series of disconnected raids on nature but the various steps of a strategically coherent invasion—an invasion which intends complete conquest and "occupation." The fitness, and therefore credibility, of the particular miracles depends on their relation to the grand miracle; all discussion of them in isolation from it is futile.

The fitness or credibility of the grand miracle itself cannot, obviously, be judged by the same standard. And let us admit at once that it is very difficult to find a standard by which it can be judged. If the thing happened, it was the central event in the history of the Earth—the very thing that the whole story has been about . . . it is easier to argue, on historical grounds, that the incarnation actually occurred than to show, on philosophical grounds, the probability of its occurrence. The historical difficulty of giving for the life, sayings, and influence of Jesus any explanation that is not harder than the Christian explanation is very great. The discrepancy between the depth and sanity and (let me add) shrewdness of His moral teaching and the rampant megalomania which must lie behind His theological teaching unless He is indeed God, has never been satisfactorily got over.

READ: LUKE 1:30-35

December 17
The Lord Is with Us
John Paul II | 1980

John Paul II (1920-2005) reigned as pope of the Roman Catholic Church from October 16, 1978, until his death on April 2, 2005.

Emmanuel! You are in our midst. You are with us, coming down to the uttermost consequences made from the beginning with man, and in spite of the fact that it was violated and broken so many times . . . You are with us! Emmanuel! In a way that really surpasses everything that man could have thought of you. You are with us as a man. You are wonderful, truly wonderful, O God, Creator and Lord of the universe.

God with the Father Almighty! The Logos! The only Son! God of power! You are with us as man, as a newborn baby of the human race, absolutely weak, wrapped in swaddling clothes and placed in a manger, "because there was no place for them" in any inn (Luke 2:7). Is it not precisely that because you became man in this way, without a roof to shelter you, that you became nearest to man? Is it not precisely because you yourself, the newborn Jesus, are without a roof that you are nearest to those brothers and sisters . . . who have lost their homes through terrible earthquakes and storms? And the people that really come to their aid are precisely the ones who have you in their hearts, you who were born at Bethlehem without a home.

The liturgy of Advent reminds us every day that the Lord is near. This closeness of the Lord is felt by all of us: both by us priests, reciting every day the marvelous major antiphons and by all Christians who try to prepare their hearts and their consciences for his coming. I know that in this period the confessionals of churches in my country, Poland, are thronged (no less than during Lent). I think that is certainly the same in Italy also, and wherever a deep spirit of faith makes the need felt of opening one's soul to the Lord who is about to come.

Read: Matthew 1:23

DECEMBER 18

THE CHRISTMAS CRÈCHE

BONAVENTURE | 1263

Bonaventure (1221-1274) was an Italian scholar, philosopher, and a cardinal bishop of Albano. He completed the official biography of Saint Francis, in which he tells of the origin of the traditional Christmas celebration of the Nativity.

It happened in the third year before his death, that in order to excite the inhabitants of Grecio to commemorate the nativity of the Infant Jesus with great devotion, St. Francis determined to keep it with all possible solemnity. Then he prepared a manger, and brought hay, and an ox and ass to the appointed place. The brethren were summoned and the people ran together as the forest resounded with their voices, and that venerable night was made glorious by many and brilliant lights and echoing psalms of praise.

Francis stood before the manger, full of devotion and piety, bathed in tears and radiant with joy; chanting the Holy Gospel. Then he preached to the people around the nativity of the poor King; and being unable to utter His name for the tenderness of his love, he called Him the Babe of Bethlehem. A certain valiant and veracious soldier, Master John of Grecio, who, for the love of Christ, had left the warfare of this world and became a dear friend of this holy man, affirmed that he beheld an Infant marvelously beautiful, sleeping in the manger, Whom the blessed Father Francis embraced with both his arms, as if he would awake Him from sleep.

This vision of the devout soldier is credible, not only by reason of the sanctity of him that saw it, but by reason of the miracles which afterwards confirmed its truth. For the example of Francis, if it be considered by the world, is doubtless sufficient to excite all hearts which are negligent in the faith of Christ; and the hay of that manger, being preserved by the people, miraculously cured all diseases of cattle, and many other pestilences; God thus in all things glorifying his servant, and witnessing to the great efficacy of his holy prayers by manifest prodigies and miracles.

READ: LUKE 2:12

DECEMBER 19

A NATIVITY

RUDYARD KIPLING | 1918

Rudyard Kipling (1865–1935), an English author and poet, famously penned 1894's
The Jungle Book *and many other books and poems for children.*

The Babe was laid in the Manger
Between the gentle kine—
All safe from cold and danger—
"But it was not so with mine,
(With mine! With mine!)
Is it well with the child, is it well?"
The waiting mother prayed.
"For I know not how he fell,
And I know not where he is laid."
A Star stood forth in Heaven;
The Watchers ran to see
The Sign of the Promise given—
"But there comes no sign to me
(To me! To me!)
"My child died in the dark.
Is it well with the child, is it well?
There was none to tend him
  or mark,
And I know not how he fell."
The Cross was raised on high;
The Mother grieved beside—
"But the Mother saw Him die
And took Him when He died.

(He died! He died!)
"Seemly and undefiled
His burial-place was made—
Is it well, is it well with the child?
For I know not where he is laid."
On the dawning of Easter Day
Comes Mary Magdalene;
But the Stone was rolled away,
And the Body was not within—
(Within! Within!)
"Ah, who will answer my word?"
The broken mother prayed.
"They have taken away my Lord,
And I know not where He is laid."
"The Star stands forth in Heaven.
The watchers watch in vain
For Sign of the Promise given
Of peace on Earth again—
(Again! Again!)
"But I know for Whom he fell"—
The steadfast mother smiled,
"Is it well with the child—is it well?
It is well—it is well with the child!"

READ: JOHN 11:25

DECEMBER 20

OF LIFE AND DEATH

FREDERICK BUECHNER | 2004

Frederick Buechner (b. 1926) is a Presbyterian minister, author, and theologian.

The young clergyman and his wife do all the things you do on Christmas Eve. They string the lights and hang the ornaments. They tuck in the children. They lug the presents down out of hiding and pile them under the tree. Just as they're about to fall exhausted into bed, the husband remembers his neighbor's sheep. The man asked him to feed them while he was away, and in the press of other matters that night he forgot all about them. So down the hill he goes through the knee-deep snow.

He gets two bales of hay from the barn and carries them out to the shed. The sheep huddle in a corner watching as he snaps the baling twine, shakes the squares of hay apart, and starts scattering it. Then they come bumbling and shoving to get at it with their foolish, mild faces, the puffs of their breath showing in the air. He is turning to leave when suddenly he realizes where he is. The winter darkness. The smell of the hay and the sound of the animals eating. Where he is, of course, is the manger.

He only just saw it. He whose business it is above everything else to have an eye for such things is all but blind in that eye. He might easily have gone home to bed never knowing that he had himself just been in the manger. It is only by grace that he happens to see this other part of the miracle.

The Word became flesh. Incarnation. It is not tame. It is not touching. It is not beautiful. It is uninhabitable terror. Agonized laboring led to it, a wrenching and tearing of the very sinews of reality itself. You can only cover your eyes and shudder before it, before *this*: "God of God, Light of Light, very God of very God . . . who for us and for our salvation," as the Nicene Creed puts it, "came down from heaven."

Came down. Only then do we dare uncover our eyes and see what we can see. It is the Resurrection and the Life she holds in her arms. It is the bitterness of death he takes at her breast.

READ: LUKE 1:46-55

December 21

A Tale of Saint Nicholas

Jacopo da Varagine | 1260

Jacopo da Varagine (c. 1230-1298) was archbishop of Genoa and compiled The Golden Legend, *a collection of fanciful hagiographies that was one of the most popular religious works of the Middle Ages.*

Nicholas, a citizen of Patera, was born of rich and pious parents. On the first day of his life, the infant stood straight up in the bath. From then on he took the breast only once on Wednesdays and Fridays. As a youth he avoided the dissolute pleasures of his peers, preferring to spend time in churches; and whatever he could understand of the Holy Scriptures he committed to memory.

After the death of his parents, he began to consider how he might make use of his great wealth, not in order to win men's praise but to give glory to God. At the time a fellow townsman of his, of noble origin but very poor, was thinking of prostituting his three virgin daughters in order to make a living out of this vile transaction. When the saint learned of this, he wrapped a quantity of gold in a cloth and, under cover of darkness, threw it through the window of the other man's house and withdrew unseen. In the morning the man found the gold, gave thanks to God, and celebrated the wedding of his eldest daughter.

Some time later the bishop of Myra died, and all the bishops of the region gathered to choose a successor. Among them was one of great authority, upon whose opinion the decision of others would depend. One night, he heard a voice telling him to post himself at the doors of the church in the morning, and to consecrate the first man he saw coming in, whose name would be Nicholas. In the morning he went outside the church to wait.

Meanwhile Nicholas, miraculously guided by God, went early to the church and was the first to enter. The bishop asked his name; and he bowed his head and answered, "Nicholas, the servant of your holiness." Then all the bishops led him in and installed him on the episcopal throne. But he, amidst his honors, always maintained his former humility and gravity of manner. He was persuasive in speech, forceful in counsel, and strict when reprimands were called for.

Read: 1 Thessalonians 4:7

DECEMBER 22
CHRISTMAS BELLS
HENRY WADSWORTH LONGFELLOW | 1863

Henry Wadsworth Longfellow (1807–1882) was a well-known professor and poet. He wrote this poem one Christmas as he nursed his son, who had been critically injured in the Civil War.

I heard the bells on Christmas Day
Their old, familiar carols play,
And wild and sweet the words repeat
Of peace on earth, goodwill to men!

And thought how, as the day had come,
The belfries of all Christendom
Had rolled along the unbroken song
Of peace on earth, goodwill to men!

Till, ringing, singing on its way
The world revolved from night to day,
A voice, a chime, a chant sublime
Of peace on earth, goodwill to men!

Then from each black, accursed mouth
The cannon thundered in the South,
And with the sound, the carols drowned
Of peace on earth, goodwill to men!

And in despair I bowed my head;
"There is no peace on earth," I said;
"For hate is strong, and mocks the song
Of peace on earth, goodwill to men!"

Then pealed the bells more loud and deep:
"God is not dead; nor doth he sleep!
The Wrong shall fail, the Right prevail,
With peace on earth, goodwill to men!"

READ: LUKE 2:14

December 23

Following the Star

G. K. Chesterton | 1909

Gilbert Keith Chesterton (1874-1936) was a prolific and diverse English writer, known as a sharp social and literary critic and Christian apologist.

There is one very vile habit that the pedants have, and that is explaining to a man why he does a thing that the man himself can explain quite well—and quite differently. If I go down on all fours to find a coin, it annoys me to be told by a passing biologist that I am really doing it because my remote ancestors were quadrupeds. I concede that he knows all about biology, or even a great deal about my ancestors; but I know he is wrong, because he does not know about the coin. If I climb a tree after a stray cat, I am unconvinced when a stray anthropologist tells me that I am doing it because I am essentially arboreal and barbaric. I happen to know I am doing it because I am amiable and somewhat overcivilized.

Scientists will talk to a man on general guesswork about things that they know no more about than about his pocket money or his pet cat. Religion is one of them. When a learned man tells me that on December 25th I am really worshipping the sun, I answer that I am not. I am practicing a particular personal religion, the pleasures of which (right or wrong) are not in the least astronomical. If he says that the cult of Christmas and the cult of Apollo are the same, I answer that they are utterly different; and I ought to know, for I believed in Apollo when I was quite little; and I believe in Christmas now that I am very, very big.

Let us not surrender to assertions that Christmas is pagan in origin. Our knowledge amounts to this—primitive Scandinavians did hold a feast in midwinter. What the dickens else could primitive Scandinavians do, especially in winter? Also, they put on the largest log in winter. Do professors expect such simple pagans to put on the largest log in summer? If people profess to feel "the spirit" behind symbols, I expect that they shall feel how opposite are the adoration of the sun and the following of the star.

Read: Revelation 22:16

DECEMBER 24
THE GOD-WHO-COMES
BENEDICT XVI | 2006

Pope Benedict XVI (b. 1927), born Joseph Ratzinger, was elected to the papacy of the Catholic Church in 2005.

At the beginning of a new year, the liturgy invites the Church to renew her proclamation to all the peoples and sums it up in two words "God comes." These words, so concise, contain an ever-new evocative power. Let us pause a moment to reflect: it is not used in the past tense—God *has* come, nor in the future—God *will* come, but in the present—"God comes."

At a closer look, this is a continuous present, that is, an ever-continuous action: it happened, it is happening now, and it will happen again. In whichever moment, "God comes." The verb "to come" appears here as a theological verb, since it says something about God's very nature. Proclaiming that "God comes" is equivalent, therefore, to simply announcing God himself, through one of his essential and qualifying features: his being the God-who-comes.

Advent calls believers to become aware of this truth and to act accordingly. It rings out as a salutary appeal in the days, weeks, and months that repeat: Awaken! Remember that God comes! Not yesterday, not tomorrow, but today, now!

The one true God, "the God of Abraham, Isaac, and Jacob," is not a God who is there in Heaven, unconcerned with us and our history, but he is the God-who-comes. He is a Father who never stops thinking of us; he wants to come, to dwell among us, to stay with us. His "coming" is motivated by the desire to free us from evil and death, from all that prevents our true happiness. God comes to save us.

The Fathers of the Church observe that the "coming" of God—continuous and, as it were, co-natural with his very being—is centered in the two principal comings of Christ: his Incarnation and his glorious return at the end of time. The Advent season lives the whole of this polarity. But between these two "manifested" comings it is possible to identify a third, which occurs in the souls of believers and, as it were, builds a "bridge" between the first and the last coming.

READ: JOHN 6:33

DECEMBER 25

AS CHRISTMAS FOLLOWS

WALTER A. MAIER | 20TH CENTURY

Walter A. Maier (1893-1950) was a noted radio personality, public speaker, author, university professor, theologian, and scholar. He is best known as the speaker for "The Lutheran Hour" radio broadcast from 1930-1950.

As Christmas follows Christmas, many of you think that you know the whole story, because you have heard it so often, when in truth you can never begin to exhaust the treasures of its grace. The most deep-rooted enemy of American Christianity in our time is not the brazen atheist who boldly brandishes his blasphemy, for only "the fool hath said . . . There is no God" (Psalm 14:1 ASV). It is not the sarcastic Modernist who often preaches only to a handful of people, nor the down-with-religion Communist who threatens to destroy our churches, for God laughs at this bombastic boasting.

As menacing as all these opponents of our faith may be, the most dangerous enemies of the Redeemer's gospel are the easygoing, self-confident Americans within the churches and without who hear Heaven's invitation and then quickly dismiss it from their minds to live and act as though there were no Savior, no Christmas with its message: God is "manifest in the flesh" (1 Timothy 3:16 KJV). These, I repeat, are the most dangerous foes because they are counted by the millions.

Now to all of you who are hurrying madly through life, with no time for the Holy Child, no heart-and-soul interest in the promise of His redemption, I say, in His name and with the plea that involves your salvation, your blessed eternity, your promise of heaven: celebrate the Savior's birthday every day! Take as your example our Lord's mother, of whom it is written that after the first Christmas had come and gone, after the shepherds had worshiped and departed, "Mary kept all these things, and pondered them in her heart" (Luke 2:19 KJV).

READ: LUKE 2:19

December 26

My Lord and Brother

Alexander of Cappadocia | 3rd century

Alexander (170-251) was Bishop of Cappadocia. During the Decian persecution he was thrown into prison at Cæsarea and died there.

Alexander, a servant and prisoner of Jesus Christ, sends greeting in the Lord to the blessed church of Antioch. Easy and light has the Lord made my bonds to me during the time of my imprisonment since I have learned that in the providence of God, Asclepiades—who, in regard to the right faith, is most eminently qualified for the office—has undertaken the episcopate of your holy church of Antioch.

And this epistle, my brethren and masters, I have sent by the hand of the blessed presbyter Clement, a man virtuous and well tried, whom you know already, and will know yet better; who also, coming here by the providence and supervision of the Master, has strengthened and increased the Church of the Lord.

For this, as you know, was the will of God, that the friendship subsisting between us from our forefathers should be maintained unbroken, yea rather, that it should increase in fervency and strength. For we are well acquainted with those blessed fathers who have trodden the course before us, and to whom we too shall soon go: Pantænus, namely, that man verily blessed, my master; and also the holy Clement, who was once my master and my benefactor; and all the rest who may be like them, by whose means also I have come to know you, my lord and brother, who excels all.

Read: 1 Thessalonians 3:7

DECEMBER 27

NO NEED TO WORRY

CHARLES SWINDOLL | 2008

Charles Rozell "Chuck" Swindoll (b. 1934) is an American evangelical pastor, author, educator, and radio preacher.

On the day Jesus was crucified, it would have appeared to anyone seeing through eyes of flesh that the darkness, the devil, and death had defeated the Son of God once and for all. I will admit that those three D's lie at the root of almost every worry I suffer. I worry about *death*—in particular, the death of the people I love. I worry about *darkness*, both literal and figurative. I worry about what the *devil* is up to. All three worked diligently throughout the ministry of Jesus to bring about this long and anguishing day. But what no one could see was that the Messiah's death would strike at the very heart of evil.

Three days after Jesus was placed in the grave, Mary Magdalene and a group of women converged on the tomb. As they approached, they saw that the giant stone had been tossed aside. Mary Magdalene immediately ran to tell Peter and John. While she was away, the other women took a closer look. The grave wrappings lay there, still together and intact, but empty. The body was gone. They stood dumbstruck until they realized two angels were behind them. One sat on the stone while the other stood nearby. "Why do you look for the living among the dead? He is not here, but has been raised!" (see Luke 24:5-6).

As word spread, the responses of the people who knew Jesus parallel the reactions I encounter every day as a modern-day bearer of this good news:

Some believed immediately. They remembered what Jesus had predicted during His ministry, and accepted His resurrection as genuine.

Some believed with indirect evidence. They initially doubted, but when they saw the empty tomb—they knew He had risen.

Some believed with direct evidence. They only believed that Jesus had risen after seeing Him with their own eyes.

Demons, darkness, and death have been vanquished, yet they continue to lash out in desperate hatred against everything in God's creation. But the forces of evil are breathing their last. So there's no need to worry . . . He has risen! He has risen, indeed!

READ: REVELATION 1:18

DECEMBER 28

THE BOND OF LOVE

JOHN OWEN | 17TH CENTURY

John Owen (1616-1683) was an English nonconformist church leader and theologian.

We know that God has styled himself the God of love, peace, and order in the church, because they are eminently from him, and highly accepted with him. And as love is the new commandment that Jesus Christ has given unto his disciples, so he has appointed it to be the bond of perfection unto them; which nothing else will ever be. Without this love, we are but as "sounding brass and tinkling cymbals" (see 1 Corinthians 13:1).

It is indispensably required of us to endeavor to be of one mind and one judgment, among all believers, to help keep the "unity of the Spirit in the bond of peace" (Ephesians 4:3). And, therefore, whenever any opinion or practice, in or about religion or the worship of God, hinders the gracious, holy principles of love and peace, or keeps men from fulfilling any duties that those principles require, it is a great and weighty prejudice against their truth and acceptance by God.

Our love is to be far reaching, unconfined as the beams of the sun, or as the showers of rain that fall upon the whole earth. Nothing of God's rational creation in this world is to be exempted from being the object of love. And where any exception might seem to be warranted by some men's causeless hatred, with unjust and unreasonable persecution of us, there we are given the particular and strictest charge in the exercise of it; which is one of the noble singularities of Christian religion. But whereas men are cast into various conditions on account of their relation unto God, the actual exercise of love towards them is required of us in a suitable variety; for it is God himself, in his infinite excellencies, who is the first and adequate object of our love.

READ: PHILIPPIANS 2:2

December 29
Escape the Wrath to Come
Jonathan Edwards | 1741

Jonathan Edwards (1703-1758) was an American preacher, theologian, author, and missionary to Native Americans; he played a critical role in shaping the First Great Awakening.

How dreadful is the state of those that are daily and hourly in the danger of this great wrath and infinite misery! But this is the dismal case of every soul in this congregation that has not been born again, however moral and strict, sober and religious, they may otherwise be. Oh that you would consider it, whether you be young or old!

There is reason to think, that there are many now hearing this message who will actually be the subjects of this very misery to all eternity. How many of you will remember this discourse in hell? And it would be no wonder, if some who are now present should be in hell in a very short time, even before this year is out. And it would be no wonder if some who sit here in health, quiet and secure, should be there before tomorrow morning.

Those of you that keep out of hell longest will be there in short order! Your damnation does not slumber; it will come swiftly, and, in all probability, very suddenly upon many of you. You have reason to wonder that you are not already in hell. It is doubtless the case of some you have known. Their case is past all hope; they are crying in extreme misery and perfect despair; but here you are in the land of the living and in the house of God, and have an opportunity to obtain salvation. What would those poor damned hopeless souls not give for one day's opportunity such as you now enjoy!

Christ has thrown the door of mercy wide open, and stands calling with a loud voice to poor sinners. Let everyone who is hanging over the pit of hell now hearken to God's word and providence. Let everyone who is not in Christ, now awake and fly from the wrath to come. The wrath of Almighty God is now undoubtedly hanging over a great part of this congregation. "Haste and escape for your lives, look not behind you, escape to the mountain, lest you be consumed" (see Genesis 19:17).

Read: Zephaniah 2:2-3

DECEMBER 30

THE GOSPEL IS . . .

ZACHARIAS URSINUS | 16TH CENTURY

Zacharias Ursinus (1534-1583) was a German Reformed theologian who is best known as the principal author and interpreter of the Heidelberg Catechism.

The term "gospel" signifies three things: a joyful message, or good news; the sacrifice which is offered to God for this good news; and the reward which is given to him who announces these joyful tidings. Here it signifies the doctrine, or joyful news of Christ manifested in the flesh; as "Behold, I bring you good tidings of great joy, . . . for unto you is born this day in the city of David a Saviour, which is Christ the Lord" (Luke 2:10-11 KJV).

The gospel is, therefore, the doctrine which the Son of God, our Mediator, revealed from heaven in Paradise, immediately after the fall, and which he brought from the bosom of the Eternal Father. It promises and announces, in view of the free grace and mercy of God, to all those that repent and believe, deliverance from sin, death, condemnation, and the wrath of God. Which is the same thing as to say that it promises and proclaims the remission of sin, salvation, and eternal life, by and for the sake of the Son of God, the Mediator; and is that through which the Holy Spirit works effectually in the hearts of the faithful—kindling and exciting in them faith, repentance, and the beginning of eternal life.

Or, we may define the gospel to be the doctrine which God revealed first in Paradise, and afterwards published by the Patriarchs and Prophets, which he was pleased to represent by the foreshadows of sacrifices, and the other ceremonies of the law, and which he has now accomplished through his only begotten Son. This teaches that the Son of God, our Lord Jesus Christ, is made unto us wisdom, righteousness, sanctification, and redemption; which is to say that he is a perfect Mediator, satisfying for the sins of the human race, restoring righteousness and eternal life to all those who by a true faith are ingrafted into him, and embrace his benefits.

READ: LUKE 2:10-11

DECEMBER 31
KEEP YOUR SOUL AT PEACE
MIGUEL DE MOLINOS | 17TH CENTURY

Miguel de Molinos (c. 1628-1697) was a Spanish priest and the chief apostle of the religious revival known as Quietism.

You ought to know that your soul is the center, habitation, and the kingdom of God. That therefore, in order that the Sovereign King may rest on the throne of your soul, you should take pains to keep it clean, quiet, void, and peaceable; clean from guilt and defects; quiet from fears; void of sinful affections, desires, and thoughts; and peaceable in temptations and tribulations.

You should always keep your heart in peace; that you may keep that temple of God pure, and with right and pure intentions, you are to work, pray, obey, and suffer, without being in the least moved, whatever it pleases the Lord to send you. Because it is certain that, for the good of your soul and for your spiritual profit, God will allow the envious enemy to trouble that city of rest and throne of peace with temptations, suggestions, and tribulations and, by the means of the natural world, with painful troubles and grievous persecutions.

Do not be upset or discouraged if you feel fainthearted, for he will return to quiet you, that he may still stir your heart. Because this divine Lord will fill you and rest in your soul, forming a rich throne of peace. He does this by means of internal recollection and through his heavenly grace, so that within your own heart, you may look for silence in the tumult, solitude in the crowd, light in darkness, forgetfulness in trials, strength in weakness, courage in fear, resistance in the midst of temptation, peace in war, and quiet in tribulation.

READ: EPHESIANS 3:16-19

CHRONOLOGICAL READING PLAN

AUTHOR INDEX

REFERENCES

January 1 – Saint Benedict. *Benedict's Rule*, Chapter VII, "Of Humility," and Chapter XX, "Of Reverence at Prayer."

January 2 – Charles Spurgeon. *Spurgeon's Practical Wisdom*. 19th century.

January 3 – George Eldon Ladd. *The Gospel of the Kingdom*. Wm. B. Eerdmans Publishing. 1959.

January 4 – George Fox. From the introduction written for the author's collected letters.

January 5 – Catherine of Siena. From a letter to Monna Agnese. c. 1374.

January 6 – Daniel Defoe. *Robinson Crusoe*. 1719.

January 7 – Ambrose. From the author's letter to the Church at Vercellae.

January 8 – Robert Hawker. *The Poor Man's Morning and Evening Portions*. 1801.

January 9 – William Barclay. "The First Beatitude." 1956.

January 10 – John Calvin. *Commentary on the Synoptics*. c. 1550.

January 11 – Anselm of Canterbury. *Proslogion*, Chapter 1, in *Basic Works 12th Century*.

January 12 – Descartes. *Meditation IV: On Truth and Falsity* and *Meditation V: On the Essence of Material Objects and More on God's Existence*. 1641.

January 13 – Thomas Merton. *Thoughts in Solitude*. Farrar, Straus, and Giroux. 1956.

January 14 – Pope Urban II. From his speech at Council of Clermont, ordering the First Crusade; version by Fulcher of Chartres. 1095.

January 15 – Billy Sunday. "Backsliding." Boston, MA, c. 1917.

January 16 – Richard Rolle. *The Fire of Love*. 1347.

January 17 – Clement of Rome. *First Letter of Clement to the Corinthians*, Roberts-Donaldson translation. c. 96

January 18 – Martin Luther. *Table Talk*. 1566.

January 19 – John of Damascus. *An Exact Exposition of the Orthodox Faith, Book One*. Translated by Rev. S.D.F. Salmond, 1898.

January 20 – Samuel Willard. "Christ Humbled Himself." 1701.

January 21 – William Gurnall. *The Christian in Complete Armor*. 1655.

January 22 – Robert McCheyne. *Sermon XIV*. 1839.

January 23 – Hilary. *On the Trinity Book XII*. c. 350.

January 24 – Sir Walter Raleigh. *Preface to the History of the World*. 1614.

January 25 – John of the Cross. *Dark Night of the Soul*. c. 1580.

January 26 – Saint Patrick. *The Confession of Saint Patrick of Ireland*. c. 460.

January 27 – John Wycliffe. *English Prose*, ed. Henry Craik. The Macmillan Company. 1916.

January 28 – Huldrych Zwingli. *The 67 Articles of Zwingli*. 1522.

January 29 – Theognostus of Alexandria. *Hypotyposes*. c. 260

January 30 – Williams Pantycelyn. *Savior, Lead Us by Thy Power*. c. 1770.

January 31 – Vatican II. *Constitution on the Sacred Liturgy*. 1964.

February 1 – John Knox. *The Scottish Confession of Faith*. 1559.

February 2 – Samuel Rutherford. *Letter 87*, written to Elizabeth Kennedy. 1637.

February 3 – *The Passion of the Scillitan Martyrs*. Roberts-Donaldson English translation.

February 4 – Francis Asbury. *The Goodness of God*. 1812.

February 5 – William Wilberforce. *A Practical View of the Prevailing Religious System of Professed Christians*. 1797.

February 6 – St. Gregory of Nyssa. "On the Baptism of Christ." c. 380.

February 7 – Watchman Nee. *The Normal Christian Life*. Gospel Literature Service, Bombay. 1957.

February 8 – Philip Schaff. *Creeds of Christendom*. Baker Books; Revised edition. 1984.

February 9 – Fanny Crosby. "Blessed Assurance." 1873.

February 10 – Alexander Maclaren. *The Gospel According to St. John, Volume 3*. A.C. Armstrong and Son. 1908.

February 11 – Robert Louis Stevenson. *Prayers Written at Vailima*. 1910.

February 12 – Ambrose. From the letters of Ambrose; addressed to the Bishop of Milan.

February 13 – G. K. Chesterton. *Orthodoxy*, Chapter 6. 1908.

February 14 – Henry Drummond. *The Greatest Thing in the World*. c. 1874.

February 15 – Bernard of Clairvaux. *On Loving God*. c. 1130.

February 16 – Copernicus. From the Dedication of the *Revolutions of the Heavenly Bodies*, to Pope Paul III. 1543.

February 17 – Jeremiah Burroughs. *The Rare Jewel of Christian Contentment*. 1651.

February 18 – Soren Kierkegaard. *Purity of Heart Is to Will One Thing*; translated by Douglas Steere. 1843.

February 19 – Leo the Great. *Letter to Provence of Vienne*. c. 445.

February 20 – Octavius Winslow. *Evening Thoughts*. 1858.

February 21 – Gilbert Tennent. "The Danger of Unconverted Ministry." 1739.

February 22 – Tatian. *Address to the Greeks*, Schaff translation.

February 23 – Augustine. *Confessions*, Book 1, E. B. Pusey translation. 1838.

February 24 – Aimee Semple McPherson. *The Second Coming of Christ*. 1927.

February 25 – James Gibbons. *The Act of Contrition*. 1884.

February 26 – William Gurnall. *The Christian in Complete Armor*. 1655.

February 27 – Origen. *Second Book of the Commentary on the Gospel According to Matthew*. 246-248

February 28 – John Paul II. From the encyclical *Evangelium Vitae (Gospel of Life)*, March 25, 1995.

February 29 – Robert Traill. "Examine Yourselves in the Light of God's Grace." c. 1690.

March 1 – *The Heidelberg Catechism*. 1563.

March 2 – Thomas Aquinas. *Summa Theologica*, question 12. 1270.

March 3 – Ron Sider. *Rich Christians in an Age of Hunger: A Biblical Study*. InterVarsity Press. 1977.

March 4 – William Lloyd Garrison. *Declaration of Sentiments Adopted by the Peace Convention*. Boston, 1838.

March 5 – *The Westminster Confession of Faith*. 1646.

March 6 – Ignatius. *The Spiritual Exercises of St. Ignatius of Loyola*, translated by Elder Mullan. 1914.

March 7 – Dionysius. *Works*. London: James Parker and Co. 1897.

March 8 – John Huss. *The Church*. Charles Scribner and Sons. 1915.

March 9 – J. Gresham Machen. "Christianity and Culture." *The Princeton Theological Review*, Vol. 11. 1913.

March 10 – Albert Barnes. "The Way of Salvation." Morristown, New Jersey. 1839.

March 11 – From the Catechism of the Catholic Church. c. 360

March 12 – Richard Sibbes. *Bruised Reeds*; translated by Nichol Series. 1630.

March 13 – Charles Dickens. *A Christmas Carol*. Chapman & Hall. 1843.

March 14 – Isaac Backus. "An Appeal to the Public for Religious Liberty, Against Oppressions of the Present Day." 1773.

March 15 – Eusebius. *The History of the Church*, Book III. 314

March 16 – Dr. Norman Vincent Peale. *The Power of Positive Thinking*. Foundation for Christian Living. 1952.

March 17 – Aristedes. Fragments of his Apology preserved from the writings of Eusebius and Jerome. 128

March 18 – Andrew Murray. *Waiting on God*. 1896.

March 19 – Teresa of Avila. *The Interior Castle*. 1577.

March 20 – Wilhelmus à Brakel. *The Christian's Reasonable Service*. c. 1690.

March 21 – Jan van Ruysbroeck. *The Adornment of the Spiritual Marriage*; translated by C.A. Wynschenk Dom, 1916.

March 22 – St. Nilus. *Works about Virtues and Vices in General*. Fifth Century.

March 23 – John Darby. *Notes on the Gospel of Luke*. c. 1865.

March 24 – John Foxe. *Foxe's Book of Martyrs*, Chapter 1. 1559.

March 25 – Karl Barth. "Jesus Is the Victor." 1933.

March 26 – Frederic Farrar. *The Life of Jesus*. 1878.

March 27 – Peter Abelard. *The Story of My Misfortunes*, Chapter XV; translated by Henry Adams Bellows. 1922.

March 28 – The Unknown Mystic. *The Cloud of Unknowing*, translated by Evelyn Underhill. 1922.

March 29 – Arthur Pink. From the Introduction to *The Sovereignty of God*. 1918.

March 30 – Sozomenus. *History of the Church*. 443.

March 31 – Isaac of Nineveh. *Homilies*. c. 685.

April 1 – John Fletcher. *Christ Manifest*. 1777.

April 2 – Malcom Muggeridge. "Another King." 1968.

April 3 – Archibald Alexander. *Practical Directions: How to Grow in Grace and Make Progress in Piety*. 1844.

April 4 – The Synod of Dort. 1618-1619.

April 5 – Gregory. *Oration 38—On the Birthday of Christ*. 381

April 6 – John Darby. *Notes on the Gospel of Luke*. c. 1760.

April 7 – Hesychius. From "On Watchfulness and Holiness" in the *Philokalia*. 1979.

April 8 – Martyn Lloyd-Jones. *"Saving Faith" An Exposition of* [Romans] *Chapter 10*, 1997.

April 9 – Claudius. *Apology of Claudius*, translated by Thomas Head. c. 815.

April 10 – Bonaventure. *The Mind's Road to God*. c. 1263.

April 11 – Charles Sheldon. *In His Steps*. Chicago Advance. 1897.

April 12 – Aphraates. *The Homilies of St. Aphraates*. 4th Century.

April 13 – Theodore the Studite. *Catechism*. 9th Century.

April 14 – F. J. Huegel. *Bone of His Bone*. 1957.

April 15 – Henry van Dyke. *The Other Wise Man*. 1896.

April 16 – Athanasius. *The Life of Antony*. c. 472

April 17 – John Flavel. From the Introduction to *The Mystery of Providence*. 1678.

April 18 – Phillips Brooks. "The Beauty of a Life of Service." c. 1853.

April 19 – Andrew of Crete. *Great Canon of Repentance*. c. 715.

April 20 – Dorothy L. Sayers. *The Mind of the Maker*. London: Methuen. 1941.

April 21 – George Fox. *Letters of George Fox*, letter 16. c. 1671.

April 22 – F. B. Meyer. *The Secret of Guidance*. 1896.

April 23 – The Unknown Mystic. *The Cloud of Unknowing*, translated by Evelyn Underhill. 1922.

April 24 – Ignatius. *The Spiritual Exercises of St. Ignatius of Loyola*, translated by Elder Mullan. 1914.

April 25 – Philip Schaff. *Creeds of Christendom*. Baker Books; Revised edition. 1984.

April 26 – Samuel Brengle. "When the Holy Ghost Has Come." c. 1914.

April 27 – Jessie Penn-Lewis. *The Centrality of the Cross*. c. 1910.

April 28 – Bede. *Ecclesiastical History of England*, edited by A.M. Sellar. 1907.

April 29 – Albert the Great. *The Works of Albert the Great*. 13th century.

April 30 – Catherine Booth. *Woman's Right to Preach the Gospel*. 1859.

May 1 – B. B. Warfield. *The Power of God Unto Salvation*. Presbyterian Board of Publication. 1903.

May 2 – Ralph Erskine. *God's Great Name*. 1842.

May 3 – Thomas Doolittle. *Love to Christ Everlasting*. 17th century.

May 4 – Jude. From the Epistle of Jude (Jude 17-25 NIV).

May 5 – Dwight L. Moody. *Prevailing Prayer*. 1873.

May 6 – Johannes Eriugena. *Prologue to the Gospel of John*. c. 854.

May 7 – Martyn-Lloyd Jones. "On Romans 10:3." 1961.

May 8 – Tacitus. *Annals of Tacitus*. 115

May 9 – Edward Grim. *Life of Thomas Becket*. 1180.

May 10 – Leslie Weatherhead. *The Significance of Silence and Other Sermons*. 1945.

May 11 – Augustine Baker. *Holy Wisdom*. c. 1636.

May 12 – Salvian. *On the Government of God*. c. 437

May 13 – G. A. Chadwick. *The Gospel of Mark*. 1896.

May 14 – Joseph Addison. *The Evidences of the Christian Religion*. c. 1714.

May 15 – Peter Marshall. "Confessional Prayer for America." 1944.

May 16 – John Foxe. *Foxe's Book of Martyrs*. 1559.

May 17 – Desmond Tutu. *Greater Good* magazine, Fall 2004.

May 18 – Lancelot Andrewes. *Devotions of Bishop Andrewes*. c. 1611.

May 19 – Paul. From the First Epistle to the Corinthians (1 Corinthians 15:12-28 ASV).

May 20 – Frances Havergal. *Kept for the Master's Use*. 1879.

May 21 – Meister Eckhart. *"Abgesschiedenheit" and the True Possession of God*. 14th century.

May 22 – John Baillie. *A Diary of Private Prayer*. Scribner & Sons. 1936.

May 23 – From *The Martyrdom of Polycarp*. c. 160

May 24 – Anton Praetorius. *Thorough Report about Witchcraft and Witches*. 1598.

May 25 – Robert Hawker. *The Poor Man's Portions*. 1855.

May 26 – Girolamo Savonarola. *Triumph of the Cross*. 1497.

May 27 – G. Campbell Morgan. *The Westminster Pulpit: The Preaching of G. Campbell Morgan*. 1937.

May 28 – Antony. *Life of Antony*. c. 347

May 29 – Frederic Farrar. From the preface of *Gathering Clouds: A Tale of the Days of St. Chrysostom*. 1874.

May 30 – Galileo. From a letter to Christina of Lorraine, Grand Duchess of Tuscany. 1615.

May 31 – Donald Barnhouse. "Pursuing the Love of God." 1950.

June 1 – Odo of Cluny. *The Life of St. Gerald of Aurillac*. c. 927.

June 2 – Wilhelmus à Brakel. *The Christian's Reasonable Service*, Volume 4; translated by Bartel Elshout. 1700.

June 3 – Clement of Alexandria. *Epistle to the Corinthinas*. c. 215

June 4 – William Sangster. *Can I Know God? And Other Sermons*. c. 1950.

June 5 – Susanna Wesley. From a personal letter to John Wesley, March 30, 1734.

June 6 – Gardner C. Taylor. *The Words of Gardner C. Taylor: 50 Years of Timeless Treasures*. 1974.

June 7 – John. From the book of 1 John (1 John 2:1-12, 14-15 ASV).

June 8 – George Herbert. *A True Hymn*. 1633.

June 9 – Sojourner Truth. From *The Narrative of Sojourner Truth*, dictated by Sojourner Truth; edited by Olive Gilbert. 1850.

June 10 – John Calvin. *Institutes*. 1536.

June 11 – Tertullian. *The Account in Tertullian's Apology*. c. 197

June 12 – John Trapp. "Anger Is a Tender Virtue." c. 1652.

June 13 – John Wimber. *Power Healing*. HarperOne. 1991.

June 14 – Richard Allen. *The Life, Experience, and Gospel Labors of the Rt. Rev. Richard Allen*. c. 1830.

June 15 – Henry Venn. *The Complete Duty of Man*. 1811.

June 16 – Isidore. *Etymologies*. 7th century.

June 17 – Nicholas of Cusa. *On the Vision of God*. 1453.

June 18 – Stephen Charnock. *A Discourse of God's Being the Author of Reconciliation*. c. 1669.

June 19 – James Gibbons. *Our Christian Heritage*. 1889.

June 20 – Charles Kingsley. "The Glories of the Cross." c. 1852.

June 21 – John Chrysostom. "Christian Example to the Greeks." 387

June 22 – Martin Luther. "A Mighty Fortress." 1527.

June 23 – Billy Graham. "Your Authority to Be Heard." Billy Graham Evangelistic Society. 2010.

June 24 – John Stott. *Basic Christianity*. InterVarsity Press. 1958.

June 25 – Fyodor Dostoyevsky. *The Brothers Karamazov*. 1880.

June 26 – Sir Thomas More. *Epigrams*. 1522.

June 27 – Isaac Watts. "Alas! and Did My Savior Bleed." 1707.

June 28 – John. From the book of Revelation (Revelation 21:1-8 NIV).

June 29 – Governing Council of Charlestown, Massachusetts. From *The First Thanksgiving Proclamation*. June 20, 1676.

June 30 – Mother Teresa. From a speech given at the National Prayer Breakfast, Washington, D.C. February 3, 1994.

July 1 – Horace Bushnell. *Christ and His Salvation*. 1864.

July 2 – Thomas Fuller. *Good Thoughts in Bad Times*. c. 1665.

July 3 – Jerome. *Prefaces to the Vulgate Version of the New Testament*. 383

July 4 – James Allen. *The Way of Peace*. 1910.

July 5 – John of Ruysbroeck. *Adornment of the Spiritual Marriage*. c. 1358.

July 6 – Reginald Heber. "Holy, Holy, Holy!" c. 1809.

July 7 – Sir Thomas More. *The Four Last Things*. 1522.

July 8 – Ralph Sockman. *Now to Live!* Stone & Pierce.1946.

July 9 – Eucherius. *Formulae of St. Eucherius of Lyons*. c. 448

July 10 – Karl Wuttke. *Christian Ethics*. 1873.

July 11 – Boethius. *Consolation of Philosophy*. c. 523

July 12 – Hannah Hurnard. *Hinds' Feet on High Places*. 1955.

July 13 – Albert the Great. *Cleave to God*. 13th century.

July 14 – Adam Clarke. *Christian Theology*. 1851.

July 15 – Miguel de Molinos. *Darkness to Light*, 1675.

July 16 – R. G. Lee. "Payday Someday." 1957.

July 17 – Jacobus de Voragine. *The Golden Legend*. c. 1281.

July 18 – Gustav Oehler. *Theology of the Old Testament*. 1884.

July 19 – Stephen Charnock. *Discourse on the Cleansing Virtue of Christ's Blood*. C. 1667.

July 20 – A. T. Robertson. "Realizing God's Plan in Life." 1954.

July 21 – Luke. From the Acts of the Apostles (Acts 2:14, 29-41 NIV).

July 22 – Jacobus Arminius. *Remonstrantice*. 1610.

July 23 – Harvey Cox. *The Future of Faith*. HarperOne Publishers. 2009.

July 24 – Charles Hodge. *Systematic Theology*. 1873.

July 25 – Henry Suso. *The Little Book of Eternal Wisdom*. 14th century.

July 26 – Matthew. From the Gospel according to Matthew (Matthew 5:1-12 NIV).

July 27 – Francis Schaeffer. *The Mark of a Christian*. InterVarsity Press. 1976.

July 28 – John Ryle. *Holiness: Its Nature, Hindrances, Difficulties and Roots*. 1879.

July 29 – George Herbert. *Discipline*. 1633.

July 30 – Jurgen Moltmann. *Jesus Christ for Today's World*; translated by Margaret Kohl. Augsburg Fortress. 1995.

July 31 – Paul Tillich. "The New Beginning." 1955.

August 1 – Maria Skobtsova. *Taking Up the Cross*. c. 1937.

August 2 – From *The Gospel of the Hebrews*. c. 179

August 3 – Moses Amyraut. *A Treatise on Religions*. 1660.

August 4 – Walter Martin. *Kingdom of the Cults*. Zondervan. 1965.

August 5 – Ebenezer Erskine. "A Robbery Committed." 1746.

August 6 – Philo. *On the Embassy to Gaius*. c. 50

August 7 – Polycarp. *Polycarp's Letter to the Philippians*, translated by Kirsopp Lake. 1912.

August 8 – A. B. Bruce. *The Training of the Twelve*. 1870.

August 9 – Amy Carmichael. *If*. 1940.

August 10 – Asterius. "On Divorce." c. 368.

August 11 – Desiderius Erasmus. *A Blessing*. 1531.

August 12 – Donald Gee. *Wind and Flame*. 1949.

August 13 – William Carey. *Enquiries*. 1792.

August 14 – Gordon Clark. *Religion, Reason, and Revelation*. Presbyterian & Reformed Publishing Company. 1965.

August 15 – John Wycliffe. *Select English Works of Wycliffe*, edited by T. Arnold. Clarendon Press. 1869.

August 16 – Thomas Aquinas. *The Scholastic Resolution of Abelardian Dialectic: the Theological Virtues and Man's Supernatural Beatitude*. c. 1270.

August 17 – R. A. Torrey. *The Power of Prayer and Prayer of Power*. 1903.

August 18 – Pliny the Younger. *Letters*, 10.96-97; to the Emperor Trajan. c. 103

August 19 – Hudson Taylor. *A Retrospect*. 1894.

August 20 – Matthew Henry. *Commentary on Lamentations 3*. 1706.

August 21 – George Buttrick. *So We Believe So We Pray*. Cokesbury Press. 1950.

August 22 – Saint Benedict. *Rule, Prologue*, Schmidt translation. 6th century.

August 23 – Thomas Shepard. *The Sincere Convert*. C. 1634.

August 24 – J. B. Phillips. *Your God Is Too Small*. Simon & Schuster. 1952.

August 25 – Origen. *On First Principles*. 3rd century.

August 26 – Adam Clarke. *Entire Sanctification*. 1826.

August 27 – Johannes Tauler. *Sermons*. 1498.

August 28 – W. A. Criswell. "The Last Beatitude." 1963.

August 29 – Hugh of St. Victor. *Sacraments of the Christian Faith*. c. 1120.

August 30 – Paul. From the Epistle to the Romans (Romans 8:31-39 NIV).

August 31 – Robert McCheyne. "A Vision of Dry Bones." c. 1837.

September 1 – George Kulp. "Apostolic Practices." c. 1937.

September 2 – Francis of Assisi. *A Last Will and Testament*. 1226.

September 3 – Richard Niebuhr. *Christ and Culture*. Torchbooks. 1951.

September 4 – Basil the Great. *The Benefit of NonChristian Literature*; Padelford translation of 1902.

September 5 – John Woolman. *The Journals of John Woolman*. 1754.

September 6 – J. I. Packer. *Knowing God*. InterVarsity Press. 1973.

September 7 – Augustine. *On Christian Doctrine*. 5th century.

September 8 – Daniel Steele. *Love Enthroned*. 1875.

September 9 – Hugh Binning. "Lecture 14 on Christian Doctrine." 1650.

September 10 – Abraham Kuyper. *Sanctification—from the Work of the Holy Spirit*. 1900.

September 11 – Jacques de Vitry. *Historia*. 1229.

September 12 – David Burrell. *The Christ Child and the Emperor*. c. 1883.

September 13 – Gregory Palamas. "Homily 4." c. 1338.

September 14 – Ephrem. *Above Fear*. 4th century.

September 15 – Thomas Brooks. *Christ's Love to Poor Sinners*. c. 1652.

September 16 – Clarence E. Macartney. *The Greatest Questions of the Bible and of Life*. Abingdon-Cokesbury Press. 1948.

September 17 – William Cowper. "The Christian." c. 1780.

September 18 – Tertullian. *The Shows*. c. 210

September 19 – George Muller. *The Life of Trust*. 1873.

September 20 – Jan van Ruysbroeck. *The Sparkling Stone: Our Lord Jesus Christ A Shining Forth of the Eternal Light*. c. 1357.

September 21 – Leonard Ravenhill. "The Prophet." 1955.

September 22 – Thomas Ken. *Awake My Soul*. c. 1685.

September 23 – Billy Graham. "Sound the Call." The Billy Graham Evangelistic Association. 2010.

September 24 – Josephus. *Jewish Antiquities*. 93

September 25 – De Witt Talmage. "The Name of Jesus." c. 1869.

September 26 – W. A. Criswell. "The Pleading of Paul." 1963.

September 27 – William Law. *The Spirit of Love in Two Parts*, reprinted in the 1974 Georg Olms Verlag (Hildesheim NewYork) edition of *The Works of the Reverend William Law*.

September 28 – Ignatius. *Epistle to the Ephesians*. 2nd century.

September 29 – Hugh Latimer. "Kingdom Responsibility." 16th century.

September 30 – James Orr. "Sketch of the Christian View of God and the World." 1886.

October 1 – George W. Truett. "We Would See Jesus." 1915.

October 2 – Edward Griffin. "Arrows Sharp in the Heart of Enemies." c. 1820.

October 3 – Catherine of Genoa. *The Life and Doctrine of St. Catherine of Genoa*. c. 1560.

October 4 – Thomas Boston. "Christ's Name Wonderful." 18th century.

October 5 – Joseph Parker. "The Revival of Religion." *The People's Bible*. c. 1872.

October 6 – Max Lucado. "Prayer: A Heavenly Invitation." UpWords. 1996.

October 7 – Athenagoras. *A Plea for the Christian*. 4th century.

October 8 – Louis de Blois. *Devotions to Our Blessed Savior*. c. 1547.

October 9 – John Chapman. "Grieving the Spirit." c. 1892.

October 10 – Cyrus Scofield. *Rightfully Dividing the Word of Truth*. 1897.

October 11 – Richard Baxter. *How to Spend the Day with God*. 1671.

October 12 – John A. Broadus. *The Savior Praying for Us*. c. 1861.

October 13 – Ignatius. *Ignatius' Letter to Polycarp*, the J.B. Lightfoot translation. 1891.

October 14 – Harry Ironside. "The Ministry of Peter." 20th century.

October 15 – Brother Lawrence. *The Sweet and the Bitter*. From an English translation published c. 1785.

October 16 – Charles Finney. "Revelation of God's Glory." 1843.

October 17 – From the Epistle to the Hebrews (Hebrews 10:19-25, 36-39 NIV).

October 18 – Alexander Pope. *The Dying Christian to His Soul*. c. 1719.

October 19 – John Cassian. *Institutions*. 5th century.

October 20 – Karl Barth. "Jesus is Victor." 1933.

October 21 – Socrates. *Church History*. 439.

October 22 – Thomas Doolittle. *A Complete Body of Practical Theology*. 1723.

October 23 – James. From the Epistle of James (James 1:19-27 NIV).

October 24 – Andrew Murray. *Waiting on God: For the Coming of His Son*. Fleming H. Revell. 1894.

October 25 – Madame Guyon. *Method of Prayer*. c. 1720.

October 26 – Justin Martyr. *First Confessions*, translated by Philip Schaff. 1895.

October 27 – John Bunyan. *The Pilgrim's Progress from This World to That Which Is to Come*. 1678.

October 28 – Thomas à Kempis. *If You Were to Die Today*, Ries translation of 1940.

October 29 – Oswald Chambers. *My Utmost for His Highest*. 1927.

October 30 – The *Didache*, Kirsopp Lake translation of 1912.

October 31 – John Milton. *Paradise Lost*. 1667.

November 1 – Charles Haddon Spurgeon. "Cleansing of the Leper." New Park Tabernacle, 1860.

November 2 – Smith Wigglesworth. "Willing to Give." 1937.

November 3 – George Whitefield. "The Potter and the Clay." 1760.

November 4 – John Calvin. *John Calvin's Institutes*, iii.7; translated by Henry Beveridge. 1845.

November 5 – Augustine. *Confessions*, VIII; translated by Dr. Pusey. 1838.

November 6 – St. Francis de Sales. *The Introduction to the Devout Life* (Pars 1, cap. 3), translated by Charles Dollen. 1923.

November 7 – Francois Fenelon. *The Seeking Heart*, published as *Spiritual Letters* in the 18th century; translated by Robert J. Edmonson. 1725.

November 8 – Hannah Whitall Smith. *The Christian's Secret of a Happy Life*, 1916 edition.

November 9 – Martin Luther. *Heidelberg Disputation*, numbers 3 and 25. 1518.

November 10 – Papias. *A Vision of Paradise*, the Roberts Donaldson translation, 1893.

November 11 – John Wesley. "God's Love to Fallen Man." c. 1764.

November 12 – Sir Walter Raleigh. *Into the Light*. 1618.

November 13 – John Knox. *On the First Temptation of Christ*. c. 1558.

November 14 – *Book of Common Prayer*. 1662.

November 15 – E. M. Bounds. *The Reality of Prayer*. 1913.

November 16 – Paul. From the Book of Philippians (Philippians 2:1-11 NASB).

November 17 – Dietrich Bonhoeffer. *The Cost of Discipleship*. Macmillan. 1937.

November 18 – Anthony the Great. *Discourses on Demons*. 4th century.

November 19 – Friedrich Schleiermacher. *On Religion*. c. 1822.

November 20 – Martin Luther King Jr. "Loving Your Enemies." 1957.

November 21 – The Confession of Chalcedon. 451

November 22 – Charles Wesley. "Amazing Love." 1738.

November 23 – Dwight L. Moody. From a sermon delivered in Dr. Bonar's church, Edinburgh, Scotland. 1873.

November 24 – Max Lucado. *When God Whispers Your Name*. UpWords. 1999.

November 25 – From the 7th Chapter of the *Shepherd of Hermes*, the Roberts-Dodds translation, 1930.

November 26 – David Livingstone. *Missionary Travels and Researches In South Africa*. 1857.

November 27 – Richard Baxter. "The Written Word." 17th century.

November 28 – A. B. Simpson. "The Uplift of the Cross." 1909.

November 29 – Isaac Penington. *The Way of Life and Death*. 1658.

November 30 – Phillips Brooks. "The Dangers of Success." c. 1872.

December 1 – Charles Jefferson. "Liberty: Its Dangers and Duties." c. 1931.

December 2 – John Wesley. *Journals of the Rev. John Welsey*. 1738.

December 3 – Reinhold Niebuhr. *Beyond Tragedy*. Charles Scribner & Sons. 1937.

December 4 – Robert Coleman. *The Master Plan of Evangelism*. Revell. 1963.

December 5 – Kenneth E. Hagin. From the commencement message given at RHEMA Bible Training Center, Tulsa, OK. May 1979.

December 6 – William Booth. "A Sea of Humanity." 19th century.

December 7 – J. R. R. Tolkien. "On Fairy Stories." 1938.

December 8 – The Athanasian Creed. 500

December 9 – Henri Nouwen. *The Way of the Heart*. HarperSanFrancisco. 1981.

December 10 – Philipp Melanchthon. *Apology of the Augsburg Confession*, Article III. 1531.

December 11 – Jeremy Taylor. *Holy Living*. 1650.

December 12 – Eugene Peterson. *A Year With Jesus*. HarperOne. 2006.

December 13 – E. Stanley Jones. "Our Christmas Meditation." 1942.

December 14 – John Young. *The Christ of History*. 1857.

December 15 – Phillips Brooks. *Christmas Everywhere*. 1903.

December 16 – C. S. Lewis. "The Grand Miracle." 1947.

December 17 – John Paul II. "Advent Meditation." 1980.

December 18 – Bonaventure. *The Origin of the Christmas Crèche*. 1263.

December 19 – Rudyard Kipling. *A Nativity*. 1918.

December 20 – Frederick Buechner. *Beyond Words*. HarperOne. 2004.

December 21 – Jacopo de Voragine. *The Golden Legend*. c. 1281.

December 22 – Henry Wadsworth Longfellow. *Christmas Bells*. 1863.

December 23 – G. K. Chesterton. *Christmas and the Professors*. 1909.

December 24 – Benedict XVI. "The God-Who-Comes." 2006.

December 25 – Walter A. Maier. "Hold Fast to Christmas." c. 1940.

December 26 – Alexander of Cappadocia. *The Epistles of Alexander*. c. 225

December 27 – Charles Swindoll. "Not to Worry . . . He's Risen!" *Insights*. March 2008.

December 28 – John Owen. *Discourse Concerning Evangelical Love, Church Peace, and Unity*. c. 1658.

December 29 – Jonathan Edwards. "Sinners in the Hands of an Angry God." 1741.

December 30 – Zacharias Ursinus. *What Is the Gospel?* c. 1566.

December 31 – Miguel de Molinos. *Spiritual Guide Which Disentangles the Soul*. c. 1658.